National

Gallery of Art

WASHINGTON

NEW AND REVISED EDITION

BY JOHN WALKER DIRECTOR EMERITUS

FOREWORD BY J. CARTER BROWN, DIRECTOR

ABRADALE PRESS

HARRY N. ABRAMS, INC., PUBLISHERS

TO PAUL MELLON   A PERFECT TRUSTEE

Library of Congress Cataloging-in-Publication Data

Walker, John, 1906 Dec. 24–
   National Gallery of Art, Washington / by John
Walker ; foreword by J. Carter Brown.—New and rev. ed.
      p.   cm.
   Includes index.
   ISBN 0–8109–8148–3 (hardcover)
   1. National Gallery of Art (U.S.)   I. National Gallery of
Art (U.S.)   II. Title.
N856.W33   1995   95–1028
708.153—dc20

Note: Parts of this book have been previously published in *Art in America, Ladies' Home Journal,
National Geographic Magazine, Twin Editions, Great Paintings of the World, Connoisseur, Atlantic
Monthly*, and certain National Gallery of Art publications and catalogues. I am very grateful for
permission to reprint this material.   J.W.

Acknowledgments

This new edition of a book published in 1975 brings the collection of the National Gallery of Art up to date. Many treasures have been added in ten years, and a new emphasis has been placed on contemporary art. This, however, does not diminish my indebtedness to those who helped with the first edition.

Without the assistance of Carolyn H. Wells I would not have undertaken this work. She has done much of the research and aided me in every way in preparing the text. But the book was made possible only by the full cooperation which I received from the staff of the National Gallery of Art.

My successor as Director of the Gallery, J. Carter Brown, has written the foreword and some passages of the introductory text. His unfailing interest and encouragement, despite the pressure of his multitudinous duties, have been invaluable. I am most grateful also to Charles P. Parkhurst, Assistant Director, who brought together the resources of the various curatorial departments to assist me, and to Elizabeth Foy, formerly Administrative Assistant to the Director. I greatly appreciate the specialized advice, in their respective fields, of David A. Brown, Curator of Early Italian Painting; William P. Campbell, late Curator of American Painting; E. A. Carmean, Jr., Curator of Twentieth-Century Art; Sheldon Grossman, Curator of Northern and Later Italian Painting; John O. Hand, Curator of Northern European Painting; Parker Lesley, late Curator of Decorative Arts; David E. Rust, former Curator of French Painting; Anna Voris, former Museum Curator; Ross Watson, former Curator of British Painting; and Arthur K. Wheelock, Jr., Curator of Flemish and Dutch Painting. Miss Voris was also of the greatest assistance in reading proof.

Douglas Lewis, Curator of Sculpture, and Andrew Robison, Curator of Graphic Arts, advised me in the selection of works of art in their departments and contributed introductory essays which add greatly to the reader's understanding of the Gallery's collections in fields other than painting.

Kathleen Ewing, former Coordinator of Photography, and her staff accomplished in record time the tremendous task of furnishing color transparencies for the more than one thousand color plates which illustrate my text. Henry B. Beville, retired Chief Photographer, returned to work long hours to complete the necessary photography.

I am also indebted to J. M. Edelstein, Chief Librarian; David Scott, Planning Consultant; Richard Bales, Assistant to the Director for Music; and Margaret Bouton, Curator in Charge of Education, for information on those functions of the Gallery under their supervision.

The chapter on scientific work at the Gallery is largely based on a report prepared for me by Dr. Robert Feller, Senior Fellow, National Gallery of Art Research Project. His investigations, together with those of his colleague Dr. Bernard Keisch, in a program begun in 1950 at the Mellon Institute, Carnegie-Mellon University, Pittsburgh, have led to the discovery of many vital tools for the preservation and authentication of works of art.

I am particularly grateful to the two eminent scholars cataloguing the Samuel H. Kress Collection of paintings, Dr. Fern Rusk Shapley and Dr. Colin Eisler, who made their notes available to me in advance of publication. Professor John Rewald was good enough to allow me to use his notes on the *Portrait of the Artist's Father* by Cézanne. I would also like to thank Miss Mary Davis, Vice-President of the Samuel H. Kress Foundation, for her constant helpfulness.

To the late Harry N. Abrams, my thanks for his exciting concept for this book, and for the professionalism of his staff, in particular Darlene Geis, Margaret Kaplan, Patricia Gilchrest and Howard Morris, who brought that concept into being.

To these must be added Ellyn Allison, Senior Editor at Harry N. Abrams, and William James Williams, Education Editor at the National Gallery. Mrs. Allison coordinated the preparation of the revisions for the new edition and Mr. Williams provided me with the information on which my text for the new works is based. He also undertook the delicate and difficult job of rearranging the plates to include the additional paintings. Dirk Luykx supervised the design and production of the new edition, and I am grateful to him. I would also like to acknowledge the help of the staff of the National Gallery, especially Robert Bowen, Special Assistant to the Director, Frances Smyth, Editor, and Carroll Cavanagh, Secretary-General Counsel.

John Walker

Contents

Foreword

Museums have walls. Since the caveman days of Lascaux and Altamira, Homo sapiens has found the wall a handy device to support works of art. But museum walls have at least two other functions. One is to protect—from wind and pollutants; from humidity drops and the thief in the night; from time, the quiet, gradual destroyer of the few remaining objects mankind has been able to hand down. The other function of a museum wall is to dissolve. That function is made possible by a book like this.

The National Gallery of Art has a special role by virtue of its very name, and the federally appropriated support that its name implies. It is a national institution if only by the importance of the objects it conserves, as even the most cursory examination of this volume will suggest. It is national, as well, in the scope of its some five million annual visitors, so many of whom come to the capital, as on a pilgrimage, to rediscover a national past and to search for a national identity. The large and growing number of international visitors to the National Gallery bears witness, what is more, to one of its founding functions of showing our guests that the concerns of this country and of its government are not simply those of technological ingenuity or mercantile and military strength.

There is, however, a national audience that the Gallery serves which may never get to Washington from one end of the year to the other. Through its Extension Service (which reaches communities in all fifty states) and through the free circulation of films, produced by or with the cooperation of the Gallery's multimedia programs, the Gallery reaches each year an estimated audience many times the number of those who actually have the privilege of visiting it here. With public and educational television, the Extension Programs reached almost one hundred million viewers in 1983. It is this wider audience that this book will so ably serve.

It is hard for a book on the National Gallery to be up to date. The collections keep growing, with a continuing emphasis on individual quality in every period, as in Rubens's *Gerbier Family* or Georges de La Tour's *Repentant Magdalen*, but with a special emphasis on the achievements of the twentieth century, as in the Harriman *Lady with a Fan* by Picasso, and more recent accessions by Ernst, Matisse, Pollock, and other twentieth-century artists. The collections simultaneously are being enriched by important additions in the fields of drawings and small sculpture. Just since 1980 major gifts from the collections of Mr. and Mrs. Paul Mellon, the late John Hay Whitney, and the late Edgar William and Bernice Chrysler Garbisch have meant significant additions to the Gallery's holdings.

Perhaps the most visible and dramatic change has been the completion of the Gallery's East Building, the gift of Paul Mellon, the late Ailsa Mellon Bruce, and the Andrew W. Mellon Foundation. The story of its genesis and realization is recounted in Mr. Walker's chapter on the two structures that house the Gallery's collections. With the transfer of the Gallery's offices from the West Building to the East, a vast amount of space in John Russell Pope's original structure became available for conversion. Completed in 1983, a major remodeling of more than 40,000 square feet produced a museum-within-a-museum which exhibits nearly 2,000 prints, drawings, paintings, small-scale sculpture, and related decorative arts objects from the National Gallery's permanent collection of Western European and American art, ranging in date from the twelfth century to the present. One of the facilities of these new galleries is a space dedicated to displaying selections from the Gallery's own collection of prints and drawings. Because these works, by virtue of their sensitivity to light, cannot be on constant view, it is now possible to exhibit, on a rotating basis, a chronological survey of graphic arts which parallels the installation of paintings always on view in the Main Floor galleries.

A comparable exhibition of small sculpture, including the highly important Renaissance bronzes from the Kress Collection, has been made possible by the renovation of the West Building's Ground Floor. The Kress holdings are so vast that it was decided to place many of the plaques and medals in a secure, open storage area, where they are accessible to scholars and students. The Chinese porcelains from the Widener Collection are now reinstalled in their specially designed, mirrored cases, where they were displayed when the Gallery opened in 1941. Also, the select examples of fine French furniture given by the Wideners have been placed in refurbished rooms which more accurately suggest their original eighteenth-century context.

Although the major construction at the National Gallery is now finished, minor modifications continue. An oculus is being cut in the North Lobby just off the West Building Rotunda. This aperture will give the visitor who enters via Constitution Avenue an immediate visual clue to the grandeur of the Main Floor. Certain spaces there have never been finished. Designed by John Russell Pope as painting galleries, these will be systematically completed over the next few years in order to house the Gallery's growing permanent collection.

In its activities, too, the Gallery's efforts have increased. With additional exhibition space, the new construction has provided for expanded Extension Service activity, including a television studio, and for the launching of the Gallery's Center for Advanced Study in the Visual Arts, where visiting scholars come to avail themselves of the greatly expanded library and national photographic archive. The Gallery has begun to utilize new and sophisticated technologies to improve various aspects of the museum's program. Computerization is underway, providing automated record keeping and reporting functions. The system chosen provides the capability for building an art-data base which can later be used for research

and study purposes. Moreover, the Gallery is one of seven museums participating in the Museum Prototype Project funded by the J. Paul Getty Trust. This undertaking will make accessible the research records which now exist on collection catalogue cards in individual museums. At the same time it will provide a model for operating an integrated system.

The first videodisc devoted to an entire American museum has as its subject the National Gallery. One side of the disc is interactive, allowing the viewer to locate over 1,600 masterpieces in the collection while benefiting from color standards which provide new levels of reproduction fidelity. The other side of the disc comprises a tour past collective highlights in both buildings, interspersed with the history of this institution. The result is yet another avenue whereby the treasures of the National Gallery can be accessible to those not actually in Washington.

Even now, the National Gallery is engaged in producing a scholarly catalogue of its holdings. These detailed publications will provide the most complete source of information concerning the objects in the collection. Their eventual appearance, however, will not obviate the need and value of a book like this one. Since the first appearance in 1944 of a slim volume called *Masterpieces of Painting from the National Gallery of Art*, there has been published a succession of books illustrated in color, with texts wholly or in part by John Walker, the Chief Curator from the Gallery's inception in 1939 until he succeeded David E. Finley as Director in 1956. Each book has served to document the growth of the collections and the scholarship that surrounds them. Each book has, in turn, gone out of print, while the collection reflected within its pages has continued to grow with startling rapidity. It is therefore a cause for rejoicing that Mr. Walker, Director Emeritus of the Gallery since 1969, has produced this new edition of the present publication. No one has been more intimately connected with the Gallery's growth. May this volume serve as a magic solvent to the Gallery's marble walls, not crumbling them, but rendering them transparent, so that our national audience may better benefit from the delights and the illumination they conserve.

J. Carter Brown
Director

The National Gallery of Art

The National Gallery of Art

Although the National Gallery of Art is the youngest of the world's great national galleries, in the character of its collections it resembles the oldest of the European museums. For, like the galleries of Paris, Vienna, Munich, Leningrad, and Madrid, it reflects the taste of discerning private collectors. They are the American successors to those princely amateurs who founded the national collections of Europe—the rulers of France, the Emperor Rudolph, the Archduke Leopold, Philip IV of Spain, Catherine the Great, and others—and it has been their generosity that has made possible the growth of a great national collection in just over thirty years. Such collections have been formed most frequently by individuals, seldom by committees, and almost never by governments.

Some governments have at times even shown themselves more ready to disperse than to assemble works of art. Consider, for example, the history of Raphael's *St. George and the Dragon*, one of the supreme works of art in the National Gallery in Washington. In three hundred years this panel has been twice sold by governments. It was first commissioned by Duke Guidobaldo da Montefeltro, ruler of Urbino, as a present for Henry VII of England. The English king had made the Italian ruler a Knight of the Garter, and Raphael was told to paint on the armor encasing St. George's leg the emblem of that knightly order. After the execution of Charles I, the revolutionary government of England sold this panel along with the rest of his collection. It was bought privately in France, where it remained until, under the shadow of the French Revolution, it was acquired by Catherine the Great and taken to Russia. Another revolution and another government, that of the Soviet Union, and it was sold again, this time from the Hermitage, the museum of Leningrad. Andrew Mellon acquired it for the National Gallery of Art, along with twenty other paintings. In the same way Hitler ordered to be sold from the German museums paintings which eventually entered the Kress and Mellon collections.

Many governments have had fluctuating attitudes toward their works of art. Sometimes they have looked upon paintings and sculpture as a form of national wealth, the equivalent of a gold reserve, intrinsically useful only to sustain the value of their currencies, but at other times paintings and sculpture have been promoted to the position of a cultural heritage. Today the pendulum has swung from improbable sales to impossible restrictions, and it is with the greatest difficulty that important works of art, even though privately owned, can be exported from most European countries.

From the opening years of the twentieth century the United States has been the greatest importer in history of works of art, but now only a trickle of masterpieces crosses the ocean. If the National Gallery of Art had been established in the 1980s instead of the 1930s, all the resources of the federal government would not have sufficed to buy the paintings and sculpture which are now in Washington. To form a comparable National Gallery today, one would have to resort to the methods of Hitler and Napoleon, gunfire and looting. But the nine Founding Benefactors of the National Gallery—Andrew W. Mellon, Samuel H. Kress, Rush H. Kress, P. A. B. and Joseph Widener, Chester Dale, Lessing J. Rosenwald, Paul Mellon, and Ailsa Mellon Bruce—used nothing more lethal than a bank account. Their contributions will be discussed later, but to understand the significance of their donations it is necessary to describe the slow growth of the idea and the realization of a national gallery in the capital of the United States.

Genesis

Until recent times, the American continent was destitute of Old Masters. Many of the leading artists of this country, from Copley in the eighteenth century to Mary Cassatt, who died in 1926, have recorded their lamentations. There was nothing for them to study. They had to go abroad to learn to paint. The New World might afford political liberty, freedom of worship, and unsurpassed prosperity, but it did not offer models for their work. That grindstone of the achievements of the past against which they needed to polish their own attainments was nowhere to be found.

Not that Americans were indifferent to art. We seem always to have had a surprising passion for paintings. Like the Dutch in the seventeenth century, we have eagerly commissioned portraits of ourselves, our possessions, our way of life, and, in our mementos and memorials, our way of death. As John Neal, the first important American art critic, wrote in 1829: "You can hardly open the door of a best-room any where, without surprising or being surprised by, the picture of somebody, plastered to the wall and staring at you with both eyes and a bunch of flowers."

But until the end of the last century Americans, with rare exceptions, had no time for connoisseurship—for that lust of the eye which, coupled with a sense of possession, leads to the formation of great collections. As John Adams, the second President of the United States, wrote to his wife in 1780: "I must study politics and war, that my sons may have liberty to study mathematics and philosophy. My sons ought to study mathematics and philosophy, geography, natural history and naval architecture, navigation, commerce, and agriculture in order to give their children a right to study painting, poetry, music, architecture, statuary, tapestry, and porcelain." One can see the stages outlined by Adams clearly reflected in the changing conceptions, over a period of a century and a half, of the nature and role of a national gallery of art in this country.

The two or three generations that followed Adams were indeed interested primarily in science and the practical arts, though the crafts and portrait painting found widespread support. The Old Masters, however, continued to be out of reach. The nature of the collection of the Washington Museum, the first institution of its kind in the capital, is characteristic. The so-called museum, which was opened in 1836, consisted of two rooms in which the proprietor had arranged "between 400 and 500 specimens." These included objects of natural history, historical relics, coins, and miscellaneous art objects. Of the works of art exhibited, only three paintings, a portrait of Cardinal Mazarin, a *Massacre of the Innocents*, and a *Turkish Battle Piece*, all by unknown artists, are still traceable; but these indicate the type of minor painting collected in this country at the beginning of the last century.

In the following years, the evolution foretold by John Adams gradually produced an increasing emphasis on the fine arts. The Washington Museum was incorporated into the National Institute, established in 1840. In the new museum, the fine arts began to assume a greater importance, although natural history continued to be the major interest. The Director of the Institute, the Honorable Joel R. Poinsett, was also Secretary of War, a bizarre combination of responsibilities which suggests his transitional role in the chronology outlined by John Adams. In a speech delivered in 1841, the only American museum director ever to obtain cabinet rank (and the only museum director after whom a flower, the poinsettia, has been named) made an impassioned plea for the arts:

"Here, the people reign—all power is centered in them; and if we would have them not only maintain their ascendancy, but use their power discreetly, no expense or pains should be spared to inspire them with a love of literature, and a taste for the fine arts. To effect this, the effort must be made here. It must originate at the seat of Government, and spread from this place over the populous plains and fertile valleys of the land."

It was a noble and enlightened attitude. Poinsett, however, labored under a handicap. He had no way of spreading "a taste for the fine arts" over "the populous plains and fertile valleys." Faced with the problem, he offered a brave though alarming solution. He recommended disseminating throughout the country copies of pictures, statues, and medals that had been commissioned by Congress. Fortunately the project was never carried out. Nevertheless, throughout the nineteenth century the position of art in this country was improving. In the capital, improvement was aided by an unexpected bequest. An Englishman, James Smithson, left $550,000 to the United States for "the increase and diffusion of knowledge among men."

Every American has heard of "The Smithsonian," but few know who Smithson was. An Englishman of noble lineage, his father was the Duke of Northumberland. Fortunately for the United States, as it later turned out, the Duke philandered, and Smithson was born out of wedlock. Precluded by illegitimacy from assuming any of his father's titles, he was nevertheless brought up as a man of wealth and given the best possible education. He graduated from Oxford at twenty-one and a year later was made a member of the Royal Society of London, one of the youngest scientists upon whom this honor was ever conferred. His subsequent researches in mineralogy proved so significant that an ore, smithsonite, bears his name.

Except in the case of royalty, a bar sinister has usually proved a bar, and Smithson found himself deprived of what he considered to be his rightful place in society. A deep bitterness poisoned his life. "The best blood of England," he wrote, "flows in my veins; on my father's side I am a Northumberland, on my mother's I am related to Kings, but this avails me nought. My name shall live in the memory of men, when the titles of the Northumberlands and the

Percys are extinct and forgotten." This must have seemed a most unlikely hope. Yet, as an adjective at least, his name has achieved immortality.

James Smithson died in Genoa in 1829. A nephew who had a life interest in the estate died six years later, and in 1835 President Jackson notified Congress of a legacy to the United States from an unknown Englishman who had never even visited this continent. No famous institution ever had an odder beginning than the Smithsonian Institution. One Congressman, Senator Preston of South Carolina, declared in a flood of oratory that it was beneath the dignity of the Republic to accept the bequest. If an institution of this kind were desired, he would prefer it to be established out of United States funds, and not have Congress pander to the paltry vanity of an individual. If Congress accepted this donation, Preston concluded, "every whippersnapper vagabond that has been traducing our country might think [it] proper to have his name distinguished in the same way."

John Quincy Adams, the sixth President of the United States, who had been elected to Congress after completing his presidential term, succeeded in persuading his fellow legislators that Smithson's far-seeing benefaction would prove a national asset; and in due course the legacy, entirely in gold sovereigns, was loaded on board a ship and landed in New York. Again difficulties arose over the testator's language. What did Smithson mean by that ambiguous statement that his bequest should be used "for the diffusion of knowledge among men"? Did this imply an institution of advanced studies? Advocates were found for an agricultural school, a research laboratory, a meteorological bureau. But in the end it was decided that Smithson had in mind something of a more general nature. In 1846, eleven years after the bequest was received, Congress finally established the Smithsonian Institution.

A Board of Regents was selected, and almost immediately adopted a resolution providing that endowment funds be appropriated for the "procuring, arranging, and preserving of the various collections of the institution, as well of natural history and objects of foreign and curious research and of elegant art, as others."

Art, it is evident, is still at the bottom of the hierarchy, below "natural history and objects of foreign and curious research." Though the Regents granted to art the adjective "elegant," they still did not grant to it much else. In half a century, apart from absorbing the National Institute in 1862, the only important support for art granted by the Smithsonian was three thousand dollars spent for the Marsh Collection of prints, an acquisition which today could be sold for many times its cost. Meanwhile the other departments of the Smithsonian were growing with phenomenal rapidity.

A change, however, was about to occur. A portent was the publication by Franklin Webster Smith in 1891 (revised and enlarged in 1900) of *A Design and Prospectus for National Galleries of History and Art in Washington.* Smith (1825–1911), though himself not an architect (he was a former hardware merchant), had a hobby of making models of famous buildings and sights he had seen on his trips abroad; one of his most famous reconstructions of ancient architecture, prior to the schemes for transforming Washington into a new Athens on the Potomac, was his Pompeia or House of Pansa in Saratoga Springs, New York. Smith's book is a mirror of the taste and culture of the United States at the turn of the century. Enthusiasm, grandiose conceptions, missionary zeal, mechanical inventiveness, and a typical desire for a shortcut to all the benefits associated with the fine arts are reflected in his plans. It was proposed to erect within the District of Columbia a wonderful agglomeration of magnificent edifices, a whole city "with walls and towers . . . girdled round." These buildings were to be full-size models of various monuments of all ages. They were to cover sixty-two acres southwest of the Washington Monument. They were to be constructed of Portland cement and decorated with paintings corresponding to the styles of the various countries. Displayed within were to be copies of great works of art. The United States was to be represented on the principal site by a reconstruction of the Acropolis with a model of the Parthenon, which, on the popular theory of the bigger the better, was to be half again larger than the original. This "pleasure dome" of art and culture was to have a device installed which might well, if adopted today, provide the solution to "museum fatigue." Smith suggested that his National Galleries be provided with "slow, auto-

matic, moving seats facing both walls," which, he said, "will be of great luxury, alike to casual observers and students."

How incredible it seems that this vast, permanent World's Fair in the middle of Washington, our first concept of a national gallery, should have won widespread support! Yet members of Congress took it up, prominent architects helped with plans, and European museum authorities wrote letters of approval. In view of all this enthusiasm it is amazing that this fantastic national gallery was never built!

An assumption underlying Smith's scheme, warmly approved by European museum directors, was that America must satisfy herself with copies. An eminent professor of architecture was quoted by Smith's supporters as saying that he "should restrict a national institution to casts of antiquarian remains, considering the fictitious value of originals in comparison." The argument was advanced that "these reproductions were in every way as valuable for education as originals."

Though reproductions represented a strong temptation—an easy access to treasures that otherwise seemed out of reach—magnificent works of art began to be acquired in Europe and to cross the ocean. As few Americans intended to leave their collections to their descendants, a stream of these masterpieces gradually flowed to public galleries. But Washington, in spite of the establishment in 1869 of the Corcoran Gallery of Art, a privately endowed institution with many important paintings and sculptures, lagged behind half a dozen other cities.

In 1906 the courts decreed that the art department of the Smithsonian Institution should be the recipient of the Harriet Lane Johnston Collection and was, in fact, the National Gallery of Art. Other gifts and bequests were added to the newly christened department. Charles Lang Freer, a Detroit railroad financier famous for his patronage of Whistler, went further and decided to build and give to the federal government a gallery for his own collection of Eastern art, and for the work of certain American painters he admired. Nevertheless, the federal government still lacked an adequate gallery of Western art; its National Gallery was still handicapped by its traditional position as an adjunct to a museum of natural history. The country had reached the third stage envisaged by John Adams, and the people were beginning to claim their right to study the fine arts, but the capital still could not provide the opportunities offered by such cities as New York, Boston, Philadelphia, Chicago, Cleveland, and Detroit.

The first real step toward the founding of an adequate national gallery was made by Andrew Mellon, as we shall see presently in dealing with his collection. It was during the period while he was Secretary of the Treasury and afterward while Ambassador to the Court of St. James's that he came to his important decision about the original National Gallery. He realized that it would always be handicapped by a position subordinate to the great scientific and historical collections of the Smithsonian Institution, and that the only solution was to establish a new gallery, in a building of its own, with its own endowment, its own appropriation from the federal government, and its own Board of Trustees. At the same time, he thought it wise to place the contemplated gallery under the aegis of the Smithsonian Institution, which had always been free from political interference. He wished the new institution to have complete independence. He offered to erect a building, to donate his collection, and to provide an endowment on the condition that Congress would appropriate funds to support the new museum. He requested that the title "National Gallery of Art" be removed from the small collection then housed in the Museum of Natural History—and that it be used instead to designate the gallery he was founding. The Smithsonian's art collection then took the title "National Collection of Fine Arts" (now renamed "National Museum of American Art") and was ultimately housed in a building of its own. Congress accepted Mr. Mellon's offer and the necessary legislation was quickly enacted.

Andrew Mellon's action was the more remarkable because he had no reason to be grateful to the federal government. He had been harassed by a mean and politically motivated tax trial which dragged on so long that vindication came only after his death. Yet he spent over $50 million, when the purchasing power of the dollar was far greater than it is today, to give the American people a National Gallery in their capital.

He was profoundly anxious that it should rate high among the great national galleries of the world, and he thought long and hard about the institution he was founding. He had stipulated that the building should not bear his name, for he felt that only a co-operative enterprise could create a great museum, and he was right. He also stipulated that the federal government pledge its word to maintain the Gallery, and he devised a governing board of nine Trustees, five of them private citizens who elect their successors. From the federal government he chose four ex-officio members: the Secretary of State, the Secretary of the Treasury, the Secretary of the Smithsonian Institution, and, as Chairman, the Chief Justice of the Supreme Court. This division of five and four has meant that though the National Gallery of Art is governmentally supported, it is controlled by private citizens, an ingenious protection against the hazards of political pressure.

The Two Buildings

The National Gallery of art comprises two buildings, both in the shadow of the Capitol, one opened in 1941 and the other in 1978. Although the addition of 1978, known as the East building, is smaller in its outside dimensions, it contains five exhibition levels rather than two, as well as eight floors for the library and the office area; consequently the usable space in both is roughly equal. Their architectural idioms, however, are quite different, reflecting the differences in taste of Andrew Mellon and his son, Paul. The earlier building was designed by the last outstanding master of Neo-Classicism, John Russell Pope. The new addition, a consummate example of contemporary style, is the work of I. M. Pei. The change in taste between the 1930s and the 1980s, as seen in these two edifices, is a striking illustration of the mutations of fashion. Yet the two buildings are remarkably harmonious. They have been related by the use of the same material, a rose Tennessee marble, by their axial placement, and by the maintenance of a uniform height for various components. Each is, in a way, expressive of its contents: the Neo-Classical building of paintings from Duccio to Cézanne and sculpture from Nino Pisano to Maillol; the modern addition, of the work of subsequent artists.

John Russell Pope created the noblest tribute of the twentieth century to Classicism. He was a martyr to his desire to erect one last monument to that great artistic tradition, which began with the Greeks and Romans and continued through the Renaissance until its final extinction in our own time. Knowing himself desperately ill, Pope worked feverishly at his designs. His doctor told him in the spring of 1937 that he had cancer and that an immediate operation offered a good chance of survival, otherwise the disease would be terminal in six months. In order to continue working on the drawings for the Gallery, Pope refused the operation. Within six months he was dead. Just twenty-four hours earlier, Andrew Mellon had died. But the plans for the Gallery were completed organizationally and architecturally.

The exterior was influenced by George Hadfield's Old District Court House erected in 1820. On the east and west ends are lofty portals and on the north and south monumental Ionic porticoes. Otherwise the exterior is adorned only with niches and pilasters, and the beauty of the building lies in its marble masonry, delicately rose in color, and in its harmony of proportion.

Pope was an architect preeminent in his ability to handle classical forms dramatically. As the main feature of the Gallery he designed a rotunda with a great coffered dome upheld by towering columns of green-black marble. This central area, in its proportions, its concept of space, its classical orders, is a free adaptation of the interior of the Pantheon in Rome, though actually departing further from its model than, say, Bernini's church in Ariccia. Joined to the rotunda by halls for monumental sculpture are two garden courts where changing exhibitions of flowers, grown in the Gallery's greenhouses, are always displayed. Around these architectural features are grouped the rooms for paintings and smaller sculpture.

The building was intended to satisfy an often unrecognized desire on the part of the public. In this country there is a lack of the magnificent churches, public buildings, and palaces of Europe; Americans living for the most part in apartments and small houses feel the need for buildings more sumptuous, more spacious, and less utilitarian than their everyday surroundings. The satisfaction of this desire has a psychological value as definite as it is difficult to analyze. From architecture that has dignity, splendor, permanence, people seem to gain an enhancement of their own personalities. There can be no doubt that, disregarding the collections, visitors receive great pleasure from the National Gallery simply as architecture.

But there is always a danger that the museum building will dominate its contents. This, I believe, the National Gallery of Art has avoided. David E. Finley, the first Director, who greatly influenced all the plans, and I, who had just become Chief Curator when the earlier building was begun, were determined that attention should be focused on the works of art. It seemed to us a mistake to clutter up the painting and sculpture galleries with antique furniture, statuary, tapestries, and other decorative arts, as is the practice in some museums. In the National Gallery the picture galleries are galleries of pictures; the sculpture galleries, galleries of sculpture. Commodious sofas there are; but these are to rest the weary, not to indicate the type of settle used by Lorenzo the Magnificent.

To avoid monotony and to harmonize with the styles of painting, we selected different backgrounds for the different rooms: plaster for the early Italian, Flemish, and German pictures; damask for later Italian paintings; oak paneling for Rubens, van Dyck, Rembrandt, and the other Dutch; and painted paneling for the French, English, and American canvases. A suggestion of the architectural styles prevalent when these schools flourished is indicated in wainscoting, moldings, and overdoors.

But we kept in mind our basic goal: to permit the visitor a concentrated and undistracted scrutiny of each work of art. Therefore we decided to hang the pictures twice as far apart as one usually sees them in other galleries—a method of installation which has been generally commended though very little imitated. In many rooms we used paneling to achieve greater isolation for each painting. The separation thus afforded a second frame, so to speak, which we believe more than compensates for any loss of flexibility. How taste has changed in the arrangement of works of art in the last forty years, how the individual object has gained more and more isolation, is clearly illustrated in two photographs of the Widener Collection: as it was first shown at Lynnewood Hall, and as it appears in the National Gallery of Art.

Thus the whole installation of the Gallery was determined by a basic assumption: that the work of art is not a specimen, not primarily a historical document, but a source of pleasure. Accepting this premise it seemed to us that the major purpose of the National Gallery of Art was to allow each painting, piece of sculpture, or other object of art to communicate to the spectator, with as little interference as possible, the enjoyment it was designed to give. An art gallery and a concert hall, we felt, have much in common: one affords delight to the eye, the other to the ears.

The museum director and the conductor of an orchestra are also comparable: both present as satisfactorily as possible the works of others, both have an interpretative function to perform, much greater, of course, in the case of the conductor. But the museum director has a further responsibility which the conductor is spared. He must preserve what he presents. In recent years this task of preservation has been immeasurably aided by air conditioning. The National Gallery is the largest completely air-conditioned art museum in the world; and the system works so well that atmospheric variations can be controlled to within five degrees of relative humidity. This stability has proved a vital factor in increasing the longevity of paintings, especially those executed on wood. For all pictures are vulnerable to fluctuations of humidity. These changes cause the support—the substance on which the picture is painted—to expand and contract at a rate different from the expansion and contraction of the surface of the picture. Consequently, blisters and cracks occur, which in turn cause the pigment to flake and chip away. The National Gallery of Art has one of the largest collections in the world of early Italian paintings, which are especially fragile. Yet, because of the stability of the atmosphere, almost no restoration has been required once these pictures have grown accustomed to their environment.

Before I retired in 1969, it became apparent that space in the original building had been used up. We could not show all the works of art we had been given, the library could not expand, the staff was cramped. Since neither we nor the architect we chose wanted to deface the symmetry of the existing building by tacking on an appendage, a second, separate building was essential. That it could be erected was owing to the foresight of Andrew Mellon, who stipulated at the time of his original gift that an additional area on the Mall be reserved by Congress for the Gallery's future expansion. This plot, the most prominent unused site left in Washington, lay between the original building and the Capitol. Thirty years passed, and it remained unoccupied. Meanwhile the Gallery's claim to an invaluable piece of real estate had become so tenuous that there was doubt in 1967 as to whether Congress would enact the necessary legislation to permit its use. Fortunately, however, I was able to tell the Committee on Public Buildings, much to their astonishment, that the money to erect the new building would be provided privately. Their relief on hearing this assured their concurrence, and with the support of President Johnson a bill authorizing the National Gallery's expansion was passed unanimously.

I retired from the Gallery shortly thereafter and my successor, J. Carter Brown, has been entirely responsible for the East Building. I would like to quote from him the following comments on its design.

*   *   *

"After an analysis of the site and its potentials by Pietro Belluschi, himself not a candidate for the commission, the architect I. M. Pei was selected. The Trustees asked for a solution that would take maximum advantage of the site, which represented the last opportunity the National Gallery would ever have to expand into contiguous space.

Pei utilized the site fully by fitting a trapezoidal plan on the trapezoidal plot; this he divided diagonally into two complementary triangles, one devoted to exhibition space and the other to the Center for Advanced Study in the Visual Arts. Thus, from the beginning, two sets of functions were envisaged for the East Building. The exhibition area accommodates changing exhibitions and provides for the growth of the permanent collections. This is particularly necessary, as the survey of Western painting and sculpture that the National Gallery offers will continue to grow into the twentieth century and beyond. The Study

Center provides offices for scholars, major library and photographic archives, and office space for Gallery administration.

Mr. Pei and his associates had also started with an analysis of the Gallery's needs, of which one of the most important was the maintenance of a homogenous environment for delicate works of art when they had to be transported to any point in the new complex. It was their suggestion that the Registrar's office and the Photographic and Conservation laboratories, which handle a steady flow of art objects, be brought close together at the east end of the original building and connected to an underground route linking the two buildings. This route lies behind the walls of the underground concourse used by the public, and it is here that the Gallery carries on certain vital service functions for both buildings. Thus the entire complex has the same environmental controls.

The architect gave early consideration to the problem of the new building's responsibility to its urban site, at the juncture of two major axes designed by Pierre L'Enfant in the eighteenth century. Its exterior had to relate to Pennsylvania Avenue, with its Federal Triangle cornice line, the highest in the city, and in scale it had to be commensurate with the neighboring museums of American and Natural History, the existing National Gallery building, and the Capitol itself. The intersection of Pennsylvania and Constitution avenues had previously been spatially undefined, but now in accordance with Pei's vision the East Building of the Gallery heads the parade of monumental federal structures leading from the Capitol to the White House and the Washington Monument.

Another challenge facing the architect was that of relating the new building to the older one across Fourth Street. An early decision was made to construct it of exactly the same rose-colored Tennessee marble. The original building, with its towering rotunda and majestic, day-lit sculpture halls and garden courts filled with natural light, was an eloquent expression by its architect, John Russell Pope, of the Beaux-Arts tradition. Pei felt that the new building also should be organized around a great orientation space that could be used for the exhibition of sculpture. However, he felt that the rigorous symmetry of Pope's circulation plan was confusing to the visitor.

Therefore he differentiated the central interior space of the East Building enough to allow the visitor to keep track at all times of where he is in relation to the rest of the building.

To make it still more evident that the old and new structures form one complex, Pei projected the axis of the Pope building through the new galleries and, astride this axis connecting the buildings, he designed a plaza which links the facades firmly together, overcoming the intrusion of Fourth Street. In many ways this was a virtuoso solution, in that the center of the new site is considerably south of that axis, and most of the area covered by the new building is asymmetrical in relation to the old.

The outdoor plaza is paved in the European manner with concentric fans of Belgian block granite. In the center, as a visual focus, is a cluster of great glass tetrahedrons, flanked to the north by a line of fountain jets from which water rushes down an open slide to form a waterfall in the underground concourse below. The tetrahedrons provide daylight to this below-grade section of the connecting link.

The visitor coming through the underground concourse from the original building will find a lively area equipped with a 'sidewalk' café, a large self-service facility, including a snack bar, a museum shop, and, at the end, a moving walkway angled upward, leading directly into a lower lobby of the East Building. On that level there is access to a large and a small auditorium and a large, flexible space for temporary exhibitions.

Visitors entering the East Building from the outdoor plaza pass through a broad, low-ceilinged reception area into a great glass-roofed courtyard, opening to four levels of courts or balconies. Besides providing a spacious setting for sculpture, the space, with its greenery and sense of openness to the sky, creates a transition from the plaza and the Mall park and acts as a natural orientation space. Open stairs and escalators lead to the various exhibition levels, housed in three gallery towers connected by bridge galleries and access bridges. A terrace café on the fourth floor provides visitors with a convenient place to rest.

The second triangle of the East Building houses the Center for Advanced Study and the library and offices. At the heart of this building is a lofty reading room with adjoining book stacks. There are large areas above and below ground for a photographic archive, reference works, and storage. Space has been provided for three hundred thousand volumes, with room for further expansion."

* * *

Recent purchases for the new library are an indication of its importance. They include the Sallemi and Reti collections on Leonardo da Vinci, making the Gallery a major center of Vincian studies; part of the huge Ugo Ojetti collection; the equally large Lubin library; the libraries formed by the art historians Rudolf Wittkower, Wolfgang Lotz, and Carl Nordenfalk; and the reference library of the late Lessing J. Rosenwald. Other special acquisitions include the Kate Steinitz collection on Kurt Schwitters, monographs and periodicals on Swedish and Russian architecture, and major collections on surrealism and French nineteenth-century art. It is the Gallery's policy to buy books whenever they are available. The supply is quickly dwindling, and prices are steadily rising. Today it is not easy to build a great library in a short period of time, but with luck and industry this can be done. What has already been accomplished at the National Gallery of Art is proof.

The Founding Benefactors

At the entrance of the West Building, the earlier of the two National Gallery edifices, there is a tablet listing the principal benefactors in chronological order of their donations: Andrew W. Mellon, the founder, Samuel H. Kress, Rush H. Kress, P. A. B. and Joseph E. Widener, Chester Dale, Lessing J. Rosenwald, Paul Mellon, and Ailsa Mellon Bruce. It is to these nine Founding Benefactors that the Gallery owes its phenomenal development. Without their gifts—entire collections assembled over many years as well as large funds for purchase—the Gallery might have developed as slowly as other museums; today, with the diminution of available masterpieces, this gradual growth would be at a snail's pace. I can think of no museum in America which has opened with comparable masterpieces. For example, the Metropolitan Museum of Art in New York and the Museum of Fine Arts in Boston, which were founded almost simultaneously, possessed mediocre collections for their first thirty years—only slightly less time than the National Gallery has existed. During those early years, from 1870 to about 1900, they could boast of little more than faith that someday they would be able to replace their casts with original works of art. And even this faith was shared by few of their Trustees and only some members of their staffs. The torrent of great paintings and sculpture from Europe had not yet swept over the United States.

I knew all of the Founding Benefactors of the National Gallery with varying degrees of intimacy, except P. A. B. Widener, who had died in 1915. They were as diverse a group as American plutocracy could produce, but they had two common denominators: great wealth and a passion for collecting. Why did they spend vast sums of money and a large proportion of their available energy and time acquiring works of art? The answer, if it can be stated at all, is bound to be complex; no generalization will satisfactorily apply to people of such varied character and temperament. But I would say that basically they shared a belief that their works of art would be of public benefit. They did not try to define this benefit, nor is it probable that they would have agreed on any definition. They were not like collectors for dynastic enrichment, such as Charles I of England, Queen Christina of Sweden, or Catherine the Great of Russia. Nor were they in the same category as such private collectors as Arundel, Crozat, or Ellsmere, who intended their treasures for their families and for the delectation of an elite body of connoisseurs like themselves. Nor did these Founding Benefactors make their donations to avoid taxation, as is too commonly asserted. If there had been no inheritance taxes in America, the donations to the Gallery in my opinion would have been very little affected. For I am convinced that these collectors looked upon themselves as the temporary custodians of a heritage belonging to all mankind. Their belief in private property did not extend to artistic property. Here they were Marxists. Although they might condemn communism, their motivation in matters of art was communistic. The duration of possession, they believed, was limited by mortality. Chester Dale was fond of saying, "A shroud has no pockets."

Meditating on their portraits hung on the walls of the Founders' Room, how often have I tried to understand the psychology of these nine remarkable people, all but one of whom are dead. Thinking of those I knew intimately, it occurs to me that most of them had in common some inner loneliness, some unsatisfied desire for friendship, which mere gregariousness could not satisfy. Several referred to their works of art as their children. They seem to have established a companionship with these silent canvases, these marble or bronze effigies, whose company was undemanding and whose presence could always be counted on. Whether looking at portraits, landscapes, still lifes, or devotional pictures, the collectors I have known appear to have felt an ineffable happiness in their presence. Possession was an important element; the magic did not work with public collections or the collections of others. This possessive relationship was like some affinity which would endure until mortality intervened. Then they wished their works of art to enter recognized and established museums and to become the permanent heritage of the people, as a father might wish to give his children security and public approbation.

Andrew W. Mellon

The Mellon family came from Ireland and settled in Pittsburgh, where Thomas Mellon became a Judge of the Court of Common Pleas, and was active in real estate, coal, and banking. By the standards of the time he was a rich man. Thus even in his youth Andrew Mellon was able to buy an occasional picture; but, as he once noted somewhat wryly, his friends and business associates looked askance when he paid as much as a thousand dollars for one of his earliest purchases. In the Pittsburgh of the 1870s collecting was not encouraged. Such a hobby was looked upon as particularly strange in a young banker who was in other respects not only full of common sense but who was admired by the whole community for his financial acumen. Yet he and his close friend Henry Clay Frick, who later established the Frick Collection in New York, persisted in their extravagance. They traveled to Europe together and continued to collect, buying works of art at the rate of a few thousand dollars a trip—expenditures which, as the years passed, increased by geometric progression until each had disbursed scores of millions of dollars on the most expensive of all pastimes.

Andrew Mellon's collecting began with seventeenth-century Dutch and eighteenth-century En-glish painting. Living a somewhat solitary life, he found his Dutch and English portraits companionable. With them he perhaps enjoyed imaginary friendships unspoiled by that sense of shyness he always felt with people. In the same way, his views of Holland and England opened windows on a world more attractive than the smoky atmosphere of Pittsburgh, where at night every aperture was covered with cheesecloth and all the furniture draped in sheets to keep out the constantly settling soot.

Mr. Mellon looked a great deal at his works of art. He learned to discriminate and developed a remarkably good eye. For example, one of the few pictures he ever returned to a dealer was a portrait of Giuliano de' Medici, now in the Bache Collection of the Metropolitan Museum. At that time it was considered to be by Raphael, and the attribution had never been questioned. The picture is now, however, considered by scholars and the Metropolitan itself to be a copy. Did Mr. Mellon have some intuition about the picture's authenticity? More probably it was the personality of the sitter which he found distasteful. Giuliano's face may have reminded him of the vulgar and grasping politicians who were his enforced associates.

Throughout his life Andrew Mellon had an aversion to nudes and Crucifixions. There are no nudes in the collection, and when he was finally persuaded to buy a *Crucifixion* by Perugino it was only because this central scene of Christianity was depicted without the slightest indication of suffering. Nevertheless when he began to think of his collection as the nucleus of a national gallery his selectivity became less personal. The exact date of his decision to found a museum in Washington is difficult to establish. In 1926 he wrote the Duchess of Rutland, "I have only those paintings and a few tapestries which I have acquired from time to time when I had suitable places in my residence. I have not had occasion to consider acquisition of such for public purposes."

However, in the latter part of 1927 he seems to have made up his mind about the future of his collection. It was at that time that he told David Finley, his special assistant in the Treasury, that he intended to build a national gallery and that he wanted Finley to be the first director. In a diary entry of 1928 Andrew Mellon noted: "Ailsa [his daughter] telephoned in morning from No. 1 Sutton Place. Has just arrived from Boston. Asks if I have given art gallery to the Government." This is the first documented mention of his intentions. From then on there are frequent references to his search for a suitable site for the new building.

For many years Mr. Mellon bought from only one dealer, M. Knoedler and Company; later he made a number of purchases from Duveen Brothers. But these two firms were the only ones with whom he dealt. It was a shrewd policy, for, as he was the principal patron of each dealer, he could count on being offered the best works of art each could procure. He never bought at auction. In those days it was customary in America for the dealers to negotiate purchases. Few sales were made in any other way.

His greatest coup as a collector was his acquisition in 1930 and 1931 of twenty-one masterpieces from the Hermitage Gallery in Leningrad. The complexity of these Russian sales is difficult to describe. In the late 1920s the Soviet Union was swarming with hopeful art dealers, like bees buzzing around sugar. But the Hermitage, the richest treasure trove, remained inviolable until Calouste Gulbenkian, having successfully advised the Russians how to unload their oil on the world market, also persuaded them that the sale of some of the works of art from their great museum would increase their reserves of hard cash. Then, however, this usually most secretive of men revealed his valuable secret. He asked a young German art historian, later head of the Matthiesen Gallery in Berlin, to act as his agent in acquiring the works of art from Russia. Matthiesen, realizing that he had stumbled on the Golden Apples of the Hesperides as far as art dealers were concerned, refused the offer; and Gulbenkian, in his anger with himself for making one of the few mistakes of his life, withdrew entirely from the Russian market, a decision he was always to regret.

Young Matthiesen soon ascertained that the Russians were willing to have him act on their behalf. But he felt he lacked experience and he knew he lacked capital for such a venture. In this crisis he turned to the partners of Colnaghi's, a leading London art dealer, and together they got in touch with the Knoedler partners.

Knoedler and Company had as a client the world's leading art collector, Andrew Mellon, then Secretary of the Treasury. Carman Messmore, the Knoedler partner who dealt with Mr. Mellon, immediately went to Washington. He explained that in return for the necessary capital his firm would buy a number of Hermitage paintings. They would be offered first to Mr. Mellon at a commission of 25 percent. Any paintings he did not find acceptable, Knoedler's would sell and pay him 25 percent of the profit, which they estimated would be at least 50 percent of the purchase price. It was a deal no collector with sufficient funds could have resisted. During the next two years Andrew Mellon bought all the paintings from Russia Knoedler's brought to America—a total of twenty-one—for which he paid just over $7 million. This seemed a high price at the time, but in 1970 the Metropolitan Museum at public auction paid $5.5 million for a single painting, the Velázquez *Portrait of Juan de Pareja*. Today, the Mellon Hermitage paintings, which include Raphael's *St. George and the Dragon* and the *Alba Madonna*, Botticelli's *Adoration of the Magi*, Perugino's *Crucifixion with Saints*, Titian's *Venus with a Mirror*, Veronese's *Finding of Moses*, van Eyck's *Annunciation*, Velázquez's *Study for Innocent X*, and numerous works by van Dyck, Frans Hals, and Rembrandt, could be sold for more than $30 million. Thus Mr. Mellon's acquisitions from the Soviet Union will always rank among the greatest transactions in the history of collecting.

Shortly after these purchases from the Hermitage were made, Mr. Mellon became Ambassador to the Court of St. James's, where he remained from 1932 to 1933. It was a happy year in his life. From the time of his earliest trips to Europe he had gone repeatedly to look at the pictures in the British National Gallery. It had become his favorite collection. The size, the installation, the high level of quality, all appealed to him. He determined that it should be the model for the Washington National Gallery of Art. One might have seen this delicate, patrician, impeccably dressed figure with his high cheekbones, his carefully trimmed gray moustache, his silver-white hair, sometimes alone, sometimes accompanied by David Finley, intensely scrutinizing paintings, teaching himself to discriminate, trying always to learn what made certain works of art greater than others.

This world of aesthetic contemplation, however, did not last. The Depression arrived and Herbert Hoover went down in defeat. On the election of Franklin D. Roosevelt, lawyers from the Department of Justice and the Treasury descended on Mr. Mellon. President Roosevelt and his followers, who had victoriously overthrown twelve years of Republican supremacy, looked upon Andrew Mellon as a symbol of all they opposed. They were determined to discredit him. They asserted that he had committed fraud on his federal income-tax return. On these grounds they attempted to procure a criminal indictment, but the grand jury flatly refused to indict. A civil trial to collect penalties dragged on, overshadowing the last years of his life. When the court finally handed down the verdict, it was a complete vindication of any wrongdoing, but Mr. Mellon was no longer alive.

Yet, during a trial of extraordinary bitterness, he never lost his stoical detachment, never permitted the cruelty of the attack to cause him to deviate from his purpose of building a great national gallery in Washington. In December 1936 he wrote to Mr. Roosevelt, "My dear Mr. President: Over a period of many years I have been acquiring important and rare paintings and sculpture with the idea that ultimately they would become the property of the people of the United States and be made available to them in a national art gallery to be maintained in the city of Washington for the purpose of encouraging and developing a study of the fine arts." And on December 26, Mr. Roosevelt replied, "My dear Mr. Mellon: When my uncle handed me your letter of December 22 I was not only completely taken by surprise but was delighted by your very wonderful offer. . . . This was especially so because for many years I have felt the need for a national gallery of art in the Capital. . . . Furthermore, your offer of an adequate building and an endowment fund means permanence in this changing world."

All during the tax trial Mr. Mellon continued to collect, spending vast sums to assemble the works of art he felt would provide the nucleus for the Gallery. In the last twelve months of his life he acquired twenty-six paintings, ranging from works by Cimabue and Masaccio to Gainsborough's *Landscape with a Bridge.* Only a few weeks before his death he acquired Duccio's *Nativity,* once part of the *Maestà* of the Cathedral of Siena. This marvelous panel had been exchanged by the Kaiser Friedrich Museum in Berlin for a German painting to satisfy the wishes of Hitler for more Teutonic art.

Andrew Mellon wanted his collection to provide a framework on which the collection of the National Gallery of Art might grow. Therefore he intended his pictures to recapitulate the development of Western painting. His gift begins with a Byzantine Madonna of the thirteenth century and ends with a Turner landscape of the nineteenth century. Between these terminal paintings there is an example by almost every artist who strongly influenced the development of style. Though his collection contains only 115 pictures, exclusive of American portraits, these were chosen with such discrimination that they provide a nearly complete outline of seven centuries of European painting.

He did not collect paintings of the second half of the nineteenth century. He rightly considered American collections to be very rich in the work of the French Impressionists and Post-Impressionists, the most significant schools of the last hundred years, and he believed that the Gallery through gifts would ultimately receive an ample representation of these movements—a judgment which has been proved correct.

But American painting he did wish to provide and to that end he bought en bloc the most important private collection of American portraits ever assembled, the Thomas B. Clarke Collection. He knew that the quality of these portraits, ranging from our pioneer painters to Frank Duveneck, was uneven; but he wished the National Gallery of Art and a future National Portrait Gallery, which he hoped would be established, to be enriched by a judicious selection from among them.

Originally it was Andrew Mellon's intention to restrict his gift to painting, but he came to the conclusion that to understand the development of Italian art it is also necessary to know the works of the great sculptors of the Renaissance. With this in mind, especially during the last months of his life, he began to acquire magnificent statues of the fifteenth and sixteenth centuries, when Florentine sculpture reached the peak of its development.

Like the collection of paintings, the number of pieces of sculpture he bought is small, just over a score, principally from the famous Dreyfus Collection. But in both painting and sculpture the quality of the works of art shows an exacting connoisseurship. Mr. Mellon wished his collection to establish a measuring rod which would guide future Trustees in their acceptance of gifts for the Gallery. Thus he set himself the difficult task of acquiring nothing but masterpieces, an undertaking which can fail with even the greatest financial resources. Andrew Mellon, however, was astoundingly successful.

Unfortunately he did not live to see his collection installed in the National Gallery. Thus he did not witness and enjoy that moment which would have meant so much to him, when, with all his paintings and sculptures in place, he might have said to himself in Louis MacNiece's words, "Hundreds of windows are open . . . on a vital but changeless world, a daydream freed from doubt."

P. A. B. and Joseph E. Widener

Of the principal donations to the National Gallery of Art, the Widener Collection is the only one assembled for the most part before 1920. It was brought together when two factors were uniquely in balance: opportunities of purchase and sophistication of judgment.

Peter A. B. Widener and his son, Joseph, were introduced into the world of art by a poker-playing friend, John G. Johnson. Mr. Johnson was among the few dedicated American collectors of his generation. Compared to the Wideners, he was merely well-to-do, but he loved his collection of paintings, a very mixed bag with a few works of outstanding importance, yet for the most part consisting of minor examples that appealed to him. He was, however, a true dilettante in the eighteenth-century sense, and unlike most of the American millionaires of the time, he collected with no ulterior social motive.

P. A. B. Widener was a very different type. According to his grandson the motivation for his collecting was directly related to Philadelphia society. He wished to rise above their snobbery on the wings of his art collection, and he triumphantly succeeded, though his son, Joseph, seems to have remained permanently embittered. P. A. B. Widener in his portrait by Sargent looks as though he might have been a recently enriched alderman; Joseph Widener, in his portrait by Augustus John, looks more like a neurotic peer. The evolution of American families is rapid.

When P. A. B. Widener died in 1915 he left his son the disposition but not the ownership of the collection. Under his will the Widener works of art could be given to a museum in Philadelphia, New York, or Washington, or they could be sold for the benefit of the Widener family. Meanwhile they were displayed at Lynnewood Hall, where the Wideners lived, a house which over the years became a pilgrimage site to all who were interested in art.

In the 1930s Andrew Mellon and Joseph Widener discussed the proposed National Gallery and the future of the Widener Collection without a definite decision being reached. After Mr. Mellon's death, and when the construction of the Gallery was under way, David Finley went to Lynnewood Hall and urged Mr. Widener to give his collection to the National Gallery in Washington. Mr. Widener seemed inclined to do so. David Finley, with his wonderful intuition of how to persuade donors to give collections, asked Otto Eggers, the successor to John Russell Pope as architect of the Gallery, to make renderings of the rooms where the Widener Collection might be placed, showing each work of art installed. Joseph Widener was entranced, but still reluctant to decide. After an agonizing period of uncertainty, he finally offered to designate the National Gallery of Art the fortunate museum provided three conditions could be met: (a) that the collection should be shown as a unit; (b) that the entire collection including Chinese porcelains, Renaissance furniture, tapestries, ceramics, jewelry, and rock crystals, and French eighteenth-century decorative arts, books, and engravings be accepted; (c) that the gift be without taxes of any kind to the Widener estate.

The Widener Collection was a museum in itself and its acquisition of greatest importance to the new National Gallery. The first condition, that the collection be shown as a unit, would, however, have nulli-

The Original Widener Gallery at Lynnewood Hall

The Widener Rembrandt Room at the National Gallery

fied Mr. Mellon's desire for a strictly chronological installation. This principle of an arrangement showing the historical development of painting and sculpture has remained a basic Gallery policy; but it is one that has cost the National Gallery of Art two collections only a little less important than the Widener Collection. The first demand, therefore, the Trustees refused, and Joseph Widener finally accepted a compromise which has been satisfactorily employed with other collectors. He agreed that the Widener Collection should not be shown in contiguous rooms; but in return the Trustees also agreed that when there were enough paintings by one artist or a single school of artists, these would be kept together. The location of the room in which they would be shown, however, would conform with the pattern of the Gallery's chronological arrangement. Thus all the Widener van Dycks are placed in one room, but this room is adjacent to another gallery containing further works by van Dyck from various collections. In a similar way the Widener English paintings are installed in two rooms, at the opposite end of the building, where there are other galleries devoted to this school.

The second condition, that all the important Widener works of art, including decorative arts, be accepted, was easier to satisfy. The original edifice of the National Gallery is built on two floors. The main floor has a skylight with natural illumination in the daytime and artificial illumination at night. It provides ample space for a collection somewhat larger than the collection on exhibition in the National Gallery in London. The ground floor, beside areas for temporary exhibitions, a print cabinet, and storage rooms, offered an ideal location for the Widener decorative arts. Though such works of art fall outside the scope of the collection as planned by Andrew Mellon, they represent some of the greatest masterpieces in the Gallery, objects of inestimable value—for instance, the Suger Chalice, one of the most renowned examples in the world of the minor arts of the Middle Ages; the Mazarin Tapestry, the outstanding illustration in the United States of the achievement of Flemish weaving about 1500; and a superbly chosen collection of Renaissance jewels, rock crystals, and Chinese porcelains.

The third condition, that the gift should be tax free,

was the most difficult to fulfill. Pennsylvania was one of the states in the Union which assessed a tax on bequests made to charitable institutions located outside the state. Ironically, under the Pennsylvania law, if Joseph Widener had decided to sell the Widener Collection for the benefit of his father's heirs, there would have been no state tax; but if these works of art were to be given to the federal government, then a 5 percent tax would have to be paid to Pennsylvania. Efforts were made by the Gallery to have this law altered, but to no avail. The Pennsylvania legislators proved obdurate and difficult. They refused to estimate the value of the collection until the Gallery agreed to pay the tax, but to accede to this meant accepting an unlimited commitment. The problem therefore seemed insoluble.

President Roosevelt took a personal interest and sent a message to Congress asking that the tax to Pennsylvania be paid regardless of the amount. The bill was passed and may well represent the only blank check ever written by Congress. It was this blank check which finally made possible one of the greatest donations in the history of museums.

There remained only the question of a valuation. The State of Pennsylvania appointed an appraiser, as did the Treasury and the National Gallery of Art. The results were significant. The date of the appraisal was 1940, when the gift was made. The three appraisals in the order mentioned were: $7,141,060; $3,877,010; and $4,953,060.

From documents in our files it is evident that P. A. B. and Joseph Widener paid between $20 and $25 million for their collections during the first two decades of the twentieth century, when the purchasing power of the dollar was very high. Yet by 1940 the value of the collection had declined 72 percent in terms of more inflated dollars. It is often assumed that the monetary value of works of art steadily increases. This is not true. The fluctuations are staggering. Today with $200 million I could not begin to assemble another Widener Collection. Yet thirty years ago its value for tax purposes was just over $7 million.

There is about the Widener Collection a certain unity of selection difficult to describe. Both father and son showed a concentration of rare intensity in their collecting. They were the type of devoted amateur that has become scarce in the world today. Although they sought advice from scholars and experts, the ultimate decision was always theirs, and for this reason, perhaps, they soon freed themselves from those fads and fashions that have characterized modern taste. Barbizon canvases, which once hid the walls of American houses under drifts of gray-green foliage, they avoided or disposed of, being satisfied with a few magnificent Corots. The present ubiquitous vogue of the Impressionists they anticipated by half a century. Manet's *The Dead Toreador* entered the collection in 1894, to be followed by important works by Degas and Renoir, at a time when these artists were still not fully appreciated even in their own country.

Yet the instinctive taste of the Wideners was for an earlier age and an earlier style. Their real feeling was for the grand manner: for the High Renaissance in Italy, for the seventeenth century in the Netherlands, and the eighteenth century in England. Their aesthetic sense was close to that of the English milords, those landed amateurs portrayed by Reynolds and Gainsborough, whose galleries showed their love of Raphael, Titian, van Dyck, and Rembrandt. For it is the work of these masters of the grand style which both Wideners tirelessly sought throughout Europe

Decorative Arts from the Widener Collection

Upper left: Pair of stained-glass windows representing the Annunciation. Florentine, c. 1500. Executed by Giovanni di Domenico for the choir chapel of Sta. Maria Maddalena dei Pazzi. Height 78½".

Upper right: Flemish tapestry representing the Lamentation. Brussels, c. 1520. Woven by Pieter van Pannemaker the Elder to designs by Bernaert van Orley. Wool, silk, gold and silver threads. 84 x 133".

Lower left: Pair of celadon fish-beast vases in seaweed mountings. Chinese porcelains in French gilt-bronze, c. 1725. Height 12½".

Lower right: Chalice of Abbot Suger. French, Saint Denis, c. 1140. Sardonyx cup with silver-gilt mounting, encrusted with filigree, jewels, pearls, and glass. Height 7¹⁷/₃₂".

and which today makes up the great treasures of their collection.

Like eighteenth-century connoisseurs, Mr. Widener and his son felt no interest in the styles of the thirteenth and fourteenth centuries, so highly esteemed in our time. Castagno, Neroccio de' Landi, Lorenzo di Credi, Mantegna, along with a few other fifteenth-century artists, seemed sufficiently archaic to indicate the origins of the Italian school. One painting by each of these masters was acquired, but what paintings they are! The unparalleled shield by Castagno; the rare example of Sienese portraiture of the fifteenth century by Neroccio; the only existing self-portrait by Lorenzo di Credi; as well as one of the most marmoreal and exquisitely preserved of Mantegna's panels—these and a few superb paintings by less well known artists represent the Quattrocento.

Similar panels one might occasionally have found hanging on the walls of great eighteenth-century houses; but wonderful as such paintings now seem, they would once have been considered, and perhaps should still be considered, secondary to other pictures in the Widener Collection, such as *The Small Cowper Madonna* by Raphael, which Lord Cowper bought in Italy nearly two centuries ago; *The Feast of the Gods,* that most harmonious but enigmatic work of collaboration between Giovanni Bellini and Titian, which was formerly the greatest treasure in the collection of the Duke of Northumberland; and the *Venus and Adonis* by Titian, which so impressed John Evelyn, the seventeenth-century diarist, when he saw it hanging in Lord Sunderland's dining room three hundred years ago. No less pride would an eighteenth-century connoisseur have taken in the portraits by van Dyck in the Widener Collection. Early in the nineteenth century Sir Robert Peel's agent in Genoa tried unsuccessfully to buy several of these, for they were always considered the finest paintings the brilliant young Flemish portraitist had left in Italy, but several generations were to pass before the Cattaneos and certain other Genoese families were willing to part with their heirlooms.

The climax of the Widener Collection, however, by eighteenth-century or contemporary standards, would unquestionably be found in the astounding array of canvases by Rembrandt. To this group belongs perhaps the supreme painting in the entire collection, Rembrandt's great landscape *The Mill,* once owned by Lord Lansdowne. Constable and Turner, whose works are also brilliantly represented in the collection, have left records of how much they owed to this example of nature seen in the grand manner.

One characteristic of eighteenth-century amateurs the Wideners escaped or outgrew: that tedious fondness for genre or still-life subjects by the lesser Dutch masters, those canvases which so often cover, from wainscot to ceiling, the walls of English country houses. Although Hals, Cuyp, Hobbema, Ruisdael, de Hooch, Potter, Steen, and both Ostades are included in the collection, they are represented by only a few major works. And to these names, so familiar in every eighteenth-century catalogue, must also be added Jan Vermeer of Delft, whose forty-odd surviving pictures were forgotten for two centuries. *Woman Holding a Balance,* a masterpiece of tranquility and stillness, is by him; *Young Girl with a Flute,* a masterpiece of technical brio, is attributed to a member of his workshop. These pictures are two of the greatest treasures in the Widener Collection.

When the Widener works of art were being packed for shipment to the National Gallery of Art, I spent several days with Joseph Widener at Lynnewood Hall. He was old and partly paralyzed. His trained nurse would help him into the long gallery where the paintings were being removed, and as he watched this desolate scene of crates and packing materials his eyes would fill with tears. He wanted to see the treasures he and his father had brought together installed in their new setting, but at the same time their removal broke his heart. Fortunately, he was strong enough to pay one last visit to the Gallery, and from a wheelchair he saw every work of art placed exactly as he wished. He died soon after this final visit to Washington.

The dismantling of the Widener house signified the end of an epoch. The brevity of the way of life represented by Lynnewood Hall has its own historical significance. Whereas the nobility of Europe enjoyed their collections for centuries, the Widener family is remarkable in America for having possessed their works of art for two generations. How often in the United States the museum director follows the hearse!

Samuel H. Kress
and Rush H. Kress

Of the principal collections given to the National Gallery of Art, the Kress Collection has been brought together most recently. Though Samuel Kress began buying works of art as early as the 1920s, the great purchases were made between 1937, the year the Gallery was founded, and 1956. Moreover, it is the only collection formed to some extent under the influence of the staff of the Gallery—an influence at first minimal, but one which steadily increased over the years.

When I first met Samuel H. Kress he was seventy-five, in appearance stocky, rather florid, with an unusually large head and small blue eyes. He was forever taking off and putting on his jacket, as he perspired easily and was deathly afraid of catching cold. He was a confirmed bachelor, living a lonely life, and his works of art had become the center of his existence.

In his youth he had taught school, and saving his small salary had accumulated enough capital to buy a stationery and novelty store in northern Pennsylvania. His enterprise succeeded, and he expanded, selecting the South and West for the chain of stores he later established. These proved to be immensely profitable; and partly for business reasons, partly for pleasure, he began to make annual trips to Europe.

He began collecting quite by chance. He was not a man who could ever be idle; and that European ennui, which affects so many American businessmen vacationing abroad, impelled him to seek an outlet for his indefatigable energy. A friend introduced him to a dealer, Count Contini-Bonacossi, in the hope that this recently ennobled Florentine might interest him in art and thus render his European vacations less boring. The cure for boredom worked beyond all expectations and cost in the end between $50 million and $100 million. Through his contact with the Count, as Mr. Kress affectionately called him, he was soon infected with the collector's virus, succumbing

almost immediately to that passion from which he never recovered, much to the benefit of cities in various parts of the United States and particularly of the National Gallery in Washington.

But Mr. Kress's collecting was, at the beginning, of a special kind. Perhaps because of his life as a storekeeper, he often referred to his works of art in a naive but charming way as "items." These "items" were to provide the most complete and systematic collection of Italian art ever brought together. Count Contini persuaded him to assemble works not only by the principal geniuses of the Italian schools but also by their entourage, those lesser-known painters and sculptors whose work, he said, explains and gives scale to the greater artists.

Such an emphasis on the form and structure of art represents a shift in the focus of appreciation from that shared by Mr. Mellon and Mr. Widener. The Kress Collection, in its first phase, reflected a point of view which Contini encouraged and which has grown out of the characteristic twentieth-century interest in art history. It showed the full effect of the scientific approach introduced into connoisseurship, especially of Italian art, by Morelli. This system of attributing paintings was perfected by Berenson, whose remarkable, intuitive scholarship made a deep impression on Samuel Kress. In the dossier of nearly every object which he gave the Gallery were written opinions not only by Berenson, but also by Fiocco, Longhi, Van Marle, Perkins, Suida, and Adolfo Venturi.

Samuel Kress's first purchases of Italian art were made in the most logical place, in Italy, and principally from his mentor, Count Contini. But he discovered that the Italian private collections had long before yielded their greatest treasures either to the museums of their own country or to the collections of England, France, and Germany. He realized that if he were to bring together distinguished works not only by minor artists but also by the great masters, he would have to search beyond the wares being offered by a single Italian dealer. This realization, however, presented Mr. Kress with a dilemma. When he began collecting, he once told me, Andrew Mellon dominated the international art market, and everything was offered to him first. Samuel Kress was reluctant to buy what had already been, he suspected, turned down. He therefore refused for many years to trade with the principal dealers. With the death of Andrew Mellon in 1937 the situation changed, and Samuel Kress became the most important private collector in the world. But in 1938 the Kress Collection still consisted chiefly of what Mr. Kress had bought from Count Contini.

Although Samuel Kress admired Andrew Mellon as a collector, he had no idea of giving his own collection to the museum Mr. Mellon had established. The fact that in the end the Kress Collection came to Washington was almost a matter of chance. In the winter of 1938 while the Gallery was being erected, two friends, Herbert Friedmann, the Curator of Birds at the Smithsonian Institution, and Jeremiah O'Connor, the Curator of Painting at the Corcoran Gallery, made a trip to New York, intent on their favorite pastime, to see as many private collections as possible. On this expedition they arranged to visit the Kress Collection, at that time scarcely known. Although neither was an expert in Italian art, both were astute enough to realize what Samuel Kress had already collected. On their return they described to David Finley the extraordinary paintings and sculpture they had seen. They went further and wrote Mr. Kress, urging him to give his collection to Washington. They knew he was contemplating a private museum like the Frick Collection, and they argued eloquently against such an arrangement and in favor of a donation to a museum supported by the federal government where, they pointed out, the Kress Collection would be seen by more persons and have a more secure future. The result of the correspondence was an invitation from Mr. Kress to Mr. Finley, asking him to come to New York to discuss the new museum in Washington.

Mr. Kress and Mr. Finley had met once on shipboard, though with characteristic modesty Samuel Kress had scarcely mentioned his collection. When the new Director of the National Gallery of Art saw what his steamship companion had brought together, he realized the collection must be procured for Washington. He had arrived at three in the afternoon; he left at ten in the evening. During those seven hours, with his inimitable powers of persuasion, he induced Samuel Kress to give up his plan for a private mu-

seum, for which property was already under option and architectural drawings prepared, and to send his works of art instead to the National Gallery. Had David Finley not arrived when he did, the Kress Collection would have remained on Fifth Avenue in its own building.

But even after Samuel Kress had decided that the National Gallery of Art would be the recipient of his collection, there was a strong possibility that the Trustees of the Gallery would be unwilling to receive it. The problem was that Andrew Mellon had insisted that a clause be inserted in the Act of Congress establishing the Gallery stating that "no work of art shall be included in the Permanent Collection of the National Gallery of Art unless it be of similar high standard of quality to those in the Collection acquired from the donor." Mr. Kress insisted that we take a minimum of 375 paintings and 18 sculptures, and a majority of these did not meet Mr. Mellon's qualifications. David Finley was able to negotiate an arrangement whereby a segment of the gift was constituted a Study Collection. But there remained 281 paintings and 18 pieces of sculpture which Samuel Kress insisted should be shown as part of the Permanent Collection. The Trustees of the Gallery were dubious, and they asked me whether these paintings and sculptures met Andrew Mellon's stipulations. If I believed they did, would I attest to this in writing?

I faced a dilemma. On the one hand, if the Gallery opened with only the 125 paintings and the 23 sculptures provided by Andrew Mellon, the vast building with 3¼ acres of exhibition space would be so empty that visitors might have to ask the guards to direct them to the next work of art. I foresaw budgetary problems with Congress, and knowing that politicians, like nature, abhor a vacuum, I was apprehensive about what we might be forced to exhibit. Moreover, I was convinced that Samuel Kress intended to improve his collection. He had the wealth, and I could see that the virus of collecting had entered his veins.

On the other hand, the standards of the Mellon Collection were as high as those of the Frick and the Widener collections, to name the two greatest in America. What Contini had sold Mr. Kress was different in character. All the lesser Italian masters were well represented, but apart from the Allendale *Nativity* by Giorgione, which Mr. Kress had bought from Duveen, there were relatively few paintings of world renown. The sculpture was no more impressive.

I was deeply perplexed. Samuel Kress was reluctantly enthusiastic about the new Gallery, and he had no intention of modifying his terms. We accepted what he offered, he stated, or he built his own museum. In the end I felt I had no choice. I signed an affidavit that the Kress Collection met Andrew Mellon's stipulations. Luckily, events proved it was the right thing to do. Of the 393 paintings and sculptures in this first gift from Samuel Kress, only 131 remain on exhibition. Those that have been removed have been replaced by the greatest masterpieces available for purchase during the 1940s and 1950s, the last two decades when acquisitions on a large scale were possible.

It must have been very hard for Samuel Kress to face parting with all these works of art, for in many ways his paintings and sculpture were a substitute for the children he never had. After the final selection for Washington had been made, David Finley said to me, as we were leaving the Kress apartment, that our new friend seemed to look upon us with the questioning and dubious reflection of a father estimating the character of his future sons-in-law. It was an astute observation, and this somewhat delicate relationship continued for several years. About once a month we would go to New York, and Mr. Kress would walk with us on the terrace of his penthouse or sit with us in his living room, where the blank walls seemed to accuse us of the treasures which had been removed. We would discuss the collection: how it looked, how it could be improved. Even in the last tragic years, when he was almost completely paralyzed, any mention of the National Gallery of Art would stimulate him to the effort of a reply. In the end we knew to our great joy that he was satisfied with the disposition of his collection, which he had originally looked on with considerable doubt.

After Samuel Kress was stricken, his much younger brother Rush Kress took over the direction of the Samuel H. Kress Foundation and devoted much of its resources to collecting for the National Gallery of Art.

The two brothers somewhat resembled one another, except that in place of Samuel Kress's shrewd, appraising glance, Rush Kress's look was open, even ingenuous. He was certainly the handsomer of the two, and his appearance was less that of a shopkeeper than of a president of an inherited firm. He did, in fact, become president of the company and of the Foundation when his brother fell ill. It was he who was responsible for the really great Kress Collection purchases. Perhaps because Samuel Kress had made the money, he was a little parsimonious in parting with it. Rush Kress, on the other hand, felt that his brother's collection, as he always called it, should contain the noblest masterpieces which could be acquired. Although he constantly repeated that he had no real interest in collecting, but was simply completing a plan begun by his brother, urged on by the director of the Foundation's artistic program, Guy Emerson, and by Mario Modestini, the curator of the Kress Collection, he grew fascinated by the quest for masterpieces. Between 1945 and 1956 the Kress Foundation spent more than $25 million on works of art. As the Gallery had the first choice of nearly all acquisitions, and considerable influence on their selection, this vast sum of money was in many ways a purchase fund, undoubtedly the largest capital expenditure disbursed in so short a time in the history of museums.

It was an extraordinary investment, as art prices subsequently have soared, and the value of what was purchased has tripled or quadrupled in the last fifteen years. Moveover, Rush Kress allowed me to distill the collection as I wished to do from the beginning, and he broadened the Kress acquisitions from an overwhelming concentration on Italian painting and sculpture to include Flemish, Spanish, French, Dutch, and German art.

Each rise of the tide of economic prosperity in the various countries has left behind incrustations of beauty; and very little of the residuum of this treasure can be removed. In recent years, through increased export restrictions, these possessions have become still more firmly embedded. It is remarkable that the Kresses, forming their collection so late in history, could have found so many masterpieces still susceptible to the ebb and flow of wealth. But private collections in England yielded the noble Allendale Giorgione and the uncompromising *Giovanni Emo* (formerly *Portrait of a Condottiere*) by Giovanni Bellini; in France, a number of eighteenth-century paintings, including the rare Boucher portrait of Madame Bergeret; and in Germany, in this case from museums, the Filippo Lippi *Madonna and Child* and the Raphael *Portrait of Bindo Altoviti.*

In Europe it is customary to think that works of art cross the Atlantic in only one direction. During the Depression, however, a number of the greatest artistic possessions of the United States returned to Europe. For economic laws, which govern the movement of works of art, have not always been in our favor. In the 1930s when our gold reserves were being drawn to Europe, their magnetic force pulled from us, among other masterpieces, the Mackay Sassettas (now in the National Gallery, London), The Kahn Carpaccio and Frans Hals, and the Morgan Ghirlandaio (now in the Thyssen Collection, Lugano), all supreme achievements by these artists.

Only the purchases made by a few American private collectors, among whom Andrew Mellon and Samuel and Rush Kress were outstanding, checked this outflow of works of art from the United States. Samuel Kress stopped further exportation of the Mackay and Kahn pictures and bought most of the Goldman Collection as well as many fine paintings from the collections of Robert Lehman and Dan Fellows Platt. Thus the original Kress Collection contained large parts of five of the most important private collections formed in this country.

During the war a number of paintings were sent to the United States for safekeeping, and from among these Rush Kress was able to make exceptional purchases. From the Cook Collection he acquired seventeen pictures, including the famous *Adoration of the Magi* by Fra Angelico and Fra Filippo Lippi; from the Thyssen Collection the wonderfully preserved *St. Veronica* by Memling, and other paintings; and from the collection of Count Cini, the *Giuliano de' Medici* by Botticelli and the *Dance of Salome* by Gozzoli.

After the war, at Rush Kress's instigation, dealers went to Europe in a continuing search for paintings and sculpture. This resulted above all in magnificent acquisitions from the greatest of Viennese collections, those of Count Czernin and of Prince Liechtenstein.

Moreover, whatever of outstanding importance came on the New York, London, or Paris markets was likely to be offered first to the Kress Foundation. The purchases in these years altered the character of the Kress Collection. More masterpieces were acquired and less attention paid to the minor Italian artists. The schools north of the Alps received new emphasis. A room devoted to German masters was assembled; two rooms of early Flemish and Hispano-Flemish paintings were added. Two galleries of seventeenth- and eighteenth-century French paintings supplemented those Samuel Kress had given; and Spanish, Dutch, and later Flemish pictures were bought.

Some idea of the magnitude of the purchases made between 1945 and 1956 by the Kress Foundation under Rush Kress's leadership may be gained from the Kress exhibitions held in 1951 and 1956 to celebrate the tenth and fifteenth anniversaries of the opening of the National Gallery of Art. In the two exhibitions there were 208 paintings and 46 pieces of sculpture. From these shows the Kress Foundation offered the National Gallery of Art the choice of as many works of art as would strengthen and enrich the collection in Washington. The Gallery finally decided to retain 167 paintings and all the sculptures.

The rapid expansion of the Kress Collection presented the Gallery with an unusual problem. There was a danger that the collection in Washington might grow too rapidly, with undue duplication, with too many minor masters, and with unwarranted emphasis on the Italian schools. Rush Kress was well aware of the law of diminishing returns, which plagues museums with collections insufficiently distilled. He decided that his brother's conception of a study collection and a permanent collection, both located in Washington, was not the most efficient way to utilize the vast number of paintings and sculpture the Kress Foundation had acquired. He concluded that works of art in storage are of little use; whereas the same paintings and sculpture shown in a community deficient in art might have a profound effect. He therefore determined to make important donations to eighteen museums in cities stretching from Miami in the East to Honolulu in the West. He bought a number of important works for these galleries, and asked that the National Gallery of Art return to the Foundation in exchange for new gifts whatever it could spare from the Kress Foundation's previous donations.

The staff of the National Gallery of Art was thus presented with one of the most fascinating series of decisions in museum history. To discuss only paintings, the Kress Foundation owned over 1,300 canvases and panels, of which there were at least 600 up to the standard of the National Gallery of Art. The space decided upon for the Kress Collection in Washington, more than a third of the main floor of the Gallery, would hold without crowding between 350 and 400 pictures. To reduce the Kress Collection to the present 377 paintings required eliminations which were often heartbreaking. But these were made less distressing by the realization that the 250 or more pictures surrendered by the Gallery would be enjoyed elsewhere in the United States.

Although the Kress Collection has been dispersed in this way, it is recorded in a nine-volume catalogue. These books reunite and present to the world one of the greatest collections formed in this century. That the most significant part of this collection should have ended in Washington has helped to give the National Gallery its high rank among museums.

Chester Dale

The sources of the principal collections given to the National Gallery of Art are interestingly varied. Andrew Mellon bought from only two firms, M. Knoedler and Company and Duveen Brothers. The Wideners and the Kresses were patrons of all the important art dealers in Europe and America. But Chester Dale alone was shrewd enough to become a partner of a dealer—the Galerie Georges Petit, one of the best-known companies dealing in Impressionist and Post-Impressionist canvases. This allowed him to scrutinize what was going on behind the scenes. His knowledge of the world centers of the art trade—Fifty-seventh Street in New York, Bond Street in London, and the rue de la Boëtie in Paris—was unique among American collectors. It enabled him to enter the art market with complete assurance and to carry off from dealers, pri-

vate collectors, and, above all, the great auctions of Europe and America, unsurpassed treasures of French painting of the last one hundred and fifty years.

That Chester Dale would one day become a great collector must have seemed unlikely to his parents. A dropout from school, he started life as a runner on the New York Stock Exchange. His first collection had nothing to do with art; it was devoted to inactive and unlisted railway bonds. His connoisseurship in these recondite securities enabled him eventually to become a partner in Langley and Company. Gifted with an amazing memory and a quick intuitive judgment, he pioneered successfully in buying public-utility holding companies, a field of investing then relatively unfamiliar even to the investment bankers of his generation. A redhead, wiry, and quick on his feet as a welterweight boxer (which he had once been), Chester Dale with his determination and inexhaustible vitality proved himself a formidable opponent among the financiers of his time. Wall Street was a challenge to him, a place to play a game with skill and daring. He played well, and ultimately retired to devote his intensely competitive nature to a different game, the acquisition of works of art.

Here he was fortunate enough to receive indispensable assistance. Maud Dale, his first wife, was a painter and art critic who would have had a successful career in either field, had her days not been fully occupied arranging art exhibitions and finding paintings for her husband to buy. In the early years of their collecting it was she who would point to the quarry; Chester Dale would track it down and secure it. Masterpieces have their own protective coloration and are not always easy to discern. But Mr. Dale's perceptive instinct soon developed, and with its development came a passion for works of art equaled by few collectors. His paintings, and the National Gallery of Art, became the major interests of his life. He gave unstinted devotion to both. For it was the essence of his character to commit himself entirely.

When Maud Dale died in 1953 one might have supposed that he would stop collecting. They had worked so closely together that the collection was in a way a joint enterprise. But such a supposition would have been wrong. He continued buying. In spite of the growing scarcity of masterpieces, some of his greatest acquisitions were made after her death.

The great period of purchase by the Dales, however, was during the 1920s. This was a time when the values of stocks and bonds were increasing daily until they were inflated beyond all reason, whereas the prices being paid for the work of the Impressionist and Post-Impressionist painters whom the Dales especially collected were, though costly, excellent investments in relation to the market today. When the crash came, securities fell to a fraction of their former prices; but the value of French painting held up remarkably well, supported largely by Chester Dale's continuing purchases. Since 1929 stocks have risen to an average somewhat less than twice their previous high, whereas French paintings now bring many times the highest prices ever paid in the 1920s. Of all the collections in the Gallery, judged in purely monetary terms, the Chester Dale Collection has had far and away the greatest increase in value.

I had known Chester Dale in the late 1920s, when two friends and I, while undergraduates, were running a gallery we had established in Harvard Square. We had temporary shows of what was then considered avant-garde art, and we borrowed extensively from the Dales, who were generous lenders. In the autumn of 1940, with David Finley, I renewed my acquaintance with Chester and Maud Dale. After a long and earnest conversation during which we stressed our need for American and French painting, we felt we had infected them with our enthusiasm for the new Gallery, but it was too close to the time of the opening, in 1941, to install a number of rooms devoted to their collection. Nevertheless, they sent seven American pictures on indefinite loan to bolster our American section. A few months later twenty-five French nineteenth-century paintings arrived to give the Gallery its first representation of Impressionism and Post-Impressionism. In 1942 more paintings of the same period were added, and in 1951 and 1952 the School of Paris canvases previously on loan to Chicago and Philadelphia were concentrated in Washington. All these paintings were only on loan, though we tried to give the impression that they had been donated.

Meanwhile the Samuel H. Kress Foundation was acquiring and sending to Washington incredible masterpieces of earlier painting and sculpture, but Rush Kress decided that as long as Chester Dale would not make a gift, the new Kress acquisitions would maintain the same status. These concealed loans were a source of constant anxiety. At one time in the late 1950s almost half of the works of art on display at the National Gallery seemed likely to be whisked away by these two potential but rival donors, whose good manners concealed a fervent dislike. This was a critical time. It ended when in 1961 the last of the Kress loans were finally converted into gifts, and when at Chester Dale's death in 1962 his loans also became the property of the Gallery.

The National Gallery of Art has acquired its collection by taking chances. Coming so late on the museum scene, the Director and Trustees had to have faith in a few collectors. To show the brilliance of French painting during the last century and a half they had to rely on Chester Dale. For a long time there were no Dale gifts, and while this was admittedly disconcerting, they refused to let it be disheartening. They knew the magnitude of the Dale Collection and they gambled that Chester Dale's fluctuating satisfaction with the Gallery would end happily. It did; the result was a bequest of 252 paintings and sculptures, a sizable purchase fund, and money for fellowships for students in art history.

Lessing J. Rosenwald

Another of the Founding Benefactors, Lessing J. Rosenwald, has given the National Gallery of Art his collection of prints and drawings, as well as some paintings.

A retired businessman who looked more like a medieval monk, Lessing Rosenwald was at one time chairman of Sears, Roebuck and Company. In his retirement the collecting of prints, drawings, and illustrated books, once his avocation, became an all-absorbing vocation. From the beginning he sought excellence rather than volume. Nevertheless, he brought together over twenty-five thousand drawings, woodcuts, engravings, etchings, mezzotints, lithographs, and prints in other media. This is not an enormous collection, but considering that it was assembled by one collector and that the impressions are extremely fine, it is an amazing achievement. In thirty years a single individual formed a collection rivaling in quality, if not in quantity, the most important private collections of graphic art ever formed.

In the past, print collectors such as the Abbé de Marolles wanted every print ever executed. In the seventeenth century, when the abbé lived, one hundred thousand impressions would have represented printmaking completely. Today millions of examples would be required and such comprehensive collecting would be folly. Selectivity has become essential. Rosenwald discriminated carefully, basing his judgment on four criteria: beauty, content, rarity, and, above all, quality. As he has said himself, "Quality is infinitely more difficult to attain than quantity. It is dependent on at least two variables, the ability to recognize the excellence of an impression from experience and knowledge and the availability of fine prints."

Print collecting requires a special erudition. A discriminating eye, though basic, is in itself insufficient. There are matters of rarity, brilliance of impression, paper, margins, states, innumerable facts which the collector must know. In all these matters Rosenwald's knowledge was exceptional.

In recent years the availability of outstanding prints and drawings has been on the whole greater than that of paintings or sculpture. There have been wonderful opportunities for acquisition from European collections like that of Count Harrach of Vienna, and from many of the European print cabinets which, since the war, have been increasingly inclined to dispose of their duplicates. Moreover, as prints and drawings are easy to transport, refugees from Nazi and Communist persecution have brought these precious leaves of paper to the auction rooms of Europe and America. Consequently, in some areas of print collecting Lessing Rosenwald assembled examples unmatched elsewhere. For example, his collection of fifteenth-century wood- and metal-cuts is one of the finest of its kind in the world. An entire year's collecting is rewarded if a few excellent impressions of these rare prints can be found. Yet, because of several extraordinary opportunities, he assembled close to four hundred examples, many of which are unique. There are other areas of print collecting in which the Rosenwald Collection is outstanding: engravings by Northern Gothic masters and by Dürer, Lucas van Leyden, Rembrandt, and Nanteuil, to select a few artists.

Lessing Rosenwald built a small museum near Philadelphia where the collection was housed during his lifetime. From there selected prints and drawings were brought to the main Print Room at the National Gallery in Washington as they were needed for study or exhibition. Traveling exhibitions and loans also showed many choice items from the Rosenwald Collection throughout the United States.

The Rosenwald Collection has been constantly augmented, and, since it was presented to the National Gallery of Art in 1943, it has more than doubled in size. This great donation deserves a more detailed treatment, and some beginnings toward that may be found in the section on drawings at the end of this volume, as well as in the series of scholarly exhibition catalogues published by the National Gallery on the miniatures and the Old Master prints in its collection.

Paul Mellon

The Founding Benefactors represent three generations of collecting: the first, Andrew Mellon (1855–1937), P. A. B. Widener (1834–1915), and Samuel Kress (1863–1955); the second, Joseph Widener (1871–1943), Rush Kress (1877–1963), Chester Dale (1883–1962), and Lessing Rosenwald (1891–1979); and the third, the son and daughter of Andrew Mellon, Paul Mellon (b. 1907) and Ailsa Mellon Bruce (1901–1969). Paul Mellon, for many years a member of the boards of the Mellon Bank and T. Mellon and Company, which handles the Mellon financial affairs, has spent his life not making money but giving it away. The Andrew W. Mellon Foundation, the result of gifts from him and his sister, is one of the largest in the United States. Philanthropy, collecting, and sport have been his major interests. A graduate of Yale and of Clare College, Cambridge, he is a self-admitted Anglophile. A few precious weeks each year he spends in England in connection with his racing stable.

While I was Chief Curator, from 1939 to 1956, I

had no idea that someone I had known from a mutual Pittsburgh childhood would become one of the great collectors of recent years. But lurking in his unconscious, perhaps planted there by heredity and nurtured by environment, was a love of art; and there was an instinct for collecting evident already in his library. He once tried to explain the impulse to collect, which has played such an important part in the lives of his wife and himself: "There seems to be a built-in or inherited desire to own, enjoy, to savor, and to conserve rare and beautiful things, a desire which must infuse all collectors. It begins in childhood, or is perhaps there even at birth. It is the childish pleasure of searching for odd or rare or beautiful shells on a beach, the immediate and delighted relationship between the shell lying in the afternoon sun in the wet sand and the clear, unclouded vision of the child."

When fairly late in life he turned to collecting paintings, his first important purchases were canvases of the French Impressionists and Post-Impressionists. Here his second wife, a remarkably creative woman in gardening, architecture, and decorating, was certainly influential. There was also the influence of Chester Dale. But as Paul Mellon has said, "We almost never buy a painting or a drawing we would not want to live with or see constantly," and the wall space in his houses soon vanished. The collection continued to grow; as had been the case with Chester Dale, the National Gallery has benefited by gifts from this overflow of masterpieces.

Although Paul Mellon has always felt himself only a temporary custodian of the treasures he has gathered, the ephemeral nature of possession has not affected the character of his collecting. As he has written, "Although obviously some day many of our works of art will be in a public museum or museums, we have only in rare instances bought with this in mind. . . . We do not believe in giving a work of art to a museum or other institution, even anonymously, if we do not personally feel affection toward it."

Such sensibilities have given the French pictures from the collection of the Paul Mellons at the National Gallery of Art a particularly personal quality. French paintings, however, represent numerically the smaller part of the collection. Paul Mellon's holdings of British art are far more extensive. Here his interest

was somewhat fortuitous. He had for many years collected in a desultory way English pictures and books, but it was not until after 1959 that his collection took on something of its present magnitude. In that year the Virginia Museum of Fine Arts, of which he has been a Trustee for many years, asked him to help organize an exhibition entitled *Sport and the Horse*. Basil Taylor, then an official of the Royal College of Art in London, was employed as adviser. A remarkable show was assembled, and in the process of borrowing from British museums and private collectors Paul Mellon became engrossed in English art, not the full-length official or society portraits his father had bought, but scenes of sport, conversation pieces, topographical paintings, and genre and storytelling pictures, whatever offered an insight into English life between 1650 and 1850. He was enchanted by the poetry of nature in the landscapes of Wilson, Constable, and Turner; the social insight of the canvases of Hogarth and the watercolors of Rowlandson; the technical virtuosity underlying the chiaroscuro of Joseph Wright of Derby, and equally reflected in the vitreous surfaces of Stubbs; the depiction of every aspect of that delectable existence, which was the good fortune of the English upper classes in the eighteenth century, glimpsed in scenes delineated with captivating charm by scores of artists like Johann Zoffany, Arthur Devis, George Morland, and others. Some of these paintings have been given to the National Gallery, but the greater part will form the collection of the Yale Center for British Art and British Studies.

Paul Mellon has been as consistent in his support of the National Gallery as he has been varied in its expression. His donation of individual works of art has regularly strengthened the collection since 1964. Important gifts have included Cézanne's monumental portrait of his father, his magnificent portrait of his friend Antony Valabrègue, and Manet's *The Plum*, as well as over 350 oils by Catlin and canvases by Canaletto and Devis. In 1983, Paul Mellon made a stunning gift of ninety-three works of art which he and Mrs. Mellon had collected over a thirty-year period, and President Reagan accepted the gift on behalf of the American people at a dinner honoring Andrew Mellon as the Gallery's founder. The donation of these objects places Paul Mellon in a select company of the Gallery's greatest benefactors, playing a crucial role in enabling the Gallery to secure its place among the foremost cultural institutions of the world.

To a great degree, Paul Mellon is responsible for the physical plant which houses his gifts. He provided essential funding for the completion of the East Building as well as necessary money for the remodeling of the Ground Floor of the West Building. Furthermore, he can be credited not only with the walls and what they contain, but also with much of what goes on within them. Specifically, Paul Mellon has been deeply interested in scholarship. His support made possible the A. W. Mellon Lectures in the Fine Arts and their publication. These have constituted since 1952 the most distinguished lectureship on the general subject of art and aesthetics in the United States. The Center for the Advanced Study in the Visual Arts, discussed in a subsequent chapter, has also benefited from the generosity of the Andrew W. Mellon Foundation.

With a characteristic concern for the future, Paul Mellon has made a very significant contribution to the Gallery's main fund for acquisitions, the Patrons' Permanent Fund. Of all his generous gifts this may well be the most touching. Remembering Paul Mellon's intense personal interest in the shaping of this institution, from the standpoints of both its form and its content, it cannot be overlooked that the donation to the Patrons' Permanent Fund expresses a profound confidence in the Gallery's future, since the Fund by definition provides for the eventual acquisition of masterpieces which may well not yet have been created.

Ailsa Mellon Bruce

The two recently merged Mellon foundations had always worked in close conjunction, and the National Gallery has benefited by many mutual donations. But the greatest gifts of money received by the Gallery from one person have come from Ailsa Mellon Bruce herself. Her untimely death was the most disastrous blow the Gallery has sustained. She gave more than money. She had a deep love of the institution her father established. She was determined that it should become the greatest of its kind. Whenever difficulties seemed insurmountable, her support and enthusiasm always enheartened us.

Like her brother she became a collector fairly late in life. Her first important acquisition was the purchase of the entire Molyneux Collection—roughly ninety French Impressionist and Post-Impressionist pictures, all intimate in scale but of the highest quality. To this nucleus she added such masterpieces as Goya's *Condesa de Chinchón*, Monet's *The Artist's Garden at Vétheuil*, Renoir's *Pont Neuf, Paris*, Cézanne's *Riverbank*, and many more French paintings. At her death her whole collection of paintings was left to the National Gallery of Art.

I always discussed with Ailsa Mellon Bruce the pictures we intended to buy with the immense resources she provided, and almost all the greatest works of art the Gallery acquired with its own funds are the result of her generosity. To some she responded with excitement, to others with a personal indifference which, she assured me, was not to matter so long as I felt they would enrich the Gallery. When we bought Leonardo da Vinci's *Ginevra de' Benci*, it took me over a year to persuade her to allow her name to be connected with the purchase. Because of speculation as to the picture's value she thought it would be ostentatious to be mentioned as having made its acquisition possible. Such modesty is not found often among collectors and donors.

I talked to her frequently about the goal I had long dreamed of for the National Gallery of Art, a goal suggested to me over thirty years ago by Bernard Berenson. It was to create in Washington a modern equivalent of the ancient library at Alexandria, which had burned in A.D. 391. This was the center of Hellenistic scholarship. It seemed to me the National Gallery could provide the same environment—a superb collection, a magnificent library adjacent, and a group of scholars to work in both. She immediately understood and enthusiastically backed the project.

Paul Mellon also saw that this was an opportunity for the National Gallery to assist scholarship in a way never attempted by any other museum since the destruction of the Alexandrine Library. He and his sister agreed to provide the enormous resources necessary to erect an additional building at the entrance to the Mall, a building which has been described in an earlier chapter.

Other Individual Donations

At the entrance to the West Building, opposite the panel listing the Founding Benefactors, there is a second inscription recording additional donors who have been exceptionally generous. This roll of honor, which is steadily lengthening, pays tribute to gifts which have varied in number from the more than three hundred American naive paintings given by Edgar William and Bernice Chrysler Garbisch to a single great Mondrian given by Herbert and Nanette Rothschild. One of the most enheartening aspects of these gifts is that, like those made by the Founding Benefactors, they often reflect several generations of donors from a single family. For example, Mr. and Mrs. Ralph Harmon Booth of Detroit contributed Old Master paintings by Bellini, Boltraffio, Tintoretto, Cranach, and Strigel. Their son and daughter-in-law, John and Louise Booth, gave one of Gauguin's last works, *The Invocation*, in memory of their daughter. More recently, Grace Vogel Aldworth, a third-generation member of the Booth family, gave Jan Gossaert's *Madonna and Child* in memory of her grandparents. Similarly, Mr. and Mrs. Peter Frelinghuysen, the son-in-law and daughter of one of America's greatest collectors, Mrs. Henry O. Havemeyer, gave a Corot, a Courbet, and a superb pair of Goya portraits. Mrs. Frelinghuysen's nephews gave the supremely beautiful Vermeer *A Lady Writing* in memory of their father, Horace Havemeyer. Their mother made a bequest of Manet's *Ball at the Opera*, one of those bold canvases which so shocked viewers of the last century and so delight the viewers of our own era.

Many donors have tailored their generosity to a particular Gallery need. The family of Governor Alvan T. Fuller of Massachusetts donated magnificent English paintings. Both the W. L. and May T. Mellon Foundation and Mrs. Maude Monell Vetlesen saw that important American paintings were secured for the nation. David K. E. Bruce established a vital purchase fund for the library's acquisitions. In addition, a nationwide Collectors' Committee makes annual donations of twentieth-century works of art. To date, fifteen paintings and sculptures have entered the Gallery because of the generosity of this organization.

Just as the National Gallery belongs to the whole country, not to a single part, these gifts have come from all over the United States. But there have also been a number of remarkably generous Washingtonians. One was Duncan Phillips, who not only gave several important paintings but as a Trustee contributed for many years his wisdom and counsel, always valuable but especially so when the Gallery was in its formative stage and badly in need of experience. A second was Mrs. Eugene Meyer, a remarkable connoisseur in Western and Oriental art, who gave her magnificent Cézannes, her Manet *Still Life*, her Renoir, Despiau, Rodin, and Brancusi, all acquired in the beginning of this century when such acquisitions represented an adventurous appreciation. A third was Averell Harriman, who assembled one of the most distinguished collections of Impressionist and Post-Impressionist paintings brought together in this country. A fourth was Oscar L. Milmore, a foreign service officer who made his permanent home in Washington. Following his wife's death, he established a trust fund in her memory. The income from this fund is to be used in perpetuity for the purchase of works of art. The donation of an economist and former member of the Federal Reserve Board, Adolph Caspar Miller, was motivated in an unexpected way. He used to come to the Gallery regularly to sit on a sofa facing the self-portrait of Rembrandt. A few weeks before Mr. Miller died, I saw him in his usual place. He said he wanted to speak to me, then told me of his decision to leave his collection and a large donation to the National Gallery of Art. He explained that he had only one motive in making the bequest, namely to repay what he had learned from years of scrutiny of a single portrait. It was a bequest really to Rembrandt, and Mr. Miller could think of no better way of expressing his gratitude.

Some other bequests to the Gallery have been unusual. Mrs. Lillian S. Timken of New York, for example, left her large collection to both the National

Gallery and the Metropolitan Museum in New York, without indicating which works of art should go to which institution. The directors tried to divide the collection into equal groups, but in the end the presidents of the two Boards of Trustees had to toss a coin for works by such artists as Moroni, Titian, Rembrandt, van Dyck, Rubens, Boucher, Fragonard, Turner, and others.

Among the Gallery's many friends there is an especially rare category comprised of those individuals who give not only art and funds but also that most precious of resources, time. One such long-standing supporter of the Gallery was the late John Hay Whitney. He served brilliantly for eighteen years as a Trustee, from 1961 to 1979. Paintings from his great collection (including one of the rare boxing-theme pictures by George Bellows, two splendid Fauve Derains, and the first canvas by Edward Hopper to come to the National Gallery) represent significant additions to the Gallery's holdings in twentieth-century art. Mr. Whitney also channeled one of the largest contributions yet made to the Patrons' Permanent Fund.

Many donors continue to show interest in the future of the Gallery. Robert H. and Clarice Smith have established fellowships for scholars and contributed substantially to the Patrons' Permanent Fund, as well as given important Dutch paintings and Old Master drawings. Robert Smith serves as well in the capacity of Chairman of the Trustees' Council, whose members represent the Gallery's national character, advising and supporting the Board of Trustees.

The Gallery continues to depend exclusively on the generosity of private citizens for the growth of the collections and can only rejoice in the fact that over its brief history it has so often been able to compete for whatever painting or sculpture of exceptional merit has been offered for sale. So that the Gallery may remain a legitimate contender for masterpieces in the international marketplace, the Trustees have formed the Patrons' Permanent Fund. The initial money for the fund, which has come in amounts ranging from five dollars to five million dollars, is invested as principal never to be touched. The purpose of this endowment is to provide immediately available funds when an opportunity arises to purchase a needed work.

Policies

When the Gallery was established by Andrew Mellon, he had in mind, as I have said, modeling it on the example of the British National Gallery. His original concept was modified during his lifetime by the inclusion of sculpture, and after his death by the acceptance of the Widener decorative arts. But works by living artists continued to be excluded from exhibition as they are in London.

For many years I strongly advocated this restriction. During the Joseph McCarthy period, and when Representative George A. Dondero was an influential member of Congress, modern art was anathema on the Hill. Our support in the Senate and the House might have been jeopardized had we shown avant-garde work. It was essential to establish the image of the Gallery as a great repository of traditional painting and sculpture before entering the controversial field of contemporary art.

When the Kennedy administration, however, was inaugurated, there was a cultural change in the country. Washington became much more sophisticated. Congressman Dondero was defeated and the atmosphere on the Hill was transformed. Modern art was no longer considered a manifestation of communism, as it had been, even though everybody was aware that only the most reactionary examples were permitted to be shown in Russia. The Kennedys knew and spoke to many painters and sculptors. They represented a new attitude in the White House, one of sympathy and understanding for the arts. During the Kennedy administration Washington became as stimulating as it had been in the days of Franklin Roosevelt.

Chester Dale in 1951 placed his modern French paintings on loan, and there were no protests over Picasso hanging on the same floor with Perugino. Nevertheless, the Trustees' policy of discouraging the acquisition of works by painters who had not died at least twenty years earlier continued. But there was no restriction on loans, and we held a series of shows of contemporary art. When Chester Dale died in December 1962, however, the Trustees were confronted with a problem. The penalty for refusing to show the work of living painters would have been the loss of an invaluable collection. For, according to Chester Dale's will, his gift to the National Gallery of Art was subject to the condition that "said Trustees of the National Gallery of Art shall agree to accept *all* [my italics] of the property bequeathed to it." And his collection contained superb paintings by Derain, Picasso, Matisse, and Braque, all of whom were still living or had not been dead twenty years.

It did not take the Trustees long to revise their thinking. They recognized that pragmatism is of necessity the philosophy of museums. By their acceptance of the Chester Dale Collection, in January 1963, they automatically had an obligation to exhibit the work of living painters.

They went further. They began a search for important collections of contemporary artists. This quest has continued, and the gallery has now in its possession, or has been promised, a superb nucleus of work of the most significant painters and sculptors of our time.

In this book I have not, however, included works by living artists. My reason is that the number of such works in the Gallery's collection, still small, is growing at such a rapid rate that the choice I might make at this time could not be a representative one.

Activities

Education

The visual arts are playing an increasingly important role in American education. Primary schools, secondary schools, colleges, and graduate schools all over the country are teaching painting and sculpture, and to a lesser extent the history of art.

This has created responsibilities and opportunities for museums. As Carter Brown has said, in no area is creativity more easily shared than in art. A work of art exists for us today as a self-contained entity whose original purpose was communication, a communication not invalidated by the obsolescence of theory, as in science; or by the barrier of language, as in literature; or, even, by the mediation of a performer, as in the sister art of music. At the National Gallery of Art one looks at an image put on canvas by Rembrandt's own hand, and one contemplates greatness directly.

It is the purpose of the Gallery's Education Department to make people aware of the vast reservoir of pleasure and enlightenment the collections represent. We have established in the Education Department two divisions, one to look after visitors to the Gallery, the other for extension activities. The total staff devoted to educational work numbers more than forty. Each day there are three types of tours: general tours of the whole collection, tours dealing with a special field or a single school, and a lecture (of which mimeographed summaries are available) on a particular painting or sculpture. These are free and are attended annually by nearly ninety thousand people. Tours and lectures for groups of fifteen or

more people are frequently arranged by appointment.

The Extension Service of the National Gallery is the nation's largest museum producer and distributor of educational lending programs. All programs are lent free of charge and are circulated annually to over four thousand communities in all fifty states. And, with public and educational television programs, over forty-five million viewers are reached annually nationwide.

A new and far-reaching educational project, developed by the Gallery in cooperation with Scholastic Magazines, Inc., is *Art & Man*, designed to provide eight monthly multimedia packages during the school year, relating the visual arts to classroom subjects such as English, history, social sciences, and modern languages.

At the Mall entrance to the Gallery an Orientation Center has been established to serve visitors more efficiently. It is staffed by ten desk-docents. The Education Department also trains volunteer docents from the Junior League and the American Association of University Women. These in turn work closely with the schools near Washington and take about 25,000 schoolchildren a year through the Gallery.

Many persons, however, prefer to wander through the collections by themselves. To allow them to listen to talks about the works of art at their own pace, electronic guides are available. They are extremely popular, and they enable the visitor to look and listen at the same time.

For those who would rather read than listen, in most of the rooms there are leaflets describing the works of art in that particular gallery. The leaflets are free and can be taken home. Our visitors seem to realize that, when the leaflets are assembled from all the galleries, they form a free handbook of the collections and are therefore worth preserving.

On Sunday afternoons there are free lectures in the auditorium given by authorities on different aspects of art. A series of six lectures, known as the A. W. Mellon Lectures in the Fine Arts, is delivered annually. These lectures are published by the Princeton University Press as part of the Bollingen Series.

An interesting educational instrument located at the Gallery is the Index of American Design. During the Depression in the mid-1930s the government, wishing to help artists, organized over 660 painters throughout the United States and gave them the task of recording the decorative arts and crafts of this country from the seventeenth century to the end of the nineteenth century. A remarkably exacting technique of watercolor rendering was taught to these artists, and the resulting facsimiles of many varied craft products form a vivid and permanent record of the development of American folk and decorative arts. Exhibitions from this vast corpus of more than 17,000 illustrations are constantly circulated by the Gallery; publishers and industrial designers, too, frequently draw upon this source of Americana.

Music

The National Gallery of Art, so far as is known, is unique among museums in having its own orchestra, with a conductor-composer working on its staff full time. Each Sunday evening, except during the summer months, the Gallery presents a free concert in its East Garden Court. These concerts are regularly broadcast and have resulted in a number of recordings which have sold widely. The orchestra has also appeared in a telecast series of pretaped concerts, during which paintings appropriate to the musical selections are shown.

The concerts were begun during World War II, owing to the generosity of Chester Dale, and were continued with funds provided by the A. W. Mellon Educational and Charitable Trust. Recently they have received generous support from the Calouste Gul-

benkian Foundation of Lisbon, and the J. I. Foundation, Inc., and from funds bequeathed by William Nelson Cromwell and F. Lammot Belin. It is a moving experience to see the crowds, seated and standing, who attend these Sunday evening performances, which have become an important part of the cultural life of Washington.

Each spring the Gallery presents a festival of American music, often giving a first hearing to contemporary compositions. A modest beginning has been made toward commissioning works composed especially for the Gallery. Another recent development is the formation of the National Gallery Strings, a group of first-chair players from the National Gallery Symphony, which frequently plays at the openings of special exhibitions.

In the informality of the setting, in the type of small orchestra with its conductor-composer, and in its emphasis on new native compositions, the National Gallery of Art is continuing the eighteenth-century tradition of musical performances under a kapellmeister, which distinguished so many German and Austrian courts.

Science

The last century and a half has seen an advance in applied science unparalleled in history. We make better steel, build longer bridges, travel in faster vehicles than ever before and live a life completely changed by technological discoveries. Yet there are exceptions to this technical progress. While the tools used to fabricate nearly every commodity have changed, those used to produce art have remained much the same. We paint with pigments not very different and often less lasting than those of the Renaissance, and we apply them in ways generally less durable than the methods of the Old Masters.

Various reasons can be found for this technical backwardness in the fine arts, but the major explanation remains a lack of interest in the kind of full-time research which has made other scientific advances possible. Until recently there has been very little support for serious scientific investigation of artists'

Schoolchildren enrich their knowledge of art through group visits and lectures

Richard Bales conducts the National Gallery Orchestra

The Gallery offers artists opportunities to study major works

Rubens' Daniel in the Lions' Den enthralls three young visitors

Blind children examine a Donatello sculpture of David

materials. In the late 1920s Harvard established at the Fogg Art Museum the first significant laboratory experiments in the United States related to the preservation of art objects. Funds for this program, however, were never abundant, and scientific investigation had to be combined with restoration and teaching. Nevertheless, during the last war, when Harvard found it necessary to curtail work in the Fogg laboratory, American museums suffered a severe loss.

In 1950 the National Gallery of Art began a program of research in artists' materials. Funds for this project were provided by the Old Dominion and Avalon foundations, and support for the continuation of this important research has been provided by the Andrew W. Mellon Foundation, with contributions from the National Science Foundation, the Atomic Energy Commission, the National Endowment for the Arts, and the Ciba-Geigy and David L. Kreeger foundations. These funds made possible a continuation of the work begun at the Fogg Museum more than a generation ago. The Gallery's program, however, differed in a significant way from the Harvard program. The scientists had no teaching or restoration responsibilities, and consequently their investigations could proceed without interruptions of this nature. From the beginning the project has been located at the Carnegie-Mellon Institute of Research at Carnegie-Mellon University in Pittsburgh. This immense center for scientific investigation, one of the best-equipped laboratories in the world, offers important advantages. Not only are the most modern tools available, equipment often rare and costly, but scientists working on artists' materials have an opportunity for discussing their research with scores of other scientists doing related work.

It was decided when the National Gallery program began that it would be more practicable to take a chemist and make him aware of the problems of restoration rather than to take a restorer and teach him chemistry. The National Gallery of Art representative at the Carnegie-Mellon Institute, a distinguished chemist, has become familiar with the difficulties confronting museums in preserving paintings. He in turn has trained his assistants. He has worked with restorers at the National Gallery and with those in other museums in the United States and abroad.

All museums today are desperately in need of scientific advice. They are faced with many problems of a practical nature related to the conservation of their collections which the scientist alone can solve. To give only three examples: (a) the fading of pigments due to museum illumination; (b) the control of excessive heat from spotlights; (c) the discoloration of areas of repaint.

It is luck, to some extent, that the Old Masters are still as brilliant in color as they are. Most paintings in the past were intended for dimly lit churches and dark palaces. In the nineteenth century, for the first time, these panels and canvases were placed in galleries with skylights, where the natural illumination reaching the walls was often a hundred times as great in intensity as the light in the buildings where the paintings originally hung. Until recently the damage which might have been caused by this vast increase in brightness of illumination had been kept to a minimum by varnishes which had in due course turned yellow. In the past, moreover, whenever pictures seemed dull and lusterless, instead of cleaning, as we would do today, the usual procedure was to revarnish. This series of yellow coatings, like layers of yellow glass, provided an effective filter, removing to a great extent the ultraviolet rays, and reducing, with the help of a good deal of dirt, the total amount of light from the rest of the spectrum reaching the pigments themselves. Then came the modern taste for pictures cleaned of their old varnish. The protective coat of yellow dammar or mastic was thus removed along with the dirt; and the pigments, today covered with only a colorless, transparent varnish, usually a synthetic resin, were exposed under gallery skylights to illumination as high as 300 footcandles, as against five or six in the average day-lit interior of a palace or church.

The National Gallery of Art's research program has undertaken an extensive investigation of the many types of damage that light can cause. It was demonstrated that the effect of light on fugitive pigments is additive, that the light waves even in the visible spectrum can be deleterious, though ultraviolet radiation is generally the most destructive, and that more pigments than we had realized are fugitive. Experimentation is being pushed to improve ultraviolet filters, which can be used over the skylights of galleries and, possibly, infused into the varnish of the pictures themselves; and other methods of reducing the destructive effect of the invisible radiation in the light are being sought. If this search fails to find satisfactory ways of lessening the damaging power of natural light, museums may be compelled to abandon daylight altogether and resort to artificial illumination for the exhibition of particularly sensitive materials. The damaging factor in such illumination can be precisely controlled, but there is frequently a loss of aesthetic pleasure. It is to be hoped that science can offer a suitable solution to the use of natural light.

Natural illumination creates heat, but this can be controlled by airconditioning. Much more serious is the heat derived from the spotlights increasingly in use not only for photography but for exhibition purposes. The problem became critical at the National Gallery of Art when plans were made to exhibit the original waxes modeled by Degas and from which his bronzes were later cast. It became obvious, as one of these ballet dancers leaned over in a posture never sanctioned by the School of Ballet, that she was sagging under the heat of the display and threatening to melt. The first problem was to determine how hot she was. A piece of equipment was used to measure the temperature of the wax figures by determining the infrared radiation they emitted. Known as a "heat-detecting gun," this device registers the surface temperature of any work of art at which it is pointed. Once the temperature could be measured, refrigeration was introduced into the case and the ballerinas now promise to hold their poses permanently. This heat-detecting gun has since proved invaluable to the Gallery staff when it becomes necessary to measure the amount of heat to which paintings are exposed during photography, especially filming for movies and television. One stands "offstage," simply pointing the gun at a painting while it is being photographed, and without touching, the temperature is continually monitored.

Light not only fades paintings and may overheat them, but it also causes a variety of photochemical reactions. In recent years an epidemic of whitening of repaint appeared to have broken out in many galleries in Europe and the United States. Bluish white areas suddenly began to appear on paintings, like a rash. These always occurred in repainted places which were, on the whole, light in tone. Such areas, of course, had previously matched the surrounding color. In the course of a thorough investigation of the problem it has been discovered that certain restorers use mixtures of zinc white, colored pigment, and dammar varnish when they retouch lost or damaged areas. Occasionally, a form of photochemically active titanium white was also detected. The effect of light on this mixture of white pigment and varnish caused the repaint to deteriorate and take on a whitish appearance. The discovery has been widely publicized among restorers, and it is to be hoped that in the future they will avoid the combination of these particular materials.

It was the general policy in supporting this research that the problems studied would be of fundamental interest not solely to the National Gallery of Art but to museums everywhere. As the investigations into the effects of light on museum objects and the application of advanced analytical techniques in the characterization of pigments, varnishes, and solvents began to bear fruit, the findings were of such importance to the field of conservation that, through the generosity of the Andrew W. Mellon Foundation, the laboratory program was expanded in 1967 through the creation of the Research Center on the Materials of the Artist and Conservator at Mellon Institute, which at that date had just become part of the newly established Carnegie-Mellon University in Pittsburgh. The director of the Research Center continued to serve the National Gallery of Art as its scientific advisor. No longer immediately responsible for the long-term research problems being studied at Pittsburgh, the National Gallery of Art at that time began the expansion of its in-house conservation facilities and staff. Following the opening of the East Building, an extensive area was constructed in one wing of the original building to provide special rooms for the treatment of sculpture, of prints and drawings and of paintings. Jointly funded from private sector sources, these facilities also included a suite of laboratories for the technical examination of the collections and the testing and evaluation of the materials used in their care and treatment. The continued growth of the conservation staff from two to over twenty members and the addition of sophisticated equipment has assured that the National Gallery of

Art will keep well abreast of the latest methods for the examination and conservation of the works in its custody, in applying the best materials and procedures as currently accepted and understood, and in contributing to the world's fund of knowledge and information on this subject through its encouragement of research and internship training in conservation.

Similar studies of pigments, supports, varnishes, solvents, adhesives, light, and other problems related to the preservation of works of art are being undertaken by an increasing number of major laboratories, particularly in European countries, and the most heartening aspect of this scientific research into the nature of artists' materials is the amount of international cooperation taking place. We are rapidly catching up with technical advances in other fields. In the next ten years it seems likely that restorers will be given new materials as revolutionary and as useful as antibiotics in medicine. For this reason it is the policy of the National Gallery of Art to restrict restoration to work necessary for preservation, and to clean paintings as little as possible consistent with their conservation.

One of the problems confronting every restorer is the introduction of new synthetic materials in place of the traditional ones. How can he be sure that these will last equally well? There are on the market today a number of synthetic resins which exhibit little tendency to discolor, but is it possible that the use of these materials will have distressing side effects? For example, research showed that it is possible for certain synthetic varnishes to become so tough over a period of time that it will be almost impossible to remove them without damaging the paint underneath. The laboratory initiated an elaborate program of "accelerated aging tests" to provide evidence for and against the use of new materials. The findings were reported in a handbook, *On Picture Varnishes and Their Solvents,* first published in 1959. It proved to be so valuable to conservators that it was revised and enlarged in 1971.

But the scientist's usefulness is not limited to the restorer's studio. He can also assist a curator in determining authenticity. One of the most helpful tools developed through the National Gallery of Art's sponsorship of this research program has been the ability to determine the age of white lead pigments. In the past white lead was used by artists in virtually every picture painted. The scientists at the Carnegie-Mellon Institute of Research knew that lead-bearing minerals exhibit a low degree of radioactivity owing to the presence of uranium as an impurity which produces a radioactive variety of lead, known as lead-210. They speculated that when the ore was refined and the uranium removed, the decomposing lead-210 would soon decay, losing half of its radioactivity every twenty years. Thus paint in which lead-210 had vanished almost entirely would be roughly a century old, whereas paint with a measurable amount of lead-210 could be judged to be of more recent manufacture.

Many tests were made to prove the validity of this assumption. A worldwide search for samples of lead of known date and origin was instituted. Among others the radioactivity of the white lead in the forgeries of Vermeer done by van Meegeren was measured. In every case the results proved the hypothesis to be correct.

The newest twist in this search for greater skills in identifying the white lead used by an artist is the use of a mass-spectrometer that is able to count the kind of lead atoms in the pigment. By this means scientists at Carnegie-Mellon University now can tell us the country and sometimes even the mine itself that the lead came from.

The Atomic Energy Commission became interested in the National Gallery of Art's project and as a joint venture a program was undertaken to determine radioactive contamination of artists' materials by the atmosphere. Because of the explosion and testing of atom and hydrogen bombs there has been a great increase in the amount of radioactive carbon in the air. Linseed oil and paper made from growing plants that have existed in the atomic era contain a significantly high proportion of carbon-14, which has been released by such explosions. The possibility of detecting this by advanced scientific methods of analysis now makes it impossible for a forger to use modern linseed oil and paper to fabricate works of art that are supposedly more than a decade or two old.

From these advances in the scientific study of works of art it might seem as though connoisseurship would someday come out of a test tube. It never will.

The scientists' contributions increase the range of capabilities that aid the curator and the conservator to do their work, but no laboratory or computer center can measure "quality"—that indescribable property of the greatest masterpieces which Andrew Mellon insisted should be evident in every painting and piece of sculpture in the National Gallery.

Center for Advanced Study in the Visual Arts

As I have already said, to establish a research center for scholars within the National Gallery was for many years a cherished ambition of mine. In 1980, after I had left the Gallery, the Center for Advanced Study in the Visual Arts opened its doors in the new East Building. Its activities are many and its benefits to the scholarly community have proved manifold and far-reaching, as the following description of the first three years of the CASVA program indicates.

* * *

"The idea of establishing a center for advanced study at the National Gallery of Art dates from a conversation between David E. Finley, John Walker, and Paul Mellon in which the creation of a new Alexandrine Library became a goal for the Gallery, then still quite new. In the mid-1950s, after consultation with Professor Millard Meiss of New York University's Institute of Fine Arts, the idea took the form of a research facility for the study of Renaissance art and conservation, perhaps, like the Hellenic Center and Dumbarton Oaks for Byzantine Studies, to be part of Harvard University in Washington. It was later decided that the program need not be restricted to Renaissance art. In 1965 the Gallery took an initial step toward forming the Center by establishing a program of predoctoral fellowships and appointing a professor-in-residence. Support for the new program came primarily from the Kress Foundation and endowments in honor of Chester Dale and David E. Finley.

When J. Carter Brown came to the National Gallery as Assistant Director, he undertook a detailed study of the desirability and feasibility of setting up an advanced research institute within the Gallery. His report was based on interviews in the United States and abroad by himself and John Walker with the faculty of graduate departments in the history of art and with directors of public and university museums, research institutes, foundations, libraries, and government commissions and agencies. Not only did those surveyed endorse the project, they also agreed about the needs that such a center should meet. Brown's report cited the benefit to the mature scholar of uninterrupted time for research and writing, for reflection and the completion of long-term projects; of adequate financial support for research, travel, and accommodations; of libraries, photographic archives, and other research facilities; of easy access to the collections of the National Gallery; and, perhaps most important, of personal exchanges with other scholars on questions of methodology, theory, evidence, and opinion. A center that provided such opportunities, support, and facilities, it was felt, would contribute significantly to the quality of art-historical studies. At the same time, the National Gallery would be enriched by contact with resident scholars and with the academic community throughout the United States and abroad. It would also increase the value of its service to the discipline of art history and to the nation.

Brown's report also contained a set of specific recommendations for the location, organization, programs, facilities, and intellectual scope of the proposed research institute. The Gallery's Board of Trustees soon initiated planning for the Center as an integral part of the then-projected East Building. A new librarian was appointed in 1972 and the acquisition of books and photographs was accelerated.

In September 1977 the Board of Trustees adopted a formal resolution to establish the Center as an integral yet independent part of the National Gallery and to authorize a senior fellowship program, which would be supported by private funds. At the same time, it was decided to incorporate the existing predoctoral fellowship program and the Kress Professorship into the Center. Within two years, a Board of Advisors was chosen, composed of seven senior art historians from the United States and abroad. Henry A. Millon, Professor of History and Architecture at

the Massachusetts Institute of Technology, and former Director of the American Academy in Rome was appointed Professor-in-Charge (a title later changed to Dean) and made a member of the Executive Committee of the National Gallery. The first fellowship appointments were made in the spring of 1980, and a full program of scholarly activities was initiated in September of the same year.

The Center's purpose is first to encourage advanced study of the history and theory of art, architecture, and urbanism in an environment that places value on works of art; second, to support a scholarly community and provide a forum for ideas about the history, themes, theories, methods, criticism, and historiography of art. Through its fellowship program and its scholarly activities, the Center fosters the

study of the production, use, and cultural meaning of art and artifacts from prehistoric times to the present. The Center encourages study of these objects by historians and critics of all the visual arts, and by scholars from cognate disciplines in the humanities and social sciences. The Center advocates the practice and study of criticism in the visual arts, including critical studies leading to the formation of aesthetic theories. The projects it sponsors need not necessarily be related to the collections or exhibitions of the National Gallery.

The topics studied at the Center since its inception reflect the institution's historical, cultural, and methodological breadth. They have included the service systems in the Greek colonies of Sicily; Piranesi's drawings of architectural fantasies; the twilight paintings of Frederic Church; the iconographic significance of the lām/alif ligature in medieval Islam; chiaroscuro woodcuts of sixteenth-century Italy; medieval stained glass in western France; studies in the social functions of art and architecture; the relationship of photography and surrealism in the early twentieth century; and Vermeer's painting techniques.

The Center sponsors four privately funded programs. The fellowship program provides for the members of the Center, its core. The Center now supports annually a Kress Professor, a number of Senior Fellows, Visiting Senior Fellows, and Associate and Predoctoral Fellows. Every year, one National Gallery of Art Curatorial Fellow is also appointed; this fellowship enables a curator to obtain a leave of absence from the Gallery and spend time on research usually unrelated to curatorial projects. Ordinarily, there are about fifteen people in residence at the Center as members. The professional staff gathers with the members at weekly lunches. These lunches provide an opportunity for scholarly exchange of information and ideas, for discussion of a paper delivered during the previous week, and for discourse on a diverse and continually changing range of issues. Colleagues visiting the Washington area are frequent guests at these lunches, where they may speak about their research interests and activities.

A program of meetings at the Center is designed to gather art historians and critics to discuss issues of art-historical interest. These meetings range in size from small seminars to full-scale symposiums. The Center also periodically holds meetings at which art historians in the metropolitan area hear the results of research in progress and discuss approaches and solutions to critical problems that derive from specific studies. These programs may take different forms—lectures, panel discussions, film screenings—and they often have a specific theme.

The Center's interest in scholarship extends beyond the local area, and it has hosted a number of special events with an international roster of participants. At a two-day symposium in November 1980 on the art and architecture of the late fourth century and Hellenistic period in Macedonia and the rest of Greece, held in conjunction with the opening of the National Gallery's exhibition *In Search of Alexander*, papers on the architecture, painting, sculpture, decorative arts, history, and literature of the Greek world were delivered by scholars

from the United States, Greece, England, and Australia. Other symposiums have explored such topics as 'The Renaissance of Islam: Art of the Mamluks' (co-sponsored with the Freer Gallery of Art); 'Claude Lorrain 1600–1682'; 'Raphael before Rome'; 'Perspectives on Manet,' 'Recent Research in Italian Art,' and 'Pictorial Narrative in Antiquity and the Middle Ages' (these three were co-sponsored with the Department of History of Art at Johns Hopkins University); 'Italian Bronze Medals'; 'Hermeticism and the Renaissance' (jointly sponsored with the Catholic University of America and The Folger Institute); and 'El Greco y Toledo' (co-sponsored with the Instituto Diego Velásquez in Madrid and held in Toledo, Spain). The Center also joins the Department of Art of the University of Maryland in sponsoring the Middle Atlantic Symposium in the History of Art, at which graduate students at universities in the region present papers on their dissertation or other advanced research.

The Center's seminars are smaller gatherings of scholars knowledgeable in a specific field, often the province of one of the members of the Center, who assists in the definition of the theme and the organization of the meeting. No formal presentations are made, nor is any recording made of the discussion, which is intended to examine and criticize recent research and consider areas and approaches for future study. Sometimes seminars follow a Center symposium, providing an opportunity for further discussion of ideas generated by the formal presentations. The El Greco symposium held in Toledo, Spain, in April 1982 was followed that fall by a seminar entitled 'Recent Research on El Greco and Sixteenth-Century Spanish Studies.' Scholars of Byzantine, Western, medieval, and Islamic manuscripts have convened in seminars to discuss codicology and the circumstances of manuscript production. Scholars whose subject is art-historical method and theory have met to consider questions of representation and of method in twentieth-century studies. Other seminars have focused on Roman architecture, Piero della Francesca and Francesco di Giorgio, urban history, medieval architectural drawings, the Pantheon, David Smith, and a computerized inventory of American sculpture.

Each fall the Center publishes a report on its research and activities during the past academic year. This publication describes the purpose and projects of the Center and contains short essays by its members on work accomplished during their fellowship period. Another annual publication, *Sponsored Research in the History of Art,* lists research projects in art history and cognate fields in the humanities and social sciences that are supported by granting institutions in the United States and elsewhere. Projects are listed according to geographic area, period, field, theme, and medium. One of the series in the National Gallery's annual publication *Studies in the History of Art* is devoted to papers from the Center's symposiums and conferences.

The fourth program of the Center is research. All of the Fellows are engaged in work on projects that they themselves have proposed. But by its very nature as an ongoing, permanent institution, the Center is also able to sponsor continuing research, research that cannot be accomplished by a single individual in a year, or even over a number of years, projects that require teamwork—a team within a discipline or an interdisciplinary task force. In 1982 the Center initiated a program of long-term research projects. One such project, under the direction of the Dean and with the participation of two research assistants, involves the compilation of a photographic archive of architectural drawings and the development of an automated system for cataloging. The archive will eventually include photographs of architectural drawings dating before 1800 that are held in public collections in North America and Europe. An advisory group comprised of representatives of research institutes, libraries, museums, and archives in the United States, Canada, and England has been called upon to establish standard cataloging forms and terms.

In the next decades, museums can become principal centers for advanced research in art history. The Center for Advanced Study in the Visual Arts at the National Gallery represents the kind of independent research facility, with programs both relating to and reaching beyond the collections and activities of the parent institution, that can link scholars and scholarship in academia and museums on an international front and thereby further significantly the advancement of knowledge in the history of art."

Conclusion

Visitors to the Gallery often express surprise when they learn that it opened as recently as 1941. Since then, the National Gallery of Art has had a growth which might never have occurred if it had been established a few years later. Coming when it did, it has proved to be a magnet for those last great American collections not already given or promised elsewhere. Thus, in the Gallery's few decades of life, treasures have flowed to Washington at an unprecedented rate. It is difficult to believe that there will ever again be a similar influx of masterpieces to any museum.

The National Gallery of art holds a unique position in America. Over its short history, the Gallery has been called upon to undertake many of the functions performed elsewhere by Ministries of Fine Arts. These responsibilities have varied from assisting in the designs of stamps and inaugural medals to organizing exhibitions offered by foreign governments. The Gallery's creation thus helped to fill a void in the governmental structure.

Its establishment presented the President and the Congress with the challenge of maintaining a federal art museum for which there was no real precedent. Until then the government's support of museums was directed mainly to the outstanding departments of science and history at the Smithsonian Institution. But with the acceptance of Andrew Mellon's gift the experiment of creating a distinguished National Gallery was undertaken. This book is in some ways a balance sheet of accomplishment.

Italian Schools

XIII THROUGH EARLY XVI CENTURY

Byzantine School

(XIII CENTURY)

1   ENTHRONED MADONNA AND CHILD

Panels like this *Madonna and Child* by an anonymous artist represent the Byzantine tradition out of which Western painting developed. "Monuments of unaging intellect," such devotional pictures were also considered in the East to be a medium of occult power. Justinian advanced behind a representation of the Virgin to reconquer Italy and much of Africa, and icons were supposed to heal the sick and give sight to the blind.

The style in which such Byzantine icons were painted was the product of two incongruous elements: one, a tradition of forms naturalistically modeled in light and shade, the Byzantine heritage of Roman painting; and opposed to this, the Oriental taste for flat pattern and calligraphic line, a taste derived from those Eastern peoples who rose to power during the last centuries of the Roman Empire. That these components never completely fused is apparent in the icon reproduced. The heads, especially that of the Christ Child, give that illusion of roundness, of three-dimensional form, which is to be found in classical painting. But the gold and ivory throne, the flattened bodies of the figures, the emphasis on abstract pattern, all are elements Oriental in origin.

In the drapery especially, one can see the hybrid nature of Byzantine art. The striated folds, which appear purely conventional, are in fact derived from the modeling of drapery in classical painting. The areas of gold, with their radiating lines, represent the highlights on the tops of the folds of a cloth woven with gold thread. Those folds, under the influence of Oriental taste, have become stylized until there is only a remote connection with naturalistic light and shade. Here, as in many Byzantine mosaics, the real purpose is to make the figures harmonize with the gold background, and to emphasize, by repetition of accent, a rhythmic sequence that has the same function as a recurrent beat in music.

Byzantine painting flourished throughout much of Europe until the dawn of the Italian Renaissance. This panel, together with a companion piece in the Andrew W. Mellon Collection at the National Gallery of Art (plate 2), was discovered in a church in Spain in the early twentieth century. It may have been executed in Constantinople in the year 1200, and brought to Aragon by a crusading knight or militant ecclesiastic returning from his long pilgrimage to the East. Recently some critics, however, have dated both this and the Mellon panel late thirteenth or even early fourteenth century, and theorize that they were painted in one or another of the Italian centers, possibly by artists of the Sicilian School.

Collections: Church in Calahorra (Aragon), Spain (from an unknown date until first quarter of twentieth century); Weissberger, Madrid; Emile Pares, Paris; G. W. Arnold. *Gift of Mrs. Otto Kahn*, 1949. Wood, 51⅝ x 30¼" (131.2 x 76.9 cm.).

2

5

3

4

These paintings further illustrate the dominance of the Byzantine tradition in Italian art. *Madonna and Child on a Curved Throne* (plate 2) is similar to plate 1. Both came from the same church in Spain and were painted at approximately the same time. The artists responsible for such icons are usually anonymous. One of the first names we know in art is that of Margaritone of Arezzo who signed plate 5. His *Madonna and Child Enthroned* must have been wonderfully impressive when seen by candlelight in a dimly lit church. Illuminated manuscripts also significantly influenced thirteenth-century painting. The effect of the manuscript style can be clearly seen in the panel by the Master of St. Francis.

Under the leadership of Duccio, Siena in the fourteenth century became one of the two great centers of art, the other being Florence. Local schools also developed in various other city-states. Of these, one of the most creative was located at Rimini on the Adriatic. Here a painter called Baronzio flourished, and the picture now labeled Master of the Life of St. John the Baptist was once ascribed to him. When research fails to establish the identity of an artist, he often becomes known as the "Master" of his most famous work. We do, however, know the name of the first great Venetian painter, Paolo Veneziano. In the beauty of its color his *Coronation of the Virgin* recalls the Byzantine enamels of the Golden Altar of San Marco in Venice.

2 Byzantine School (XIII century): *Madonna and Child on a Curved Throne*. Wood, 32⅛ x 19⅜″ (81.5 x 49 cm.). Andrew W. Mellon Collection

3 Master of St. Francis (Umbrian, active second half XIII century): *St. John the Evangelist*. Probably c. 1270/80. Wood, 19½ x 9½″ (49.5 x 24 cm.). Samuel H. Kress Collection

4 Master of the Life of St. John the Baptist: *Madonna and Child with Angels*. Probably c. 1330/40. Wood, 39⅝ x 18⅞″ (100.5 x 48 cm.). Samuel H. Kress Collection

5 Margaritone (Arezzo, active second half XIII century): *Madonna and Child Enthroned*. Signed. c. 1270. Wood, 38⅛ x 19½″ (97 x 49.5 cm.). Samuel H. Kress Collection

6 Lippo Memmi (Sienese, active 1317–1347): *Madonna and Child with Donor*. Probably c. 1335. Wood, 22¼ x 9½″ (57 x 24 cm.). Andrew W. Mellon Collection

7 Paolo Veneziano (Venetian, active 1324–1358): *The Coronation of the Virgin*. Dated 1324. Wood, 39 x 30½″ (99.1 x 77.5 cm.). Samuel H. Kress Collection

8 Duccio di Buoninsegna (Sienese, active 1278–1318/19): *Nativity with the Prophets Isaiah and Ezekiel*. Between 1308 and 1311. Wood, middle panel 17¼ x 17½″ (43.8 x 44.4 cm.); side panels, each 17¼ x 6½″ (43.8 x 16.5 cm.). Andrew W. Mellon Collection

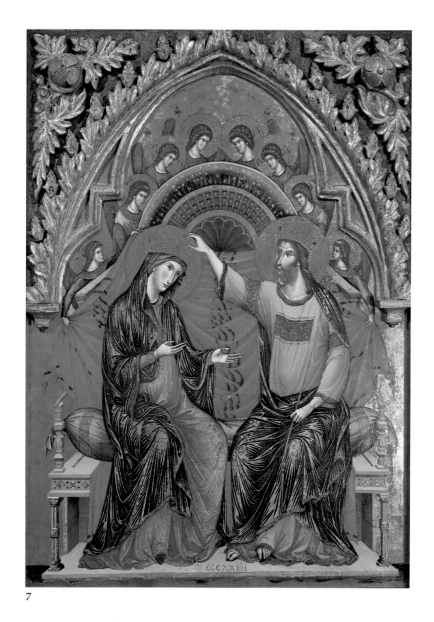

7

6

8

67

Duccio di Buoninsegna

(SIENESE, ACTIVE 1278–1318/19)

9 THE CALLING OF THE APOSTLES PETER AND ANDREW

The greatest single creation of the Byzantine School was painted not in Byzantium but in Siena. The Byzantine tradition culminated in the *Maestà—The Virgin in Majesty*—painted for the Cathedral of Siena between 1308 and 1311 by Duccio di Buoninsegna. This altarpiece is a compendium of all that men had learned during a thousand years about the craft of painting. Within the Byzantine style there is no more skillful use of line, pattern, and composition, no finer example of dramatic power and significant characterization.

Duccio's altarpiece was not only the most perfect expression of medieval painting, it also contained the seeds of future development. In *The Calling of the Apostles Peter and Andrew*, a panel which once formed part of the predella of the *Maestà*, there is evidence that the hieratic rigidity of the Byzantine style has changed. There is a tender awareness of human life, of its daily activity. The apostles busily netting their fish, and the aquatic life itself, open new vistas in art. This rudimentary naturalism was stimulated by the growing popularity of the Franciscan interest in nature. But the figure of Christ has still the austerity of Byzantine art. The edge of His robe is still touched with gold, which, like a flash of lightning, sets Him apart from common humanity. When the *Maestà* was completed, the Sienese realized that their altarpiece was, of its type, the supreme masterpiece of the age. A great procession was formed to carry it in triumph to the high altar of the Cathedral, and a whole day was devoted to prayers and hymns to the Virgin.

Duccio's masterwork was dismembered in 1771 and again in 1878, but most of it may still be seen in the Museo dell'Opera del Duomo in Siena, where it remains one of the principal treasures of the city. Ten sections of the predella were dispersed to England and the United States, and two of these, the one reproduced here and a scene of the Nativity (plate 8), are now in the National Gallery of Art.

Collections: Cathedral of Siena; Robert H. and Evelyn Benson, London; Clarence H. Mackay, Roslyn, New York. *Samuel H. Kress Collection*, 1939. Painted between 1308 and 1311. Wood, 17⅛ x 18⅛″ (43.5 x 46 cm.).

Giotto

(FLORENTINE, 1266?–1337)

10   MADONNA AND CHILD

Duccio sums up the past; Giotto foretells the future. Both artists typify the spirit of the cities in which they lived. Siena was conservative, sophisticated, overrefined; Florence was experimental, vigorous, dynamic. Duccio's style was the flowering of an ancient tradition, but Giotto's paintings, based on study of the human form and stimulated by intellectual curiosity, tore apart the formulas of the immediate past. Duccio developed the Eastern elements of Byzantine art—line, pattern, and composition on a flat plane. Giotto emphasized instead form, mass, and volume—the almost forgotten tradition of classical painting.

To appreciate the difference between these two approaches to painting, compare the figures in *The Calling of the Apostles Peter and Andrew* by Duccio, on a preceding page, and the figures of the *Madonna and Child* by Giotto. One feels intuitively something like a difference in specific gravity, as though Duccio's figures were made of aluminum and Giotto's of lead. It was Giotto's passion for solidity that determined the appearance of his figures, that caused him to depict large-boned, massive models. He willingly sacrificed superficial physical beauty to convey more intensely physical existence. This *Madonna and Child*, which may once have formed part of a celebrated altarpiece painted by Giotto for the Church of Santa Croce in Florence, is typical. It seems carved from a monolith as solid as a piece of granite. Every device is used to enhance the feeling of substance. Look, for instance, at the powerful rendering of the hands, the thickness and roundness of the fingers, the sense of existence conveyed by the manner in which the Christ Child grasps His Mother's forefinger.

Here Giotto has given us the essential quality of significant Florentine painting. Two hundred years later, Leonardo da Vinci was to define this quality in the following words: "The first object of the painter is to make a flat plane appear as a body in relief and projecting from that plane." In Giotto's work this suggestion of relief is rendered with a power that has never been surpassed.

Collections: Edouard-Alexandre Max, Paris; Henry Goldman, New York. *Samuel H. Kress Collection*, 1939. Painted probably between 1320 and 1330. Wood, 33⅝ x 24⅜" (85.5 x 62 cm.).

71

11

Giotto's master was Cimabue, to whom two of these pictures are ascribed. His style was essentially Byzantine, but in drawing his figures he shows a new observation and articulation. Bernardo Daddi and Agnolo Gaddi were followers of Giotto, and in their work a diminution of Giotto's mastery of form is apparent. Giottesque artists are to be found throughout Italy. Two of these, one from Florence, the other from Umbria, evidently worked on the same altarpiece (plate 17). Some damage must have occurred, for years after the picture had been painted, Allegretto Nuzi was called in to do some restoration work on it. He executed the left panel, but so little stylistic change had taken place that his work harmonizes perfectly with that of his anonymous predecessor.

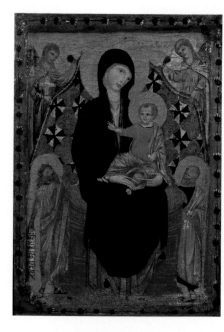

12

13

14

16

15

17

11　**Attributed to Cimabue** (Florentine, mentioned 1272–1302): *Christ between St. Peter and St. James Major*. Soon after 1270. Wood, center panel, 31 x 21¾″ (79 x 55 cm.). Andrew W. Mellon Collection

12　**Bernardo Daddi** (Florentine, active 1312–c. 1348): *St. Paul*. Dated 1333. Wood, 92 x 35⅛″ (234 x 89 cm.). Andrew W. Mellon Collection

13　**Agnolo Gaddi** (Florentine, active 1369–1396): *The Coronation of the Virgin*. Probably c. 1370. Wood, 64 x 31¼″ (162.6 x 79.4 cm.). Samuel H. Kress Collection

14　**Attributed to Cimabue**: *Madonna and Child with the Baptist and Saint Peter*. Probably c. 1290. Wood, 13½ x 9¼″ (34.3 x 24.8 cm.). Samuel H. Kress Collection

15　**Bernardo Daddi**: *Madonna and Child with Saints and Angels*. 1330s. Wood, 19¾ x 9½″ (50.2 x 24.2 cm.). Samuel H. Kress Collection

16　**Agnolo Gaddi**: *Madonna Enthroned with Saints and Angels*. c. 1380/90. Wood, 80⅝ x 96⅝″ (205 x 245 cm.). Andrew W. Mellon Collection

17　**Master of the Fabriano Altarpiece and Allegretto Nuzi** (Florentine, active probably c. 1335–c. 1365; Umbrian, active 1345–1373): *Madonna Enthroned with Saints*. Dated 1354. Wood, center panel 42¾ x 23⅜″ (108.6 x 59.4 cm.). Andrew W. Mellon Collection

Masaccio

(FLORENTINE, 1401–1428)

18   PROFILE PORTRAIT OF A YOUNG MAN

Giotto's attainment of the suggestion of sculptural form died with him. His followers lost sight of his objective. They were seduced by a love of accessories, by a desire to represent rich stuffs for their own richness, by graceful gestures for their own grace. Thus these artists sacrificed form for pattern and modeling for calligraphy. This attractive heresy culminated in the so-called International Style, which at the end of the fourteenth century flourished throughout Europe.

At the beginning of the fifteenth century, however, Florentine artists were recalled to the true faith, so to speak, by a fanatic for form, Tommaso di Ser Giovanni Guidi, called Masaccio. His panel paintings are extremely rare. Bernard Berenson, the great critic of Italian art, lists only fourteen. Though it is difficult to attribute with complete conviction profile portraits of the fifteenth century, the qualities of sculptural form which distinguish this painting tend to support Berenson's ascription of the panel to Masaccio. Note its subtle qualities of relief achieved by delicate transitions of value from light to shade, which model the lid of the eye, the concavity under the jaw, and the plastic convolutions of the ear.

Rendering three-dimensional form with a new flexibility, Masaccio adapted it to new purposes. The discovery in the fifteenth century of classical coins and busts stimulated a desire for portraiture and the perpetuation of personality which it can give. Masaccio endowed his sitters with this immortality. Like Shakespeare, he could assert:

> So long as men can breathe, or eyes can see
> So long lives this, and this gives life to thee.

Collections: Artaud de Montor, Paris. *Andrew W. Mellon Collection*, 1937. Painted c. 1425. Wood, 16⅝ x 12¾" (42 x 32 cm.).

19

19 Lorenzo Monaco (Florentine, c. 1370–1422/24): *Madonna and Child*. Dated 1413. Wood, 46 x 21¾" (117 x 55 cm.). Samuel H. Kress Collection

20, 21 Masolino da Panicale (Florentine, 1383/84– active to 1432): *The Archangel Gabriel, The Virgin Annunciate*. Probably c. 1420/30. Wood, each panel 30 x 22⅝" (76 x 57 cm.). Samuel H. Kress Collection

22 Gentile da Fabriano (Umbrian, c. 1360/70–1427): *A Miracle of St. Nicholas*. 1425. Wood, 14¼ x 14" (36 x 35 cm.). Samuel H. Kress Collection

23 Gentile da Fabriano: *Madonna and Child*. c. 1422. Wood, 37¾ x 22¼" (96 x 57 cm.). Samuel H. Kress Collection

24 Andrea del Castagno (Florentine, c. 1417/19– 1457): *Portrait of a Man*. c. 1450. Wood, 21¼ x 15⅞" (54 x 40.5 cm.). Andrew W. Mellon Collection

25 Masolino da Panicale: *The Annunciation*. Probably c. 1425/30. Wood, 58¼ x 45¼" (148 x 115 cm.). Andrew W. Mellon Collection

The grace and charm of the International Style referred to in the note to *Profile Portrait of a Young Man* (plate 18) are brilliantly illustrated in the Annunciation by Masolino da Panicale (plates 20, 21) and the *Madonna and Child* by Lorenzo Monaco (plate 19), Masolino's somewhat older contemporary. The dissemination of this International Style is to be seen in Germany, France, and Spain. It is evident all over Italy, most es-

20

21

22

23

pecially in the work of the first great Umbrian Master, Gentile da Fabriano. The discursive naturalism and linear beauty of late Gothic painting did not last, however, and one of the finest portraits in Florentine art, Castagno's *Portrait of a Man* (plate 24), introduces the severe, uncompromising realism which was a reaction against a sweetness that had begun to cloy.

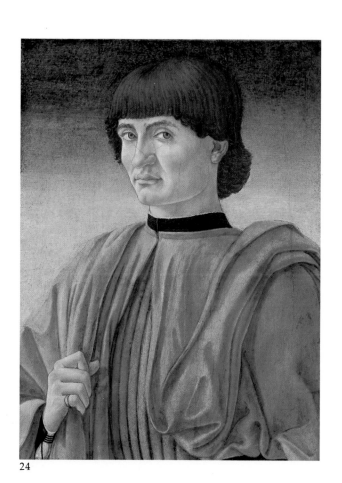

24

25

Sassetta and Assistant

(SIENESE, ACTIVE 1423–1450)

26 THE MEETING OF ST. ANTHONY AND ST. PAUL

In the early decades of the fifteenth century the late Gothic style flowered in such enchanting paintings as this. In spite of medieval characteristics such as the high horizon line and the method of continuous narration whereby three scenes from the life of St. Anthony are shown at once, Sassetta reveals a sensitive observation of nature as advanced as any painter of his age. The landscape with its arid hills, its groves of dark, dense foliage, is the distilled essence of the *Senese*, of that beautiful region of Tuscany near Siena where Sassetta lived and worked.

Sassetta was one of the most gifted of narrative painters. In a series of predella panels, four of which are in the National Gallery of Art (plates 26, 27, 28, 29), he has told, more poetically than any other artist, the legend of St. Anthony Abbot. The panel reproduced here, the seventh of the series, tells of his journey to meet St. Paul. The tradition is that St. Anthony, after having a vision of a fellow hermit, St. Paul, who had attained greater sanctity, decided to pay him a visit. In the upper left-hand corner, staff in hand, St. Anthony sets out on his travels. On his way he meets a centaur, a symbol of the gods of paganism, fast vanishing from the Christian world. The centaur, holding a palm branch, beats on his breast as a sign of his penitence, and receives a blessing—an indication of the conversion to Christianity of the ancient divinities of the woods.

At the bottom of the picture the two old men at last find each other. Their deep emotion is beautifully suggested by their tender embrace. As they incline their bodies one toward the other, their halos overlap, and the two figures form a pyramid whose shape is echoed in the opening of the cave and in the barren hill beyond. The intensity of feeling Sassetta conveys gives this small panel an impressive grandeur, making it one of the noblest creations of Sienese painting.

Collections: G. E. H. Vernon, Nottinghamshire; Wentworth Blackett Beaumont, First Lord Allendale; Viscount Allendale, London. *Samuel H. Kress Collection*, 1939. Painted c. 1440. Wood, 18¾ x 13⅝" (47.5 x 34.5 cm.).

27

28

27 Sassetta (Sienese, active 1423–1450) **and Assistant**: *St. Anthony Distributing His Wealth to the Poor.* c. 1440. Wood, 18⅝ x 13⅝″ (47.5 x 34.5 cm.). Samuel H. Kress Collection

28 Sassetta and Assistant: *St. Anthony Leaving His Monastery.* c. 1440. Wood, 18½ x 13¾″ (47 x 35 cm.). Samuel H. Kress Collection

29 Sassetta and Assistant: *The Death of St. Anthony.* c. 1440. Wood, 14⅜ x 15⅛″ (36.5 x 38.3 cm.). Samuel H. Kress Collection

30 Francesco di Giorgio (Sienese, 1439–1501/2): *God the Father Surrounded by Angels and Cherubim.* c. 1470. Wood, 14⅜ x 20⅜″ (36.5 x 51.8 cm.). Samuel H. Kress Collection

31 Giovanni di Paolo (Sienese, active 1420–1482): *The Annunciation.* c. 1445. Wood, 15¾ x 18¼″ (40 x 46 cm.). Samuel H. Kress Collection

32 Neroccio de' Landi (Sienese, 1447–1500): *Madonna and Child with St. Anthony Abbot and St. Sigismund.* c. 1495. Wood, 62⅜ x 55⅞″ (158.5 x 142 cm.). Samuel H. Kress Collection

33 Giovanni di Paolo: *The Adoration of the Magi.* c. 1450. Wood, 10¼ x 17¾″ (26 x 45 cm.). Andrew W. Mellon Collection

32

29

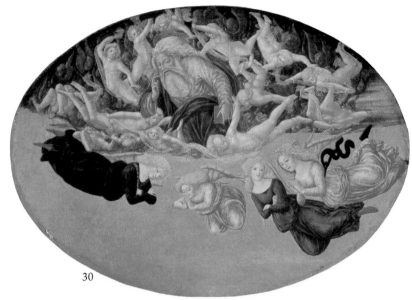

30

With *The Meeting of St. Anthony and St. Paul* (plate 26) we return to the International Style. Three more panels by Sassetta and his Assistant from the same altarpiece are reproduced in plates 27, 28, and 29. Paintings by Sienese contemporaries and followers of Sassetta are shown in the other reproductions. All these paintings have in common the characteristics of late Gothic art: linear beauty and languid grace. Siena was a center of stylistic conservatism. Forty miles away Florentines were experimenting with anatomy and perspective. Portraiture also flourished in Florence, whereas Sienese painters ignored these new trends. The portrait by Neroccio (plate 35) is virtually unique in Sienese art. Why, one wonders? The Sienese were known to be amazingly superstitious; perhaps having one's portrait painted was considered unlucky. There seems to be no other rational explanation.

31

33

34

34   Master of the Griselda Legend (Umbrian-Sienese active late XV century): *Eunostos of Tanagra.* c. 1495/1500. Wood, 34⅞ x 20⅝" (88.5 x 52.5 cm.). Samuel H. Kress Collection

35   Neroccio de' Landi (Sienese, 1447–1500): *Portrait of a Lady.* c. 1490. Wood, 18⅜ x 12" (46.5 x 30.5 cm.). Widener Collection

36   Benvenuto di Giovanni (Sienese, 1436–c. 1518): *The Adoration of the Magi.* c. 1470. Wood, 71¾ x 54⅛" (182 x 137 cm.). Andrew W. Mellon Collection

37   Andrea di Bartolo: (Sienese, first mentioned 1389–1428): *Joachim and the Beggars.* c. 1400. Wood, 17⅜ x 12¾" (44.2 x 32.4 cm.). Samuel H. Kress Collection

38   Andrea di Bartolo: *The Nativity of the Virgin.* c. 1400. Wood, 17⅜ x 12¾" (44.2 x 32.4 cm.). Samuel H. Kress Collection

39   Andrea di Bartolo: *The Presentation of the Virgin.* c. 1400. Wood, 17⅝ x 12¾" (44.2 x 32.4 cm.). Samuel H. Kress Collection

37

35

QVANTVM·HOMINI·FAS·EST·MIRA·LICET·ASSEQVAR·ARTE
NIL·AGO·MORTALIS·EMVLOR·ARTE·DEOS

36

38

39

Fra Angelico and Fra Filippo Lippi

(FLORENTINE, ACTIVE 1417–1455; PROBABLY c.1406–1469)

40   THE ADORATION OF THE MAGI

This tondo ranks among the greatest Florentine paintings in the world. It is a climax of beauty, a summary in itself of the whole evolution of the Italian schools of painting in the first half of the fifteenth century, for it stands at a crossroads of art. The old style, the gay, colorful, fairy-tale painting of the Middle Ages, is ending in an outburst of splendor; and the new style, scientific in observation, studious in anatomy and perspective, realistic in its portrayal of life, is beginning its long development. Two harbingers of the future are the row of naked youths who watch the procession—an early indication of that preoccupation with human anatomy which was to obsess Italian artists until it reached its climax in Michelangelo and the Sistine Chapel—and the scene in the stable, which foretells the flowering of genre painting at a still later date. It is interesting to note the degree to which Florentine style for the next fifty years fell under the spell of the two monks who collaborated on this *Adoration of the Magi*. It is almost as though the Kress Collection tondo seeded a whole garden of art.

Berenson was the first to indicate the probable collaboration of two artists on this panel, concluding that it was probably left unfinished when Fra Angelico departed for Rome in 1445. Though he subsequently came to agree with most critics that the painting was largely by Fra Filippo Lippi, the influence of Fra Angelico is everywhere apparent, and in some cases his touch can be discerned. The tondo has been connected with an entry in the Medici inventory of 1492 made after the death of Lorenzo the Magnificent, which reads: "A tondo with its golden frame representing the Madonna and Our Lord and the Magi offering gifts, from the hand of Fra Giovanni [Fra Angelico] worth 100 florins." This was the highest price for a painting in the inventory.

Collections: Possibly Medici family; Guicciardini Palace, Florence; probably M. Dubois, Florence; William Coningham, London; Alexander Barker, London; Cook, Doughty House, Richmond, Surrey. *Samuel H. Kress Collection*, 1952. Painted c. 1445. Wood, diameter 54″ (137.2 cm.).

41

42

The three pictures by Fra Angelico reproduced here are medieval in feeling. His Madonna, for example, is placed against a traditional gold background. But with Fra Filippo Lippi the full Renaissance has arrived. His Madonna is in a shell niche, a favorite motif of Renaissance architects. The two narrative pictures, *St. Benedict Orders St. Maurus to the Rescue of St. Placidus* (plate 43), and *The Healing of Palladia by St. Cosmas and St. Damian* (plate 44), are also quite different in style. Although both follow the ancient tradition of representing more than one scene in a single picture, the figures in the Fra Angelico are like the actors on the stage of a miracle play, whereas the monks in the Fra Filippo are depicted out-of-doors, performing their drama in a landscape still primitive but beginning to suggest actuality.

41   Fra Angelico (Florentine, active 1417–1455): *The Madonna of Humility*. c. 1430/35. Wood, 24 x 17⅞" (61 x 45.5 cm.). Andrew W. Mellon Collection

42   Attributed to Fra Angelico: *The Entombment*. c. 1445. Wood, 35 x 21⅝" (89 x 55 cm.). Samuel H. Kress Collection

43   Fra Filippo Lippi (Florentine, probably c. 1406–1469): *St. Benedict Orders St. Maurus to the Rescue of St. Placidus*. c. 1445. Wood, 16⅜ x 28" (41.6 x 71.1 cm.). Samuel H. Kress Collection

43

44

44 **Fra Angelico**: *The Healing of Palladia by St. Cosmas and St. Damian*. Probably between 1438 and 1443. Wood, 14⅜ x 18⅜″ (36.5 x 46.7 cm.). Samuel H. Kress Collection

45 **Fra Filippo Lippi**: *Madonna and Child*. 1440/45. Wood, 31⅜ x 20⅛″ (80 x 51 cm.). Samuel H. Kress Collection

46 **Fra Filippo Lippi**: *The Annunciation*. Probably soon after 1440. Wood, 40½ x 64″ (103 x 163 cm.). Samuel H. Kress Collection

45

46

Domenico Veneziano

(FLORENTINE, ACTIVE 1438–1461)

47   ST. JOHN IN THE DESERT

The Renaissance artist was confronted with the conflict between paganism and Christianity. How could he bring into harmony the classical world he was learning to love, as he came to know it, and the Christian doctrines and traditions which were his immediate heritage? He rarely solved this problem, rarely achieved complete reconciliation. When, however, he managed to bring the two forces into perfect balance, as they are in this painting by Domenico Veneziano, there is a magic calm, a breathless moment, in which the underlying tensions of Renaissance art are miraculously resolved.

Few pictures present so perfectly the essence of the Quattrocento—the youthful spirit of a new world emerging from the shadows of the Middle Ages into the cold beauty of the dawning Renaissance. St. John is a nude athlete with a body that might have been carved by Polycleitus, but above his head appears a golden halo, the emblem of his sanctity. The panel has always been thought to represent, in a virtually unique form, the moment when St. John put aside his worldly clothes and assumed the rough garb of the wilderness. But is there also a second meaning, another interpretation more subtle, more in keeping with the classical spirit which permeates the picture? Is this youth putting aside instead the drab clothes of his mortal body and reaching for the iridescent garments of a spiritual realm he is about to enter? As the panel was a part of an altarpiece whose main panel is now in the Uffizi, undoubtedly the usual Christian story of St. John donning his hair shirt was the interpretation intended for the public. But there is throughout the picture an evocative fancy, a suggestion of some half-disclosed symbolism, perhaps some Neoplatonic theory of the progress of the soul, which makes this second and quite different meaning not impossible.

Regardless of iconography, this panel and a few other works by Domenico Veneziano must have had a revolutionary effect on the painting of their day. Here for the first time we find a landscape filled with sparkling air, like a high plateau swept clean with cool winds. To be able to convey the mood of a particular place was new in art, and it has remained rare.

Collections: Santa Lucia dei Magnoli, Florence; Bernard Berenson, Florence; Carl W. Hamilton, New York. *Samuel H. Kress Collection*, 1943. Painted c. 1445. Wood, 11⅛ x 12¾" (28.5 x 32.5 cm.). Another panel from the same predella, *St. Francis Receiving the Stigmata* (plate 50), is in the National Gallery of Art.

48

49

48 Assistant of Piero della Francesca (Umbrian, c. 1416–1492): *St. Apollonia*. Toward 1470. Wood, 15¼ x 11″ (39 x 28 cm.). Samuel H. Kress Collection

49 Domenico Veneziano (Florentine, active 1438–1461): *Madonna and Child*. c. 1445. Wood, 32½ x 22¼″ (83 x 57 cm.). Samuel H. Kress Collection

50 Domenico Veneziano: *St. Francis Receiving the Stigmata*. c. 1445. Wood, 10⅞ x 12″ (26.7 x 30.5 cm.). Samuel H. Kress Collection

51 Francesco Pesellino (Florentine, c. 1422–1457): *The Crucifixion with St. Jerome and St. Francis*. Probably c. 1440/45. Wood, 24½ x 19″ (62 x 48 cm.). Samuel H. Kress Collection

52 Benozzo Gozzoli (Florentine, 1420–1497): *The Dance of Salome*. 1461/62. Wood, 9¾ x 13½″ (23.8 x 34.3 cm.). Samuel H. Kress Collection

53 Benozzo Gozzoli: *The Raising of Lazarus*. Probably 1497. Canvas, 25¾ x 31¾″ (65.5 x 80.5 cm.). Widener Collection

50

51

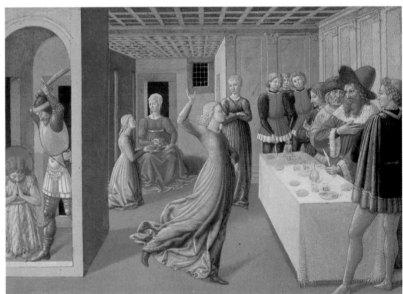

52

Bernard Berenson, the outstanding authority on Italian Renaissance painting, lists only thirteen works by Domenico Veneziano. It is remarkable that of these the National Gallery of Art possesses three. This rare painter shows his originality not only in his rendering of light and air but in his unique color sense, delighting in acidulous contrasts of pale green and pink. All the paintings reproduced here were done toward the middle of the fifteenth century, when Florentine art exerted its hegemony over the other Italian schools. Newly discovered principles of optics, a closer observation of nature, and, in the *Dance of Salome* by Benozzo Gozzoli (plate 52), psychological drama are Florentine innovations which were destined to have a significant influence on subsequent Italian art.

53

Andrea del Castagno

(FLORENTINE, c. 1417/19–1457)

54   THE YOUTHFUL DAVID

One of the most vivid tales in Vasari's *Lives of the Painters* is the description of the brutal murder of Domenico Veneziano by his pupil Andrea del Castagno. We now know that Vasari's account is fictitious, for Domenico outlived his supposed murderer, but if a man's personality is reflected in his creations, then Vasari's characterization of Castagno is true. Truculence, bravado, a brutal power, these are the qualities that emanate from his work.

In his interpretation of the triumphant David, he is less aggressive, less savage than one would expect, but he displays, nevertheless, his power to overwhelm us with the sheer impact of emotion. The intense vitality of this heroic youth, vibrant with energy, anticipates the Romanticism of Géricault and Delacroix.

David is a symbolic figure, the ideal warrior, hard, resolute, conscious of his power, but conscious at the same time of its tragic implications. The head of the slain Goliath already lies at his feet. To the modern spectator this may seem an inconsistency in the sequence of events, but it did not disturb Castagno's contemporaries, for the picture is symbolic. It is not the representation of a historic occurrence. Consequently the act and the result of the act are shown simultaneously. For the meaning of the scene, the triumph of freedom over tyranny, could best be expressed this way.

The painting is on a leather shield and was probably carried in the processions which preceded the jousts, or tournaments, popular in the fifteenth century. Other ornamental shields exist, though they are rare, but this example is the only one by a great master that has survived.

Collections: Drury-Lowe, Locko Park, England. *Widener Collection*, 1942. Painted c. 1450. Leather, 45½ x 30¼" (115.5 x 77 cm.).

Botticelli

(FLORENTINE, 1444/45–1510)

55 THE ADORATION OF THE MAGI

With this *Adoration of the Magi* we reach the last quarter of the fifteenth century and the reign of Lorenzo de' Medici. Florence had become a center of Greek studies, Neoplatonism almost a religion. Refinement, a fastidious sensibility, a mood of poetic reverie had come into fashion. It was a time when pageants and ceremonials were popular and families took pride in having themselves portrayed as the principal actors in the dramas of Christianity. In the present painting, which Botticelli probably executed during his sojourn in Rome while he was working in the Sistine Chapel, the portraits have never been identified in spite of their incisive characterizations.

But the wonder of this *Adoration* does not consist so much in these portrait studies as in the subtle disposition of the figures, their vibrant movement, and their poetic setting. Amid the ruins of the classical world, symbolized by fragments of ancient architecture, the new order of Christianity is born. From the calmness of the central group, from the mystical yet human serenity of the Madonna and Child, movement radiates in waves of increasing activity through the gestures of awe and of prayer of the onlookers, and reaches a climax in the youthful grooms on the far right.

Beyond this human activity stretches a landscape suggestive of the serene spaces of the Campagna. It is impossible to let the eye travel into the tranquil beauty of this countryside without some relief of the spirit, some sense of refreshment and calm. The breadth, serenity, and restraint which are so conspicuous in this *Adoration* disappeared shortly thereafter from Botticelli's work. With the exile of the Medici he came under the spell of Savonarola, and his last years were overclouded by the feverish visions of the Dominican reformer.

Collections: Purchased in Rome by the engraver Peralli, it was acquired in 1808 for the Hermitage Gallery, Leningrad, by Czar Alexander I. *Andrew W. Mellon Collection*, 1937. Painted early 1480s. Wood, 27⅝ x 41" (71 x 103.5 cm.).

56

57

The paintings reproduced here are by two of the greatest Florentine masters working at the turn of the fifteenth century: Botticelli and Filippino Lippi. Their styles are so similar that it is hard to distinguish one from the other. For example, both *Portrait of a Youth* (plate 58) and the *Coronation of the Virgin* (plate 56), now generally considered to be by Filippino, were once ascribed to Botticelli. This confusion is evidence of the difficulties of attributing unsigned pictures. But the portrait of Giuliano de' Medici, aesthetically and historically one of the most important of Florentine paintings, shows the handwriting of Botticelli so clearly that no other authorship has ever been suggested.

58

56 **Filippino Lippi** (Florentine, probably 1457–1504): *The Coronation of the Virgin.* c. 1480. Wood, 35½ x 87½" (90 x 222 cm.). Samuel H. Kress Collection

57 **Filippino Lippi**: *Tobias and the Angel.* Probably c. 1480. Wood, 12⅞ x 9¼" (32.5 x 23.5 cm.). Samuel H. Kress Collection

58 **Filippino Lippi**: *Portrait of a Youth.* c. 1485. Wood, 20 x 13⅞" (51 x 35.5 cm.). Andrew W. Mellon Collection

59 **Botticelli** (Florentine, 1444/45–1510): *Giuliano de' Medici.* c. 1478. Wood, 29¾ x 20⅝" (75.6 x 52.6 cm.). Samuel H. Kress Collection

60 **Botticelli**: *The Virgin Adoring the Child.* c. 1480–90. Wood, diameter 23⅜" (59.6 cm.). Samuel H. Kress Collection

61 **Botticelli**: *Portrait of a Youth.* Early 1480s. Wood, 16¼ x 12½" (41.2 x 31.8 cm.). Andrew W. Mellon Collection

59

60

61

Leonardo da Vinci

(FLORENTINE, 1452–1519)

63   GINEVRA DE' BENCI

62   Leonardo da Vinci: Reverse of *Ginevra de' Benci*

On the reverse of the portrait of Ginevra de' Benci is the only painted still life by Leonardo da Vinci, if so heraldic a design can be thus designated.

The cost per square inch of paint of the portrait of Ginevra de' Benci is the greatest in the history of collecting. Why is the likeness of a young, seemingly disgruntled Florentine heiress so precious? Paintings by Leonardo da Vinci are indeed rare, but rarity in itself is only a cipher, dependent on the numbers that precede it. Furthermore, how can one be sure the picture is by that most extraordinary genius? True, all recent critics have agreed to this attribution, but on what is their judgment based? First, there is external evidence. We know from contemporary sources that Leonardo painted someone called Ginevra de' Benci. The juniper bush, so prominent in the portrait and repeated symbolically on the back, is considered to identify the sitter as that lady, the name *Ginevra* being a dialect form, in the feminine, of the Italian word for juniper (*ginepro*). A pun of this kind would certainly have appealed to Leonardo. Second, and much more important, is the internal evidence. The portrait reveals Leonardo's incomparable technical skill. There are passages, such as the modeling of the lips, which Leonardo never surpassed in delicacy. Such value transitions are miracles of technique, and Leonardo was the first painter to have the perfect control of his medium necessary to make light and shade merge imperceptibly.

In his notebooks, Leonardo compares curls of hair to swirling water. The ringlets which frame Ginevra's face resemble cascading whirlpools. These curls are so like Leonardo's rendering both of hair in his other paintings and of water in his drawings as to be a virtual signature. Lastly, there are Leonardo's colored reflections, discussed at length in his *Treatise on Painting*. In Ginevra's portrait such reflected colors reverberate through the painting and cause the flesh to glow as if, like the moon, it reflected some hidden radiance.

But we still have not answered the question of why the portrait is of such significance. The answer is that this is the first psychological portrait ever painted. Leonardo's tremendous innovation was developed in his three portraits of women. Each expresses a different mood: the earliest, *Ginevra*, withdrawn sadness; the next, *Cecilia Gallerani*, now in Krakow, appealing wistfulness; and the last, the *Mona Lisa*, mirthless amusement. Of these, the most original is the enigmatic melancholy of Ginevra de' Benci. Sadness has rarely been represented in portraiture. I know of no other instance in painting before the seventeenth century, and even then the tragic view of life was usually conveyed by portraits of men, not of women.   *(continued)*

(continued)

The date of the portrait is in dispute. The staff of the National Gallery believes the painting to have been a gift to the bridegroom made in 1474 at the time of Ginevra's marriage. If so, it is one of the most lugubrious likenesses ever given to a groom! The bride must have taken a bleak view of her prospects! Many critics, however, believe the painting was executed a few years later. A date of about 1480 offers a more likely and a more romantic explantation of Ginevra's gloom. In March of that year Ginevra was deserted by her lover, the Venetian Ambassador to Florence, Bernardo Bembo. The Renaissance poet Braccesi wrote: "May Ginevra shed tears as you go, Bembo. May she desire long delays and beseech the gods above that every difficulty may hinder your journey. And may she wish that the kindly stars with adverse winds and heavy storms prevent your departure."

The gods, however, favored Bembo, and sail he did. No wonder Leonardo's sitter, weeping on the Pisan shore, was melancholy and withdrawn.

Collections: Possibly Niccolini and Benci families; possibly Prince Carl Eusebius of Liechtenstein; The Princes of Liechtenstein from 1733. *Ailsa Mellon Bruce Fund,* 1967. Painted c. 1474 or c. 1480. Wood, 15⅛ x 14½" (38.2 x 36.7 cm.).

64

65

64   Studio of Leonardo da Vinci (early XVI century): *Portrait of a Young Lady.* Transferred from wood to hardboard, 18⅝" x 13½" (47.3 x 34.3 cm.). Samuel H. Kress Collection

65   Bernardino Luini (Milanese, c. 1480–1532): *Portrait of a Lady.* c. 1520/25. Wood, 30⅜ x 22½" (77 x 57.5 cm.). Andrew W. Mellon Collection

66   Circle of Verrocchio (possibly Leonardo) (Florentine, c. 1470/75): *Madonna and Child with a Pomegranate.* Wood, 6⅛ x 5" (15.7 x 12.8 cm.). Samuel H. Kress Collection

67   Bramantino (Milanese, c. 1465–1530): *The Apparition of Christ among the Apostles.* c. 1500. Wood, 9⅜ x 7⅝" (23.8 x 19.5 cm.). Samuel H. Kress Collection

68   Andrea Solario (Milanese, active 1495–1524): *Pietà.* c. 1515. Wood, 66⅜ x 59⅞" (168.6 x 152 cm.). Samuel H. Kress Collection

69   Jacopo del Sellaio (Florentine, 1441/42–1493): *St. John the Baptist.* c. 1480. Wood, 20⅜ x 12⅞" (52 x 33 cm.). Samuel H. Kress Collection

66

67

68

69

Except for *St. John the Baptist* by Jacopo Sellaio (plate 69) and the picture called "Circle of Verrocchio" (plate 66), which is so close to the early Leonardo as to have been attributed to him at one time, all these pictures are by Milanese followers of the master. Leonardo's presence in Milan (1482–99 and 1506–13) gave a new direction to the provincial Lombard style of the Renaissance. His dark shadows, meticulous gradations of tone to express form, and *sfumato*—softening of contours to express space and atmosphere—were eagerly adopted by local artists and combined with native traits and influences from Northern Europe to produce a distinctive Lombard style.

Piero di Cosimo

(FLORENTINE, 1462–c.1521)

70   THE VISITATION WITH ST. NICHOLAS AND ST. ANTHONY ABBOT

Piero di Cosimo possessed the artistic temperament, as we think of it, to an exceptional degree. Vasari has written so delightfully about Piero and this particular painting that I cannot do better than quote the famous sixteenth-century biographer at length.

"And in truth, in all that there is to be seen by his hand, one recognizes a spirit very different and far distant from that of other painters, and a certain subtlety in the investigation of some of the deepest and most subtle secrets of Nature, without grudging time or labor, but only for his own delight and for his pleasure in the art. And it could not well be otherwise; since, having grown enamoured of her, he cared nothing for his own comfort, and reduced himself to eating nothing but boiled eggs, which, in order to save firing, he cooked when he was boiling his glue, and not six or eight at a time, but in fifties; and, keeping them in a basket, he would eat them one by one. . . . He could not bear the crying of children, the coughing of men, the sound of bells, and the chanting of friars; and when the rain was pouring in torrents from the sky, it pleased him to see it streaming straight down from the roofs and splashing on the ground. He had the greatest terror of lightning; and, when he heard very loud thunder, he wrapped himself in his mantle, and having closed the windows and the door of the room, he crouched in a corner until the storm should pass. He was very varied and original in his discourse, and sometimes said such beautiful things, that he made his hearers burst with laughter. But when he was old, and near the age of eighty, he had become so strange and eccentric that nothing could be done with him. He would not have assistants standing round him, so that his misanthropy had robbed him of all possible aid. He was sometimes seized by a desire to work, but was not able, by reason of the palsy, and fell into such a rage that he tried to force his hands to labor; but, as he muttered to himself, the mahl-stick fell from his grasp, and even his brushes so that it was pitiable to behold. Flies enraged him, and even shadows annoyed him.

"For the Chapel of Gino Capponi, in the Church of S. Spirito at Florence, he painted a panel wherein is the Visitation of Our Lady, with S. Nicholas, and a S. Anthony who is reading with a pair of spectacles on his nose, a very spirited figure. Here he counterfeited a book bound in parchment, somewhat old, which seems to be real, and also some balls that he gave to the S. Nicholas, shining and casting gleams of light and reflections from one to another; from which even by that time men could perceive the strangeness of his brain, and his constant seeking after difficulties."

Collections: Chapel of Gino Capponi, Santo Spirito, Florence; Villa Capponi a Legnaia, near Florence; The Hon. Mrs. Frederick West, Chirk Castle, Denbigh; Frederick Richard West, Ruthin Castle, Denbigh; Colonel W. Cornwallis-West, later Lord Lascelles, Newlands Manor, Hampshire. *Samuel H. Kress Collection*, 1939. Painted probably c. 1495. Wood, 72½ x 74¼" (184 x 189 cm.).

71   Filippino Lippi (Florentine, probably 1457–1504): *Pietà.* c. 1490. Wood, 6⅞ x 13¼″ (17.5 x 33.7 cm.). Samuel H. Kress Collection

72   Domenico Ghirlandaio (Florentine, 1449–1494): *Lucrezia Tornabuoni.* Toward 1475. Wood, 21 x 15¾″ (53.3 x 39.9 cm.). Samuel H. Kress Collection

73   Domenico Ghirlandaio: *Madonna and Child.* c. 1470. Transferred from wood to hardboard, 28⅞ x 20″ (73.4 x 50.8 cm.). Samuel H. Kress Collection

74   Lorenzo di Credi (Florentine, c. 1458–1537): *Self-Portrait.* Probably 1488. Transferred from wood to canvas, 18 x 12¾″ (46 x 32.5 cm.). Widener Collection

75   Piero di Cosimo (Florentine, 1462–c. 1521): *Allegory.* c. 1500. Wood, 22⅛ x 17⅜″ (56 x 44 cm.). Samuel H. Kress Collection

76   Piero di Cosimo: *The Nativity with the Infant St. John.* c. 1500. Canvas, diameter 57⅜″ (146 cm.). Samuel H. Kress Collection

71

73

72

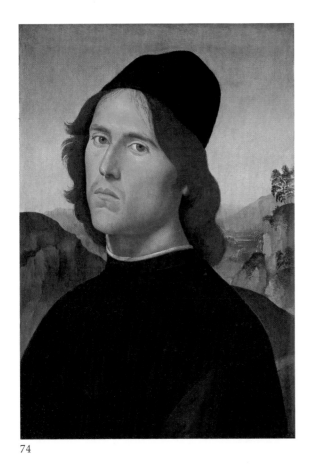

74

75

The "strangeness of Piero's brain," which Vasari notes (see commentary 70), gives his pictures an odd fascination. Why should St. Joseph in *The Nativity* (plate 76) be shown descending a flight of stairs, or the dove, symbolizing the Holy Ghost, perch on the ground, or the Christ Child turn away from those who adore him? And what is the symbolism of the surrealist *Allegory* (plate 75) with its stallion, its winged maiden, and its swimming mermaid? There are no answers known to us. It is something of a relief to turn from these puzzles to the straightforward portrait of a great Florentine lady, Lucrezia Tornabuoni, the mother of Lorenzo the Magnificent, or to the haunting self-portrait of Lorenzo di Credi, whose introspection and self-doubt, so clearly conveyed, led him to burn his secular paintings at the behest of the fanatical priest Savonarola.

76

Pietro Perugino

(UMBRIAN, c.1445–1523)

77 THE CRUCIFIXION WITH THE VIRGIN, ST. JOHN, ST. JEROME, AND ST. MARY MAGDALENE

In his *Journal intime*, Henri-Frédéric Amiel meditates on Good Friday: "You desire to know the art of living, my friend? It is contained in one phrase: make use of suffering. . . . O Death, where is thy sting? O Grave, where is thy victory? From a long contemplation of this theme—the agony of the Just, peace in the midst of agony, and glory in such peace—mankind came to understand that a new religion had been born, that is, a new way of explaining life and of understanding suffering. . . ."

Perugino's paintings create to a degree rare in art a mood of tranquil veneration, in which such religious truths appear self-evident or demonstrable. It is surprising therefore to learn from Vasari that Perugino was a person of little religion and disbelieved in the immortality of the soul.

The present triptych was formerly ascribed to Perugino's pupil Raphael, but as we know that it was given to the Church of San Domenico at San Gimignano by Bartolommeo Bartoli, who died in 1497, when Raphael was only fourteen, we can be certain that the attribution was incorrect. The picture is now unanimously ascribed to Perugino. It is one of the greatest treasures acquired by Andrew Mellon from the Hermitage Gallery, Leningrad. (For a complete contrast in the treatment of this theme compare Grünewald's *Crucifixion*, plate 146.)

Collections: Bartolommeo Bartoli, Bishop of Cagli, ordered the painting for the Church of San Domenico, San Gimignano; Antonio Moggi; Dr. Buzzi; Prince Alexander Galitzin; Prince Theodore Galitzin; Galitzin Museum; Hermitage Gallery, Leningrad. *Andrew W. Mellon Collection*, 1937. Painted c. 1485. Transferred from wood to canvas. Center: 39⅞ x 22¼" (101.5 x 56.5 cm.). Sides: 37½ x 12" (95 x 30.5 cm.).

78 Pietro Perugino (Umbrian, probably 1445–1523): *St. Jerome in the Wilderness.* Probably c. 1481/82. Wood, 24⅝ x 16½" (63 x 42 cm.). Samuel H. Kress Collection

79 Pietro Perugino: *Madonna and Child.* Soon after 1500. Wood, 27⅝ x 20" (70 x 51 cm.). Samuel H. Kress Collection

80 Giannicolo di Paolo (Umbrian, active 1484–1544): *The Annunciation.* Wood, 15⅞ x 14⅛" (40 x 36 cm.). Samuel H. Kress Collection

81 Luca Signorelli (Umbrian, c. 1441–1523): *Calvary.* Probably c. 1505. Wood, 28⅜ x 39½" (72.1 x 100.4 cm.). Samuel H. Kress Collection

82 Master of the Barberini Panels (Umbrian-Florentine, active third quarter XV century): *The Annunciation.* c. 1450. Wood, 34½ x 24¾" (88 x 63 cm.). Samuel H. Kress Collection

83 Luca Signorelli: *The Marriage of the Virgin.* c. 1491. Wood, 8½ x 19" (21.6 x 48.2 cm.). Samuel H. Kress Collection

79

80

78

The two paintings by Perugino both create the same mood of calm reverence conveyed in his *Crucifixion* (plate 77). The spirit of his contemporary and fellow Umbrian, Signorelli, was totally different. His figures seem to swagger assertively. His *Calvary*, for instance, is filled with horsemen and his *Marriage of the Virgin* with truculent suitors. By contrast the rare Master of the Barberini Panels, also an Umbrian, was an artist who, like Perugino, could create a feeling of stillness, of serene devotion. But he was aware as well of the scientific investigations of his time. Not even Paolo Uccello in Florence ever delineated a more pronounced linear perspective.

82

81

83

Giovanni Bellini

(VENETIAN, c. 1430–1516)

84   GIOVANNI EMO

When this portrait was painted, between about 1475 and 1483, Giovanni Bellini, who lived to be over eighty, was the acknowledged leader of the Venetian School of painting. As Vasari, writing in the sixteenth century, said, "Since he had the habit of painting portraits from life, he made it the fashion in that city for anyone of prominence to be portrayed by him or someone else." Not only did Giovanni Bellini popularize portraiture in Venice, he was one of the first to start the vogue for a three-quarter view of the sitter, replacing the older, profile type exemplified by Ercole Roberti's portrait of Ginevra Bentivoglio (plate 89). This new way of posing the sitter was probably introduced into Italy by artists from Flanders, who also brought with them the technique of painting in oil. Giovanni Bellini, always alert to innovations, recognized that the three-quarter view permitted better characterization and that the use of oil instead of tempera allowed a greater refinement of modeling. Stimulated by this fresh approach, he executed a series of small portraits of famous Venetians which rank among the finest masterpieces of portraiture.

Certain critics have felt that this may be a posthumous portrait of Bartolommeo Colleoni, who died in 1475; others have suggested Giacomo Marcello. Many scholars favor Bartolommeo d'Alviano, for two reasons: first, Vasari records that Bellini painted his portrait, and second, the Kress painting bears a strong resemblance to known likenesses of this condottiere, who defeated the troops of Emperor Maximilian in 1508 in the decisive battle of the Cadore Mountains.

The staff of the National Gallery has recently identified the sitter as Giovanni Emo, a high official of Venice who served as general in the Venetian army during the war against Ferrara in the early 1480s. The identification of fifteenth-century portraits is extremely difficult, as the above indicates, but Emo is perhaps the best candidate. Nevertheless, I feel a question mark is desirable. Regardless of such scholarly controversy, it is obvious that Giovanni Bellini has brilliantly represented the universal type of military leader—hard, resolute, relentless—while at the same time revealing the personality of an individual whose thin and tightly closed lips suggest a character not devoid of cruelty.

Collections: Sir Abraham Hume (bought in Venice, 1786) and his descendants to Adelbert Wellington, Third Earl Brownlow, Ashbridge Park, Berkhamsted. *Samuel H. Kress Collection*, 1939. Painted c. 1475-83. Wood, 19¼ x 13⅞″ (49 x 35 cm.).

85

86

85 **Ambrogio de' Predis** (Milanese, c. 1455–c. 1508): *Bianca Maria Sforza.* Probably 1493. Wood, 20 x 12¾" (51 x 32.5 cm.). Widener Collection

86 **Giovanni Bellini** (Venetian, c. 1430–1516): *Portrait of a Young Man in Red.* c. 1480. Wood, 12½ x 10⅜" (32 x 26.5 cm.). Andrew W. Mellon Collection

87 **Giovanni Bellini**: *St. Jerome Reading.* c. 1480/90. Wood, 19¼ x 15½" (49 x 39 cm.). Samuel H. Kress Collection

88 **Ercole Roberti** (Ferrarese, active 1479–1496): *Giovanni II Bentivoglio.* c. 1480. Wood 21⅛ x 15" (54 x 38 cm.). Samuel H. Kress Collection

89 **Ercole Roberti**: *Ginevra Bentivoglio.* c. 1480. Wood, 21⅛ x 15¼" (54 x 39 cm.). Samuel H. Kress Collection

90 **Venetian School** (c. 1505): *Portrait of a Young Man.* Wood, 11 x 9" (28 x 23 cm.). Widener Collection

87

88

89

90

Portrait painters at the turn of the fifteenth century placed their sitters either in the old-fashioned profile pose or in the newer three-quarter view. The more primitive method was derived from classical coins and medals, which were passionately collected during the Renaissance; the more innovative style, with the sitter's head turned three-quarters, usually to the right, illustrated by *Giovanni Emo* (plate 84) and by plates 86 and 90, seems to have been first developed in the North. With the model in silhouette there is very little opportunity for psychological characterization, but by delineating the two eyes and two cheeks, the painter has a much greater opportunity to convey his sitter's personality.

Andrea Mantegna

(PADUAN, 1431–1506)

91   JUDITH AND HOLOFERNES

The search for actuality and the discovery of archaeology molded fifteenth-century Italian painting. Padua, where Mantegna was born, was a center of antiquarianism. Even in a scene from the Old Testament Apocrypha, Judith decapitating Holofernes, we find the Jewish drama transformed into a Greek tragedy. Thus the actors, in spite of the gruesomeness of the event, are as impersonal as the sculptured figures of the Parthenon. Judith turns away from her bloody prize with a look of calm detachment; she accepts impassively her predestined triumph. The stone-colored panel seems chiseled rather than painted, like an enlarged cameo which has survived from the ancient world.

Such Classicism appealed strongly to seventeenth-century taste, especially in England. The first recorded owner of this panel was Charles I, who believed it to be by Raphael. Later he exchanged it with the Earl of Pembroke for paintings by Bellini and Parmigianino. Thus it escaped one of the tragic consequences of Cromwell's Revolution, the dispersal of the Royal Collection. It remained in England instead, a part of the famous Pembroke Collection at Wilton House, until brought to America by P. A. B. Widener. The subject of Judith and Holofernes was treated several times by Mantegna and his school. Among the drawings of this scene are one in the Uffizi, Florence (dated 1491), and one in the Samuel H. Kress Collection, National Gallery of Art. A grisaille of almost identical dimensions, showing the same subject, with the composition in reverse, is in the National Gallery, Dublin. Judith, the unscrupulous murderer of tyrants, was the most popular heroine of the Renaissance.

Collections: King Charles I of England; Pembroke Collection, Wilton House. *Widener Collection,* 1942. Painted c. 1495. Wood, 11⅞ x 7⅛" (30 x 18 cm.).

92

93

94

92 **Andrea Mantegna** (Paduan, 1431–1506): *Portrait of a Man*. Probably c. 1460. Transferred from canvas to hardboard, 9½ x 7½" (24.3 x 19.1 cm.). Samuel H. Kress Collection

93 **North Italian School** (c. 1460): *Portrait of a Man*. Wood, 22¼ x 15¾" (56.5 x 40 cm.). Samuel H. Kress Collection

94 **Andrea Mantegna:** *The Christ Child Blessing*. Probably c. 1480/90. Canvas, 27⅝ x 13¾" (70.3 x 35 cm.). Samuel H. Kress Collection

95 **Andrea Mantegna:** *St. Jerome in the Wilderness*. c. third quarter of XV century. Wood, 31¾ x 21⅝" (80.5 x 55 cm.). Andrew W. Mellon Collection

96 **Carlo Crivelli** (Venetian, active 1457–1493): *Madonna and Child Enthroned, with Donor*. c. 1470. Wood, 51 x 21⅜" (129.5 x 54.5 cm.). Samuel H. Kress Collection

97 **Cosimo Tura** (Ferrarese, c. 1430–1495): *Madonna and Child in a Garden*. c. 1455. Wood, 20¾ x 14⅝" (53 x 37 cm.). Samuel H. Kress Collection

98 **Francesco del Cossa** (Ferrarese, c. 1435–c. 1477): *The Crucifixion*. Soon after 1470. Wood, diameter 25⅛" (64 cm.). Samuel H. Kress Collection

99 **Francesco del Cossa:** *St. Florian*. Soon after 1470. Wood, 31¼ x 21⅝" (79 x 55 cm.). Samuel H. Kress Collection

95

116

96

98

97

99

The National Gallery's collection is especially rich in the work of Mantegna and of the numerous artists who came under his influence in Lombardy, Venice, Ferrara, and even as far south as Sicily, the home of Antonello da Messina. Mantegna's imprint on his followers was extremely strong; thus it is quite possible that the panel representing St. Jerome (plate 95), which is usually attributed to him, was painted by some contemporary Paduan. This picture, of jewel-like beauty, shows the saint kneeling in his flinty desert and beating his breast with a stone. The *Portrait of a Man* (plate 92) and *The Christ Child Blessing* (plate 94), ascribed with more certainty to the master, also show his sculptural style.

Crivelli, active in Venice, also models his elegantly mannered figures as though they were made of some tangible precious stone. And Ercole Roberti,

(continued)

100

101

100 Francesco del Cossa (Ferrarese, c. 1435–1477): *St. Lucy.* Soon after 1470. Wood, 31¼ x 22" (79 x 56 cm.). Samuel H. Kress Collection

101 Antonello da Messina (Sicilian, active 1456–1479): *Madonna and Child.* c. 1475. Wood, 23¼ x 17¼" (59 x 44 cm.). Andrew W. Mellon Collection

102 Antonello da Messina: *Portrait of a Young Man.* Probably 1475. Wood, 13 x 9¾" (33 x 25 cm.). Andrew W. Mellon Collection

103 Ercole Roberti (Ferrarese, active 1479–1496): *The Wife of Hasdrubal and Her Children.* c. 1480/90. Wood, 18½ x 12" (47.1 x 30.6 cm.). Ailsa Mellon Bruce Fund

102

(continued)

Cosimo Tura, and Francesco del Cossa, the greatest Ferrarese artists, also looked to Padua and to Mantegna for their sharply delineated contours and infrangible surfaces. This austere, Mantegnesque style, with its hard, monumental forms, was softened and humanized by Antonello da Messina. He was one of the painters who introduced into Italy the use of oil as a medium, a procedure he must have learned through some contact with Northern artists. This new method of painting, which gradually replaced *tempera*, gives his figures a glow of light which seems to come from some interior illumination. It represents a technical innovation which was destined to have a profound effect all over Italy, but especially in Venice, Antonello's adopted city.

103

Northern Schools

XV AND XVI CENTURY

Jan van Eyck

(FLEMISH, 1380/1400–1441)

104   THE ANNUNCIATION

In many ways the founder of all Northern painting was Jan van Eyck, who died in Bruges in 1441. He is traditionally considered the discoverer of oil painting, a technique in which linseed oil serves as the solvent for pigment, rather than egg, which was used in the Italian technique of tempera. This made possible a new flexibility and delicacy of handling.

Whether or not van Eyck actually did discover oil painting may be debated, but certainly he was the first to achieve a naturalistic rendering of interior space, or in less technical terms, the effect of looking through an open window or door into a room. It is this new power of representation which is van Eyck's most salient characteristic. Note his masterful suggestion of atmosphere through subtle gradations of light, and his supreme skill in the definition of detail. Contrast the barely visible frescoes at the top of the dimly lit walls of the church, painted with an impalpable delicacy, and the hard microscopic clarity of the jewels on the angel's robes. No artist has ever had a greater range of visual effects. *The Annunciation*, however, is more than a record of new technical attainment; it is a masterpiece of Christian symbolism. It expounds the significance of the Annunciation, the momentous event in history which divides the Era of Law from the Era of Grace, the Dispensation of the Old Testament from the New. The dark upper part of the church with its single window on which is depicted Jehovah, the Lord of the Old Testament, is contrasted with the lower half illumined by three windows, symbolic of the Trinity, through which shines the Light of the World. The angel addresses Our Lady with the words *Ave Gratia Plena*, to which She answers *Ecce Ancilla Domini*, the words reversed and inverted so they can be read by the Holy Ghost, descending in rays of light.

The building cannot be identified with an existing church, but it suggests the late Romanesque style of Maastricht and Tournai. It would seem as though van Eyck designed this building in an architectural style which had not been practiced for several centuries, perhaps the first example of "revivalism" in architecture.

Collections: William II, King of the Netherlands; Hermitage Gallery, Leningrad. *Andrew W. Mellon Collection*, 1937. Painted c. 1425/30. Transferred from wood to canvas, 36½ x 14⅜" (93 x 36.5 cm.).

Petrus Christus

(FLEMISH, c. 1410–1472/73)

107   THE NATIVITY

105, 106   Petrus Christus: *A Donor and His Wife.* c. 1455. Wood, two panels, each 16½ x 8½″ (42 x 21.6 cm.). Samuel H. Kress Collection

Glimpses of landscape in Flemish painting are always rewarding. The background of the Petrus Christus *Nativity* shows how pleasant the countryside must have been in the fifteenth century. The town walls kept building within bounds. There were no suburbs. One stepped from the gate of the city directly into meadowland. Nothing could seem closer to an earthly paradise than the world the Flemish artists portrayed. Fortunately, the smells, the dirt, the lack of sanitation of urban life in the Middle Ages had no place in the visual arts.

Painters were not paid to represent the facts of life. Theirs was a different task—to portray the facts of religion. In the foreground of his painting Petrus Christus tells us the story of Man's Fall and Redemption; Adam and Eve stand on columns supported on the backs of stooped figures, symbolizing mankind burdened with Original Sin. Above on the arch are scenes showing the Expulsion from Eden, Cain slaying Abel, and other episodes from the Old Testament. In the spandrels are two battling figures, mankind in hopeless conflict and enmity as a consequence of sin.

These simulated sculpture groups provide the historical antecedents for the action in the center, where Mary and Joseph, accompanied by angels, worship the Redeemer. This moment of dramatic stillness, so portentous for mankind, must often have been acted out in a similar way in mystery plays, even to the wooden shoes of Joseph, which lend a sense of actuality to the scene. In the middle distance are four spectators, symbols of humanity, for whose Redemption the Incarnation has taken place. Confronted by a vision of compelling eloquence their indifference, so characteristic of mankind, remains tragically unchanged.

Collections: Prince Manuel Yturbe, Madrid; Duchess of Parcent, Madrid. *Andrew W. Mellon Collection*, 1937. Painted c. 1445. Wood, 51¼ x 38¼″ (130 x 97 cm.).

123

108

109

Petrus Christus was a superb portrait painter as well as a painter of altarpieces. His double portrait *A Donor and His Wife* (plates 105, 106) once formed the wings of a triptych, the center panel of which has been lost. Another Flemish portraitist of exceptional skill was Dirk Bouts, who like Petrus Christus was strongly influenced by Jan van Eyck. The newly perfected technique of painting in oils made possible the minute realism of these likenesses. From Flanders, realism spread to France; its influence is evident in the somewhat unusual representation of Our Lady pregnant with the Saviour.

110

111

112

113

114

108   School of Amiens (French, c. 1437): *The Expectant Madonna with St. Joseph*. Wood, 27⅝ x 13⅝" (70.2 x 34 cm.). Samuel H. Kress Collection

109   Hispano-Dutch School (probably last quarter XV century): *The Adoration of the Magi*. Wood, 73 x 65⅜" (185.4 x 166.1 cm.). Samuel H. Kress Collection

110   Dirk Bouts (Dutch-Flemish, c. 1420–1475): *Portrait of a Donor*. c. 1455. Wood, 10⅛ x 8" (25.6 x 20.4 cm.). Samuel H. Kress Collection

111   Franco-Flemish School (early XV century): *Profile Portrait of a Lady*. c. 1415. Wood, 20⅜ x 14⅜" (52 x 36.5 cm.). Andrew W. Mellon Collection

112   Miguel Sithium (Flemish, c. 1469–1525): *A Knight of the Order of Calatrava*. c. 1515. Wood, 13⅛ x 9¼" (33.5 x 23.5 cm.). Andrew W. Mellon Collection

113   Master of Flémalle and Assistants (Flemish, first half XV century): *Madonna and Child with Saints in the Enclosed Garden*. Wood, 47⅛ x 58½" (119.9 x 148.8 cm.). Samuel H. Kress Collection

114   Circle of Rogier van der Weyden (c. 1460): *Christ Appearing to the Virgin*. Wood, 64 x 36⅝" (163 x 93 cm.). Andrew W. Mellon Collection

115   Rogier van der Weyden (Flemish, 1399/1400–1464): *St. George and the Dragon*. c. 1432. Wood, 5⅝ x 4⅛" (14.3 x 10.5 cm.). Ailsa Mellon Bruce Fund

Rogier van der Weyden's *St. George and the Dragon* (plate 115), reproduced here actual size, is the smallest painting in the National Gallery. It is also among the most valuable. It was bought at auction, and the final bid represented a price of $26,552 per square inch. Among the other reproductions shown here, the Franco-Flemish *Portrait of a Lady* (plate 111) is particularly interesting. Formerly ascribed to Pisanello, it was long considered a masterpiece of Italian art. The costume, however, is Burgundian, and the picture is now correctly placed on the other side of the Alps. This example demonstrates the international character of late Gothic portraiture.

115

Rogier van der Weyden

(FLEMISH, 1399/1400-1464)

116   PORTRAIT OF A LADY

Among the hundreds of portraits at the National Gallery of Art there is one as beautiful as it is baffling. It is the portrait by Rogier van der Weyden of a young lady tentatively identified as a famous heiress of the fifteenth century, Marie de Valengin, daughter of Philip the Good, Duke of Burgundy. The painting's attraction is twofold: its excellent preservation and the fascination of the lady who sat for it. As is usual with Flemish pictures of this period, it is painted on a piece of wood overlaid with white gesso. On this prepared panel the figure was first painted in monochrome, and the underpainting then covered with thin glazes of colored oil. With this newly discovered oil technique the artist was able to render the most subtle gradations of light, especially noticeable in passages such as the transparent wimple. With age such Flemish panels have acquired a web of minute cracks, a surface as beautiful in its way as the surface of old porcelain.

Although the precision of Flemish painting was suited to the firm structure and sharp contours of Marie de Valengin's features, if the sitter is she, the clarity of this style only stresses her somewhat eccentric appearance. She is too thin, her lips too thick, her forehead too high. Her looks are outré, defensible only on the basis of Sir Francis Bacon's axiom, "There is no excellent beauty that hath not some strangeness in the proportion." But ugly as her features may be individually, still they combine to suggest a personality so enigmatic, with so many conflicting tendencies, that one becomes absorbed and ends by finding Rogier van der Weyden's model not only enthralling but, in some way, strangely beautiful.

The first impression is of her preoccupation. Her stare, so oblivious of the spectator, is like a challenging withdrawal; she looks out from a citadel of secrecy. Then one notices her meager body made to appear still thinner by her silken girdle, and afterward her high, intellectual forehead, its domelike appearance exaggerated by its diaphanous covering. All this is psychologically consistent, every detail indicative of a contemplative, somewhat ascetic nature. But this is only one aspect of her character. There is another side, eagerly sensuous and fiercely passionate. It is shown by the thick underlip and the full mouth. Thus the actions of this Burgundian princess must always have been unpredictable, always determined by an unresolved conflict in her personality. She remains an enigma, with something of the perplexing quality of that Gothic lady whom John Skelton paradoxically describes:

> As midsummer flower
> Gentle as falcon
> Or hawk of the tower.

Collections: Duke of Anhalt-Dessau, Gotisches Haus, Wörlitz, and Herzogliches Schloss, Dessau, East Germany. *Andrew W. Mellon Collection*, 1937. Painted c. 1455. Wood, 14½ x 10¾" (37 x 27 cm.).

Hans Memling

(FLEMISH, c. 1430/35–1494)

117   THE PRESENTATION IN THE TEMPLE

The problem of attribution grows especially complicated when it seems possible that two artists have worked on the same picture. Among the most beautiful and best preserved of Flemish Primitives is *The Presentation in the Temple*, a panel now generally ascribed to the youthful Hans Memling, working in the studio of Rogier van der Weyden.

The two enchanting children in the scene, however, look different from Memling's typical portraits, as the Belgian critic Hulin de Loo first pointed out. They are more delicately painted and convey a greater sense of form than the other figures. Were they, as Hulin de Loo insists, painted by Rogier van der Weyden, and thus an addition by the old master to his pupil's panel? This seems not unlikely; indeed, the theory is strengthened by X-rays of the two girls' heads, which indicate a higher concentration of lead white than is found in other parts of the panel.

In order to convey the teachings of Christian theology in visual terms, Hans Memling has employed symbolic devices. The church in which the Presentation of Our Lord takes place is Romanesque on the inside and Gothic on the outside. The change in architectural style indicates the change from the Old to the New Dispensation which will result from the Incarnation. The stained-glass windows in the background illustrate the Fall of Man, whereas the foreground prefigures his Redemption. Thus in one scene the artist symbolically portrays the basic principles of Christian doctrine.

Collections: Count Johann Rudolf Czernin von Chudenitz, Vienna; Czernin Gallery, Vienna. *Samuel H. Kress Collection*, 1961. Painted c. 1463. Wood, 23½ x 19″ (59.8 x 48.3 cm.).

118

119

118, 119   Hans Memling (Flemish, c. 1430/35–1494):
Obverse, *St. Veronica*; reverse, *Chalice of St. John the
Evangelist*. c. 1480. Wood, 12¼ x 9½″ (31.1 x 24.2
cm.). Samuel H. Kress Collection

120   Hans Memling: *Madonna and Child with
Angels*. c. 1480. Wood, 23⅛ x 18⅞″ (59 x 48 cm.). Andrew W. Mellon Collection

121   Hans Memling: *Portrait of a Man with an Ar-
row*. c. 1470. Wood, 12⅝ x 10¼″ (32 x 26 cm.). Andrew
W. Mellon Collection

122   Bernaert van Orley (Flemish, c. 1488–1541):
Christ among the Doctors. c. 1513. Wood, 21⅛ x 12¾″
(53.7 x 32.5 cm.). Samuel H. Kress Collection

123   Bernaert van Orley: *The Marriage of the Virgin*.
c. 1513. Wood, 21⅛ x 12⅝″ (53.7 x 32.3 cm.). Samuel
H. Kress Collection

120

The National Gallery's collection of works by Hans Memling, the leader among Flemish painters of the generation after Jan van Eyck, is unsurpassed outside Belgium. Particularly interesting is one of the earliest of all still-life paintings (plate 119), the reverse of the panel representing St. Veronica. The viper emerging from the chalice is a reference to the cup of poisoned wine offered to St. John the Evangelist. When the saint made the sign of blessing, the venom, in the form of a snake, was miraculously drawn from the liquid. The pictures by van Orley, which are later, show by their architecture that the Italian Renaissance had reached the North.

121

122

123

Gerard David

(FLEMISH, c. 1460–1523)

124   THE REST ON THE FLIGHT INTO EGYPT

Flemish painting is characterized by a curious mixture of observation and tradition. In this connection the small wicker basket in the foreground of David's *Rest on the Flight into Egypt* is revealing. It is only natural that Our Lady should have taken a traveling bag on her journey, and for this accessory David designed a little reticule which was to prove so popular that it appears sporadically in other paintings for almost a hundred years. The scene depicted, a pause on a journey, is one he must often have seen. In the middle distance, the father, beating chestnuts from a tree, is gathering food, while in the foreground the mother has already begun to feed her child. But there is more in this scene than a glimpse of a family at mealtime. A transcript of actuality is combined with an ancient symbolism. A family pauses to eat, but the food, the grapes, are a sign of the Eucharist, a prefiguration of the Last Supper and of the suffering which awaits Our Lord. Early Flemish painting has often a double significance: as a mirror of everyday life and as a symbol of the life to come.

The popularity of David's painting is attested by the many existing copies and altered replicas. Possibly its charm for contemporaries lay in the originality of its coloring. The misty landscape, illumined with an azure light so characteristic of the Belgian countryside, echoes the color of the sky and of the Virgin's mantle. Four hundred years later Whistler might have entitled such a painting *A Symphony in Blue*. Is it perhaps the earliest tonal symphony with a dominant color in the history of art?

Collections: Rev. Montague Taylor, London; Rodolph Kann, Paris; J. Pierpont Morgan, New York. *Andrew W. Mellon Collection*, 1937. Painted c. 1510. Wood, 17¾ x 17½" (45 x 44.5 cm.).

125

126

127

The development of Northern landscape painting was erratic. How far ahead of his time Gerard David was can be seen by comparing his *Rest on the Flight into Egypt* (plate 124) with the *St. Jerome* of his younger contemporary Gossaert (plates 131, 132). The background of stylized rocks in Gossaert's painting can be traced to Byzantine icons. There is no observation of nature. Joachim Patinir, however, introduced a landscape style as atmospheric and naturalistic as David's. In his work all the Gothic conventions had disappeared. The same development is evident in portraiture. The natural gesture of Joos van Cleve's man pulling on a glove, for example, is not to be found in the fifteenth century.

128

129

130

125–27 Gerard David (Flemish, c. 1460–1523): *The St. Anne Altarpiece.* c. 1500/1510. Wood, middle panel 94 x 38″ (239 x 96.5 cm.); side panels, each 94 x 28″ (239 x 71 cm.). Widener Collection

128 Follower of Joachim Patinir (Flemish, XVI century): *The Flight into Egypt.* c. 1550. Wood, 9⅜ x 5⅞″ (23.7 x 15 cm.). Samuel H. Kress Collection

129 Joos van Cleve (Flemish, active 1511–1540/41): *Joris W. Vezeler.* c. 1520. Wood, 22⅞ x 15¾″ (58 x 40 cm.). Andrew W. Mellon Fund

130 Joos van Cleve: *Margaretha Boghe, wife of Joris W. Vezeler.* c. 1520. Wood, 22½ x 15⅝″ (57.1 x 39.6 cm.). Andrew W. Mellon Fund

131, 132 Jan Gossaert (Mabuse) (Flemish, c. 1478–1532): *St. Jerome Penitent.* c. 1512. Wood, two panels, each 34 x 10″ (86.4 x 25.4 cm.). Samuel H. Kress Collection

131   132

135

Master of the St. Lucy Legend

(FLEMISH, ACTIVE 1480–1489)

133   MARY, QUEEN OF HEAVEN

The panel reproduced, which is exceptionally large, is outstanding among Flemish paintings in both preservation and color. It is interesting therefore that it should have been executed with an unusual technique. Whereas nearly all Flemish paintings have a coat of gesso made of white chalk and glue covering the wood, here the paint is laid on a thinner, less rigid type of primer. One is reminded of the famous altar by Nuño Gonçalves in Lisbon, painted almost contemporaneously and with a similar technique, and likewise unusual in scale and perfectly preserved. It is possible that this variation from the normal Flemish method represented an improvement in the durability of large panel paintings. In any case, it was a technique which must have been simpler to handle.

The originality of the St. Lucy Master also appears in the iconography. Paying tribute to the New Marian devotion, the artist has combined in one scene the Immaculate Conception, the Assumption, and the Coronation of the Virgin. According to Colin Eisler, "This brilliantly colored altarpiece, placed in the capital of old Castile, may well have played an influential role in determining later representations of the same subject."

Musicologists as well as iconographers have found this panel particularly fascinating. The instruments played by the angels and the grouping of the heavenly choir illustrate medieval musical practice. Emanuel Winternitz, the eminent musicologist, has pointed out that "all the instruments are contemporary with the painting and depicted with the greatest exactness as if the artist had transplanted into Heaven a musical performance of his own time. Equally precise is the rendering of the finger positions, the holding of the bow, etc. Also, the organization of the two orchestras and their quantitative relation to small vocal groups is by no means fanciful; it is quite in line with contemporary practice. The music sheets are clearly legible."

The St. Lucy Master also used color in a musical way. The angels' robes, like chromatic chords, form a polyphonic harmony of hues. Though apparently trained in Flanders, this artist was probably active in Spain, as the panel came from a convent near Burgos.

Collection: Convent near Burgos, Spain. *Samuel H. Kress Collection*, 1952. Painted c. 1485. Wood, 85 x 73" (215.9 x 185.4 cm.).

134 **Miguel Sithium** (Flemish, c. 1469–1525): *The Assumption of the Virgin.* c. 1500. Wood, 8⅜ x 6½" (21.2 x 16.4 cm.). Ailsa Mellon Bruce Fund

135 **Juan de Flandes:** *The Temptation of Christ.* c. 1500. Wood, 8¼ x 6¼" (21 x 15.8 cm.). Ailsa Mellon Bruce Fund

136 **Juan de Flandes** (Hispano-Flemish, active 1496–c. 1519): *The Annunciation.* Probably c. 1510. Wood, 43¼ x 31¼" (109.9 x 79.4 cm.). Samuel H. Kress Collection

137 **Juan de Flandes:** *The Nativity.* Probably c. 1510. Wood, 43½ x 31" (110.5 x 83.2 cm.). Samuel H. Kress Collection

138 **Juan de Flandes:** *The Adoration of the Magi.* Probably c. 1510. Wood, 49⅛ x 31¼" (124.8 x 79.4 cm.). Samuel H. Kress Collection

139 **Juan de Flandes:** *The Baptism of Christ.* Probably c. 1510. Wood, 49½ x 32" (125.7 x 81.1 cm.). Samuel H. Kress Collection

134

136

137

135

During the latter part of the fifteenth century, several provinces of the Netherlands became linked to Burgundy and Spain as a result of political alliances. A consequence of this union was that a number of artists trained in the Low Countries and eastern France traveled south. Many of them settled in Spain, where a fusion of Northern and Hispanic artistic traditions took place. Two of these itinerant artists collaborated on an altar for Queen Isabella, Sithium painting two scenes and Juan de Flandes, the court painter, forty-five. A panel by each artist is shown (plates 134, 135). Albrecht Dürer wrote of the altarpiece, which he saw in the Netherlands, "I saw about 40 little panels in oil color, such as I have never seen for precision and excellence."

The other pictures reproduced here show further work by Juan de Flandes, the finest of these Hispano-Flemish artists: four panels painted for the High Altar of the Cathedral of Palencia.

138

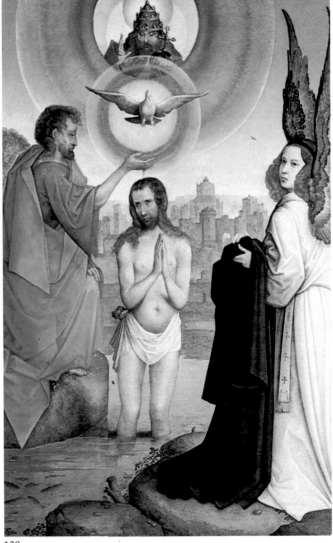

139

Master of St. Giles

(FRANCO-FLEMISH, ACTIVE c. 1500)

140 THE BAPTISM OF CLOVIS

The Flemish technique of painting spread over northern Europe and Spain. The panel reproduced is by an artist strongly influenced by Hugo van der Goes. His birthplace is unknown, but his Parisian residence is certain. The baptism is shown as occurring in Sainte-Chapelle on the Île de la Cité in Paris. The upper church is suggested by the statue on the central pier and the door on the right, but otherwise the scene seems to take place on the ground level. Through the door of the chapel can be seen the former royal palace and its courtyard, Place du Parvis, as they appeared about 1500. The gabled edifice and the corner tower were built about 1323 and are thought to have housed the king's chaplains. Just beyond, one has a glimpse of the royal apartments. This picture and a companion piece (plate 142), also in the National Gallery of Art, are, except for manuscript illumination, the earliest accurate views of the city of Paris. Thus, apart from the beauty of the paintings, they are archaeological documents of outstanding significance.

Clovis was baptized at Rheims, not Paris, and William M. Hinkle has suggested that the scene represents instead the baptism of Lisbius by St. Denis. Lisbius was the first Christian martyr of Paris. His martyrdom was brought about by the denunciation of his wife, Larcia, who is identified as the grim lady standing behind the baptismal font. Colin Eisler, however, has found an illustration of 1488, approximately the date of the panel reproduced, which shows the scene in much the same fashion. He believes the forbidding expression of the lady in the background was due less to hostility toward her husband than to repainting by an inept restorer. Thus she and her two companions are more likely to have been donors. That the figure being baptized wears a crown indicates that he could be Clovis, who was king of the Franks. Assuming that the naked man with the far-away look is the king, the description of his baptism, one of Gibbon's most delightful passages, is worth quoting: "The important ceremony was performed in the cathedral of Rheims, with every circumstance of magnificence and solemnity that could impress an awful sense of religion on the minds of its rude proselytes. The new Constantine was immediately baptized, with three thousand of his warlike subjects; and their example was imitated by the remainder of the *gentle Barbarians*, who, in obedience to the victorious prelate, adored the cross which they had burnt, and burnt the idols which they had formerly adored."

Collections: Probably commissioned for the church of St.-Leu–St.-Giles, Paris; Chevalier Lestang-Parade; Comte Melchior de Lestang-Parade, Aix-en-Provence; Baron E. de Beurnonville; M. Watil, Paris. *Samuel H. Kress Collection*, 1952. Painted c. 1500. Wood, 24¼ x 18⅜" (61.6 x 46.7 cm.).

141

141

141 Corneille de Lyon (French, active 1534–1574):
Portrait of a Man. c. 1540. Wood, 6½ x 5⅝" (16.5 x 14.3
cm.). Ailsa Mellon Bruce Fund

142 Master of St. Giles (Franco-Flemish, active c.
1500) and Assistant: *Episode from the Life of a Bishop
Saint.* Wood, 24¼ x 18" (61.6 x 45.8 cm.). Samuel H.
Kress Collection

143 Master of the Retable of the Reyes Católicos
(Spanish, late XV century): *Christ among the Doctors.*
Wood, 61½ x 37" (156.3 x 94 cm.). Samuel H. Kress
Collection

144 Master of the Retable of the Reyes Católicos:
The Marriage at Cana. Wood, 60⅜ x 36⅜" (153.4 x 92.6
cm.). Samuel H. Kress Collection

145 French School (XV century): *Portrait of an Ecclesiastic.* c. 1480. Wood, 11⅜ x 8¾" (28.8 x 22.2 cm.).
Samuel H. Kress Collection

142

143

144

145

The companion piece to *The Baptism of Clovis* (plate 140) is *Episode from the Life of a Bishop Saint*. The saint stands on the steps of the church of Saint-Jean-le-Ronde in Paris. Until the eighteenth century this building served as the Baptistry of Notre Dame, the façade of which is faithfully represented. Also represented here are a characteristic French portrait of the fifteenth century, an unusually fine work by Corneille de Lyon, and two panels painted by a Spanish artist trained in Flanders. In one of these panels, representing the Marriage at Cana, the portraits suggest a connection with the marriages in 1496–97 of the children of Ferdinand and Isabella to those of the Emperor Maximilian.

Mathis Grünewald

(GERMAN, c. 1465–1528)

146 THE SMALL CRUCIFIXION

Heir to the Gothic and precursor of the Baroque, Grünewald has in this painting attained an unsurpassed intensity of expression. The hands and feet of Christ stab at one's heart. Twisted and tortured, they are visual symbols of physical agony. His torso, "dark smirched with pain," is drawn in by a paroxysm of suffering. John and the two Marys show their anguish with gestures prayerful but helpless. The mood of ineffable woe is enhanced by the dark gloom of night, and by the colors: murky greens, livid blues, and blood reds.

The Small Crucifixion is one of scarcely more than a dozen paintings by Grünewald, whose most famous picture is the great *Isenheim Altarpiece* at Colmar. It was known to Sandrart, who saw the panel in the possession of Duke Maximilian I of Bavaria. It had previously been owned, Sandrart tells us, by Maximilian's father, Duke William V of Bavaria, an "intelligent judge and connoisseur of fine art." Sandrart writes of it as follows: "[Duke William] had a small Crucifixion with Our Dear Lady and St. John, together with a kneeling and devoutly praying Mary Magdalen, most carefully painted by his [Grünewald's] hand, and he [the Duke] loved it very much, even without knowing whom it was by. On account of the wonderful Christ on the Cross, so suspended and supported on the feet, it is so very rare that real life could not surpass it and certainly it is more true to nature and reality than all Crucifixions when one contemplates it with thoughtful patience for a long time. For this reason it was, on the gracious order of the honorable Duke, engraved, half a sheet large, on copper in the year 1605 by Raphael Sadeler, and I pleased His Highness, the Great Elector Maximilian, of blessed memory, greatly since I made known the master's name." It is a name that has fascinated art historians ever since. A list made thirty years ago of the most significant publications on Mathis Grünewald since 1914 listed 436 books and articles.

Collections: Probably the Collegiate Church (*Stift*) of Aschaffenburg; Duke William V of Bavaria; Duke Maximilian I of Bavaria; Landrat Dr. Friedrich Schöne, Essen; Franz Wilhelm Koenigs and heirs, Haarlem. *Samuel H. Kress Collection*, 1961. Painted c. 1510. Wood, 24¼ x 18⅛" (61.6 x 46 cm.).

145

147

148

149

150

151

152

147   Master of the St. Bartholomew Altar (School of Cologne, active c. 1470–c. 1510): *The Baptism of Christ.* c. 1500. Wood, 41¾ x 67⅛" (106.1 x 170.5 cm.). Samuel H. Kress Collection

148   Master of Heiligenkreuz (Franco-Austrian, early XV century): *The Death of St. Clare.* c. 1410. Wood, 26⅛ x 21⅜" (66.4 x 54.5 cm.). Samuel H. Kress Collection

149   Master of St. Veronica (School of Cologne, active early XV century): *The Crucifixion.* c. 1400/1410. Wood, 18⅛ x 12⅜" (46 x 31.4 cm.). Samuel H. Kress Collection

150–52   Workshop of Albrecht Altdorfer (German, before 1480–1538): *The Fall of Man.* Probably c. 1535. Wood, middle panel 15¼ x 12" (38.7 x 35 cm.); side panels, each 15¼ x 6¼" (38.7 x 15.9 cm.). Samuel H. Kress Collection

153   Johann Koerbecke (German, active 1453–1491): *The Ascension.* 1457. Wood, 36½ x 25½" (92.6 x 64.8 cm.). Samuel H. Kress Collection

German painting in the early fifteenth century formed part of the International Style already mentioned in connection with the works of Lorenzo Monaco, Masolino, and Gentile da Fabriano. In the North, even more than in Italy, this mode of representation stressed bright, clear colors, flat patterns, and minute detail rendered with precise brushwork. The figures are usually two-dimensional, drawn with a mannered grace. The style is well illustrated by these paintings. Toward the end of the century, however, a totally different manner of painting appeared, introduced by such geniuses as Grünewald, Dürer, and Cranach.

153

Albrecht Dürer

(GERMAN, 1471–1528)

154   MADONNA AND CHILD

In the year 1506 Albrecht Dürer wrote a famous letter to his friend Willibald Pirckheimer in which he said, "But Sanbellinus [Giovanni Bellini] has praised me highly before several noblemen and he wishes to have something of my painting. He came himself and asked me to do something for him, saying that he would pay me well for it and all the people here tell me what a good man he is, so that I also am greatly inclined to him. He is very old, but yet he is the best painter of them all."

The epistolary tribute to Giovanni Bellini is well known. But a still greater compliment from the Northern painter to the Venetian master is the Madonna reproduced here, which was once thought to be by Bellini himself, so close is it to the work of that artist. Here Dürer was searching, as have many other Germans, for absolute beauty, which he hoped to find in the work of Italian painters. But his creation remained as essentially Northern as the landscape glimpsed through the window, or the escutcheons at the lower corners, one of which has been identified as belonging to the Haller family, who came from Dürer's home town, Nuremberg.

A number of critics have dated the painting in the last years of the fifteenth century, but more recently there has been a tendency to place it sometime after 1504 for a very good reason. The position of the Child's left arm, with the hand holding an apple, agrees almost precisely with the left arm and hand of Eve in Dürer's engraving of Adam and Eve dated 1504. Did Dürer intend this detail of the painting to refer to the Fall, repeating in the Child born to redeem Mankind the gesture of the Eve in his recently executed engraving?

Collections: Possibly Willibald Imhof the Elder; possibly Paul von Praun; Colonel Charles a'Court-Repington, Amington Hall, near Tamworth, Warwickshire; Mrs. Phyllis Loder, London; Baron Heinrich Thyssen-Bornemisza, Lugano. *Samuel H. Kress Collection*, 1952. Signed *verso* with monogram. Painted c. 1505. Wood, 19¾ x 15⅝" (50.2 x 39.7 cm.).

149

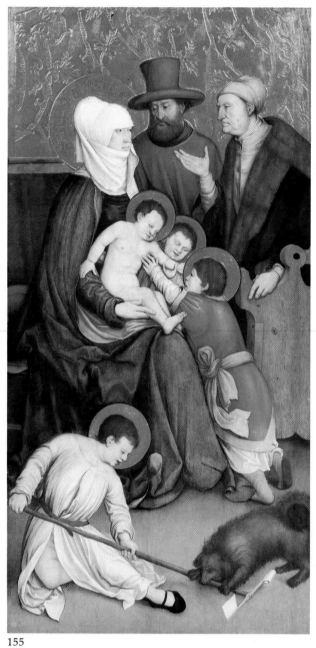

155

156

The reverse of Dürer's *Madonna and Child* (plate 154) shows Lot fleeing with his daughters (plate 157) from what looks like an atomic attack on Sodom and Gomorrah while Lot's wife, paralyzed in her saline state, stands statuesquely in the middle distance. This scene seems to me delightfully comic, but the other paintings reproduced here are depressingly serious. Baldung Grien and Bernhard Strigel are admirable craftsmen, but German art wnen not fanciful tends to be ponderous; and both these worthy painters are, for the most part, a trifle boring. More interesting is the anonymous artist of the *Crucifixion* and the *Christ in Limbo* (plates 159, 160). The large crowds pushing against the narrow frames, the ghostly light, and the strangely cut-off bodies give these panels a visionary intensity.

157

158

155   **Bernhard Strigel** (German, 1460/61–1528): *St. Mary Cleophas and Her Family.* 1520/28. Wood, 49 x 24¾″ (124.4 x 62.9 cm.). Samuel H. Kress Collection

156   **Bernhard Strigel:** *St. Mary Salome and Her Family.* 1520/28. Wood, 49⅜ x 25⅞″ (125.4 x 65.8 cm.). Samuel H. Kress Collection

157   **Albrecht Dürer** (German, 1471–1528): *Lot and His Daughters,* reverse of *Madonna and Child* (plate 154). Wood, 19¾ x 15⅝″ (50.2 x 39.7 cm.). Samuel H. Kress Collection

158   **Hans Baldung Grien** (German, 1484/85–1545): *St. Anne with the Christ Child, the Virgin, and St. John the Baptist.* c. 1511. Transferred from wood to hardboard, 34¼ x 29⅞″ (87 x 75.9 cm.). Samuel H. Kress Collection

159, 160   **German School** (c. 1570): *The Crucifixion* and *Christ in Limbo.* Wood, each 42⅞ x 16¼″ (108.9 x 41.5 cm.). Samuel H. Kress Collection

159

160

151

Albrecht Dürer

(GERMAN, 1471–1528)

161   PORTRAIT OF A CLERGYMAN

This famous portrait from the Czernin Collection, Vienna, is signed with Dürer's monogram and dated 1516. Though the subject has not been identified, the portrait is a brilliant example of Dürer's ability to "lay open the fine net-work of the heart and brain of man," to make us see deep into the soul until we understand, for example, the character of this ugly, resolute individual, whose personality, flashing out through luminous and asymmetrical eyes, exerts a powerful spell. His is the face of the Reformation. Here one sees that burning fanaticism which, occurring on both sides, caused the religious wars and, after a deluge of blood and destruction, left northern Europe bleak and desolate.

Dürer was not only capable of suggesting in his portraits the universal in the individual, he was also able to give a remarkable record of physical appearance. Trained by his work as an engraver and designer of woodcuts, he drew every form with the utmost precision. A trick of verisimilitude he often employed, until it became almost a signature, was to delineate the windowpanes of his studio as though reflected in the pupils of his sitter's eyes.

The technique of this painting is unusual: it is executed on parchment. Artists were constantly seeking new methods and materials, and in 1516 Dürer twice tried the skin of a goat or sheep as a support for his painting. Though the experiment apparently did not satisfy him, this portrait has lasted without a blemish, and one wonders why he abandoned an interesting innovation.

Collections: Paul von Praun, Nuremberg; Count Johann Rudolf Czernin von Chudenitz, Vienna; Czernin Gallery, Vienna. *Samuel H. Kress Collection*, 1952. Signed with monogram, and dated 1516. Parchment on canvas, 16⅞ x 13″ (42.9 x 33.2 cm.).

153

162

164

163

165

154

162   Bernhard Strigel (German, 1460/61–1528): *Margaret Vöhlin, Wife of Hans Rott.* Dated 1527. Wood, 17¼ x 12¼" (43.8 x 31.1 cm.). Ralph and Mary Booth Collection

163   Bernhard Strigel: Reverse of *Margaret Vöhlin, Wife of Hans Rott*

164   Bernhard Strigel: *Hans Rott, Patrician of Memmingen.* Dated 1527. Wood, 17¼ x 12¼" (43.8 x 31.1 cm.). Ralph and Mary Booth Collection

165   Bernhard Strigel: Reverse of *Hans Rott, Patrician of Memmingen*

166   Nicolaus Kremer (German, c. 1500–1553): *Portrait of a Nobleman.* Signed with initials, and dated 1529. Wood, 23½ x 17⅜" (59.9 x 44.5 cm.). Ralph and Mary Booth Collection

167   Hans Schäufelein (German, c. 1470/85–1538/40): *Portrait of a Man.* Dated 1507. Wood, 15⅝ x 12⅝" (40 x 32 cm.). Andrew W. Mellon Collection

167

166

German painters were often superb portraitists, although few reached the level of Dürer. The painting attributed to Schäufelein bears the false initials "A.D." (Albrecht Dürer), a favorite device to give a picture greater importance. This brilliant characterization, however, needs no misrepresentation to be considered a masterpiece. The sitter's ruthless and determined face reveals the fanaticism that made possible the cruelty and intolerance of the Reformation. The portraits by Strigel of Hans Rott and his wife, two patricians from Memmingen, seem by comparison far too mild and inexpressive. Their coats of arms on the reverse are more interesting than their likenesses. This often happens with German painters who delighted in decorative calligraphy for its own sake.

Hans Holbein the Younger

(GERMAN, 1497–1543)

168   SIR BRIAN TUKE

As Hazlitt said, Holbein's portraits are like state documents. In them we find recorded objectively, but with impressive dignity, the great figures who surrounded Henry VIII. Sir Brian Tuke was Governor of the King's Post "in England and in other parts of the King's domain beyond the sea." He was also secretary and treasurer of the royal household, and he has been credited with the responsibility of bringing Holbein to England, possibly to paint this portrait, which is the finest of a number of versions.

Droit et avant (upright and forward) was the sitter's personal motto, one that seems to have been justified by his life. On the folded paper near his hand can be discerned with difficulty the Latin words from Job 10:20, "Are not my days few? cease then, and let me alone, that I may take comfort a little." Sir Brian was fifty-seven when he was painted, an old man by the standards of his time. He accepted that he had but a short while to live, for in the Renaissance death was always imminent. The plague still ravaged Europe, and an outbreak of the pestilence in London some years later carried off Holbein himself when only forty-six and at the peak of his career. If a courtier escaped death by disease there was still the enmity of his monarch to be feared, and this could be mortal, too, as it was in the case of St. Thomas More, the friend of both Tuke and Holbein, who died with many others for refusing to say "yes" to the King. Sir Brian never lost his sovereign's favor, but in his twisted smile, full of pain, and in the wistful plea on the folded paper, we sense the desperate insecurity of life in the England of Henry VIII.

Collections: Philip Sidney, Third Earl of Leicester; Sir Paul Methuen and descendants, among whom the last owner was Paul, First Lord Methuen, Corsham Court, Chippenham, Wiltshire; Richard Sanderson, Edinburgh; Richard, Second Marquess of Westminster; Lady Theodora Guest, Inwood, Templecombe, England; Watson B. Dickerman, New York. *Andrew W. Mellon Collection,* 1937. Painted c. 1527. Wood, 19⅜ x 15¼" (49 x 39 cm.).

169

169 Jan Gossaert (Mabuse) (Flemish, c. 1478–1532): *Portrait of a Banker.* c. 1530. Wood, 25 x 18¾" (63.6 x 47.5 cm.). Ailsa Mellon Bruce Fund

170 Hans Holbein the Younger (German, 1497–1543): *Portrait of a Young Man.* c. 1520. Wood, 8⅝ x 6¾" (21.9 x 17 cm.). Samuel H. Kress Collection

171 South Netherlandish School (Antwerp?): *A Member of the de Hondecoeter Family.* Dated on reverse 1543. Wood, 10 x 7⅞" (25.5 x 19.9 cm.). Gift of Adolph Caspar Miller

172 South Netherlandish School (Antwerp?): *Wife of a Member of the de Hondecoeter Family.* 1543. Wood, 10⅛ x 7⅞" (25.9 x 19.9 cm.). Gift of Adolph Caspar Miller

173 Jan Gossaert (Mabuse): *Madonna and Child.* c. 1532. Wood, 13½ x 9¾" (34.4 x 24.8 cm.). Gift of Grace Vogel Aldworth in memory of her grandparents Ralph and Mary Booth

174 Adriaen Isenbrant (Flemish, active c. 1510–1551): *The Adoration of the Shepherds.* Wood, 29¼ x 22½" (74.3 x 57.1 cm.). Ailsa Mellon Bruce Fund

175 British School (c. 1597): *The Earl of Essex.* Wood, 45⅛ x 34½" (114.7 x 87.7 cm.). Gift of Mrs. Henry R. Rea

170

171

172

173

175

174

The fascination of portraits comes partly from the way they entrap the past. They catch in the mirror of art the reflections of a vanished life. Five of these reproductions show the face of the sixteenth century, revealing how men and women looked in the Netherlands, Germany, and England when Europe was being torn apart by dynastic wars and the Reformation and Counter-Reformation.

Hans Holbein the Younger

(GERMAN, 1497–1543)

176 EDWARD VI AS A CHILD

This panel, painted soon after Holbein's second arrival in England, was given to Henry VIII on New Year's Day, 1539. It is listed in the Royal Inventory as "By Hanse Holbyne a table of the pictour of the p'nce [Prince's] grace." The King was undoubtedly pleased with the likeness, for according to the same document, he gave "To Hanse Holbyne, paynter, a gilte cruse [a type of cup] wt a cover Cornelis weing X oz. quarter."

The poem at the bottom of the picture was written by Cardinal Morison, an influential figure of the Church and Court. It urges Edward to emulate his illustrious father in every way, presumably in matrimony as in other matters. Healthy as the young Prince seems in this portrait, fate did not give him time to marry even once, for he died at the age of fifteen.

The English were easily pleased in matters of art. Since the monkish illuminators of the Middle Ages they had never produced or imported a painter of the first rank. Therefore when Holbein arrived from Switzerland his popularity was enormous. He was particularly admired for his ability to ennoble his sitters. Here, commissioned to paint a portrait of a child not yet two years old, he manages to convey rank and majesty. The future monarch of England is dressed in courtly clothes of gold and velvet; he holds his rattle as though it were a scepter, and he raises his right hand in a gesture of royal magnanimity. Thus an effigy becomes a symbol rather than a portrait. Holbein has presented the quintessence of royalty, the embodiment of the princely infant.

Collections: English Royal Collection; Arundel (where engraved in 1650); Provincial Museum, Hanover (from the Royal and Ducal Hanoverian Collections). *Andrew W. Mellon Collection, 1937.* Painted presumably in 1538. Wood, 22⅜ x 17⅜" (57 x 44 cm.).

PARVVLE PATRISSA, PATRIÆ VIRTVTIS ET HÆRES
ESTO, NIHIL MAIVS MAXIMVS ORBIS HABET.
GNATVM VIX POSSVNT COELVM ET NATVRA DEDISSE,
HVIVS QVEM PATRIS, VICTVS HONORET HONOS.
ÆQVATO TANTVM, TANTI TV FACTA PARENTIS,
VOTA HOMINVM, VIX QVO PROGREDIANTVR, HABENT
VINCITO, VICISTI. QVOT REGES PRISCVS ADORAT
ORBIS, NEC TE QVI VINCERE POSSIT, ERIT. Ricardi Morysini Car.

Lucas Cranach the Elder

(GERMAN, 1472–1553)

177   A PRINCE OF SAXONY

Lucas Cranach painted the two famous portraits of a young prince and princess tentatively identified by Friedländer and Rosenberg as the children of Duke George the Bearded, of Saxony. The brother and sister, with their long flaxen hair, their brocaded clothes and intricate jewelry, have the unembarrassed serenity of children taught to face the ritual of social life with complete self-assurance. In all of Northern art no more sympathetic studies of childhood are to be found (see also plate 180).

It is interesting to contrast these portraits with Holbein's *Edward VI* (plate 176). Cranach's children are young nobles dressed up for a party, whereas Holbein's prince is an infant monarch in his robes of state. Cranach was a regional painter working in an unsophisticated principality; Holbein, a cosmopolitan artist familiar with the great courts of Europe. But of the two it is Cranach who, in his prosaic way, appeals to us, for it is he who has penetrated to what we deem the reality of childhood, to what we adults like to consider, rightly or wrongly, the wistfulness and guilelessness of youth.

Collection: A. Salomon, Dresden. *Ralph and Mary Booth Collection*, 1947. Painted c. 1517. Wood, 17⅛ x 13½" (43.5 x 34.5 cm.).

178

179

Lucas Cranach the Elder was one of the three greatest German painters, the other two being Dürer and Grünewald. The seven panels by Cranach in the National Gallery's collection are evidence of his ability as a portraitist, religious painter, and delineator of seductive nudes. His portraits and devotional pictures, however, have never been as popular with collectors as his enticing nymphs and naked goddesses. He was Hermann Goering's favorite artist, and the field marshall managed to loot a large number of Cranach nudes from all over Europe.

180

181

Lucas Cranach the Elder   (German, 1472–1553)

178   *Portrait of a Man.* Dated 1522. Wood, 22⅜ x 15⅛″ (56.8 x 38.4 cm.). Samuel H. Kress Collection

179   *Portrait of a Woman.* 1522. Wood, 22⅜ x 15″ (56.8 x 38.1 cm.). Samuel H. Kress Collection

180   *A Princess of Saxony.* c. 1517. Wood, 17⅛ x 13½″ (43.6 x 34.3 cm.). Ralph and Mary Booth Collection

181   *The Crucifixion with the Converted Centurion.* Dated 1536. Wood, 20 x 13¾″ (50.8 x 34.9 cm.). Samuel H. Kress Collection

182   *Madonna and Child.* Probably c. 1535. Wood, 28 x 20½″ (71.1 x 52.1 cm.). Gift of Adolph Caspar Miller

183   *The Nymph of the Spring.* After 1537. Wood, 19 x 28⅝″ (48.5 x 72.9 cm.). Gift of Clarence Y. Palitz

182

183

Hieronymus Bosch

(FLEMISH, c. 1450–1516)

184   DEATH AND THE MISER

The Dance of Death and the *Ars Moriendi* obsessed many European artists in the fifteenth and sixteenth centuries. However, death's conquest has never been treated more dramatically than in this wing from an altarpiece by Hieronymus Bosch. On this long, narrow panel a sermon on avarice is enacted. In the foreground are weapons and pieces of armor, symbols of power, the original source of wealth. With age, wealth is first hoarded; then increased through usury; and in the end rats and salamanders become its agents. The rich man has his rosary and the key to his strongbox tied to his waist. These determine the final scene, the last transaction. Which will he choose? If he chooses the rosary he will look up, as his guardian angel pleads, yearning that he shall see the crucifix and be saved. If the key to his earthly treasures is also the key to his heart, the demon peering down from above the bed will be the victor. We can find the answer in the *Ars Moriendi*. According to its anonymous author the sleeper awakens, cries to God to protect him, and thereafter dedicates himself to religion. Thus the dying man gives back his gold to Mammon, whose toad face appears under the curtain, and the drama has a happy ending. But we have overlooked one character in the scene. Leaning on the threshold is a winged manikin. He appears so often in paintings by Bosch that he is almost a signature. Is this perhaps a portrait of the artist himself, who, with a twisted, sardonic smile, meditates skeptically on his own sermon?

Collection: Baron Joseph van der Elst, Bruges. *Samuel H. Kress Collection*, 1952. Probably painted c. 1490, as the outside of the left wing of an altarpiece. Wood, 36⅝ x 12⅛" (93 x 31 cm.).

185 Follower of Pieter Bruegel the Elder (XVI century): *The Temptation of St. Anthony*. Wood, 23 x 33¾" (58.4 x 85.7 cm.). Samuel H. Kress Collection

The sixteenth century in the Netherlands was an age of anxiety, an age of conflicting ideologies not unlike our own. There was, on the one hand, the anguish and fanaticism of reform and, on the other, the soldiers of the Duke of Alva trying in vain with blood and fire to reforge the lost unity of Europe. The tensions are reflected in the work of Pieter Bruegel the Elder and his School. Another manifestation of the stress of Flemish life during this period was an excessive affectation, an exaggeration of style known as Mannerism, illustrated by the painting by van Scorel (plate 189) and the one attributed to van Hemessen (plate 188). By contrast, in *The Card Players* (plate 187) the source of strain is not political. It is merely the fever of gambling. Yet this picture is the most significant of all, for it is one of the first genre scenes ever painted.

(See overleaf) ▶

186

186 Antwerp School (c. 1540): *The Martyrdom of St. Catherine.* Wood, 24½ x 46½" (62.3 x 118.3 cm.). Samuel H. Kress Collection

187 After Lucas van Leyden (Dutch, 1494–1533): *The Card Players.* Wood, 22⅛ x 24" (56.4 x 60.9 cm.). Samuel H. Kress Collection

188 Jan van Hemessen (Flemish, c. 1500–1566?): *"Arise, and take up thy bed, and walk."* c. 1555. Wood, 42½ x 30" (108 x 76 cm.). Gift of Chester Dale

189 Jan van Scorel (Dutch, 1495–1562): *The Rest on the Flight into Egypt.* c. 1530. Wood, 22¾ x 29½" (57.8 x 74.9 cm.). Samuel H. Kress Collection

187

189

188

Italian Schools

XVI AND XVII CENTURY

Raphael

(UMBRIAN, 1483–1520)

190 ST. GEORGE AND THE DRAGON

Raphael was in his early twenties when he painted *St. George and the Dragon*. He had already become one of the most accomplished masters in Italy. No painting reveals more clearly his serenity, his effortless achievement. But there has been a reaction against "the very rightness of Raphael's perfection." Appreciation has shifted. The lofty pinnacles of art are today often considered boring, and critics prefer to study the arduous ascent to these heights, to trace the tortuous route leading from the incompetent to the proficient. Thus the romantic basis of contemporary aesthetics has blinded many people to the beauty of Raphael's paintings.

This point of view, the exaltation of the half-realized, the half-expressed, accords with the art of our time. Modern painters lack the very qualities for which Raphael was preeminent. For more than a century painters have brought to their craft less and less of that easy fluency of draftsmanship, that simple felicity of composition, which Raphael took for granted. We have come to despise facility largely because facility of a high order has almost ceased to exist. Drawn by instinctive sympathy to contemporary art, many people, especially painters, have come to look on Raphael's work with prejudice. But his great paintings, such as the picture reproduced, should not be judged by the standards prevalent today. They should be judged by the standards which Sir Joshua Reynolds termed "the great style," and which in Italy is termed the *gusto grande* and in France the *beau idéal*. For these are the terms of excellence which people of culture have accepted for over four hundred years. If we use them as a measure of Raphael's achievement, we shall find that he has given us a supreme expression of the classical style.

Collections: Commissioned by Duke Guidobaldo da Montefeltro, the ruler of Urbino, and taken as a gift to Henry VII of England by Count Baldassare Castiglione; Third Earl of Pembroke (engraved by L. Vorsterman in 1627); Fourth Earl of Pembroke gave it to Charles I of England in exchange for the Holbein drawings now at Windsor Castle; Charles d'Escoubleau, Marquis de Sourdis, Paris; Laurent de Tessier de Montarsy; Pierre Crozat; Louis-François Crozat, Marquis de Châtel; Louis-Antoine Crozat, Baron de Thiers; Catherine II, Empress of Russia; Hermitage Gallery, Leningrad. *Andrew W. Mellon Collection*, 1937. Signed. Painted 1504/6. Wood, 11⅛ x 8⅜" (28.5 x 21.5 cm.).

171

191

192

193

191 **Bacchiacca** (Florentine, 1495–1557): *The Flagellation of Christ.* Wood, 22 x 18⅞″ (55.9 x 48.1 cm.). Samuel H. Kress Collection

192 **Bacchiacca:** *The Gathering of Manna.* c. 1540/55. Wood, 44 x 37½″ (112 x 95 cm.). Samuel H. Kress Collection

193 **Andrea del Sarto** (Florentine, 1486–1530): *Charity.* Shortly before 1530. Wood, 47¼ x 36½″ (120 x 92.7 cm.). Samuel H. Kress Collection

194 **Italian School** (XVI century): *Portrait of a Man.* c. 1515. Wood, 24¾ x 18½″ (63 x 47 cm.). Widener Collection

195 **Circle of Raphael** (c. 1500): *Putti with a Wine Press.* Wood, diameter 13⅛″ (33.3 cm.). Samuel H. Kress Collection

196 **Amico Aspertini** (Ferrarese-Bolognese, c. 1474–1552): *St. Sebastian.* c. 1505. Wood, 45¼ x 26″ (115 x 66 cm.). Samuel H. Kress Collection

194

Raphael's effortless achievement is at the core of what we call Classicism. Of the paintings reproduced here, *The Flagellation of Christ* (plate 191) and *Putti with a Wine Press* (plate 195) are so close to the master's style that they were formerly ascribed to him. Andrea del Sarto, Bacchiacca, and Aspertini, whose work is shown here, were completely under his influence. The *Portrait of a Man* (plate 194) has traditionally been identified as Baldassare Castiglione, who knew Raphael at the court of Urbino, and whose handbook, *The Courtier*, describes the *beau idéal* of social intercourse.

195

196

Raphael

(UMBRIAN, 1483–1520)

197 THE SMALL COWPER MADONNA

The Small Cowper Madonna was purchased in Italy in the eighteenth century by that remarkable Earl Cowper who is referred to frequently in Horace Walpole's correspondence with Sir Horace Mann, and the painting hung for over a century in Lord Cowper's country estate of Panshanger. A great connoisseur with an instinctive sympathy for the Renaissance, Lord Cowper was so drawn to Italy that he spent most of his life in Florence and became a prince of the Holy Roman Empire. Horace Walpole wrote scathingly of this eighteenth-century expatriate, "He has the awkward dignity of a temporary representative of nominal power."

Although Walpole might despise Lord Cowper's choice of titles, he could not but envy his choice of pictures. For this eccentric English earl was the only collector of his time who could show the span of Raphael's development during his Florentine period. The two Madonnas, which were in his collection and which are now both in the National Gallery of Art (see plate 198), reveal the quintessence of Raphael's early and best manner of painting on panel. Giovanni Morelli, the founder of the system on which the modern attribution of Italian painting is based, considered *The Small Cowper Madonna* to be "perhaps the most lovely of all Raphael's Madonnas . . . [It] sets the young artist before our eyes in the full blaze of his independence." In the half-century that has elapsed since Morelli made this statement, no serious critic has questioned either his evaluation or his placing of the picture in Raphael's development. There has been general agreement among critics that *The Small Cowper Madonna* was probably painted sometime in the year 1505, shortly after Raphael achieved his mature style in Florence. Our Lady's expression still retains the dry, tired wistfulness we find in the Madonnas and saints painted by his master, Perugino, but the figures are drawn with more certainty, their forms modeled with more solidity, than in any work of the Umbrian period. The buildings in the background, however, seem quite definitely to be the convent and church of San Bernardino on the outskirts of Urbino. Thus even though the picture may have been painted in Florence, it was probably commissioned by an Umbrian patron.

Collections: Purchased in Florence by Lord Cowper about 1780, the present painting remained in the possession of his family at Panshanger, Hertfordshire, until 1913. *Widener Collection*, 1942. Painted probably c. 1505. Wood, 23⅜ x 17⅜" (59.5 x 44 cm.).

Raphael

(UMBRIAN, 1483–1520)

198   THE NICCOLINI-COWPER MADONNA

Signed and dated 1508, *The Niccolini-Cowper Madonna* was probably one of the first pictures Raphael painted in Rome, at the end of his Florentine period. It was a work for which he must have made innumerable studies. There is a drawing for the head of the child in the Lille Museum, and another drawing of heads in the British Museum in London. The latter study bears a close relation to the painting reproduced here, though it has also been connected with other works. A master of composition, Raphael never achieved a more intricately and satisfactorily balanced design of two figures.

The early history of the painting is unknown. It is first recorded in the Casa Niccolini in 1677. It seems to have been bought from the Niccolini family by the painter and art dealer Johann Zoffany shortly after his arrival in Florence in 1772. He had been commissioned by Queen Charlotte of England to paint a view of the Tribuna, the room in the Uffizi which housed many of the greatest art treasures of the Grand Dukes of Tuscany. In many ways a precursor of Lord Duveen, Zoffany did not hesitate to get as much publicity as possible from his *Tribuna*. In the painting (which is now at Windsor), he has shown himself offering for sale the *Casa Niccolini Madonna* to Earl Cowper and to the other English cognoscenti sojourning in Florence. In 1826 the *Literary Gazette* ran an amusing account of Zoffany's dealings. "He was wont to ask all English comers to Florence, 'Have you seen my Raffael?—Ah! den you must see it.' . . . His lordship [Lord Cowper] paid down a certain liberal sum [five hundred guineas according to the Panshanger papers], and granted, by way of residue, an annuity of a hundred pounds, which the fortunate painter (who lived, as is said and pretty generally believed, to be between ninety and a hundred) enjoyed to the last. Hence this 'Madonna', perhaps, whatever may be its merits, is the dearest Raffael that ever was purchased, even by a traveling English lord!"

Actually, Zoffany lived to be only seventy-seven. He had originally asked five thousand guineas for his Raphael and, in spite of his long life, did not quite realize this figure. Lord Cowper in turn tried to sell the *Madonna* to George III at a very low price, hoping this bargain would cause him to be made a Knight of the Garter. Fortunately for the National Gallery of Art, the King did not accept the offer and Lord Cowper never got the Garter. The painting was finally sold by his heirs through Duveen Brothers to Andrew Mellon. In the end, Zoffany's *Madonna* brought 170,000 guineas, thirty-four times his original asking price.

Collections: Casa Niccolini, Florence (as early as 1677); Johann Zoffany; Earl Cowper and his heirs, Panshanger, Hertfordshire, until 1928. *Andrew W. Mellon Collection*, 1937. Signed with initials, and dated 1508. Wood, 31¾ x 22⅝" (81 x 57 cm.).

176

Raphael

(UMBRIAN, 1483–1520)

199   THE ALBA MADONNA

The Alba Madonna was painted about 1510, after Raphael had arrived in Rome and had fallen under the spell of Michelangelo. It is one of the supreme compositional achievements of Renaissance painting, for balance in a tondo, or round picture, required the utmost delicacy in adjustment. If the masses are not in equilibrium, the picture will seem to roll like a wheel. In the *Alba Madonna* this complex problem is solved and the result is one of extraordinary stability. The compact group of figures in the foreground is also related to the surrounding landscape, with that feeling for perfect spatial composition which was Raphael's greatest achievement.

The picture was taken to Spain at the end of the seventeenth century by the Spanish viceroy in Naples, Don Gaspar de Guzmán; shortly thereafter it entered the collection of the Duchess of Alba, where it remained for more than a hundred years, thus acquiring its present name. Powerful as the Albas were, they were nonetheless forced by Charles IV to allow Manuel Godoy to buy the picture for his palace of Buenavista, even though it was entailed in their estates. A handsome profligate, Godoy depended for his power on the infatuation of the Queen and the curious complaisance of her cuckold husband. Married to the King's niece (whose portrait by Goya is shown in plate 568), Godoy became prime minister and virtual ruler. But he was so inept, first opposing the leaders of the French Revolution and then toadying to them, that when Napoleon's armies moved into Spain, he was arrested by the Prince of the Asturias, the King's eldest son, who controlled the government for a short time. Godoy's collection was immediately confiscated and put up for sale. The Albas tried through a lawsuit to recover their *Madonna*, but failed. Instead, the Danish Ambassador in Madrid, Count de Bourke, bought it, took it to London, and sold it at auction for £4,000 to W. G. Coesvelt—a thousand pounds less than Zoffany had asked for his Raphael a quarter-century earlier. Prices were rising, however, and Coesvelt made a handsome profit a few years later when he sold the *Alba Madonna* to the Curator of the Hermitage Gallery for £14,000. The Russians in turn waited a hundred years and sold the picture to Andrew Mellon for £233,000. Even though somewhat out of fashion today, Raphael's paintings have continued to rise in price, and his Madonnas are still the soundest of investments.

Collections: Church of Monteoliveto, Nocera di Pagani, near Naples; Don Gaspar Méndez de Haro y Guzmán, Naples; the Dukes of Alba, Madrid; Don Manuel Godoy, Principe de la Paz; Count Edmond de Bourke, Danish Ambassador to Spain; W. G. Coesvelt, London; Hermitage Gallery, Leningrad. *Andrew W. Mellon Collection*, 1937. Painted c. 1510. Transferred from wood to canvas, diameter 37¼" (94.5 cm.).

179

Raphael
(UMBRIAN, 1483–1520)

200 BINDO ALTOVITI

Bindo Altoviti was a Florentine banker, born in 1491, who lived in Rome. Vasari says he commissioned Raphael to paint two pictures, a Madonna known as the *Madonna dell'Impannata*, now in the Pitti Gallery, and *il ritratto suo quando era giovane* ("his portrait when he was young"). But, critics have asked, does the *suo* ("his") refer to Bindo Altoviti or to Raphael himself? The ambiguity of the biographer's phrase led earlier writers to believe Vasari was speaking of a self-portrait of Raphael. Recent scholars now agree that he was referring instead to a likeness of Raphael's patron.

There is not the same uniformity of opinion, however, in attributing the portrait to Raphael. Although the inspiration is certainly his, some students have believed the execution to be by Giulio Romano. But even if one must recognize that by 1515, when the portrait was probably painted, there were numerous assistants executing the master's designs, still he was responsible for painting some pictures entirely himself, and a number of recent critics have seen his touch throughout the portrait. Thus such eminent experts as Sir John Pope-Hennessy, Cesare Brandi, and Konrad Oberhuber have joined Bernard Berenson in believing this to be an autograph work by Raphael.

The history of the painting is reassuring. From the time Vasari saw it—a few years after it was painted—until shortly before 1790, it remained in the Altoviti Palace in Rome, whence it was moved to the Altoviti Palace in Florence. In 1808 it was purchased for Crown Prince Ludwig of Bavaria (later King Ludwig the First), who gave it to the Alte Pinakothek in Munich, which he wished to make, he said, "the most glorious collection of pictures on earth."

Ludwig was a remarkable connoisseur and was largely responsible for the great collections in Munich, not only of painting but most particularly of classical sculpture. An admirer of ancient art and, among moderns, of Canova and Thorwaldsen, his taste in painting was equally classical. Raphael was the painter he loved above all others, and the portrait of Bindo Altoviti was the crowning jewel of his picture collection. Until the arrival of Hitler it also remained one of the proudest possessions of Bavaria. But the Führer's fanatical passion for Teutonic art led to an arrangement with Lord Duveen whereby *Bindo Altoviti* came to America in exchange for several skillfully repainted German pictures from the unsold stock of Duveen Brothers.

Collections: Palazzo Altoviti, Rome (until shortly before 1790); Palazzo Altoviti, Florence; Crown Prince Ludwig of Bavaria; Alte Pinakothek, Munich. *Samuel H. Kress Collection*, 1943. Painted c. 1515. Wood, 23½ x 17¼″ (60 x 44 cm.).

201 Ridolfo Ghirlandaio (Florentine, 1483–1561): *Lucrezia Sommaria.* c. 1510. Wood, 24¾ x 18″ (63 x 46 cm.). Widener Collection

202 Girolamo di Benvenuto (Sienese, 1470–1524): *Portrait of a Young Woman.* c. 1505. Wood, 23⅝ x 17⅞″ (60 x 45 cm.). Samuel H. Kress Collection

203 Il Rosso (Florentine, 1494–1540): *Portrait of a Man.* Early 1520s. Wood, 34⅞ x 26¾″ (88.7 x 67.9 cm.). Samuel H. Kress Collection

204 Giuliano Bugiardini (Florentine, 1475–1554): *Portrait of a Young Woman.* c. 1525. Canvas, 22¾ x 19½″ (57.8 x 49.6 cm.). Samuel H. Kress Collection

205 Agnolo Bronzino (Florentine, 1503–1572): *Eleonora di Toledo.* c. 1560. Wood, 34 x 25⅝″ (86.4 x 65.1 cm.). Samuel H. Kress Collection

206 Perino del Vaga (Central Italian, 1501–1547): *The Nativity.* Signed, and dated 1534. Transferred from wood to canvas, 108¼ x 87⅛″ (274.4 x 221.1 cm.). Samuel H. Kress Collection

202

201

203

204

206

205

The influence of Raphael on his contemporaries, as well as on the next generation, is evident in these six portraits. With Bronzino, however, a certain glacial detachment is added. His sitters seem chiseled from cold marble, their physical refinement exaggerated. We have passed the summit of classical art, and Mannerism lies ahead. *The Nativity* by Perino del Vaga (plate 206) illustrates the overemphasized grace, the affectations of this new style.

Florentine School

(XVI CENTURY)

207 ALLEGORICAL PORTRAIT OF DANTE

This portrait of Dante is a remarkable discovery made quite recently in an English collection. Its attribution remains a mystery. Pontormo has been suggested; Bacchiacca is another candidate. More recent scholarship favors two lesser-known artists: Battista Naldini and Gerolamo Macchietti. But none of these ascriptions is entirely satisfactory. There can, however, be no doubt that whoever painted this canvas has given us the noblest ideal portrait of Dante which has survived from the Renaissance.

The poet sits brooding over the mystery of the temporary and the eternal, the city of man and the city of God. Below his protective hand is Florence, fitfully illumined by the fires of Hell. Dante looks across the Stygian river at the Monte Sancto di Dio silhouetted against the ineffable light of Paradise. His left hand holds a manuscript codex of the *Paradiso* open to a page of *Canto* XXV, "Se mai continga . . ." ("If it should ever happen . . ."), the famous passage which expresses his wistful hope that one day he might be welcomed back from exile and crowned poet laureate in the Baptistery opposite the Cathedral which was for so long the center of his life.

This moving tribute to the most famous of all Florentines was painted two centuries after his death. The independence of Florence, for which so many of her citizens had died, was lost; Florentine literature, which had promised so much, was bankrupt; and Florentine painting, which had once lighted up the world with that great fire of achievement kindled by Giotto, Dante's friend and contemporary, was now only an afterglow. Yet an unknown painter envisaged this tragic symbol of the greatness of his beloved Florence and in so doing created one of her last masterpieces.

Collections: William Graham, London; Viscount Hailsham, London. *Samuel H. Kress Collection,* 1961. Painted probably late sixteenth century. Wood, 50 x 47¼" (126.9 x 120 cm.).

208

209

210

The afterglow of Florentine art produced several paint-ers of genius, among whom Pontormo was the most original and accomplished. As Raphael's work is the su-preme expression of Renaissance Classicism, so Pon-tormo's paintings offer the most beautiful examples of early Mannerism. This style, which flourished in the second half of the sixteenth century, has three major characteristics: the chiaroscuro of Leonardo, the con-tours of Raphael, and the exaggerated *contrapposto* and restless compositions of Michelangelo. To these is later added an element of distortion, of elongation, which reaches its climax in the work of El Greco.

211

212

208 **Pontormo** (Florentine, 1494–1556/57): *The Holy Family*. c. 1525. Wood, 39⅞ x 31″ (101 x 79 cm.). Samuel H. Kress Collection

209 **Pontormo**: *Portrait of a Young Woman*. c. 1535. Wood, 22 x 17″ (56 x 43 cm.). Widener Collection

210 **Pontormo**: *Ugolino Martelli*. c. 1545/50. Wood, 36 x 26¾″ (91 x 68 cm.). Samuel H. Kress Collection

211 **Pontormo**: *Monsignor della Casa*. Probably 1541/44. Wood, 40⅛ x 31″ (102.1 x 78.8 cm.). Samuel H. Kress Collection

212 **Federico Barocci** (Roman, 1535–1612): *Quintilia Fischieri*. Probably c. 1600. Canvas, 48¾ x 37½″ (124 x 95 cm.). Samuel H. Kress Collection

213 **Domenico Beccafumi** (Sienese, c. 1485–1551): *The Holy Family with Angels*. c. 1545/50. Wood, 32 x 24¼″ (81 x 62 cm.). Samuel H. Kress Collection

213

Lorenzo Lotto

(VENETIAN, c. 1480–1556)

214   ALLEGORY

In July 1505, Lorenzo Lotto completed a portrait of Bernardo Rossi, who was Bishop of Treviso from 1499 to 1527. This painting is now one of the masterpieces of the Naples museum. Some years ago the picture reproduced here was discovered, and on the back of the panel was an inscription identifying it as the cover for Rossi's portrait. As further identification, propped against the tree is his coat-of-arms, showing a lion rampant on a blue shield, which also appears on his signet ring in the Naples portrait. Such covers were often hinged, thus forming with the portrait itself a diptych. Their purpose remains obscure: perhaps the sitter wished his likeness to be seen only by intimate friends; perhaps he wished to protect the portrait itself; or perhaps he welcomed the opportunity that this additional panel offered for a further symbolic interpretation of his character or his life. This latter allegorical intention seems to have motivated Bernardo Rossi. That he was interested in allegory is indicated by his portrait medal, which is also in the National Gallery of Art. This has on the reverse a female figure in tunic and mantle, holding a sunflower and standing in a car drawn by an eagle and a winged dragon (see plates 215, 216).

The meaning of Lotto's *Allegory* is less baffling than its medallic counterpart. The painted cover seems to present in figurative terms the desirability of choosing virtue instead of vice. On the left, a naked child bathed in sunlight is picking up instruments—a compass, a carpenter's square, a flute, a scroll—symbols of cultural pursuits and thus, for the Renaissance man, symbols of the virtuous life. The right side of the picture is devoted to an allegory of vice. The light has gone, and in the umbrageous gloom a drunken satyr sprawls among overturned vessels, while in the distance a ship founders in the storm. Lotto tactfully indicates that his sitter has triumphed over passion and won his way to virtue. Rossi's winged spirit is shown climbing rapidly upward on a steep and stony path toward the summit of a mountain where the sky is clearing.

Collections: Probably Garden Palace of the Farnese, Parma (seventeenth century); Antonio Bertioli, Parma; Giacomo Gritti, Bergamo. *Samuel H. Kress Collection*, 1939. Painted 1505. Wood, 22¼ x 16⅝" (56 x 42.2 cm.).

215

217

216

Lotto's inventiveness is often enigmatic. It is not at first apparent why a mousetrap is included with the Nativity, or why flowers rain down on a sleeping maiden. The symbolism is elusive. Cima's paintings are never obscure. The beauty of his work consists in its marvelous preservation and exquisite lighting. Both artists, though minor compared to Titian, Veronese, and Tintoretto, made important contributions to the Venetian School.

218

219

220

215 , 216   School of Francesco Francia (Bolognese, c. 1450/53–1517): *Portrait Medal of Bernardo de' Rossi, Bishop of Treviso.* Bronze, diam. 2 9/16″ (6.5 cm.). Samuel H. Kress Collection

217   Cima da Conegliano (Venetian, 1459/60–1517/18): *St. Helena.* c. 1495. Wood, 16 x 12¾″ (40.4 x 32.4 cm.). Samuel H. Kress Collection

218   Cima da Conegliano: *St. Jerome in the Wilderness.* c. 1495. Canvas, 19 x 15¾″ (48 x 40 cm.). Samuel H. Kress Collection

219   Lorenzo Lotto (Venetian, c. 1480–1556): *A Maiden's Dream.* c. 1505. Wood, 16⅞ x 13¼″ (43 x 34 cm.). Samuel H. Kress Collection

220   Lorenzo Lotto: *The Nativity.* Signed, and dated 1523. Wood, 18⅛ x 14⅛″ (46 x 36 cm.). Samuel H. Kress Collection

221   Lorenzo Lotto: *St. Catherine.* Signed, and dated 1522. Wood, 22½ x 19¾″ (57 x 50 cm.). Samuel H. Kress Collection

221

Dosso Dossi

(FERRARESE, ACTIVE 1512–1542)

222   CIRCE AND HER LOVERS IN A LANDSCAPE

There are paintings which, like "huge cloudy symbols of a high romance," never cease to challenge the imagination, to promise the revelation of some hidden secret. In the canvas by Dosso Dossi a nude woman, seated in an idyllic landscape, is surrounded by birds and beasts. Who is she and why does she point, like one of Michelangelo's sibyls, toward an inscribed tablet? The scene fits the legend of Circe, who turned men into animals; but absent are those wolves, lions, and swine Ulysses saw when he encountered "that awful Goddess of the luxuriant tresses, own sister to the wizard Aeëtes." A transformation in the story has taken place. The animals are now the most charming and gentle of beasts, and even the lioness is more heraldic than savage. Nature seems under a spell, so that the spoonbill and the owl do not fear the falcon, nor the stag and the doe, the dogs. It is a scene of sorcery based on the legend of Circe, but transformed from the Olympian realm of the *Odyssey* into the fairy-tale world of *A Midsummer Night's Dream*.

There is a clue to this change. In the court of Ferrara, where this picture was probably painted, Ariosto had composed his famous *Orlando Furioso*, setting forth a new version of the Circean myth. In his romantic epic Alcina is the perfect example of the beautiful and seductive woman. Like Circe she changes her lovers into animals, but instead of doing this with the touch of a wand, as Homer describes the transformation of the followers of Ulysses, she uses esoteric incantations. These in Dosso Dossi's canvas are symbolized by the tablet and the cabalistic book with which Alcina—for the nude figure is probably she—holds her court of wild creatures spellbound.

And there is perhaps a parallel here to the human admirers who were also enthralled by Dosso Dossi's patroness, Lucrezia Borgia, then Duchess of Ferrara. For she, too, wove a spell over her lovers, whether poets, courtiers, or princes. One wonders whether she may have felt some instinctive sympathy for the entrancing witch in *Orlando Furioso*. Does this perhaps explain why Alcina in Dosso Dossi's picture is portrayed in such an appealing way, with a look of innocent expectancy? It is easy to speculate, to imagine that Lucrezia Borgia, considering herself a blameless victim of the sinister forces aroused by her beauty, may have identified herself with the wistful enchantress depicted by her court painter, Dosso Dossi, as she may have considered herself eulogized in the tribute to Alcina composed by her court poet, Ariosto,

> Her matchless person every charm combined
> Formed in the idea of a painter's mind.

Collections: William Graham; Robert H. and Evelyn Benson, London. *Samuel H. Kress Collection*, 1943. Painted c. 1525. Canvas, 39⅝ x 53½" (100 x 136 cm.).

223

224

225

During the Renaissance wealthy patrons often commissioned artists to paint the walls of their palaces and villas with episodes from some mythological story. This series is devoted to the legend of Cephalus and Procris, a commentary on jealousy. Procris is accused of infidelity by her husband, Cephalus. The quarrel is resolved through the mediation of the goddess Diana. Procris in turn becomes jealous of Cephalus and spies on him while he is hunting. Hearing her footsteps, he mistakes her for a wild animal, hurls his spear, and kills her.

228

229

194

226

227

231

230

Bernardino Luini (Milanese, c. 1480–1532): Frescos transferred to canvas. c. 1522/23. Samuel H. Kress Collection

223 *Procris' Prayer to Diana.* 90 x 55¼" (228.6 x 140.3 cm.)

224 *Cephalus Hiding the Jewels.* 87¼ x 59⅛" (221.6 x 150.2 cm.)

225 *Cephalus and Pan at the Temple.* 89 x 40¾" (226 x 103.5 cm.)

226 *Cephalus at the Hunt.* 83¼ x 43⅝" (211.4 x 110.3 cm.)

227 *Procris Pierced by Cephalus' Javelin.* 56¾ x 48½" (144.1 x 123.2 cm.)

228 *The Illusion of Cephalus.* 89¾ x 49" (228 x 124.5 cm.)

229 *The Despair of Cephalus.* 71⅝ x 46⅝" (181.9 x 118.4 cm.)

230 *The Misfortunes of Cephalus.* 69⅜ x 42¼" (176.2 x 107.3 cm.)

231 *Procris and the Unicorn.* 90 x 42½" (228.6 x 108 cm.)

Giorgione

(VENETIAN, c. 1478–1510)

232 THE ADORATION OF THE SHEPHERDS

What we have come to call the Giorgionesque was as revolutionary in the Renaissance as was Cubism at the beginning of the twentieth century. In the early Renaissance, paintings were thought of as colored drawings modeled in light and shade to suggest relief. Later artists observed that we do not normally see the separate contours of objects but that their forms seem to melt into each other and to fuse with the surrounding atmosphere. The crystalline clarity of early morning, which is characteristic of the fifteenth century and can be seen in the Botticelli *Adoration* (plate 55), changes in the new style to the misty sunlight of late afternoon. This soft illumination increases unity of effect. Giorgione, who died in 1510, presumably at the age of thirty-two, has been credited with these innovations, which found their fullest development among Venetian painters. But actually the Giorgionesque, like Cubism, was a way of painting adopted simultaneously by a number of artists. *The Adoration of the Shepherds*, for example, has been attributed in turn to the three leading painters of Venice at the beginning of the sixteenth century, Giorgione, Bellini, and Titian.

Today, an increasing number of experts believe the picture to be by Giorgione, and this is the attribution which most clearly describes its style. Bernard Berenson, the most famous of all critics of Italian art, remained adamant for many years in his opposition to ascribing this painting to Giorgione. Joseph Duveen, the art dealer who owned the picture at the time, tried in every way to make Berenson alter his opinion. This led to their celebrated quarrel. At the end of his life, however, Berenson did change his mind and concluded that the painting was at least in part by Giorgione, working in collaboration with Titian. Berenson's theory is borne out by X-rays which show a number of changes from the original composition. Similar alterations, but on a much greater scale, were made by Titian when he repainted Giovanni Bellini's *Feast of the Gods* (plate 239).

Collections: Cardinal Joseph Fesch, Rome; Claudius Tarral, Paris; Thomas Wentworth Beaumont, Bretton Hall, Yorkshire; Wentworth Blackett Beaumont, First Lord Allendale; the Viscounts Allendale, London. *Samuel H. Kress Collection*, 1939. Painted c. 1505/10. Wood, 35¾ x 43½" (91 x 111 cm.).

233

These paintings further illustrate the Giorgionesque style. *The Holy Family* (plate 236) is gaining gradual acceptance as a work by the master; the *Portrait of a Venetian Gentleman* (plate 238), like *The Adoration of the Shepherds* (plate 232), seems to have been worked on by both Titian and Giorgione; the idyllic *Orpheus*, now ascribed to Bellini, and plates 234 and 235 are pastoral scenes in the Giorgionesque manner. Titian's *Madonna and Child* (plate 233), painted as late as the 1550s, shows how long this style endured.

234

235

236

237

233 **Titian** (Venetian, c. 1477–1576): *Madonna and Child and the Infant Saint John in a Landscape.* Toward 1550. Canvas, 11 x 22¾″ (28 x 58 cm.). Andrew W. Mellon Collection

234 **Venetian School, possibly Giorgione** (c. 1505): *Venus and Cupid in a Landscape.* Wood, 4⅜ x 8″ (11 x 20 cm.). Samuel H. Kress Collection

235 **Venetian School** (c. 1530): *Allegory.* Wood, 17 x 15⅜″ (43 x 39.2 cm.). Gift of Dr. and Mrs. G. H. Alexander Clowes

236 **Giorgione** (Venetian, c. 1478–1510): *The Holy Family.* Probably c. 1500. Transferred from wood to hardboard, 14⅝ x 17⅞ (37.3 x 45.6 cm.). Samuel H. Kress Collection

237 **Giovanni Bellini** (Venetian, c. 1430–1516): *Orpheus.* c. 1515. Transferred from wood to canvas, 18⅝ x 32″ (39.5 x 81 cm.). Widener Collection

238 **Giorgione and Titian:** *Portrait of a Venetian Gentleman.* c. 1510. Canvas, 30 x 25″ (76 x 64 cm.). Samuel H. Kress Collection

238

Giovanni Bellini

(VENETIAN, c. 1430–1516)

239   THE FEAST OF THE GODS

The connoisseurship of painting offers, from time to time, investigations as fascinating and complex as a detective story. *The Feast of the Gods*, for example, is signed by Giovanni Bellini. Yet Titian, according to Vasari, brought it to completion. A composite X-ray of the painting indicates that the picture has had three backgrounds. There is evidence that the final alterations, and perhaps the earlier changes as well, are due to Titian. As far as one can tell, his motives were mixed; but the impelling reason seems to have been that the original design did not harmonize with the other pictures in the same room in the Castle of Ferrara which Alfonso d'Este asked him to paint: *Bacchus and Ariadne*, now in London, and *The Venus Worship* and *The Andrians*, now in Madrid.

Although Titian finally transformed the background of *The Feast of the Gods* into a landscape which has been judged "the finest that up to that time had ever been painted . . . an epoch in the history of art," still, from the beginning, Bellini's painting was an astounding innovation. One remarkable feature is the representation of the gods and goddesses in the guise of everyday people. It is as though they had become players in a Renaissance masque. The scene they act out, a story told by Ovid, explains the annual sacrifice made by the Romans to Priapus. On the left the ass of Silenus brays and arouses the drowsy deities as, on the right, the god of fertility secretly approaches the goddess of chastity. Then, as Ovid says, "The nymph in terror started up . . . and flying gave the alarm to the whole grove; . . . the god in the moonlight was laughed at by all." However, at the touch of Bellini's brush the ribald joke undergoes a metamorphosis, becomes a noble Dionysiac mystery, much as Shakespeare's alchemy transmutes leaden stories into golden plays.

Collections: Duke Alfonso I d'Este, Ferrara; Cardinal Pietro Aldobrandini and family, Rome; Vincenzo Camuccini, Rome; Duke of Northumberland, Alnwick Castle, England. *Widener Collection*, 1942. Signed, and dated 1514. Canvas, 67 x 74" (170 x 188 cm.).

240

Paintings of the Virgin and Christ Child similar to plates 243 and 244, many bearing the signature "Giovanni Bellini" or some variation of the name, are the products of a studio which became virtually a factory. The comeliness and dignity of Our Lady have made these panels immensely popular. A generation later Carpaccio introduced a Madonna with broader and less appealing features. In *The Flight into Egypt* (plate 240) we see her riding through the Veneto; and in the background we catch a glimpse of a countryside so striking in its actuality as to be one of the earliest examples of landscape in the modern sense.

241

242

243

244

240 Vittore Carpaccio (Venetian, c. 1460/65–1523/26): *The Flight into Egypt.* c. 1500. Wood, 28¼ x 43⅞″ (72 x 111.5 cm.). Andrew W. Mellon Collection

241 Vittore Carpaccio: *Madonna and Child.* c. 1505. Wood, 33⅜ x 26⅞″ (84.8 x 68.3 cm.). Samuel H. Kress Collection

242 Vittore Carpaccio: *The Virgin Reading.* c. 1505. Wood, 30¾ x 20″ (78 x 51 cm.). Samuel H. Kress Collection

243 Giovanni Bellini (Venetian, c. 1430–1516): *Madonna and Child with Saints.* c. 1490. Wood, 29¼ x 20″ (76 x 51 cm.). Samuel H. Kress Collection

244 Giovanni Bellini: *Madonna and Child in a Landscape.* c. 1480. Wood, 28¼ x 20⅞″ (72 x 53.2 cm.). Ralph and Mary Booth Collection

245 Giovanni Bellini: *The Infant Bacchus.* Probably 1505/10. Wood, 18⅞ x 14½″ (48 x 36.8 cm.). Samuel H. Kress Collection

245

Titian

(VENETIAN, c. 1477–1576)

246   DOGE ANDREA GRITTI

The seal of Charles I of England and a label reading, "Bought for his Majesty in Italy, 1626," are still preserved on the back of the canvas of this stupendous portrait, more recently in the Czernin Collection in Vienna. The royal catalogue also listed it: "Duke Grettie, of Venice, with his right hand holding his robes. Bought by the King, half figures so big as the life, in a black wooden gilded frame." Perhaps Charles saw in the stern, implacable face of the Venetian Doge those traits of character he himself lacked. Titian has dowered Gritti with a grim, ruthless personality and made him a symbol of the power of the galleys that, under the patronage of St. Mark, caused Venice to be honored and feared along the trade routes of the world. But Gritti was also a patron of the arts. At his order, a considerable number of Titian's large religious, historical, and allegorical pictures, now mostly lost, were painted.

The hand with which the Doge grasps his flowing cape may be based upon the hand of Moses in the famous statue by Michelangelo in Rome. A Venetian sculptor, Jacopo Sansovino, is believed to have brought a cast of this hand to Venice, where Titian probably studied its massive power to help him create an image of uncompromising majesty, the archetype of the imperious ruler moving forward in a ceremonial procession.

Collections: King Charles I of England; Wenzel Anton, Prince von Kaunitz-Rietburg, Chancellor of Empress Maria Theresa; Count Johann Rudolf Czernin von Chudenitz, Vienna; Czernin Gallery, Vienna. *Samuel H. Kress Collection*, 1961. Signed. Painted probably between 1535 and 1540. Canvas, 52½ x 40⅝" (133.6 x 103.2 cm.).

205

247

248

249

247 **Titian** (Venetian, c. 1477–1576): *Cardinal Pietro Bembo.* c. 1540. Canvas, 37⅛ x 30⅛″ (94.5 x 76.5 cm.). Samuel H. Kress Collection

248 **Titian:** *Ranuccio Farnese.* Signed. 1542. Canvas, 35¼ x 29″ (89.7 x 73.6 cm.). Samuel H. Kress Collection

249 **Titian:** *Vincenzo Capello.* c. 1540. Canvas, 55½ x 46½″ (141 x 118 cm.). Samuel H. Kress Collection

250 **Sebastiano del Piombo** (Venetian, c. 1485–1547): *Portrait of a Young Woman as a Wise Virgin.* c. 1510. Wood, 21 x 18⅛″ (53.4 x 46.2 cm.). Samuel H. Kress Collection

251 **Sebastiano del Piombo:** *Portrait of a Humanist.* c. 1520. Wood mounted on hardboard, 53 x 39¾″ (134.7 x 101 cm.). Samuel H. Kress Collection

252 **Sebastiano del Piombo:** *Cardinal Bandinello Sauli, His Secretary, and Two Geographers.* Dated 1516. Wood, 47⅞ x 59″ (121.6 x 149.8 cm.). Samuel H. Kress Collection

250

Like Andrea Gritti, Vincenzo Capello, his contemporary and the admiral of the Venetian fleet, looks as though he might have spoken those impressive lines from *Othello*: "I have done the state some service, and they know't." All three of Titian's sitters have been dowered with an enlargement of personality that distinguishes the work of the greatest portraitists. Sebastiano del Piombo reduces his models to a more human scale. The Cardinal (plate 252), about to be incarcerated for conspiring to poison the Pope, becomes a pathetic terrorist, and the humanist (plate 251) a neurotic scholar.

251

252

Titian

(VENETIAN, c. 1477–1576)

253   VENUS WITH A MIRROR

Titian, more than any other Renaissance artist, understood the spirit of classical art. Yet he was nearly seventy when he went to Rome and had his first opportunity to visit the capital of the ancient world and to see the great works of art accumulated there. When he was not executing his many important missions at the Vatican and among the Roman nobility, he was, as he said, "learning from the marvelous, ancient stones." Although he regretted that he had not received this inspiration earlier, still it came at a time when he was about to enter upon his period of supreme achievement, which lasted until he was well into his nineties. Under the influence of classical art his late nudes gained an amplitude of form, a heavy magnificence which suggests Greek sculpture of the Golden Age.

From his earliest masterpieces like the Bacchanals, painted for the Duke of Ferrara, to canvases like this, painted when he was over seventy, Titian repeatedly celebrated the goddess of love. All these pictures are permeated with a sensuality which deepens with age, growing always more impersonal. In his final work he expresses the indwelling power of feminine beauty, a quality which transcends the loveliness of any individual woman. These pictures are his final homage to Venus, as moving in their way as the late love poems of Yeats.

But Titian's amatory tribute was not arrived at suddenly. From data revealed by recent X-rays it appears that the canvas was used previously for two other compositions, which Titian abandoned in succession. The first was a horizontal composition of a man and a woman standing together, possibly an allegory of marriage with the bride and groom in the roles of Venus and Mars. The second was a vertical composition representing a Venus with two cupids; the head and pose of the Venus were retained in the final picture.

Having found the composition he wanted, Titian painted several further variations on this theme, and still others were produced by followers and imitators, but this particular canvas he kept for himself, feeling for it perhaps some special affection. After his death it was sold by his son Pomponio to the Barbarigo family, and remained in their possession until it was purchased by Nicholas I for the Hermitage Gallery, Leningrad.

Collections: Pomponio Vecellio, Venice; Barbarigo family, Venice; Hermitage Gallery, Leningrad. *Andrew W. Mellon Collection*, 1937. Painted c. 1555. Canvas, 49 x 41½" (124.5 x 105.5 cm.).

254

254 **Titian** (Venetian, c. 1477–1576): *Portrait of a Lady.* c. 1555. Canvas, 38½ x 29⅛″ (98 x 74 cm.). Samuel H. Kress Collection

255 **Titian:** *Cupid with the Wheel of Fortune.* c. 1520. Canvas, 26 x 21¾″ (66 x 55 cm.). Samuel H. Kress Collection

256 **Follower of Titian:** *Emilia di Spilimbergo (?).* Canvas, 48 x 42″ (122 x 106.5 cm.). Widener Collection

257 **Follower of Titian:** *Irene di Spilimbergo (?).* Canvas, 48 x 42″ (122 x 106.5 cm.). Widener Collection

258 **Titian:** *St. John the Evangelist on Patmos.* Probably 1544. Canvas, 93½ x 103½″ (237.6 x 263 cm.). Samuel H. Kress Collection

Evidently Titian's heart was not in painting women sitters, and he often turned such portraiture over to assistants. The Spilimbergo sisters, though eulogized in poetry, could never have seduced a poet. Painting nude goddesses Titian enjoyed, but Venetian ladies bored him. How much more interesting, he thought, to decorate a ceiling with the Evangelist's vision of the Apocalypse.

255

256

257

258

Titian

(VENETIAN, c. 1477–1576)

259   VENUS AND ADONIS

When he was over eighty years old, Titian painted this canvas showing Adonis tearing himself from the embrace of Venus to undertake his fatal hunt. These two figures from Greek mythology symbolize a recurring conflict in the human soul, the suffering that comes from unsatisfied passion, an emotion deeply rooted in human experience. Portents of the cruel death awaiting Adonis are disclosed in the stormy light bursting in the sky, the gesture of Venus clutching her lover with terror, and the attitude of Cupid huddled over his dove like an embodiment of his mother's fear.

The figures seem to transcend human form, to have become heroic shapes only vaguely related to physical reality. This gives to Titian's late works an unearthly quality, a preternatural appearance. Titian's *Venus and Adonis* is a climax of the imaginative, pictorial mode of painting which begins with such pictures as *The Adoration of the Shepherds* by Giorgione (plate 232).

Of the many versions of the composition, the present painting is considered the last executed by Titian himself. It was engraved by Sadeler in 1610, and the diarist John Evelyn records having seen the picture in 1679 in the home of the Countess of Bristol, and again in 1685 when it had passed by inheritance to her daughter, Lady Sunderland.

Collections: Lord Bristol (seventeenth century) and his descendants, among whom the last owner was the Seventh Earl Spencer. *Widener Collection*, 1942. Painted after 1560. Canvas, 42 x 53½" (106.8 x 136 cm.).

260

261

262

263

Paolo Veronese, a rival of Titian, was a less heroic, less passionate artist. But he was one of the most brilliant decorators who ever lived. Often his subjects served only as an excuse for the display of his decorative powers. He loved rich brocades, the complexities of linear and aerial perspective, the thrust and counterthrust of moving, gesticulating bodies. So interested did he become in these formal aspects of art that he grew indifferent to the content of his scenes, incurred the censorship of the Inquisition, and barely escaped prison.

Paolo Veronese (Venetian, 1528–1588)

260 *The Annunciation.* c. 1580. Canvas, 38¾ x 29⅝" (98.4 x 75.3 cm.). Samuel H. Kress Collection

261 *St. Jerome in the Wilderness.* c. 1580. Canvas, 42½ x 33⅛" (108 x 84.1 cm.). Samuel H. Kress Collection

262 *Rebecca at the Well.* 1580/85. Canvas, 57¼ x 111¼" (145.5 x 282.7 cm.). Samuel H. Kress Collection

263 *The Finding of Moses.* Probably early 1570s. Canvas, 22¾ x 17½" (58 x 44.5 cm.). Andrew W. Mellon Collection

264 *St. Lucy and a Donor.* Probably c. 1580. Canvas, 71⅛ x 45⅜" (180.6 x 115.3 cm.). Samuel H. Kress Collection

264

215

Sodoma

(SIENESE, 1477-1549)

265　ST. GEORGE AND THE DRAGON

Although the majority of the great achievements in art are in the realm of high tragedy, still there is enchantment to be found in certain paintings that come close to comedy. Sodoma's *St. George and the Dragon* is in this lighter vein. The hero's horse is much fiercer than the poor contorted monster he seems about to bite, and it is evident that St. George, with his broken barber's-pole spear, may plunge at any moment over the head of his mount. The heroine rolls her eyes to heaven, and deliciously overacts her part! The angel in the sky, who like a referee at a prize fight seems to be counting out the dragon, is unique in representations of this scene.

These comic elements do not diminish but rather increase the strange fairy-tale beauty of the painting. How lovely are the flaming red cape of the saint silhouetted against the sky, the variegated reflections shining in the pool at the feet of Princess Cleodolinda, and the landscape background bathed in a mysterious illumination, "the consecration and the poet's dream!"

When the picture was acquired from the famous Cook Collection the foreground was a flowering meadow. X-rays disclosed that some squeamish collector had completely buried under repaint the remains of the dragon's previous meal, eaten apparently just before the arrival of St. George. The meadow was cleaned away, and the picture now appears as originally painted, with just that touch of gruesomeness so characteristic of fairy tales.

In a letter of May 3, 1518, to Alfonso I d'Este, Duke of Ferrara, Sodoma wrote: "Some time ago, when I was with His Holiness Pope Leo in Florence, your ambassador gave me a commission for your Lordship to make a St. George on horseback killing the dragon; therefore I have made it and am holding it at your Lordship's pleasure." That this is the painting referred to seems likely, as the eagle on St. George's helmet is an Este symbol.

Collections: Seventeenth Earl of Shrewsbury, Alton Towers, Straffordshire; Cook, Doughty House, Richmond, Surrey. *Samuel H. Kress Collection,* 1952. Painted probably 1518. Wood, 55½ x 38⅜″ (137.8 x 97.6 cm.).

266

267

268

269

These paintings are a heterogeneous lot. Correggio is the earliest of the artists reproduced. *The Mystic Marriage of St. Catherine* (plate 266) gives no idea of his great decorations in the Parma Cathedral on which his reputation rests, but his delicate and subtle handling of chiaroscuro, for which he was also famous, is evident. Jacopo Bassano is celebrated as a precursor of El Greco and Paris Bordone as a prophet of Baroque painting. The Basaiti Madonna and the Bartolommeo Veneto portrait are particularly worth looking at for their superb condition.

266 **Correggio** (School of Parma, 1489/94–1534): *The Mystic Marriage of St. Catherine.* c. 1510/15. Wood, 10⅞ x 8⅜" (27.7 x 21.3 cm.). Samuel H. Kress Collection

267 **Correggio**: *Salvator Mundi.* c. 1515. Wood, 16¾ x 13⅛" (42.6 x 33.3 cm.). Samuel H. Kress Collection

268 **Jacopo Bassano** (Venetian, c. 1515–1592): *The Annunciation to the Shepherds.* Probably c. 1555/60. Canvas, 41¾ x 32½" (106 x 83 cm.). Samuel H. Kress Collection

269 **Bartolommeo Veneto** (Lombard-Venetian, active 1502–1546): *Portrait of a Gentleman.* c. 1520. Transferred from wood to canvas, 30¼ x 23" (77 x 58 cm.). Samuel H. Kress Collection

270 **Paris Bordone** (Venetian, 1500–1571): *The Baptism of Christ.* c. 1535/40. Canvas, 51 x 52" (129.5 x 132 cm.). Widener Collection

271 **Marco Basaiti** (Venetian, active 1496–1530): *Madonna Adoring the Child.* Signed. c. 1520. Wood, 8⅛ x 6½" (21 x 17 cm.). Samuel H. Kress Collection

272 **Sodoma** (Sienese, 1477–1549): *Madonna and Child with the Infant St. John.* c. 1505. Wood, 31 x 25½" (79 x 65 cm.). Samuel H. Kress Collection

270

271

272

219

Giovanni Battista Moroni

(BRESCIAN, c. 1520–1578)

273   A GENTLEMAN IN ADORATION BEFORE THE MADONNA

Little is known of Moroni's life except that he was active in the provincial town of Bergamo. His portraits, in which he revealed his true ability, his sensitive understanding of character, recall the work of his master, Moretto, who was active in nearby Brescia. The mood he creates is the same wistful melancholy that we find in Moretto's style. The figures in Moroni's portraits seem to implore our sympathy with a shy, solemn insistence. This elusive note of diffident sadness, so often to be found in provincial portraiture, is the opposite of the mood created by Titian, Veronese, and Tintoretto, in whose portraits we have a feeling of inner strength, a sense that the men and women they portray were destined by some ineluctable right to dominate, to possess the world.

Probably Moroni's provincial patrons lacked the self-assurance which is so conspicuous in the people who sat for the Venetian masters. Or perhaps this lack was in the artist himself, for Moroni never mastered the *gusto grande*, the grand manner, which was fashionable in his day. He never learned that art of ennobling, or amplifying, the personalities of his sitters. He painted his subjects as he saw them; he delineated with touching fidelity the commoners and the petty nobility of a provincial town, men and women who were close to their peasants, who often helped in the vineyards and fields, and were not above menial tasks. His canvases mirror, perhaps better than the work of any other artist, the personalities of a small town in the sixteenth century.

In the painting *A Gentleman in Adoration before the Madonna* Moroni was confronted with a subject common enough in Venetian art, a miraculous apparition. Titian, for instance, has often created such scenes with his easy invention, his great imaginative power, but Moroni, devoid of all visionary feeling, was paralyzed, as Berenson has said, the moment he was separated from the model. Thus in portraying the Madonna and Child he dared not trust his own creative genius. He turned instead to an engraving by Albrecht Dürer for his model. Yet the amazing fact remains that his painting triumphs over such naive imitation. Moroni's sensitive and poetic treatment of the kneeling man gives his picture a mood of intimate devotion, an atmosphere of fervent piety, which seems an echo from a simpler, more innocent world.

Collection: Casa Grimani, Venice. *Samuel H. Kress Collection*, 1939. Painted c. 1560. Canvas, 23½ x 25½" (60 x 65 cm.).

The Venetian paintings so far reproduced indicate that the leadership of the Italian Schools was gradually passing from Florence to Venice, whose suzerainty at the beginning of the sixteenth century extended from the head of the Adriatic to Lake Como. In Venice's expansion over this wide territory a number of city-states were overrun, each of which had developed its own school of painting. Although the artists of these North Italian towns accepted the preeminence of the great Venetian masters, their styles remained local and idiomatic. Thus the paintings of Savoldo and Moretto are marked by a religious feeling hard to find in Venice itself after the death of Giovanni Bellini.

275

274

276

277

278

274 Giovanni Girolamo Savoldo (Brescian, active 1508–1548): *Elijah Fed by the Raven.* c. 1510. Transferred from wood to canvas, 66⅛ x 53⅜" (168 x 135.6 cm.). Samuel H. Kress Collection

275 Giovanni Girolamo Savoldo: *Portrait of a Knight.* c. 1525. Canvas, 34¾ x 28⅞" (88.3 x 73.4 cm.). Samuel H. Kress Collection

276 Moretto da Brescia (Brescian, c. 1498–1554): *Pietà.* 1520s. Wood, 69⅛ x 38¼" (175.8 x 98.5 cm.). Samuel H. Kress Collection

277 Giovanni Battista Moroni (Brescian, c. 1520–1578): *"Titian's Schoolmaster."* c. 1575. Canvas, 38⅛ x 29¼" (97 x 74 cm.). Widener Collection

278 Giovanni Battista Moroni: *Gian Federico Madruzzo.* c. 1560. Canvas, 79½ x 46" (201.9 x 116.8 cm.). Timken Collection

279 Northern Follower of Titian (probably mid-XVI century): *Alessandro Alberti with a Page.* Canvas, 48⅞ x 40⅜" (124.2 x 102.7 cm.). Samuel H. Kress Foundation

279

François Clouet

(FRENCH, c. 1510–1572)

280 "DIANE DE POITIERS"

François Clouet's work is an example of the wide dissemination in the sixteenth century of the Italian style. This is one of three portraits he signed. In the nineteenth century the sitter was considered to be Diane de Poitiers, and the portrait retained this title for many years. The children in the painting were supposed to be the offspring of her lover Henri II and Catherine de' Medici. We know they were placed in her care. The unicorn embroidered on a chair back or firescreen was thought to be a reference to the unicorn horn purchased by Diane to preserve the health of the royal children through its supposed therapeutic properties.

More recently the date of the picture has been placed much later, toward the end of Clouet's life. The lady's coiffure, for example, resembles that of Clouet's portrait of Elizabeth of Austria, a drawing for which is dated 1571. As Diane died in 1566, scholars have gone in search of some other royal favorite. Gabrielle d'Estrées, mistress of Henri IV, and Marie Touchet, mistress of Charles IX, have had their advocates but have yet to gain general acceptance. In 1966 Roger Trinquet published the most fascinating suggestion of all. He believes the lady to be Mary Queen of Scots and the painting to have been done with satirical intent for some Huguenot patron, possibly François, Maréchal de Montmorency.

Although the lady's face is highly idealized, a beautiful feminine mask, there is no doubt that she resembles accepted portraits of the tragic Scottish queen, particularly a drawing in white mourning attire attributed to François Clouet. If this identification is correct, then the infant is her son and the crossed black bands on his swaddling clothes an allusion to the Cross of St. Andrew and possibly also to the death of Darnley, the baby's father. The same child at four or five would then be the boy reaching for the fruit, a symbol of his grasping for the crown of Scotland. There is also the supporting evidence that the unicorn and the grapes appear in emblematic devices of Mary Stuart; and Colin Eisler, who is inclined to accept this identification, has pointed out that the bather's cap "is closer to English than to French fashion."

The setting may seem unusual, but judging by the numerous copies of this picture in the sixteenth century and the variations on the theme of a lady in her bath, which continued into the seventeenth century, Clouet's painting made bathing portraits extremely fashionable. Trinquet claims that a lady shown in her bath must be

(continued)

281

French painting came under the spell of the most famous artist ever to visit France, Leonardo da Vinci. Leonardo spent the last three years of his life at Amboise, where he died in 1519. His influence, which is particularly apparent in Clouet's portrait (plate 280), was ubiquitous in France. His personality was so overwhelming that it also dominated the School of Milan, where he stayed from 1482 to 1499. We see, for example, the Leonardesque modeling in Boltraffio's Youth and the Mona Lisa smile in Luini's Magdalen.

282

(continued)

a lady of questionable virtue. If so, judging by the popularity of this setting, many sixteenth-century ladies were delighted to have their virtue questioned. If the bather is Mary Stuart, must Clouet's painting be considered satirical? May not some French admirer have wanted a portrait that would convey the fatal sexual attraction of this woman for whom so many men died or were imprisoned? Is this perhaps the finest portrait in existence of the most fascinating queen in history?

Collections: Sir Richard Frederick, Burwood Park; Cook, Doughty House, Richmond, Surrey. *Samuel H. Kress Collection*, 1961. Painted probably c. 1571. Wood, 36¼ x 32″ (92.1 x 81.3 cm.).

283

284

285

281 French School (XVI century): *Prince Hercule-François, Duc d'Alençon.* Dated 1572. Canvas, 74½ x 40¼″ (188.6 x 102.2 cm.). Samuel H. Kress Collection

282 Bernardino Luini (Milanese, c. 1480–1532): *The Magdalen.* c. 1525. Wood, 23⅛ x 18⅞″ (58.8 x 47.8 cm.). Samuel H. Kress Collection

283 Bernardino Luini: *Venus.* c. 1530. Wood, 42 x 53½″ (107 x 136 cm.). Samuel H. Kress Collection

284 Giovanni Antonio Boltraffio (Milanese, 1467–1516): *Portrait of a Youth.* Shortly before 1500. Wood, 18⅜ x 13¾″ (46.7 x 35 cm.). Ralph and Mary Booth Collection

285 French School (XVI century): *Portrait of a Nobleman.* c. 1570. Wood, 12¾ x 9¼″ (32.5 x 23.5 cm.). Gift of Chester Dale

286 Jacopo Tintoretto (Venetian, 1518–1594): *Susanna.* c. 1575. Canvas, 59⅛ x 40⅜″ (150 x 103 cm.). Samuel H. Kress Collection

286

Jacopo Tintoretto

(VENETIAN, 1518–1594)

287   CHRIST AT THE SEA OF GALILEE

Ask a contemporary painter to name the greatest of the Venetian artists, and the chances are he will choose Tintoretto. There are many reasons for this choice, but in the painting reproduced one is especially evident: Tintoretto's emotional intensity. In *Christ at the Sea of Galilee*, the event illustrated is described in John 21:7. Our Lord, standing on the shore, reveals himself to his disciples who are fishing: "Now when Simon Peter heard that it was the Lord, he girt his fisher's coat unto him (for he was naked), and did cast himself into the sea." Here almost for the first time nature becomes an actor in the drama. The driven clouds, the storm-tossed waves, the "light that never was, on sea or land," all heighten the terrible intensity of the moment of ecstatic union when man is irresistibly drawn to His Lord and Saviour. How marvelously Tintoretto conveys the towering majesty of Christ and the yearning desire of the disciple who flings himself into the sea to reach his Master!

It is interesting to note that Hans Tietze, one of the most astute authorities on Venetian painting, always believed this picture to be by El Greco. The elongation of Christ, the color and modeling of the waves, and the emotional intensity of the scene suggest the Spanish painter. But it is hard to place the picture in the chronology of El Greco's works, and the touch in the smaller figures and the painting of the sky seem typical of Tintoretto's style.

Collections: Count J. Galotti; Arthur Sachs, New York. *Samuel H. Kress Collection*, 1952. Painted c. 1575/80. Canvas, 46 x 66¼" (117 x 168.5 cm.).

229

288

Jacopo Tintoretto (Venetian, 1518–1594)

288 *Doge Alvise Mocenigo and Family Before the Madonna and Child.* Probably 1573. Canvas, 85⅛ x 164″ (216.1 x 416.5 cm.). Samuel H. Kress Collection

289 *A Procurator of St. Mark's.* c. 1575/85. Canvas, 54½ x 39⅞″ (138.7 x 101.3 cm.). Samuel H. Kress Collection

290 *The Worship of the Golden Calf.* c. 1560. Canvas, 62⅝ x 107″ (159 x 272 cm.). Samuel H. Kress Collection

291 *The Conversion of St. Paul.* c. 1545. Canvas, 60 x 92⅞″ (152.4 x 236.2 cm.). Samuel H. Kress Collection

292 *Summer.* c. 1555. Canvas, 41⅝ x 76″ (105.7 x 193 cm.). Samuel H. Kress Collection

293 *The Madonna of the Stars.* 2nd half of XVI century. Canvas, 36½ x 28⅝″ (92.7 x 72.7 cm.). Ralph and Mary Booth Collection

294 **Guercino** (Bolognese, 1591–1666): *Cardinal Francesco Cennini.* c. 1625. Canvas, 46¼ x 37⅞″ (117.4 x 96.2 cm.). Samuel H. Kress Collection

295 **Domenico Fetti** (Roman, c. 1589–1623): *The Veil of Veronica.* c. 1615. Wood, 32⅛ x 26½″ (81.5 x 67.5 cm.). Samuel H. Kress Collection

289

290

The sixteenth-century biographer Vasari said of Tintoretto that he was "extravagant, capricious, quick and determined, with the most terrific imagination in the history of painting." These qualities are especially apparent in *The Conversion of St. Paul* (plate 291). The saint lies stunned. A stricken rider on a rearing charger is carried off to the left. On the bridge a horseman struggles to hold aloft his strange banner. The ghostly faces of drowning legionnaires and the spectral boatmen contrast with the calm power of Christ, seen in the upper left. The turbulence of the scene anticipates Baroque painting.

291

292

293

294

295

296

297

298

296 **Orazio Gentileschi** (Florentine, c. 1563–1639): *St. Cecilia and an Angel.* c. 1610. Canvas, 34⅝ x 42½" (87.8 x 108.1 cm.). Samuel H. Kress Collection

297 **Orazio Gentileschi**: *The Lute Player.* Probably c. 1610. Canvas, 56½ x 50⅝" (143.5 x 128.8 cm.). Ailsa Mellon Bruce Fund

298 **Bernardo Strozzi** (Genoese-Venetian, 1581–1644): *Bishop Alvise Grimani.* Probably c. 1633. Canvas, 57¾ x 37⅜" (146.7 x 95.1 cm.). Samuel H. Kress Collection

299 **Jan Lys** (German, active chiefly in Italy c. 1600–1629): *The Satyr and the Peasant.* Probably c. 1620. Canvas, 52½ x 65½" (133.5 x 166.5 cm.). Widener Collection

The more tranquil aspects of the Baroque style are to be seen in these reproductions. The most beautiful of these is *The Lute Player.* The painting seems to preserve a moment of actuality. Time stands still as it often does in Dutch painting. The scene touches us with its simple and tender realism. In this picture, and in *St. Cecilia and an Angel,* the model is probably Artemisia Gentileschi, the artist's daughter, who was to become one of the most distinguished of women painters.

299

Spanish School

XVI AND XVII CENTURY

El Greco

(SPANISH, 1541–1614)

300 CHRIST CLEANSING THE TEMPLE

Christ Cleansing the Temple, by El Greco, an early work, perhaps the first he ever signed, reflects the influence of Titian, Tintoretto, and Veronese. It was painted after the young Greek had arrived in Venice and while he was still learning the style of these great Venetian masters. On the panel he signed in Greek his real name, Domenikos Theotokópoulos; then he added, perhaps to give himself confidence, the name of his birthplace, Crete. There is still much in this picture that reminds us of El Greco's probable training as an icon painter: the small size of the picture, the use of wood instead of canvas, the enamel-like impasto, and the deep bronze colors with less glazing than the Venetians customarily used.

But there are also borrowings from Venetian paintings. The pose of the half-nude woman, lying on the ground with her arm behind her head, was copied from the sleeping Ariadne in Titian's early *Bacchanal*; the vigorous diagonal thrusts of the composition show Tintoretto's influence; while the voluptuous female types suggest Paolo Veronese's works. There is also a debt to the greatest master of Roman painting, Michelangelo, in the half-nude figure, seen from the back, at the left of Christ, which is based on two figures in Michelangelo's *Conversion of St. Paul* in the Pauline Chapel in the Vatican. These eclectic borrowings are fused into unity by El Greco's strong personal style, which here is limited to the use of contortions, with only a hint of the distortions characteristic of his mature work. The subject, symbolizing reform within the Church, was one which proved exceptionally popular and was repeated by El Greco at least five times; the last version, in San Ginés, Madrid, painted at the end of his life, seems to have been executed with the collaboration of his son, Jorge Manuel.

Collections: J. C. Robinson, London; Cook, Doughty House, Richmond, Surrey. *Samuel H. Kress Collection*, 1957. Signed. Painted c. 1570. Wood, 25¾ x 32¾" (65.4 x 83.2 cm.).

301

Of the five pictures by El Greco shown here, three in particular throw light on his method of work. *St. Jerome* (plate 303) in its unfinished state illustrates his method of underpainting, with the figure drawn in bold contours over which brilliant glazes were added. The smaller version of *St. Martin and the Beggar* (plate 304) in the Mellon Collection may well be one of the models El Greco kept in his studio from which patrons might order other altarpieces. It was done after the far superior *St. Martin* from the Widener Collection (plate 301), a painting which was once in the chapel of San José in Toledo, along with the painting reproduced in plate 306.

302

303

304

El Greco (Spanish, 1541–1614)

301 *St. Martin and the Beggar.* 1597/99. Canvas, 76⅛ x 40½" (193.5 x 103 cm.). Widener Collection

302 *St. Ildefonso.* c. 1600/1605. Canvas, 44¼ x 25¾" (112 x 65 cm.). Andrew W. Mellon Collection

303 *St. Jerome.* c. 1610/14. Canvas, 66¼ x 43½" (168 x 110.5 cm.). Gift of Chester Dale

304 *St. Martin and the Beggar.* 1604/14. Canvas, 41 x 23⅝" (104 x 60 cm.). Andrew W. Mellon Collection

305 *The Holy Family.* Probably c. 1590. Canvas, 20⅞ x 13½" (53.2 x 34.4 cm.). Samuel H. Kress Collection

305

El Greco

(SPANISH, 1541–1614)

306   MADONNA AND CHILD WITH ST. MARTINA AND ST. AGNES

Among the Old Masters, the true prophet of modern art is El Greco. His work fore-shadows the abandonment three hundred years later of naturalism for Expression-ism, of proportions determined by nature for proportions determined by emotion. Academic critics fighting this trend used to assert that El Greco distorted the hu-man form because his eyesight was defective. We now believe that astigmatism af-fected him less, if at all, than the stylization of Byzantine icons and mosaics he had seen as a young man on his native island of Crete. But the fashion initiated by Par-migianino, that vogue for tall, slender figures with small heads, which became modish in European painting of the late sixteenth century, also played its part and prepared the public to accept the exaggerated elongations El Greco found suitable for his highly emotional style.

El Greco, however, was not merely a precursor of many contemporary artists; he also expressed, through the flamelike forms he created, the spirit of his own time, that ardent and mystical piety which followed the newly launched Counter Ref-ormation. The *Madonna and Child with St. Martina and St. Agnes*, once in the chapel of San José in Toledo, the Spanish town which became El Greco's final home, is a summit of such visionary painting. What more marvelous rendering of substance at once tangible and intangible, corporeal and incorporeal, than the cherubim who surround the Virgin? They seem modeled in ectoplasm, formed of some emanation of thought. Even the artist's signature, the initials of his Greek name (Domenikos Theotokópoulos) traced on the forehead of St. Martina's lion, seems to have taken on symbolic significance. The whole scene illustrates, so far as this is possible, the experiences described by El Greco's contemporary, St. John of the Cross, and other mystics.

But if El Greco himself was a mystic, he was a very practical one. We know that he was an efficient painter, ran a profitable shop, and was ready to repeat his pic-tures as many times as the market required. Even his distortions did not diminish his popularity, for his paintings apparently gave concrete and convincing form to visions that many pious people in Spain had seen or hoped to see.

Collection: Chapel of San José, Toledo (until 1906). *Widener Collection*, 1942. Signed with initials. Painted 1597–99. Canvas, 76⅛ x 40½" (193.5 x 103 cm.).

239

El Greco

(SPANISH, 1541–1614)

307 LAOCOÖN

The story of Laocoön is told by Arctinus of Miletus and repeated with some variations by Vergil. Laocoön was a priest of Poseidon who warned his fellow Trojans not to carry into their city the wooden horse left behind by the invading Greeks. But his famous words, "Fools, trust not the Greeks, even when bearing gifts," went unheeded. In despair he hurled his spear against the horse, a gesture of sacrilege against Minerva, to whom the wooden statue had been dedicated. The deities, perhaps portrayed on the right of the canvas, avenged this desecration by causing sea serpents to kill Laocoön and his two sons. Their deaths were interpreted by the Trojans as a sign of the anger of the gods, and the horse was brought inside the city walls. At night Greek soldiers concealed inside its belly crept out and opened the city gates, thus bringing about the fall of Troy and ending the Trojan War. In the middle distance the wooden horse can be seen, and in place of Troy is a view of Toledo, El Greco's adopted home.

Although El Greco was, as his name implies, Greek, he ignored the mythology and the history of his fatherland except for this one subject. In the inventory of his possessions made in 1614 three Laocoöns are listed, one of which is similar in measurements to the painting reproduced here. El Greco may have been working on this particular version when he died, for a recent cleaning suggests that the three figures on the right remained unfinished.

Why was the story of Laocoön of such exceptional interest to a painter whose work, apart from portraits, was almost entirely religious? Some scholars explain this by arguing that the Greek myth bears a relationship to Christianity, E. W. Palm going so far as to identify the figures on the right as Adam and Eve. (The third head is presumably a *pentimento*.) It is true that the legend of Laocoön and the beginning of Genesis both illustrate divine retribution for transgression, the serpent playing an important role in the classical and Biblical stories.

But El Greco's motivation, one feels, had little to do with Judeo-Hellenic parallels. He was more probably impelled to paint this subject by an artistic challenge, the desire to surpass the most famous of all statuary groups, the *Laocoön* of the Vatican discovered in 1506, which he must have scrutinized when he visited Rome in 1570. El Greco, one may presume, wished to show how much more effectively this legendary theme of suffering could be treated in paint than in marble; and with his masterpiece of twisting, contorted figures he has offered a strong argument for the pictorial as opposed to the sculptural.

Collections: Probably the large painting of Laocoön listed in the inventory of El Greco's estate in Toledo; Duke of Montpensier, Palace of San Telmo, Seville; Infante Don Antonio d'Orléans, Sanlúcar de Barrameda; E. Fischer, Charlottenburg; Prince Paul of Yugoslavia, Belgrade. *Samuel H. Kress Collection*, 1946. Painted c. 1610. Canvas, 54⅛ x 67⅞" (137.5 x 172.5 cm.).

241

Diego Velázquez

(SPANISH, 1599–1660)

308 THE NEEDLEWOMAN

The few pictures Velázquez painted to please himself are among his finest and most original achievements. In such paintings as the two views of the garden of the Villa Medici in the Prado and *The Needlewoman* in the National Gallery of Art, he appears a precursor of Corot, revealing a similar simplicity of treatment joined to a penetrating power of observation.

It would seem at first as though this study of a woman sewing were never finished. The left hand is merely blocked in, and the fingers of the right barely indicated. But this device of adumbrating rather than defining shapes was used by Velázquez in a number of late works to suggest motion. In the painting of Innocent X in the Palazzo Doria in Rome (for which the painting reproduced in plate 314 is a sketch) the outlines of the fingers are blurred, an indistinction which makes them seem to twitch with nervous energy. Again there is the hand of the boy with his foot on the dog in *Las Meninas*, where a flickering movement is given by making the contours seem faltering or indiscernible; and in *Las Hilanderas* if one looks at the hand of the woman in the foreground one sees what appear to be successive positions of her fingers as she winds her yarn. In all these pictures the vibrating effect of shifting planes of light conveys a sense of motion in a way that is new in art. Similarly *The Needlewoman* may not be an incomplete work but rather an experiment on the road leading to Impressionism.

A. Mayer identifies the sitter with the painter's daughter Francisca, who married his pupil Juan Bautista del Mazo; and Sánchez Cantón suggests that this painting may be a *Head of a Woman Sewing* mentioned in the inventory of Velázquez' effects at the time of his death.

Collections: Amédée, Marquis de Gouvello de Keriaval, Château de Kerlevenant, Sarzeau, Morbihan, Brittany; Mme Christiane de Polès, Paris. *Andrew W. Mellon Collection*, 1937. Painted c. 1640. Canvas, 29⅛ x 23⅝″ (74 x 60 cm.).

242

243

Bartolomé Esteban Murillo

(SPANISH, 1617–1682)

309   A GIRL AND HER DUENNA

All the paintings we have reproduced so far have been either devotional pictures, allegorical or mythological scenes, or portraits. In the seventeenth century scenes of daily life—genre subjects—came into fashion. In the past such material was to be found with rare exception only in the cheaper media of woodcut and engraving. This double portrait is essentially a genre picture. A young girl and her duenna stare boldly at the spectator, much as Murillo must have seen such women gazing from the high windows in the narrow streets of Seville. The painting was popularly known as *Las Gallegas*, the Galicians, referring to the tradition that it represents two notorious courtesans of Seville who originally came from the province of Galicia. Murillo was an artist of the people: genial, commonplace in outlook, with an easy eloquence. In religious painting his sentiment was torrential, and his immense popularity finally wore away a technical ability which was second only to that of Velázquez. Disconcertingly uneven as was his achievement, he occasionally created a masterpiece like the present picture. Here he has avoided the sticky sentimentality and trite picturesqueness which spoil so much of his work. He presents these two women with that detached observation which is the hallmark of the best Spanish painting.

What Northern artist would have treated the subject with such subtle restraint? Rembrandt alone would have had the insight to eliminate the extraneous and focus attention, as Murillo has done, on the young girl so beautifully placed in the window, so plastically rendered. But not even Frans Hals would have had sufficient alertness of vision to suggest the smile of the older woman, witty, sardonic, yet expressed by the eyes and cheek alone.

Collections: Duque de Almodóvar, Madrid; Lord Heytesbury, Heytesbury House, Wiltshire. *Widener Collection*, 1942. Painted c. 1670. Canvas, 50¼ x 41¾" (127.7 x 106.1 cm.).

310

311

Spanish painting of the seventeenth century is evidence of the erratic emergence of genius. In the sixteenth century all the painters of significance in Spain were foreigners. Then suddenly, for no apparent reason, five major native artists appeared: Velázquez, Murillo, Zurbarán, Ribera, and Valdés Leal. With their deaths foreigners took over again until, unexpectedly, Goya arrived on the scene. Then a period of sterility followed until once more three great masters, all exiled Spaniards, emerged: Picasso, Juan Gris, and Miró. After them a new aridity seems probable, though no one knows.

312

313

314

315

310 Juan de Valdés Leal (Spanish, 1622–1690): *The Assumption of the Virgin.* Signed. c. 1670. Canvas, 84⅝ x 61½" (215.1 x 156.3 cm.). Samuel H. Kress Collection

311 Juan van der Hamen y Leon (Spanish, 1596–1631): *Still Life.* Signed, and dated 1627. Canvas, 33⅛ x 44⅜" (84.2 x 112.8 cm.). Samuel H. Kress Collection

312 Francisco de Zurbarán (Spanish, 1598–1664): *St. Jerome with St. Paula and St. Eustochium.* c. 1640. Canvas, 96½ x 68⅛" (245.1 x 173 cm.). Samuel H. Kress Collection

313 Francisco de Zurbarán: *Santa Lucia.* c. 1625. Canvas, 41 x 30⅜" (104.1 x 77.2 cm.). Gift of Chester Dale

314 Diego Velázquez (Spanish, 1599–1660): *Pope Innocent X.* c. 1650. Canvas, 19½ x 16¼" (49 x 42 cm.). Andrew W. Mellon Collection

315 Circle of Velázquez (Spanish, XVII century): *Portrait of a Young Man.* Canvas, 23¼ x 18⅞" (59 x 48 cm.). Andrew W. Mellon Collection

316 Bartolomé Esteban Murillo (Spanish, 1617–1682): *The Return of the Prodigal Son.* 1670/74. Canvas, 93 x 102¾" (236.6 x 261 cm.). Gift of the Avalon Foundation

316

Flemish &
Dutch Schools

XVII CENTURY

Peter Paul Rubens

(FLEMISH, 1577-1640)

317   DANIEL IN THE LIONS' DEN

The rarest of paintings by an Old Master is one with a testimony of authenticity from the artist himself. In a letter of 1618 to Sir Dudley Carleton, the British Ambassador at The Hague, Rubens describes the picture reproduced here as "Daniel among many lions, taken from life. Original entirely by my hand, 8 x 12 ft." This document was involved in a sale being negotiated between Rubens and the Ambassador. The British diplomat had made a collection of antique marbles while *en poste* in Venice, and these marbles Rubens coveted. After several weeks of negotiations an agreement was worked out whereby Rubens would pay two thousand florins and give four thousand florins' worth of his own work, in exchange for which Carleton would let him have the classical sculpture he so ardently desired.

Carleton, though an ambassador, was also engaged in forming the art collection of the Prince of Wales, who was later to become Charles I, and whom Rubens called "le prince le plus amateur de la peinture qui soit au monde." It is probable that having been created Viscount Dorchester in 1628 and Secretary of State soon after, Carleton in gratitude presented the *Daniel* to his royal master. For some reason the painting was subsequently given by Charles to the Duke of Hamilton, and it remained in the Hamilton Collection, with one short interruption, until 1919.

In the 1960s it was put up for sale at a small London auction house. The owner was unaware that he possessed one of Rubens' greatest masterpieces. All the British art dealers, however, knew, and were waiting for the auction, ready to bid £100,000 to £200,000; but an American dealer living in London made an offer of less than a thousand pounds just before the day fixed for the sale, saying that he would be away when the auction was to take place and that he had a client named Daniel who collected such pictures. Informed by the auctioneer, the owner was delighted to be offered anything for a painting he considered worthless, and immediately accepted. His folly handed the American the chance for one of the greatest art coups of all time. Since the picture had fetched less than a thousand pounds, it could be exported legally without an examination by the British museum authorities. Taken by surprise, and helpless, they have since stated they would certainly have stopped one of their greatest works by Rubens from leaving the country had this been possible. If the American dealer had paid a shilling over a thousand pounds, a British museum might have robbed him of his fantastic profit by buying the picture in at the same price.

Collections: Sir Dudley Carleton; Charles I of England; the Marquess of Hamilton (at Hamilton Palace, with one brief interruption, until 1919); by inheritance, third Viscount Cowdray. *Ailsa Mellon Bruce Fund*, 1965. Painted c. 1615. Canvas, 88¼ x 130⅛" (224.3 x 330.4 cm.).

318

319

318 **Peter Paul Rubens** (Flemish, 1577–1640): *The Assumption of the Virgin.* c. 1626. Wood, 49⅜ x 37⅛″ (125.4 x 94.2 cm.). Samuel H. Kress Collection

319 **Peter Paul Rubens**: *The Meeting of Abraham and Melchizedek.* c. 1625. Wood, 26 x 32½″ (66 x 82.5 cm.). Gift of Syma Busiel

320 **Peter Paul Rubens**: *Decius Mus Addressing the Legions.* Probably 1617. Wood, 31¾ x 33¼″ (80.7 x 84.5 cm.). Samuel H. Kress Collection

321 **Peter Paul Rubens**: *Tiberius and Agrippina.* c. 1614. Wood, 26¼ x 22½″ (66.6 x 57.1 cm.). Andrew W. Mellon Fund

322 **Sir Anthony van Dyck** (Flemish, 1599–1641): *The Assumption of the Virgin.* c. 1627. Canvas, 46½ x 40¼″ (118 x 102 cm.). Widener Collection

320

The special qualities of Rubens' genius can be seen in the paintings reproduced here. These stylistic characteristics are: a spiritual exuberance we associate with the Counter Reformation; a sustained rhythm of twisting, turning forms; the transformation of pigment into flesh, fur, silk, and steel while remaining paint, a miraculous change which Rubens could work as no other artist; and a sumptuousness which was the goal of all Baroque decorators, among whom Rubens was supreme.

321

322

Peter Paul Rubens

(FLEMISH, 1577–1640)

323 DEBORAH KIP, WIFE OF SIR BALTHASAR GERBIER, AND HER CHILDREN

The mood of introspection of the Gerbier family is puzzling, particularly as it is virtually unique in Rubens' work. Why does Lady Gerbier appear so withdrawn, as though meditating on some inner problem, which her elder son, looking at her almost beseechingly, seems to share? The two daughters gaze appraisingly and joylessly at the spectator. Only the baby is unaffected by this atmosphere of somber contemplation, which somehow suggests unhappiness, an air of foreboding.

How easy it is to invent the psychology of others, especially in paintings! There is nonetheless in this case reason to believe that Lady Gerbier had many problems which might well have made her pensive, if not melancholy. She was married to a scoundrel, and perhaps Rubens saw reflected in her face the tragedies —debts, frauds, even murder—which were to plague her life.

We can identify these sitters because the group portrait in the National Gallery of Art has been repeated on a much larger canvas, with the additions of Gerbier, five more children, and a coat of arms. George Vertue knew both pictures and discussed them in his unpublished letters in the British Museum. In 1749 he was asked to examine a sketch, sent from Flanders, of a painting offered to the Prince of Wales purporting to be a portrait of Sir Balthazar Arundel and his family. Vertue soon established that no one of that name had ever existed. Nevertheless the picture was bought for the Prince, and Vertue was called in again. In examining the purchase he found a half-erased inscription, "La Famille de Balthasar Gerbiere Chevaliere," and he identified the Gerbier coat of arms. The Prince was shocked. "How shall I come off of this?" he said to Vertue, "I have for this month past told many persons of quality that I have purchased a family peece of the Sheffield ancestor to the late Duke of Buckingham . . . as I was assured it (was) . . . be said the truth that dealers in pictures are like false moneyers." The picture the "false moneyers" sold the Prince is now in the Rubens Room at Windsor Castle, labeled correctly *Sir Balthazar Gerbier and His Family*. It is a rather poor copy in its central part of the National Gallery of Art painting. The latter, according to Vertue, "was sold at Lord Radnor's in St. James Square, there I saw Lord Burlington bid five hundred pounds for it, and Mr. Scowen bought it. . . . many years afterwards Mr. Scowen being obliged to sell it . . . it was bot by a Gent of the Law, who lately sold it to Mr. Gideon, the Jew." One of Gideon's descendants married into the Fremantle family, and the painting was owned by the family until it was acquired by the National Gallery.

Collections: Balthazar Gerbier; First Earl of Radnor; Thomas Scowen; Sampson Gideon and descendants; Baron Eardley; Sir Culling Eardley; Mrs. W. H. Fremantle; Colonel F. E. Fremantle; E. V. Fremantle, Esq., Belvedere, Kent. *Andrew W. Mellon Fund*, 1971. Painted 1629–30. Canvas, 64¼ x 70" (165.8 x 177.8 cm.).

Sir Anthony van Dyck

(FLEMISH, 1599–1641)

324   ISABELLA BRANT

In spite of the smiling face of the sitter there is about this portrait an elusive sadness. Isabella Brant was Rubens' first wife. They were married for fifteen years. She was painted by her husband many times, and also by his pupil van Dyck. These portraits reveal the gradual change from a buxom girl to a sick, middle-aged woman. The last of the series may be the portrait reproduced here, which shows a face drawn and pinched by illness, though still with a courageous if somewhat wistful smile. In the background is the ornamental gateway which formed a part of the garden of Rubens' house in Antwerp, an entrance into what was once for Isabella her desirable life. But now her melancholy eyes seem to meditate on something else. Perhaps on the transience of beauty. Rubens seems to have loved her dearly. Shortly after her death he wrote a friend, "Such a loss seems to me worthy of deep grief. I must, no doubt, hope that the daughter of Time, Oblivion, who cures all sorrows, will grant me relief." His hope apparently was granted, for four years later he married the young and beautiful Hélène Fourment, with whom he lived happily the rest of his life.

In the eighteenth century this portrait was in the famous Crozat Collection, where Watteau and many of his contemporaries learned to paint by copying Rubens, van Dyck, and other artists. It was bought subsequently by Catherine the Great for the Hermitage Gallery in Leningrad. For many years this painting was attributed to Rubens, but more recent scholars have ascribed it to van Dyck. They tend to identify it with the picture which Félibien, writing in 1666, says van Dyck gave to his master on leaving his studio, as a token of gratitude.

Collections: Crozat, Paris; Catherine II, Empress of Russia; Hermitage Gallery, Leningrad. *Andrew W. Mellon Collection*, 1937. Painted c. 1621, the year Isabella died. Canvas, 60¼ x 47¼" (153 x 120 cm.).

325

327

326

Antonis Mor was the outstanding portraitist of an international school whose work was based on that of Titian. Since sitters of various nationalities in the sixteenth century wore similar clothes, it is difficult to tell from any portrait whether Mor was executing one of his Flemish, Italian, Portuguese, Spanish, or English commissions. The conventional stiffness of Mor's portraits is seen also in Rubens' earliest work, when he was painting in Italy (see plate 327), but it soon disappeared. *The Portrait of a Man* (plate 330) seems at first glance typical of Rubens' mature style, and the painting was long ascribed to him. With remarkable connoisseurship, Professor Michael Jaffé saw evidence pointing to Jordaens, and subsequent examination in 1969 with infrared light revealed this artist's abbreviated signature. Many Flemish portraits of the time present similar problems of attribution.

325 Antonis Mor (Flemish-Dutch, Probably 1517–1576/77): *Portrait of a Gentleman.* Signed, and dated 1569. Transferred from wood to canvas, 47⅛ x 34¾" (119.7 x 88.3 cm.). Andrew W. Mellon Collection

326 Sir Anthony van Dyck (Flemish, 1599–1641): *Portrait of a Flemish Lady.* 1618/21. Canvas, 48⅜ x 35½" (123 x 90 cm.). Andrew W. Mellon Collection

327 Peter Paul Rubens (Flemish, 1577–1640): *Marchesa Brigida Spinola Doria.* c. 1606. Canvas, 60 x 38⅞" (152.2 x 98.7 cm.). Samuel H. Kress Collection

328 Sir Anthony van Dyck: *Susanna Fourment and Her Daughter.* c. 1620. Canvas, 68 x 46¼" (173 x 117 cm.). Andrew W. Mellon Collection

329 Sir Anthony van Dyck: *Doña Polyxena Spinola Guzmán de Leganés.* Early 1630s. Canvas, 43⅛ x 38⅛" (109.7 x 97 cm.). Samuel H. Kress Collection

330 Jacob Jordaens (Flemish, 1593–1678): *Portrait of a Man.* c. 1624. Wood, 41½ x 29" (105.5 x 73.5 cm.). Ailsa Mellon Bruce Fund

329

328

330

Sir Anthony van Dyck

(FLEMISH, 1599–1641)

331 MARCHESA ELENA GRIMALDI,
WIFE OF MARCHESE NICOLA CATTANEO

Paintings have their vicissitudes, as do human beings. Van Dyck's portrait of the Marchesa Elena Grimaldi has experienced the mutability of fortune. It was probably painted in 1623, when the artist was a young man, still at the height of his vigor. He had left his native Flanders and settled temporarily in Genoa, where he became overnight the fashionable portraitist of the patrician families. There he created on canvas a race of supermen and superwomen, richly dressed, of lofty stature and aloof expression. However, of all the Genoese who sat for him, van Dyck has given to none so dignified, so majestic a pose as to the wife of the Marchese Cattaneo. He has also favored her with perhaps his most brilliant design. How skillfully the parasol is used to heighten still further the Marchesa's tallness, "towering in her pride of place" as she advances across her terrace and casts at the spectator, far below, an appraising glance! This is the ultimate in the grand manner in portraiture.

The failure of their trade and the decline of their independence, however, brought the great families of Genoa close to destitution. English collectors cast covetous eyes on their works of art, and especially on the Marchesa Grimaldi's portrait. Sir David Wilkie in 1828 wrote Sir Robert Peel saying he had heard from his agent that in the palace of Nicola Cattaneo there was a picture of "a Young Lady, with a Black Servant holding a Curious Parasol over her head," which he tried to buy. The family would not sell, but should he try once more? Apparently the later efforts of Wilkie's agent were equally unavailing, for early in this century, when the van Dyck scholar Lionel Cust gained admission to the Cattaneo palace, he was ushered into a room where he halted spellbound. "From every wall, as it seemed, Van Dyck looked down, and on one there stood and gazed at me a haughty dame, over whose head a negro-page held a scarlet parasol. All, however, spoke of dust and neglect, and when I left the palace, it was with a feeling of regret that such treasures of painting should be left to moulder on the walls." Van Dyck's masterworks were not to crumble away much longer; they had in fact reached the nadir of their fortune. A dealer bought all the Cattaneo paintings shortly before World War I, and eventually P. A. B. Widener acquired the most important of the lot, the portrait of the Marchesa Grimaldi and the portraits of her two children (plates 333 and 334). These he gave with the rest of his collection to the nation.

Collection: Palazzo Cattaneo, Genoa. *Widener Collection*, 1942. Painted probably 1623. Canvas, 97 x 68" (246 x 173 cm.).

332

333

334

As a rough generalization van Dyck can be said to have had four periods: his education in Rubens' workshop, c. 1617; his Italian period, spent mostly at Genoa, 1621–27; his second Flemish period, 1628–32; and his English period, 1632 until his death in 1641. The paintings shown here belong to van Dyck's Genoese period. This is generally considered his most creative time. He was in full possession of his immense talent, and, eager to win renown, he poured all his genius into portraying the Genoese nobility.

335

336

Sir Anthony van Dyck (Flemish, 1599–1641)

332 *Paola Adorno, Marchesa Brignole Sale, and Her Son.* c. 1625. Canvas, 74½ x 55" (189.2 x 139.7 cm.). Widener Collection

333 *Clelia Cattaneo, Daughter of Marchesa Elena Grimaldi.* Dated 1623. Canvas, 48⅛ x 33⅛" (122.3 x 84.2 cm.). Widener Collection

334 *Filippo Cattaneo, Son of Marchesa Elena Grimaldi.* Dated 1623. Canvas, 48⅛ x 33⅛" (122.3 x 84.2 cm.). Widener Collection

335 *Giovanni Vincenzo Imperiale.* Dated 1625. Canvas, 50 x 41½" (127 x 105.5 cm.). Widener Collection

336 *Marchesa Balbi.* 1622/27. Canvas, 72 x 48" (183 x 122 cm.). Andrew W. Mellon Collection

337 *The Prefect Raphael Racius.* c. 1625. Canvas, 51⅝ x 41⅝" (131 x 105.5 cm.). Widener Collection

337

263

338

Sir Anthony van Dyck (Flemish, 1599–1641)

338 *Philip, Lord Wharton.* Signed, and dated 1632. Canvas, 52½ x 41⅞″ (133 x 106 cm.). Andrew W. Mellon Collection

339 *Queen Henrietta Maria with Her Dwarf.* Probably 1633. Canvas, 86¼ x 53⅛″ (219.1 x 134.8 cm.). Samuel H. Kress Collection

340 *Henri II de Lorraine, Duc de Guise.* c. 1634. Canvas, 80⅝ x 48⅝″ (204.6 x 123.8 cm.). Gift of Cornelius Vanderbilt Whitney

341 *Lady d'Aubigny.* c. 1638. Canvas, 42 x 33½″ (106.5 x 85 cm.). Widener Collection

342 **Adriaen Hanneman** (Dutch, 1604–1671): *Henry, Duke of Gloucester.* c. 1653. Canvas, 41¼ x 34¼″ (105 x 87 cm.). Andrew W. Mellon Collection

339

340

341

There are seventeen portraits by van Dyck in the collection of the National Gallery of Art. Nowhere in the world can his work be studied more thoroughly. Plates 338-41 belong to the artist's last period. His fame had become so prodigious that he was overwhelmed with commissions; and he relied greatly on well-trained assistants who worked in his studio in England.

342

Frans Hals

(DUTCH, c. 1580–1666)

343   WILLEM COYMANS

Frans Hals is an artist difficult to evaluate. Although it can be said that there is more truth in one of his portraits than in a gallery of portraits by van Dyck, this truth is superficial. We know this young Coymans as we might know someone on shipboard who passes our deck chairs daily but whom we never meet. Was he really as jaunty as all that? Was he proud of his coat of arms, which enables us to identify his family (*koey* means "cow" therefore, *koeymans*, "the cowman")? What was he really like?

The painting is dated 1645, and it has recently been pointed out that the inscription originally gave the sitter's age as 22 (the second digit has since been clumsily altered to a 6). If the subject of the portrait was only twenty-two in 1645, he may well be Willem Coymans, born in 1623; an earlier identification was Balthasar who, born in 1618, would have been older than the originally inscribed age. Whichever young man is represented, he was the scion of a distinguished and prosperous family. Yet Hals has stressed not his wealth and position but his youth and high spirits, and with the tilt of a hat has given him the appearance of a common rake. Was Hals after all an inverted alchemist, transmuting the gold we all believe exists in our personality into its true lead? And was van Dyck the true alchemist, giving his sitters something of the sublimity they sensed in themselves? As Fromentin wrote, van Dyck was "admired everywhere, welcomed everywhere . . . the equal of the greatest lords, the favorite and the friend of kings," whereas Frans Hals died in the poorhouse. Few sitters want truth in portraiture, even a superficial truth.

Van Dyck could flatter and he was an able painter, but he was not a virtuoso like Hals. The pyrotechnics of Hals' brush remain unique. With what genius he controls its swordplay! How far he soars above his disciples, artists like Sargent and Duveneck! Those of us who love painting for its own sake will find more delight in the sleeve and collar of Coymans' shirt than in all the paint-ennobled aristocracy of Sir Anthony van Dyck.

Collections: Coymans family, Haarlem; Mrs. Frederick Wollaston, London; Rodolphe Kann, Paris; Mrs. Collis P. Huntington, New York; Archer E. Huntington, New York. *Andrew W. Mellon Collection,* 1937. Dated 1645. Canvas, 30¼ x 25'' (77 x 64 cm.).

ÆTASVA 28
1645

Frans Hals (Dutch, c. 1580–1666)

344 *Portrait of an Elderly Lady.* Dated 1633. Canvas, 40¼ x 34″ (103 x 86.4 cm.). Andrew W. Mellon Collection

345 *Portrait of an Officer.* c. 1640. Canvas, 33¾ x 27″ (86 x 69 cm.). Andrew W. Mellon Collection

346 *Portrait of a Young Man.* c. 1645. Canvas, 26⅞ x 21⅞″ (68 x 56 cm.). Andrew W. Mellon Collection

347 *Portrait of a Man.* c. 1655/60. Canvas, 25 x 21″ (63.5 x 53.5 cm.). Widener Collection

348 *A Young Man in a Large Hat.* c. 1628/30. Canvas, 11½ x 9⅛″ (29 x 23 cm.). Andrew W. Mellon Collection

349 *Portrait of a Gentleman.* c. 1650/52. Canvas, 45 x 33½″ (114 x 85 cm.). Widener Collection

350 *Portrait of a Man.* c. 1650/52. Canvas, 37 x 29½″ (94 x 75 cm.). Andrew W. Mellon Collection

344

345

346

348

347

350

Frans Hals was one of the first artists in Europe to paint *alla prima* (i.e., directly on the canvas without preliminary underpainting). This rapid technique is the one normally used by modern painters. It is especially adapted to catching momentary expressions and gestures, as one can see in these reproductions. The comment about the superficiality of Hals' interpretation of his sitters in the discussion of *Willem Coymans* (plate 343) must be modified by saying that at the end of his life he showed a far deeper insight into character (see plate 349).

349

Rembrandt van Ryn

(DUTCH, 1606–1669)

351   SELF-PORTRAIT

Rembrandt was a much more profound artist than Frans Hals. Few autobiographies are as searching as his self-portraits. The one reproduced here was signed and dated 1659, ten years before his death. In 1656 he had been declared bankrupt and during the next two years everything he owned was sold. His son and his mistress were shortly to make themselves custodians even of his still-unpainted pictures. Once more he looked in a mirror to take stock of himself, to analyze the problem of his personality. He saw reflected a face lined with age and misfortune. He saw eyes which had searched more profoundly into the human soul than those of any other artist. He saw a mouth and a chin weak, infirm of purpose, manifesting that flaw in his character which had ruined his life. His hands are grasped as though in anguish at the spectacle of a self-ruined man. There exists no painting more pitiless in its analysis or more pitiful in its implications.

Collection: Duke of Buccleuch, London. *Andrew W. Mellon Collection*, 1937. Signed, and dated 1659. Canvas, 33¼ x 26″ (84 x 66 cm.).

352

Rembrandt in his self-portraits does not always reveal his weaknesses. Many reflect the mask he held up before the world. In the *Self-Portrait* of 1650 (plate 354), in spite of reverses he had suffered, he still appears proud, self-confident, challenging. Here one sees the look of the man Saskia van Uilenburgh (see plate 352) married in 1634. Her death seven years later was an affliction which altered Rembrandt's life. Without her practicality and influence, wealth, with its concomitant compromises with the taste of his middle-class patrons, eluded him, but achievement at a far higher level followed.

353

354

355

356

Rembrandt van Ryn   (Dutch, 1606–1669)

352   *Saskia van Uilenburgh, the Wife of the Artist.* Probably 1633. Wood, 23¾ x 19¼" (60.5 x 49 cm.). Widener Collection

353   *A Polish Nobleman.* Signed, and dated 1637. Wood, 38⅛ x 26" (97 x 66 cm.). Andrew W. Mellon Collection

354   *Self-Portrait.* Signed, and dated 1650. Canvas, 36¼ x 29¾" (92 x 75.5 cm.). Widener Collection

355   *A Girl with a Broom.* Signed, and dated 1651. Canvas, 42¼ x 36" (107 x 91 cm.). Andrew W. Mellon Collection

356   *The Philosopher.* c. 1650. Wood, 24¼ x 19½" (61.5 x 49.5 cm.). Widener Collection

357   *A Turk.* c. 1630/35. Canvas, 38¾ x 29⅛" (98 x 74 cm.). Andrew W. Mellon Collection

357

273

Rembrandt van Ryn

(DUTCH, 1606–1669)

358   THE MILL

The Mill is Rembrandt's supreme achievement in landscape painting. It is usually dated about 1650, when he was still at the height of his fame. John Constable judged it "sufficient to form an epoch in the art . . . the first picture in which a sentiment has been expressed by chiaroscuro only, all details being excluded." And this melancholy sentiment, this mood of sublime sadness, which Rembrandt conveys through the stark simplicity of a windmill silhouetted in the fading light against the mist-filled sky, is indescribably moving. As Roger Fry has said, "It is surely the most complete expression of the dramatic mood in landscape that has ever been achieved in Western art."

Probably no single canvas has so strongly affected English painting. Turner admired it, and the notes in his sketchbook show that it was the basis of his conception of Rembrandt's handling of light. Sir Joshua Reynolds painted a free adaptation of it; and it was engraved by Charles Turner for his *Gems of Art*, a book to be found in the studio of nearly every nineteenth-century English painter.

In his autobiography, Peter Widener, the son and grandson of the founders of the collection, says that when Wilhelm von Bode, director of the Kaiser Friedrich Museum and an authority on Rembrandt, came to Lynnewood Hall to see the collection, he sat for half an hour contemplating *The Mill*. Finally he turned to Joseph Widener, who was waiting for his opinion, and said, "This is the greatest picture in the world. The greatest picture by any artist."

*   *   *

The above was written nine years ago for the first edition of this book. Since then the picture has been cleaned. In my opinion, it has gained in colorfulness but has lost in sublimity. The patina of time often adds to the beauty of a work of art, but how this painting looked when Rembrandt finished it we shall never know.

Collections: Duc d'Orléans, Paris; William Smith, London; Marquess of Lansdowne, Bowood Hall, Wiltshire. *Widener Collection*, 1942. Painted c. 1650. Canvas, 34½ x 41½'' (87.5 x 105.5 cm.).

Rembrandt van Ryn

(DUTCH, 1606–1669)

359   PORTRAIT OF A LADY WITH AN OSTRICH-FEATHER FAN

Were I asked to select the greatest portrait of a woman ever painted, my choice would be the *Lady with an Ostrich-Feather Fan*. Like Isabella Brant (plate 324), her looks, once beautiful, seem faded by illness. She is a woman to me infinitely sad and endlessly fascinating. I am always entranced by the simplicity of her pose, by her mood of stillness and serenity, by her seeming acceptance of life with all its richness of experience, its sorrows, and its joys.

What a strange history her portrait was to have. It hung for many years in the Yousupoff Palace, where it looked down on carnivals and balls, on the gaiety of the Ancien Régime under the shadow of the Revolution; even on Rasputin and his murderers—perhaps in the very hall where the great hulking monk himself staggered, bleeding and poisoned. Then, after the Revolution, it was smuggled out of Russia, concealed under an amateurish landscape hastily painted by the fleeing Prince.

Still to come was the adventure of one of the most famous lawsuits in the history of collecting. After having sold the painting and its pendant (plate 360) to Joseph Widener, Prince Yousupoff tried to reclaim them, asserting that they were only the collateral for a loan. His motives are easily explained. Calouste Gulbenkian had offered him the largest price ever paid up to that time for works by Rembrandt. Everything seemingly depended on a telegram from Yousupoff to Widener acknowledging the sale, and this could never be found, though an exhaustive search was made of the Widener offices, their files, and their home, Lynnewood Hall. Without being able to produce the cable, the Widener lawyers nonetheless convinced the jury of its existence and won the suit. When Lynnewood Hall was being dismantled and the works of art shipped to the National Gallery, the missing telegram fell out of an old stud book, which Joseph Widener, many years before, must have been consulting in connection with his racing stable.

Collection: Prince Yousupoff, Leningrad. *Widener Collection*, 1942. Signed; date partially effaced. Painted c. 1660. Canvas, 39⅛ x 32½" (99.5 x 82.5 cm.).

360

361

362

Rembrandt van Ryn (Dutch, 1606–1669)

360 *Portrait of a Gentleman with a Tall Hat and Gloves.* c. 1660. Canvas, 39⅛ x 32½" (99.5 x 82.5 cm.). Widener Collection

361 *A Woman Holding a Pink.* Signed, and dated 1656. Canvas, 40⅜ x 33¾" (103 x 86 cm.). Andrew W. Mellon Collection

362 *An Old Lady with a Book.* Signed, and dated (164)7. Andrew W. Mellon Collection

363 *A Young Man Seated at a Table.* Signed, and dated 1662 (or 1663). Canvas, 43¼ x 35¼" (110 x 90 cm.). Andrew W. Mellon Collection

364 *Portrait of a Man in a Tall Hat.* c. 1662. Canvas, 47¾ x 37" (121 x 94 cm.). Widener Collection

364

363

Plate 360 is the companion piece to plate 359. This unknown gentleman's face is pale and shadowed, the skin almost translucent in contrast to the strong black and white of his garments. All the portraits reproduced here bring out a quality in Rembrandt's art that has been insufficiently stressed; his mastery of volume, of three-dimensional form. The apples in *A Woman Holding a Pink*, for example, are as solid and weighty in their suggestion of specific gravity as any painted by Cézanne. The same feeling for substance is evident throughout Rembrandt's work.

Rembrandt van Ryn

(DUTCH, 1606–1669)

365   JOSEPH ACCUSED BY POTIPHAR'S WIFE

This picture is a calmer, more monumental version of the subject treated in another picture by Rembrandt in the Berlin Museum, which is also dated 1655. Joseph is falsely accused by Phraxanor, the wife of Potiphar, of trying to seduce her. The reverse is actually the case, as the story is told in Genesis 39. The scene was one which Baroque artists delighted in representing. Usually Joseph is shown fleeing from his would-be seductress, who leaps from her bed and grabs at his coat, here shown on the bedpost. But Rembrandt has interpreted the legend at the level of the highest tragedy. The aging beauty, the beautiful youth, the puzzled husband, all seem bemused by passions beyond their comprehension. One senses Rembrandt's deep compassion for each of the actors in this archetypal domestic drama, which has been the subject of many books and poems. Yet in literature there has been nothing to equal Rembrandt's insight and profundity until our own time and Thomas Mann's great novel *Joseph and His Brothers*, for which this seems an illustration. Of the many masterpieces in the collection of Catherine the Great, this painting may have had a special significance for the Empress, for she, like Phraxanor, knew the anguish of love by command.

Collections: Catherine II, Empress of Russia; Hermitage Gallery, Leningrad. *Andrew W. Mellon Collection*, 1937. Signed, and dated 1655. Canvas, 41⅝ x 38½" (106 x 98 cm.).

366

367

Of all the artists who have ever lived, Rembrandt was the greatest illustrator of the Bible. Where in art can one find the tenderness, the yearning faith, and at the same time the troubled puzzlement one sees in the face of Joseph of Arimethea, who grasps the body of Our Lord as He is lowered from the Cross? What painter has expressed pure, intense thought more clearly than Rembrandt does in the face and posture of St. Paul as he meditates on the letter he is about to write to his brothers in Christ? Rembrandt was drawn also to Roman history and legend, to which he brought his unique sense of theater. *Lucretia* (plate 369) would have been the envy of Sarah Bernhardt, or of any great actress, as she totters forward, dagger in hand, seeming to try to push away the dark fate that forces her to choose death over a life of dishonor.

368

369

Rembrandt van Ryn (Dutch, 1606–1669)

366 *The Descent from the Cross.* Signed, and dated 165(1). Canvas, 56¼ x 43¾″ (143 x 111 cm.). Widener Collection

367 *The Circumcision.* Signed, and dated 1661. Canvas, 22¼ x 29½″ (56.5 x 75 cm.). Widener Collection

368 *The Apostle Paul.* Signed. Probably 1657. Canvas, 50¾ x 40⅛″ (129 x 102 cm.). Widener Collection.

369 *Lucretia.* Signed, and dated 1664. Canvas, 47¼ x 39¾″ (120 x 101 cm.). Andrew W. Mellon Collection

370 *Philemon and Baucis.* Signed, and dated 1658. Wood, 21½ x 27″ (54.5 x 68.5 cm.). Widener Collection

370

Gerard ter Borch

(DUTCH, 1617–1681)

371   THE SUITOR'S VISIT

The easel picture, the kind of picture we are accustomed to hang in our homes, flourished in the seventeenth century, especially in Calvinistic Holland. Here a new secular style replaced the timeless dramas of Christian art, which had occupied painters in the past; and instead momentary glimpses of everyday life became the fashion. Of such genre pieces *The Suitor's Visit* is typical. We watch, as though through an open window, the suitor in all his finery forever approaching his pensive fiancée; while her father from behind looks on appraisingly and her sister or friend with self-conscious concentration strums on a theorbo. As sometimes happens in the movies, the film seems to have caught, the actors suddenly to have become immobile. Everyone, even the dog, questions the future which cannot begin while the enchanted stillness lasts. Here is a different kind of timelessness, one described by Goethe when he said to Eckermann, "Every situation—nay, every moment—is of infinite worth; for it is the representative of a whole eternity."

This new search in painting for the permanent in the ephemeral led to a more realistic transcription of appearance. The achievement of this necessitates a careful adjustment of tones and values. In the present picture the figure of the suitor, the friend, and the father are mutually consistent, but the figure of the fiancée is out of key. The highlights on her white dress and coral bodice are too bright to be justified by the apparent illumination of the room. This overemphasis on certain passages, especially of white silk, repeatedly upsets the balance of ter Borch's colors. Yet paradoxically his fame rests on this flaw in the actuality of his scenes, for the popularity of his canvases is due largely to his handling of satin, to his rendering of texture, which, skillful as it is, at the same time affects the reality of his paintings.

Collections: Charles-Auguste-Louis-Joseph, Duc de Morny, Paris; Marqués de Salamanca, Madrid; Adolphe de Rothschild, Paris; Maurice de Rothschild, Paris. *Andrew W. Mellon Collection*, 1937. Painted c. 1658. Canvas, 31½ x 29⅝" (80 x 75 cm.).

372

373

Rembrandt, Hals, and Vermeer tower high above the
other Dutch painters, but there were scores of artists
ready to satisfy the demands of the Dutch burghers for
portraits of themselves, their countryside, and their
way of life. And what a pleasant life it must have been!
Avercamp's skating scene almost makes one long en-
viously for the cold Northern winter; the Flemish artist
David Teniers depicts the festive Twelfth Night feast;
and Metsu shows an amusing and delightful flirtation,
even if it has been temporarily frustrated.

374

375

372 **Hendrick Avercamp** (Dutch, 1585–1634): *A Scene on the Ice*. c. 1625. Wood, 15½ x 30⅜″ (39.3 x 77.1 cm.). Ailsa Mellon Bruce Fund

373 **Gabriel Metsu** (Dutch, 1629–1667): *The Intruder*. Signed. c. 1660. Wood, 26¼ x 23½″ (67 x 60 cm.). Andrew W. Mellon Collection

374 **Nicolas Maes** (Dutch, 1632–1693): *An Old Woman Dozing over a Book*. c. 1655. Canvas, 32⅜ x 26⅜″ (82 x 67 cm.). Andrew W. Mellon Collection

375 **Adriaen van Ostade** (Dutch, 1610–1685): *The Cottage Dooryard*. Signed, and dated 1673. Canvas, 17⅜ x 15⅝″ (44 x 39.5 cm.). Widener Collection

376 **Judith Leyster** (Dutch, c. 1609–1660): *Self-Portrait*. c. 1635. Canvas, 29⅜ x 25⅝″ (72.3 x 65.3 cm.). Gift of Mr. and Mrs. Robert Woods Bliss

377 **David Teniers II** (Flemish, 1610–1690): *Peasants Celebrating Twelfth Night*. Signed, and dated 1635. Wood, 18⅝ x 27½″ (47.2 x 69.9 cm.). Ailsa Mellon Bruce Fund

376

377

Pieter de Hooch

(DUTCH, 1629-c.1683)

378 A DUTCH COURTYARD

Paul Claudel, the French poet, has analyzed with wonderful penetration the charm of Dutch scenes of everyday life such as the picture reproduced here. He points out that these canvases make us conscious of time. "They are the reservoir of evanescent feelings. We do not merely glance at a painting by . . . de Hooch with condescending approval; we are immediately within it, we live there." Thus, as in paintings by Vermeer and ter Borch, we share an ephemeral moment which is given an enchanted permanence.

Beyond the wall of de Hooch's courtyard is the Nieuwe Kerk in Delft. This picture was probably painted, therefore, when during the 1650s and early '60s de Hooch was living in the native city of the greatest of the Dutch genre painters, Jan Vermeer. During several years under the inspiration of Vermeer, he painted, along with his more usual interiors, an occasional scene out-of-doors. In these he catches in a web of almost invisible brushstrokes the texture of crumbling brick and mortar, the undulations of old paving, the gleam of metals, and the transparency of liquids. Masterpieces of a true visual effect, such canvases conjure up a domestic paradise of eternal sun-drenched felicity. The best painters in Holland, with the exception of Rembrandt, were in varying degrees scientific investigators of such images which the eye conveys to the mind. It is significant in this connection that the Dutch are also credited with the practical discovery of both the compound microscope and the telescope, one in 1590 and the other in 1608.

Collections: Possibly Samuel A. Koopman, Utrecht; Baron Lionel Nathan de Rothschild; Alfred Charles de Rothschild; Countess of Carnarvon, Newbury, England. *Andrew W. Mellon Collection*, 1937. Painted c. 1660. Another version, lacking the cavalier holding the beer jug, is in the Mauritshuis, The Hague (formerly Ten Cate Collection). Canvas, 26¾ x 23" (68 x 59 cm.).

289

379

380

381

382

379 Jan Steen (Dutch, c. 1626–1679): *The Dancing Couple.* Signed, and dated 1663. Canvas, 40⅜ x 56⅛″ (102.5 x 142.5 cm.). Widener Collection

380 Paul Potter (Dutch, 1625–1654): *A Farrier's Shop.* Signed, and dated 1648. Wood, 19 x 18″ (48 x 46 cm.). Widener Collection

381 Gerard Dou (Dutch, 1613–1675): *The Hermit.* Signed, and dated 1670. Wood, 18⅛ x 13⅝″ (46 x 34.5 cm.). Timken Collection

382 Pieter de Hooch (Dutch, 1629–c. 1683): *The Bedroom.* c. 1660. Canvas, 20 x 23½″ (51 x 60 cm.). Widener Collection

383 Isack van Ostade (Dutch, 1621–1649): *The Halt at the Inn.* Signed, and dated 1645. Canvas, 19½ x 26″ (49.5 x 66 cm.). Widener Collection

383

Jacob van Ruisdael

(DUTCH, 1628/29–1682)

384 FOREST SCENE

The Dutch landscape, judged by itself, rarely reaches an exalted place in the hierarchy of painting. But from the viewpoint of the development of the representation of nature, it is almost as important to modern art as is Byzantine painting in the history of Christian art. In modern times the desuetude of religious painting has resulted in Christian iconography becoming almost obsolete, and pantheism has supplanted the Church as the energizing force impelling artistic creation. The visualistic basis of Dutch art was a necessary point of departure from which to explore, with complete realism, the different aspects of natural scenery. Thus the Dutch established that iconography of nature which was to be developed in the nineteenth century by many landscapists, especially those associated with Norwich and Barbizon.

This realistic attitude toward nature appears in all the paintings by Ruisdael; but he also tried to convey an emotional response to the scene. In Claude's pictures an emotional reaction to landscape is suggested by a kind of stage scenery; in Ruisdael's canvases nature is shown in its everyday appearance. Claude recalls Vergil; Ruisdael, Wordsworth. One evokes an Arcadian world, conveying to the spectator a corresponding tranquillity of spirit; the other creates a totally different mood, either one of loneliness and foreboding before the tangled darkness of encroaching forests, or one of exaltation at distant vistas of land and water under a cold and sullen sky.

Collection: Sir Hugh Hume Campbell, Berwickshire. *Widener Collection*, 1942. Signed. Painted c. 1660/65. Canvas, 41½ x 51½" (105.5 x 131 cm.).

385

386

The birthplace of nineteenth-century landscape painting is seventeenth-century Holland. Hobbema, for example, anticipates Constable's love of a particular locality. He satisfied the tastes of his middle-class patrons who wanted portraits of the types of scenes they saw every day as they walked through the countryside. Like Joos de Momper's fanciful grotto from the early part of the century, Hobbema's compositions were painted in his studio, and not from life. Similarly, van der Heyden's *Architectural Fantasy* (plate 387) depicts an ideal château, neither too big nor too elaborate for our modern taste.

388

387

389

390

391

385 **Jacob van Ruisdael** (Dutch, 1628/29–1682): *Park with a Country House.* Signed. c. 1680. Canvas, 30 x 38⅜″ (76.3 x 97.5 cm.). Gift of Rupert L. Joseph

386 **Meindert Hobbema** (Dutch, 1638–1709): *Hut Among Trees.* Signed. c. 1665. Canvas, 38 x 42½″ (96.5 x 108 cm.). Widener Collection

387 **Jan van der Heyden** (Dutch, 1637–1712): *An Architectural Fantasy.* c. 1670. Wood, 19½ x 27¾″ (49.6 x 70.5 cm.). Ailsa Mellon Bruce Fund

388 **Joos de Momper II** (Flemish, 1564–1635): *Vista from a Grotto.* c. 1625. Wood, 20 x 20⅜″ (50.9 x 51.7 cm.). Ailsa Mellon Bruce Fund

389 **Meindert Hobbema:** *A Farm in the Sunlight.* 1660/70. Canvas, 32 x 25⅞″ (81 x 66 cm.). Andrew W. Mellon Collection

390 **Meindert Hobbema:** *A Wooded Landscape.* Signed, and dated 1663. Canvas, 37½ x 51⅜″ (95 x 130 cm.). Andrew W. Mellon Collection

391 **Meindert Hobbema:** *A View on a High Road.* Signed, and dated 1665. Canvas, 36¾ x 50½″ (93 x 128 cm.). Andrew W. Mellon Collection

295

392

The transition in Holland from land to water is so frequent that many of the landscape painters also painted seascapes and, on the whole, more satisfactorily. Seascapes, unlike forest scenes, did not encourage over-elaborate detail, and the Dutch painters instinctively hit on a successful notation for the choppy waves of their inland seas.

Cuyp's animal paintings are rarely the equal of his lesser-known pictures of the Dutch estuaries, such as the painting reproduced here, where reflected color and a broadly handled detail combine to create a masterpiece of visual truth. The aim of such paintings is portraiture, the exact appearance of the Dutch harbors filled with shipping and men-of-war. To criticize painters like Aelbert Cuyp, Jan van Goyen, and Willem van de Velde because the calmer aspect of the sea is almost invariably shown is to mistake their purpose, for portraiture presupposes that the object portrayed will remain relatively still. Moreover the Dutch wanted pleasant scenes, not shipwrecks and storms at sea. Such tragedies were more popular with the French and Italians, people less dependent than the Dutch on successful navigation.

Cuyp's painting probably represents an event that occurred during the summer of 1646. At that time, an enormous fleet of ships carrying thirty thousand soldiers was anchored at Dordrecht. The fleet seems to have been brought together for symbolic reasons, for peace was finally at hand. The Treaty of Münster, which ended all hostilities with Spain, was signed only two years later.

393

392 Aelbert Cuyp (Dutch, 1620–1691): *The Maas at Dordrecht.* Signed. c. 1650. Canvas, 45¼ x 67″ (115 x 170 cm.). Andrew W. Mellon Collection

393 Jan van Goyen (Dutch, 1596–1656): *View of Dordrecht from the Dordtse Kil.* Signed, and dated 1644. Wood, 25½ x 37¾″ (64.7 x 95.9 cm.). Ailsa Mellon Bruce Fund

394

395

396

Of all Dutch painters Cuyp is closest to the nineteenth-century landscapists. His preoccupation was theirs—the evanescence of light. His study of this phenomenon, however, is concentrated on a single form of illumination, on sunset and the golden mist of summer. The beams of the setting sun almost always flood his pastoral scenes, which are characterized by low horizon lines and figures silhouetted against the sky. J.M.W. Turner learned from such landscapes, and in *Mortlake Terrace* (plate 583) he shows his mastery of the atmospheric effect which was Cuyp's speciality.

394   Pieter Jansz. Saenredam (Dutch, 1597–1665): *Church of Santa Maria della Febbre, Rome.* Signed, and dated 1629. Wood, 14⅞ x 27¾″ (37.8 x 70.5 cm.). Samuel H. Kress Collection

395   Pieter Jansz. Saenredam: *Cathedral of Saint John at 's-Hertogenbosch.* Signed, and dated 1646. Wood, 50⅝ x 34¼″ (128.8 x 87 cm.). Samuel H. Kress Collection

396   Aelbert Cuyp (Dutch, 1620–1691): *Herdsmen Tending Cattle.* Signed. c. 1650. Canvas, 26 x 34½″ (66 x 88 cm.). Andrew W. Mellon Collection

397   Aelbert Cuyp: *Lady and Gentleman on Horseback.* Signed. c. 1660. Canvas, 48½ x 67¾″ (123 x 172 cm.). Widener Collection

398   Aelbert Cuyp: *Horsemen and Herdsmen with Cattle.* Signed. c. 1660/70. Canvas, 47⅜ x 67½″ (120 x 171.5 cm.). Widener Collection

397

398

299

Jan Vermeer

(DUTCH, 1632–1675)

399   A LADY WRITING

Vermeer is now acclaimed one of the greatest artists who ever lived. A hundred years ago he was almost unknown, and he still remains among the most mysterious figures in the history of art. We have no letters, no diary, not a single line written by him. During his lifetime he is briefly mentioned in print only three times: first, in a poem saying he was a phoenix who rose from the ashes of Carel Fabritius, a fellow painter blown to bits by an explosion in Delft; a second time, in which only his name occurs; and a third mention in the diary of a French collector to whom he refused to show his paintings.

We do know, however, that he lived all his life in Delft, that he was a picture dealer, and that on one occasion he was called in as an expert to appraise some Italian paintings, which he said were rubbish. In 1652 he became a master and thus acquired the right to sell his own work. But amazingly he seems to have sold almost nothing. Paintings generally accepted as by him number fewer than forty, and of these it is thought that he still owned twenty-nine at the time of his death.

Vermeer must have painted slowly and painstakingly, completing only two or three pictures a year. His wife or one of his eleven children were his usual models. When he died he was deeply in debt, especially for food, which he must have needed for his hungry offspring.

Why, plagued with debt, was he so reluctant to part with his own work? There were certainly buyers for his pictures, for his style was not so original that collectors could not appreciate it. He painted like many of his contemporaries, only much better. Yet when a potential purchaser, Balthazar de Monconys, came all the way to Delft in 1663 to see him, he refused to show him anything. De Monconys relates how, after this rebuff, he was taken to a bakery where he saw a canvas with a single figure priced at three hundred florins, the same amount Dou, one of the most popular of Dutch painters, would customarily receive. There is reason to think that even this picture Vermeer had not sold but that the baker was holding it as collateral for debts.

Collections: Dr. Luchtmans, Rotterdam; J. Kamermans, Rotterdam; Count F. de Robiano, Brussels; J. Pierpont Morgan; Sir Harry Oakes. *Gift of Harry Waldron Havemeyer and Horace Havemeyer, Jr., in memory of their father, Horace Havemeyer, 1962.* Signed. Painted c. 1665. Canvas, 17¾ x 15¾" (45 x 39.9 cm.).

301

Jan Vermeer

(DUTCH, 1632–1675)

400   WOMAN HOLDING A BALANCE

Jan Vermeer of Delft was a master of stillness, of those moments of life when all action has ceased, held by an ephemeral adjustment of forces. This canvas conveys a sense of dynamic quiescence; it is in fact an allegory of balances. The unmoving figure weighing gold balances in her scales her earthly treasure, while Christ, in the Last Judgment in the background, in His divine knowledge weighs human guilt. The woman is absorbed, wrapped in the serene and mysterious thought of approaching maternity; and her pregnant body half concealing the painting hung behind her suggests a further equation, as though, as in Santayana's phrase, "The truth of life could be seen only in the shadow of death; living and dying were simultaneous and inseparable."

Such symbolic profundity is rare among Dutch painters of the seventeenth century and only intermittent in Vermeer's own work. The quality for which his paintings are always distinguished is form rather than content. For Vermeer among all Dutch artists is unrivaled in his mastery of optical reality. In his paintings just so much detail is included as can be seen from a normal distance, not by focusing the eye successively on different objects, or in an instant of time, but with a steady gaze. Similarly in his treatment of tone relations, there is a perfect consistency with what we actually see. No other painter has been able to maintain such subtle distinctions of color in different planes of light, or to extend this organization of tone into such depths of shadow.

Symmetry and balance in design, consistent selection of detail, proportional organization of tone relations, these are difficult to achieve, and Vermeer must have labored long and hard over each painting. Recently a Dutchman, van Meegeren, painted a series of religious pictures in the manner of Vermeer; but of these forgeries only one, *Supper at Emmaus*, is worthy of exhibition. The rest are so poor in quality that nothing but the chaos of the years of World War II could explain their temporary success. For Vermeer's mastery of optical truth cannot be imitated by the forger and is lost to some extent in the most faithful color reproduction.

Collections: Possibly in the collection of Jac. Abrahamsz. Dissius, Amsterdam; Nieuhof, Amsterdam; van der Bogaerd, Amsterdam; King of Bavaria, Munich; Duke of Caraman, Vienna and Paris; Casimir Périer; Comtesse de Ségur (née Périer) Paris. *Widener Collection*, 1942. Painted c. 1664. Canvas, 16¾ x 15" (42.5 x 38 cm.).

Jan Vermeer

(DUTCH, 1632–1675)

402 THE GIRL WITH A RED HAT

401 Circle of Jan Vermeer (Dutch, late XVI century): *Young Girl with a Flute.* c. 1665/67. Wood, 7⅞ x 7" (20 x 18 cm.). Widener Collection

Of the pictures now attributed to Vermeer, one of the most beautiful is *The Girl with a Red Hat*. It hangs in the National Gallery with a puzzlingly similar work, *Young Girl with a Flute*, possibly painted in Vermeer's workshop. Both pictures are on wooden panels, and the same tapestried background and the same chair appear in each. They went separate ways in the seventeenth century, only to be reunited in the twentieth when Andrew Mellon gave one to the National Gallery and Joseph Widener gave the other.

The Girl with a Red Hat is a superb example of Vermeer's characteristic technique. Here one sees clearly how much more vitreous the surface is than in other Dutch paintings, with the pigments seemingly fused in a glassy medium. It has been suggested that this is the result of painting from images reflected in a mirror. But there is another possible explanation. Delft, where Vermeer worked, was closely in contact with the Orient because of its famous china. The paintings on Chinese porcelains have a vitreous look, and craftsmen in Delft studied how to imitate this effect. Is it not possible that Vermeer was seeking to achieve on wood and canvas something of the surface texture of Chinese porcelain painting? The only other artist, so far as I know, who gained a similar effect in his pictures is the English painter George Stubbs. And we know Stubbs worked for a famous porcelain manufacturer, Josiah Wedgwood. This may be a coincidence, but if not, it would seem to throw some light on the mystery of Vermeer's technical method.

Collections: [Lafontaine] sale, Paris, 1822; General Baron Althalin, Colmar; Baron Laurant Althalin. *Andrew W. Mellon Collection*, 1937. Painted c. 1665/67. Wood, 9⅛ x 7⅛" (23 x 18 cm.).

403

403 Jan Davidsz. de Heem (Dutch, 1606–1683/84): *Vase of Flowers.* Signed, c. 1645. Canvas, 27⅜ x 22¼" (69.6 x 56.5 cm.). Andrew W. Mellon Fund

404 Willem Kalf (Dutch, 1622–1693): *Still Life.* c. 1665. Canvas, 25⅜ x 21¼" (64.5 x 54 cm.). Gift of Chester Dale

405 Willem van Aelst (Dutch, 1627–1683): *Still Life with Dead Game.* Signed, and dated 1661. Canvas, 33⅜ x 26½" (84.7 x 67.3 cm.). Pepita Milmore Memorial Fund

If one were to choose a single picture to summarize the achievement of Dutch and Flemish flower painters, it might well be de Heem's *Vase of Flowers* (plate 403). Executed at the apogee of seventeenth-century still-life painting, it combines the strength of earlier work with added elegance and technical virtuosity. Such still lifes were not only decorative; they were also symbolic. Decay is indicated by the broken wheat stalk and the fallen poppy, which symbolize the vanity and transitoriness of life on earth. For the Dutch, flowers, particularly cut flowers, with the morning dew still clinging to them, epitomized the evanescent.

404

405

French &

Italian Schools

XVII AND XVIII CENTURY

Georges de La Tour

(FRENCH, 1593–1652)

406 THE REPENTANT MAGDALEN

Jan Vermeer and Georges de La Tour were born only a generation apart. Although of different nationalities, they had much in common. For several centuries both virtually disappeared as artists and existed only as names in obscure archives. Both were finally resurrected by modern art historians. Their pictures also are equally rare—we can find fewer than forty by either, a meager number by comparison with the oeuvre of other painters. But their most significant resemblance is their preoccupation with the realistic rendering of light: Vermeer with the appearance of daylight; La Tour, more and more, with the effects of chiaroscuro and the diffusion of artificial illumination.

To discover those few pictures which can be ascribed to La Tour has been relatively simple, because a number are signed and the rest stamped with a distinctive style, but to unearth biographical material has proved nearly impossible. We know he was born at Vic-sur-Seille, a village about twenty kilometers from Nancy, and spent most of his life in Lunéville in the Duchy of Lorraine. In 1639, when the Duchy was absorbed by France, he was named *peintre du roi*, a high honor. For stylistic reasons it seems likely that he went to Rome and saw the work of Caravaggio and his followers. These *tenebristi*, as they were called, may have turned his attention to night scenes with their strong contrasts of light and shadow. He could, however, have learned the same lesson in Holland from Caravaggio's Northern disciple, Gerard Honthorst. His travels outside France, if they exist, are purely conjectural.

But wherever he journeyed, though he would have seen many penitent Magdalens, none would have been as beautiful as those he was to paint in Lunéville. For him this subject, which he treated at least four times, may have had some special significance. But it was in any case a popular scene, one greatly encouraged by the Church, which during the Counter Reformation emphasized penance and absolution in contrast to the Calvinistic doctrine of predestination.

Is there really forgiveness, the young girl's eyes seem to ask as they stare introspectively beyond the mirror with its reflection of the skull? Her sensitive fingers caress the brain's empty case, while the concentrated power of her thought seems a kinetic force, which, like a current of air, bends the candle flame, the only source of light. Few paintings exist of greater psychological and spiritual intensity.

Collections: Marquise de Caulaincourt; her sister, Comtesse d'Andigné: André Fabius, Paris. *Ailsa Mellon Bruce Fund*, 1974. Painted c. 1640. Canvas, 44½ x 36½" (113 x 92.7 cm.).

Claude Lorrain

(FRENCH, 1600–1682)

407   THE JUDGMENT OF PARIS

Unknown masterpieces still come to light. One day in 1966 a lady brought to Sotheby's, the London auction house, a dirty painting which she believed to be by the eighteenth-century English landscapist Richard Wilson. It was destined for a small sale, an unillustrated item in the catalogue, when one of the Sotheby partners noticed barely visible sheep in the foreground and realized that they looked like the sheep Claude often drew. The auctioneers, uncertain whether they were selling a copy, called in Marcel Röthlisberger, the greatest living authority on Claude Lorrain. With remarkable perspicacity he recognized under yellowed varnish and accumulated grime the touch of the master. When the landscape was sold, instead of a few thousand dollars it brought $480,000. The lady was indeed fortunate, and so was the dealer who bought the painting, for though its condition was scarcely discernible, when cleaned it proved to be excellently preserved.

It is, as Röthlisberger has said, "one of the most beautiful examples of classical landscape." Reproduced in Claude's *Liber Veritatis*, the book of drawings he made to authenticate his oeuvre, it contains figures larger than those of any other painting by him of like dimensions. They are considered entirely autograph, which cannot be said of the figures in many of his canvases, for in the words of Baldinucci, a contemporary, "he took no displeasure in having the figures in his landscapes or sea pieces added by another hand."

But it is not the figures, fine as these are, which entrance the viewer of this glorious landscape. It is the vista enframed on the right by one of the most magnificent trees Claude ever painted and balanced on the left by a steep, shadowy embankment. Here, in the far distance and in the middle ground, Claude enchants us, entraps our spirit in his Arcadian world. From the sweep of space in his paintings, from the way the eye glides to distant mountains and headlands, clear in shape but impalpable in substance, comes a curious psychological release, which both Dostoevski and Nietzsche have noted—an emotion difficult to describe but one which makes Claude, for some of us, the most satisfactory of all landscape painters.

Collections: Probably Marquis de Fontenay, Rome; recorded at auction sales in Paris, 1748, and London, 1819 and 1820; Miss V. Price, London. *Ailsa Mellon Bruce Fund*, 1969. Painted 1645/46. Canvas, 44¼ x 58⅞" (112 x 149.5 cm.).

408

Contemporary biographers state that Annibale Carracci painted and sketched landscapes for his own amusement and as a form of relaxation from the arduous work of filling his many commissions for figure painting. It was not until the time of Claude, who was familiar with Annibale's rare landscapes, that connoisseurs accepted and valued pictures of classical scenery. Nevertheless, except in Holland, landscapists held an inferior place in the hierarchy of artists until well into the nineteenth century.

409

410

411

408 **Simon Vouet** (French, 1590–1649): *The Muses Urania and Calliope.* c. 1634. Wood, 31⅛ x 49⅜" (79.8 x 125 cm.). Samuel H. Kress Collection

409 **Simon Vouet:** *Saint Jerome and the Angel.* c. 1625. Canvas, 57 x 70¾" (144.8 x 179.8 cm.). Samuel H. Kress Collection

410 **Annibale Carracci** (Bolognese, 1560–1609): *Landscape.* Probably c. 1590. Canvas, 34¾ x 58¼" (88.5 x 148.2 cm.). Samuel H. Kress Collection

411 **Annibale Carracci:** *Venus Adorned by the Graces.* c. 1595. Transferred from wood to canvas, 52⅜ x 67⅛" (133 x 170.6 cm.). Samuel H. Kress Collection

412 **Claude Lorrain** (French, 1600–1682): *Landscape with Merchants.* Signed. c. 1630. Canvas, 38¼ x 56½" (97.2 x 143.6 cm.). Samuel H. Kress Collection

413 **Nicolas Poussin** (French, 1594–1665): *Holy Family on the Steps.* 1648. Canvas, 27 x 38½" (68.6 x 97.8 cm.). Samuel H. Kress Collection

412

413

Nicolas Poussin

(FRENCH, 1594–1665)

414   THE ASSUMPTION OF THE VIRGIN

This early work by Poussin is dependent on the past and predicts the future. On the one hand, it is strongly influenced by several paintings done a century earlier: Titian's *Assumption of the Virgin* and his Pesaro Altarpiece, both in the Church of the Frari in Venice, and his *Venus Worship*, now in the Prado but at that time in the Villa Aldobrandini in Frascati. On the other hand, it anticipates the freedom of brushwork and general exuberance which characterize the French Rococo. There are passages, especially in the painting of the chubby, rosy children, which might have been done by Fragonard.

It is difficult to imagine a more joyous Assumption than this. Three cherubs fill Our Lady's grave with flowers to take the place of her risen body. Accompanied aloft by swarms of other children who need no wings for their levitation, she looks upward in ecstasy while two of her entourage pull back the clouds as though they were draperies concealing Heaven. Poussin has achieved a miracle of movement, of twisting, turning *putti* that lead the eye toward a divine vision kept just out of sight. All this turbulence is controlled in turn by the verticals of two stately columns enframing the central scene and by the horizontals of the geometric sarcophagus in the foreground.

Such superb compositions are not easily arrived at. Poussin planned them carefully, often attaining his final design by placing on a miniature stage small figures which he moved around until he achieved the perfect balance of thrust and counterthrust. His intellectual approach to painting has made his work an inspiration to some of the best painters of our time. Picasso was greatly influenced by him, and the Cubists adopted many of his ideas on art, especially his emphasis on harmony, clarity, and, above all, reason.

But there is another side of Poussin as well. He could convey the sensuality of Titian and the great Venetians, a tradition continued in the eighteenth century in the work of Watteau, Fragonard, Boucher, and others, and in the nineteenth century in many artists from Delacroix to Renoir. It is an oversimplification to see the French School as a constant battle between the advocates of Rubens and the supporters of Raphael. Many of the greatest French artists, like Poussin, combined the richness of color and the fluency of brushwork of the one and the probity of draftsmanship and firmness of design of the other.

Collections: Marchese Vincenzo Giustiniani, Palazzo Giustiniani, Rome, by 1638; Conte Niccolò Soderini, Rome, by 1750; Marquis of Exeter, Burghley House, at least as early as 1794, where it is said to have come from the Palazzo Soderini, Rome. *Ailsa Mellon Bruce Fund,* 1963. Painted c. 1626. Canvas, 52⅞ x 38⅝" (134.4 x 97.8 cm.).

315

415

416

417

Lodovico Carracci, with other members of his family, helped to found in Bologna the most celebrated Academy in Europe. The style taught was an amalgam of Classicism and the painting of the High Renaissance. Sébastien Bourdon was one of the founding members of the French Academy, established a little later. French artists were instructed to paint with precision, detachment, and logic. *Omer Talon* by Philippe de Champagne (plate 420) shows the dignified and impressive treatment required in official portraits.

419

415 **Lodovico Carracci** (Bolognese, 1555–1619): *The Dream of St. Catherine of Alexandria.* c. 1590. Canvas, 54⅝ x 43½" (138.8 x 110.5 cm.). Samuel H. Kress Collection

416 **Nicolas Poussin** (French, 1594–1665): *The Feeding of the Child Jupiter.* c. 1640. Canvas, 46⅛ x 61⅛" (117.4 x 155.3 cm.). Samuel H. Kress Collection

417 **Nicolas Poussin**: *The Baptism of Christ.* 1641/42. Canvas, 37⅝ x 47⅝" (95.5 x 121 cm.). Samuel H. Kress Collection

418 **Sébastien Bourdon** (French, 1616–1671): *Countess Ebba Sparre.* Probably 1653. Canvas, 41¾ x 35½" (106.1 x 90.2 cm.). Samuel H. Kress Collection

419 **Sébastien Bourdon**: *The Finding of Moses.* Probably c. 1650. Canvas, 47 x 68" (119.6 x 172.8 cm.). Samuel H. Kress Collection

420 **Philippe de Champagne** (French, 1602–1674): *Omer Talon.* Signed, and dated 1649. Canvas, 88½ x 63⅝" (225 x 161.6 cm.). Samuel H. Kress Collection

418

420

Louis Le Nain

(FRENCH, c. 1593-1648)

421   LANDSCAPE WITH PEASANTS

Louis Le Nain has caught the exact tone of that gray wintry light so characteristic of the countryside near the Belgian border. This feeling for a particular place gives his picture a modern quality. The painting reproduced here also resembles, in the seemingly informal yet carefully staged arrangement of isolated figures, the work of certain twentieth-century Neo-Romantic artists, like Eugene Berman.

The three Le Nain brothers, all painters, were apparently trained by a Dutch artist. Their work represented a reaction against the academic style, fundamental to which was heroic subject matter. Poussin seems to have had the Le Nains in mind when he said, "Those who elect mean subjects take refuge in them because of the weakness of their talents." It is evident that the Le Nain brothers were disliked by the official court painters led by Poussin, who were occupied with religious themes or scenes of history or mythology. But there was a demand among middle-class patrons for glimpses of rural life, a demand which the three brothers helped satisfy with the canvases they exhibited and sold at popular fairs, such as those at St. Germain-des-Prés.

In the eighteenth century the same interest in everyday life appears in the work of Chardin, a style totally different from the art popular at the French court. This difference becomes especially evident when the picture reproduced here is contrasted with those by Boucher (plates 443–47, 449). A painting by Le Nain is also reproduced in plate 423, beside one by Chardin, to show the continuity of this French tradition of unadorned realism.

This picture is the canvas listed in an exhibition catalogue of 1829, in which it is said to be by "Le Nain, a favourite of Gainsborough and was twice in his collection." The sweep of landscape, with its strongly emphasized receding planes, was exactly what Gainsborough sought in his early work, usually thought to be entirely under Dutch influence. Actually this continual recession, neither interrupted by detail nor broken up by bands of light and shade, is rare in Dutch art; and Gainsborough in his handling of distance in landscape seems also to owe a debt to France, which should not be ignored.

Collections: Thomas Gainsborough, London; Dr. Didbin; Joseph Neeld, London; Sir Audley Neeld, Chippenham, Wiltshire. *Samuel H. Kress Collection*, 1946. Painted c. 1640. Canvas, 18⅜ x 22½" (46.5 x 57 cm.).

Jean-Baptiste-Siméon Chardin

(FRENCH, 1699–1779)

422   THE ATTENTIVE NURSE

Chardin was the favorite painter of Diderot, whereas Boucher was the favorite, as we shall see, of Mme de Pompadour. The editor of the Encyclopedia had different taste from that popular at Versailles. He wished to see on canvas the virtues of domesticity rather than the enticements of femininity. In the long run, however, feminine charm is more tedious than domestic virtue, especially when this virtue is interpreted by Chardin's brush, which gilds with poetic light the everyday life of the middle class in eighteenth-century France.

For it was Chardin's talent to find plastic poetry in a bowl of fruit, a blue-and-white pitcher, or a nurse preparing a meal for her convalescent patient. In the picture reproduced here the painter conveys, with his exquisite sensibility, emotions of love and tenderness, sincere feelings springing from the charity in his heart but difficult to express without banality and triteness. Nothing could be further from the sometimes delicious and always glittering artificiality preferred at Versailles. Chardin was a product of Paris—the city of merchants and bankers, of traders and shopkeepers, of encyclopedists and bluestockings. His art is an affirmation of their independently developed taste, which at its best has a great appeal. But it was also a taste in which was latent that germ of sentimentality which a hundred years later became a plague that almost destroyed French painting.

Chardin's canvases also had considerable charm for the aristocracy. *The Attentive Nurse* was purchased from the artist by the Prince of Liechtenstein when he was Austrian Ambassador to France. It was one of the few works by Chardin that were not engraved before being sold, and it has been assumed that the Prince was so enamored of the picture, when it was displayed in the Salon of 1747, that he took it immediately to Vienna. Apart from a sketch which was probably the basis for Jules de Goncourt's etching, there are no other versions, which is unusual in Chardin's genre compositions of this type.

Collections: The Princes of Liechtenstein. *Samuel H. Kress Collection*, 1952. Signed. Painted probably 1738, the date which appears on its pendant, *The Governess*, in the National Gallery of Canada, Ottawa. Canvas, 18⅛ x 14½″ (46.2 x 37 cm.).

423

A painting by Louis Le Nain is included with those of Chardin, who was born a century later, to show how a tradition of Realism continued in French painting. In spite of the dominance in the Academy of the Classicists, the new middle class was not interested in reminders of spiritual values and the glorious pages of history. They wanted instead the subjects Chardin provided: a girl being instructed, a child playing cards, a glimpse of a kitchen, scenes of everyday life with which they were familiar. Through the purity and beauty of his handling of the paintbrush, Chardin transforms these commonplace subjects into enduring works of art.

425

424

426

427

423 Louis Le Nain (French, c. 1593–1648): *A French Interior*. c. 1645. Canvas, 21⅞ x 25⅜″ (55.6 x 64.7 cm.). Samuel H. Kress Collection

424 Jean-Baptiste-Siméon Chardin (French, 1699–1779): *The House of Cards*. Signed. c. 1735. Canvas, 32⅜ x 26″ (82 x 66 cm.). Andrew W. Mellon Collection

425 Jean-Baptiste-Siméon Chardin: *The Kitchen Maid*. Signed, and dated 1738. Canvas, 18⅛ x 14¾″ (46.2 x 37.5 cm.). Samuel H. Kress Collection

426 Jean-Baptiste-Siméon Chardin: *The Young Governess*. Signed. c. 1739. Canvas, 22⅞ x 29⅛″ (58.3 x 74 cm.). Andrew W. Mellon Collection

427 Jean-Baptiste-Siméon Chardin: *Soap Bubbles*. Signed. c. 1745. Canvas, 36⅝ x 29⅜″ (93 x 74.6 cm.). Gift of Mrs. John W. Simpson

428 Jean-Baptiste-Siméon Chardin: *Still Life*. Signed. c. 1760/65. Canvas, 19½ x 23⅜″ (49.6 x 59.4 cm.). Samuel H. Kress Collection

428

Nicolas de Largillière

(FRENCH, 1656–1746)

429   ELIZABETH THROCKMORTON

Nicolas de Largillière, who lived to be ninety, was the John Singer Sargent of the age of Louis XIV. Everyone in society wanted to be painted by him. As a young man he had traveled to London to become a pupil of Lely, and while there attracted the attention of Charles II, who wished to keep him in his service. But the anti-Catholic feeling in England was so strong that he feared for his life and returned to Paris, where he spent his remaining years except for a short stay in England during the reign of James II.

While in London he had come to know the Catholic families who under Charles II and James II had enjoyed a brief respite from their disabilities. Among these families were the Throckmortons, staunch supporters of the Pope and the Stuarts. Like other recusants, numerous Throckmortons resided in France. The ladies of the family were almost invariably educated in Paris and usually by the Blue Nuns, whose Reverend Mother, Anne Throckmorton, was Elizabeth's aunt. Letters are preserved from Anne to her brother in London telling about the childhood of Elizabeth, who seems to have been very delicate and to have recovered with difficulty from smallpox. Her aunt was of sufficient distinction to be able to take her niece to tea with the royal children at Versailles, the summit of social prestige.

In 1714, at the age of twenty, Elizabeth took vows in the convent of the Augustinian Blue Sisters. She was elected Mother Superior twice, from 1736 to 1744 and from 1752 to 1760. Because of her delicate health, however, she was released from many of the austerities of the Order.

Neither the scars of smallpox nor later signs of ill health appear in Largillière's portrait. He has shown a ravishingly attractive nun whose radiant beauty, had she not spent her life in a convent, might have brought her, in those dissolute days, many lovers. When she was painted, according to an inscription on the back of the canvas, she was thirty-five years of age. Looking at her one realizes that life in a convent must have preserved feminine beauty more successfully than any method devised in the secular world. Little wonder that in the eighteenth century men often fell in love with nuns.

Collections: Family of the sitter, Coughton Court, Warwickshire. *Ailsa Mellon Bruce Fund*, 1964. Painted 1729. Canvas, 32 x 25⅞" (81.3 x 65.7 cm.).

ELIZABETH DAUGHTER OF S^R ROB^T THROCKMORTON BAR^T.

325

430

432

431

430 **Maurice-Quentin de La Tour** (French, 1704–1788): *Claude Dupouch*. Probably 1739. Pastel on paper, 23⅜ x 19⅜″ (59.4 x 49.4 cm.). Samuel H. Kress Collection

431 **Jean-Marc Nattier** (French, 1685–1766): *Joseph Bonnier de la Mosson*. Signed, and dated 1745. Canvas, 54¼ x 41½″ (137.9 x 105.4 cm.). Samuel H. Kress Collection

432 **Nicolas de Largillière** (French, 1656–1746): *A Young Man with His Tutor*. Signed, and dated 1685. Canvas, 57½ x 45⅛″ (146 x 114.8 cm.). Samuel H. Kress Collection

433 **François-Hubert Drouais** (French, 1727–1775): *Group Portrait*. Signed, and dated *ce. 1 avril. 1756.* Canvas, 96 x 76⅝″ (244 x 195 cm.). Samuel H. Kress Collection

434 **Attributed to François-Hubert Drouais**: *Marquis d'Ossun*. Probably 1762. Canvas, 85⅞ x 64⅝″ (218 x 164.1 cm.). Gift of Mrs. Albert J. Beveridge in memory of her aunt Delia Spencer Field

435 **Hubert Drouais** (French, 1699–1767): *Portrait of a Lady*. c. 1750. Canvas, 46½ x 37½″ (118 x 95 cm.). Gift of Chester Dale

French eighteenth-century portraitists were subtle analysts of character, much more so than their English contemporaries. One of the most percipient representations in art of upper-class family life is Drouais' *Group Portrait* (plate 433). The father leans forward tenderly and smiles equivocally. He doubtless has a mistress, but his wife's complacency makes one imagine that he might also be a cuckold. Only the child seems innocent, and this condition, one feels, will not last long. The painting is appropriately inscribed "First of April 1756"—April Fools' Day!

434

433

435

Antoine Watteau

(FRENCH, 1684–1721)

436   CERES (SUMMER)

Born in Valenciennes, a part of Flanders then recently acquired by France, Watteau during his brief life established French Rococo painting. *Ceres*, or *An Allegory of Summer*, shows the characteristics of this new style: its essential derivation from Rubens and the Venetians, in this case Paolo Veronese; its slighter rhythms and more delicate phrasing; and its somewhat enervated sensuality. In Watteau's work, however, the inevitable animation and somewhat affected charm of the Rococo is kept from monotony by an overtone of sadness, autumnal and pensive.

Watteau came to Paris at the age of eighteen. For a time he produced religious and popular pictures. Finally he gained access to the Louvre, where he scrutinized the paintings by Rubens in the Maria de' Medici Gallery. But, much more important, he was invited to live with Pierre Crozat, the greatest collector in France, whose drawings and paintings by Raphael, Rubens, van Dyck, Giorgione, Titian, and Veronese he was able to study. These were the artists who formed his style and taught him what he could never have learned from his contemporaries. Among the paintings he must have seen were Raphael's *St. George and the Dragon* (plate 190) and van Dyck's *Isabella Brant* (plate 324).

It was while he was living in the Crozat palace in the Rue de Richelieu that his patron asked him to decorate his dining room with allegories of the Four Seasons, one of which is the painting reproduced here. These he completed sometime between 1712 and 1716.

When Crozat died, his palace was inherited through his great-niece by the Duc de Choiseul, the most powerful man in France. Choiseul ran through his fortune, however, and on his death in 1786 his property was sold to pay his immense debts. The National Gallery painting and the *Allegory of Winter* were in the sale. The other two, *Spring* and *Autumn*, also known from engravings, had disappeared at an earlier date. *Spring* was rediscovered and identified in an English collection as recently as 1963, but three years later it was burned during a robbery. *Autumn* and *Winter* are still missing; perhaps a fortunate connoisseur will one day bring them to light. If the Crozat decorations could be reassembled, they would challenge many of the decorative cycles of G. B. Tiepolo and indicate that Watteau was capable of more than his characteristic *Fêtes Galantes*, entrancing as they are with their curious blend of gaiety and melancholy.

Collections: Pierre Crozat; Louis-François Crozat, Marquis du Châtel; Duchesse de Gontaut-Biron; Duc and Duchesse de Choiseul; Alphonse Roehn, Paris; possibly H.A.J. Munro of Novar; Lionel Phillips, Tylney Hall, Winchfield; H. Michel-Lévy, Paris; Léon Michel-Lévy, Paris; Charles-Louis Dreyfus, Paris. *Samuel H. Kress Collection*, 1961. Painted c. 1712. Canvas, oval, 56¾ x 45¾" (142 x 115.7 cm.).

329

437

438

437 Antoine Watteau (French, 1684–1721): *"Syl-via" (Jeanne-Rose-Guyonne Benozzi)*. c. 1720. Canvas, 27¼ x 23⅛" (69 x 59 cm.). Samuel H. Kress Collection

438 Antoine Watteau: *Italian Comedians*. Probably 1720. Canvas, 25⅛ x 30" (64 x 76 cm.). Samuel H. Kress Collection

439 Nicolas Lancret (French, 1690–1743): *La Camargo Dancing*. c. 1730. Canvas, 30 x 42" (76 x 107 cm.). Andrew W. Mellon Collection

440 Nicolas Lancret: *The Picnic After the Hunt*. c. 1740. Canvas, 24⅛ x 29⅜" (61.5 x 74.8 cm.). Samuel H. Kress Collection

441 Jean-Baptiste-Joseph Pater (French, 1695–1736): *Fête Champêtre*. c. 1730. Canvas, 29⅜ x 36½" (74.5 x 92.5 cm.). Samuel H. Kress Collection

442 Jean-Baptiste-Joseph Pater: *On the Terrace*. Probably c. 1730–35. Canvas, 28¼ x 39⅜" (71.8 x 100 cm.). Gift of Mr. and Mrs. William D. Vogel in memory of her father and mother, Mr. and Mrs. Ralph Harman Booth

439

440

Watteau introduced into art the *Fête Galante*, a type of painting further popularized by his followers, Lancret and Pater. Their pictures show a life of the utmost sophistication, one devoted to beauty and dalliance. This lightness appears even in sport and the dance. How different from English hunting scenes is Lancret's *Picnic after the Hunt* (plate 440), with the ladies dressed by an eighteenth-century Schiaparelli. And how enchanting is the floating, effortless grace of La Camargo and her partner, their ballet steps so irresistible that it is difficult for the spectator to remain motionless.

441

442

François Boucher

(FRENCH, 1703-1770)

443   VENUS CONSOLING LOVE

Melancholy was a rare quality in the eighteenth century, especially in France. The overtones of sadness which lend such poetry to Watteau's work never appear in the paintings of Boucher. *Venus Consoling Love* once belonged to Mme de Pompadour. It is signed and dated 1751, the year Louis XV's mistress moved into a new apartment in the north wing of Versailles, where she was to live the rest of her life. It may have adorned these rooms or else have been painted for her château at Bellevue, where Boucher was working about 1750. He was Mme de Pompadour's favorite artist. She gave him commissions for innumerable decorations and easel pictures; ordered from him an illuminated prayer book, surprising as such a commission must seem; petted and cajoled him; and wrote her counselor of state that he must be kept in a good humor. For as she said, "I'm sure you would hate to find a crippled or cock-eyed nymph in your pretty room."

Mme de Pompadour has been said to have posed for the Venus in the painting reproduced here. But this entrancing maiden is much more the product of the painter's imagination. Boucher was never tied down to a model. He had learned a language of design, and this he used with the utmost freedom. Notice with what grace the movements of Venus, Cupid, and the surrounding *putti* are suggested. Or notice the lovely passages of painting in the feathers of the dove, the flowers, and the foliage. Eighteenth-century painters delighted in the display of beautiful handling, of fine brushwork, much as a violinist might take pleasure in a virtuoso performance. In this technical dexterity lies the principal charm of Rococo art.

Collections: Probably Mme de Pompadour and her brother, the Marquis de Ménars; H. Cousin, Paris; Baron Alfred de Rothschild, Buckinghamshire; Marchioness of Curzon, Kedleston, Derbyshire. *Gift of Chester Dale*, 1943. Signed, and dated 1751. Canvas, 42⅛ x 33⅜" (107 x 85 cm.).

333

444

445

444 **François Boucher:** (French, 1703–1770): *The Love Letter.* Signed, and dated 1750. Canvas, 32 x 29⅛" (81.3 x 74.1 cm.). Timken Collection

445 **François Boucher:** *Madame Bergeret.* Signed, and dated 1746. Canvas, 56¼ x 41⅜" (143 x 105 cm.). Samuel H. Kress Collection

446 **François Boucher:** *Allegory of Painting.* Signed and dated 1765. Canvas, 40 x 51⅛" (101.5 x 130 cm.). Samuel H. Kress Collection

447 **François Boucher:** *Diana and Endymion.* c. 1765. Canvas, 37⅜ x 53⅞" (95 x 137 cm.). Timken Collection

448 **Charles-Amédée-Philippe van Loo** (French, 1719–1795): *The Magic Lantern.* Signed, and dated 1764. Canvas, 34⅞ x 34⅞" (88.6 x 88.6 cm.). Gift of Mrs. Robert W. Schuette

449 **François Boucher:** *Allegory of Music.* Signed, and dated 1764. Canvas, 40¾ x 51⅛" (103.5 x 130 cm.). Samuel H. Kress Collection

450 **Charles-Amédée-Philippe van Loo:** *Soap Bubbles.* Signed, and dated 1764. Canvas, 34⅞ x 34⅞" (88.6 x 88.6 cm.). Gift of Mrs. Robert W. Schuette

446

447

448

450

449

Boucher represents the gay, witty, artificial life of the court of Louis Quinze. This artificiality was extended to life in the country, as can be seen in *The Love Letter* (plate 444). Rural life for the French aristocracy was an imaginary idyll filled with Arcadian shepherds and shepherdesses, their sheep saturated with perfume. Even mythological scenes were often bucolic in detail, as in *Diana and Endymion* (plate 447). At home, children were well groomed, never rowdy or rambunctious, as van Loo's boys and girls clearly indicate. In plate 448 two children are looking into a magic lantern; the figures are enframed by a circular wreath, thus simulating a scene viewed through the lens of the closed box—a rare example of a visual pun.

Jean-Honoré Fragonard

(FRENCH, 1732–1806)

451   A YOUNG GIRL READING

Painted about 1776 at the peak of the artist's career, this charming study is considered by many critics to be among Fragonard's most appealing and masterly paintings. It is one of a series representing young girls in moments of solitude and relaxation, either reading a billet-doux, turning the pages of a book, or seated at a dressing table and lost in the world of their private thoughts. The identity of the sitters, as in this case, is unknown. Apparently Fragonard painted this series on speculation, hoping to interest Parisian patrons who were decorating their private apartments with intimate scenes typical of the last phase of Rococo taste.

Few paintings reveal more brilliantly that wonderful dexterity of brushwork for which Fragonard was famous. Look first at the curving fingers of the girl's hand holding the book. These fingers establish a rhythm which runs through the whole painting. The same movement, to be seen in various brushstrokes, is especially noticeable in the delicate and complicated touches which render the bows, the ribbons, and the ruffles of the young girl's costume. As in Boucher's *Venus Consoling Love* (plate 443), the quality of this brushwork has a spontaneity suggestive of a Mozartian cadenza. This virtuoso performance reaches a climax in the broad strokes of burnt umber which model the cushion and suggest its softly yielding volume. All these warm tones, placed so rapidly on the canvas, seem aglow with sunshine.

Collections: Leroy de Senneville, Paris; Duquesnoy, Paris; Marquis de Cypierre, Paris; Comte de Kergorlay, Paris; Ernest Cronier, Paris; Dr. Tuffier, Paris; Mr. and Mrs. Alfred W. Erickson, New York. *Gift of Mrs. Mellon Bruce in memory of her father, Andrew W. Mellon, 1961. Painted c. 1776. Canvas, 32 x 25½" (81.1 x 64.8 cm.).*

337

452

452 Jean-Baptiste Greuze (French, 1725–1805): *Ange-Laurent de Lalive de Jully.* Probably 1759. Canvas, 46 x 34⅞" (117 x 88.5 cm.). Samuel H. Kress Collection

453 Jean-Honoré Fragonard (French, 1732–1806): *Love as Folly.* c. 1775. Canvas, oval, 22 x 18¼" (55.9 x 46.4 cm.). In memory of Kate Seney Simpson

454 Jean-Honoré Fragonard: *Love as Conqueror.* c. 1775. Canvas, oval, 22 x 18⅜" (55.9 x 46.7 cm.). In memory of Kate Seney Simpson

455 Jean-Honoré Fragonard: *Blindman's Buff.* Probably c. 1765. Canvas, 85⅛ x 77⅞" (216.2 x 197.8 cm.). Samuel H. Kress Collection

456 Jean-Honoré Fragonard: *A Game of Horse and Rider.* 1767/73. Canvas, 45⅜ x 34½" (115 x 87.5 cm.). Samuel H. Kress Collection

457 Jean-Honoré Fragonard: *The Swing.* Probably c. 1765. Canvas, 85 x 73" (215.9 x 185.5 cm.). Samuel H. Kress Collection

458 Michel-Francois Dandré-Bardon (French, 1700–1783): *The Adoration of the Skulls.* Canvas, 20¾ x 25⅛" (52.8 x 63.6 cm.). Gift of Lewis Einstein

453

454

455

456

457

458

If one purpose of art is to represent the desirable life, then Fragonard has caught an aspect of that life, the suggestion of an enchanted world where no one grows old and pleasures are without ennui. In his paintings idyllic nature and the unthinking happiness of a carefree nobility exert their magic. But in *Blindman's Buff* (plate 455), huge cumulus clouds are gathering as though a presage of the storm that will sweep away the *ancien régime* with all its games and gaiety, and leave behind only the guillotine.

459

460

461

462

Before the storm broke, however, fashion changed from Rococo frivolity to archaeological solemnity. Pompeii and Herculaneum were excavated, and the architecture, statuary, and furniture discovered made a profound impression on society. *The Old Bridge* by Hubert Robert (plate 462) is still Rococo in style, but in spirit it foreshadows this change in taste. Elisabeth Vigée-Lebrun lived into the new epoch and modified her style accordingly (plates 463 and 464 belong to her earlier period). Many artists were never able to accomplish this transformation, and their work was rejected. Fragonard, for example, died in poverty at the age of seventy-four.

459 Jean-Honoré Fragonard (French, 1732–1806): *A Game of Hot Cockles.* 1767/73. Canvas, 45½ x 36" (115.5 x 91.5 cm.). Samuel H. Kress Collection

460 Jean-Honoré Fragonard: *The Visit to the Nursery.* Before 1784. Canvas, 28¾ x 36¼" (73 x 92 cm.). Samuel H. Kress Collection

461 Jean-Honoré Fragonard: *The Happy Family.* After 1769. Canvas, oval, 21¼ x 25⅝" (53.9 x 65.1 cm.). Timken Collection

462 Hubert Robert (French, 1733–1808): *The Old Bridge.* Probably c. 1775. Canvas, 35⅞ x 47⅝" (91.3 x 121 cm.). Samuel H. Kress Collection

463 Elisabeth Vigée-Lebrun (French, 1755–1842): *The Marquise de Pezé and the Marquise de Rouget with Her Two Children.* 1787. Canvas, 48⅝ x 61⅜" (123.4 x 155.9 cm.). Gift of the Bay Foundation in memory of Josephine Bay Paul and Ambassador Charles Ulrick Bay

464 Elizabeth Vigée-Lebrun: *Portrait of a Lady.* Signed, and dated 1789. Wood, 42⅛ x 32¾" (107 x 83 cm.). Samuel H. Kress Collection

465 Jean-Marc Nattier (French, 1685–1766): *Madame de Caumartin as Hebe.* Signed, and dated 1753. Canvas, 40⅜ x 32" (102.5 x 81.5 cm.). Samuel H. Kress Collection

463

464

465

Giovanni Battista Tiepolo

(VENETIAN, 1696–1770)

466   QUEEN ZENOBIA ADDRESSING HER SOLDIERS

The subject of this picture has for a long time mystified some of the best scholars of classical history and of Venetian painting. Lionello Venturi thought it might represent the founding of Rome, illustrating an episode in the Aeneid when Venus appeared to Aeneas and his followers to encourage them on their landing in Latium. But it is hard to recognize in this helmeted Amazon the Goddess of Love. Wilhelm Suida suggested that she was, instead, an allegorical figure of Rome urging all the legionaries to unite. This would explain the gesture of her left hand making a ring, the sign of unity.

My own preference has been for the theory put forth by Dr. Kezia Knauer, that the subject is "Agrippina Addressing the Legionaries." This is based on a passage in Tacitus: "Gaius Plinius . . . relates how she took her stand at the head of the bridge, bestowing praise and thanks on the returning legions . . . and in the most artless manner conceivable paraded the General's son about the camp in the dress of a private soldier, delighting to hear him called by the appellation of *Little Caesar in Boots*." "Little Caesar in boots" would then be the young boy about to mount the podium. This interpretation explains a figure to whom Tiepolo has given considerable importance.

However, a fourth interpretation, first proposed by Erwin Panofsky, has now been accepted and further documented by Dr. Fern Rusk Shapley in her catalogue *Paintings from the Samuel H. Kress Collection* (1973), and the National Gallery has accordingly changed the title of the painting from *A Scene from Roman History* to the more specific one given here.

Queen Zenobia's story is retold in Gibbon's *Decline and Fall of the Roman Empire* from an ancient source. She ruled Palmyra in the third century A.D. and attained such power in the East that she could defy Rome. It would appear that the painting reproduced here formed a decorative scheme with at least three others: *A Hunter on Horseback* and *A Hunter with a Stag*, probably references to Zenobia's passion for hunting, both now in the Crespi Collection, Milan; and Tiepolo's well-known *Triumph of Aurelian*, now in the Galleria Sabauda, Turin, and undoubtedly a pendant to the National Gallery painting. It is intriguing to speculate that these paintings may have been commissioned by the Zenobio family of Venice, because of the resemblance of their name to that of the famous queen. Certainly it is known that Tiepolo did decorate a room in the Zenobio palace, which still stands in Venice, sometime before 1732.

Collections: Possibly Ca' Zenobio, Venice; Villa Grimani-Valmarana, Noventa Padovana; Count Dino Barozzi, Venice; C. Ledyard Blair, New Jersey. *Samuel H. Kress Collection*, 1961. Painted c. 1730. Canvas, 102⅞ x 144" (261.4 x 365.8 cm.).

342

467

The richness of the National Gallery in eighteenth-century Italian works is indicated by these paintings. The first generation of these artists who died about 1750 is represented by Crespi, Magnasco, Sebastiano Ricci, and Piazzetta. Their dashing brushwork and dramatic gestures reach a climax in Piazzetta's *Elijah* (plate **471**), where the figures look as if they are being tossed by a whirlwind of flame, and in the two paintings by Magnasco, whose lightning-like streaks of paint lend his pictures an electric vibrancy. Tiepolo, who belongs to the next generation, was the greatest decorator of the eighteenth century. *The World Pays Homage to Spain* (plate **474**) is typical of the models for ceiling designs with which he provided his patrons, in this case the King of Spain.

468

469

470

471

472

473

472 Giovanni Battista Tiepolo (Venetian, 1696–1770): *Timocleia and the Thracian Commander.* c. 1750. Canvas, 55¼ x 43⅛″ (140.3 x 109.3 cm.). Samuel H. Kress Collection

473 Sebastiano Ricci and Marco Ricci (Venetian, 1659–1734 and 1676–1730): *Memorial to Admiral Sir Clowdisley Shovell.* Signed. c. 1725. Canvas, 87½ x 62½″ (222.3 x 158.5 cm.). Samuel H. Kress Collection

474

474 Giovanni Battista Tiepolo (Venetian, 1696–1770): *The World Pays Homage to Spain.* Probably 1762. Canvas, 71½ x 41⅛" (181 x 104.5 cm.). Samuel H. Kress Collection

475 Giovanni Battista Tiepolo: *Apollo Pursuing Daphne.* Signed. c. 1755/60. Canvas, 27 x 34¼" (68.8 x 87.2 cm.). Samuel H. Kress Collection

475

476 Giovanni Paolo Panini (Roman, 1691/92–1765): *The Interior of the Pantheon.* c. 1740. Canvas, 50½ x 39" (128 x 99 cm.). Samuel H. Kress Collection

477 Giovanni Paolo Panini: *Interior of Saint Peter's, Rome.* 1746/54. Canvas, 60¾ x 77½" (154.4 x 197 cm.). Ailsa Mellon Bruce Fund

478 Canaletto (Venetian, 1697–1768): *The Square of Saint Mark's.* Signed. Early 1730s. Canvas, 45 x 60½" (114.5 x 154 cm.). Gift of Mrs. Barbara Hutton

479 Canaletto: *View in Venice.* c. 1740. Canvas, 28 x 44" (71 x 112 cm.). Widener Collection

480 Canaletto: *The Portello and the Brenta Canal at Padua.* c. 1740. Canvas, 24⅝ x 43" (62.5 x 109 cm.). Samuel H. Kress Collection

The Italians of the eighteenth century, like the Dutch of the seventeenth, wanted portraits of places and buildings. No artist has rivaled Panini as a portrayer of interiors; nor has anyone equaled Canaletto as a painter of cityscapes. He delineated the palaces and canals of Venice so vividly that the sightseer in that city, after having looked at many of Canaletto's paintings, will sometimes, when admiring a view, find himself almost reaching out to touch a canvas before he realizes that he is not looking at a picture, but is himself part of the scene. Canaletto's nephew Bellotto does much the same for Northern cities. Guardi, by contrast, gives poetic and impressionistic visions of this aqueous Venetian scenery, enchanting views of the most beautiful city in the world.

476

477

478

479

480

481

482

481 **Canaletto** (Venetian, 1697–1768): *Venice, the Quay of the Piazzetta*. Signed. Early 1730s. Canvas, 45⅛ x 60⅜" (115.2 x 153.6 cm.). Gift of Mrs. Barbara Hutton

482 **Francesco Guardi** (Venetian, 1712–1793): *View of the Rialto*. Probably c. 1780. Canvas, 27 x 36" (68.5 x 91.5 cm.). Widener Collection

483 **Gian Antonio Guardi and Francesco Guardi** (Venetian, 1699–1760 and 1712–1793): *Carlo and Ubaldo Resisting the Enchantments of Armida's Nymphs*. 1750/55. Canvas, 98½ x 181" (250.2 x 459.8 cm.). Ailsa Mellon Bruce Fund

484 **Gian Antonio Guardi and Francesco Guardi**: *Erminia and the Shepherds*. 1750/55. Canvas, 99 x 174⅛" (251.5 x 442.2 cm.). Ailsa Mellon Bruce Fund

485 **Francesco Guardi**: *A Seaport and Classic Ruins in Italy*. 1730s. Canvas, 48 x 70" (122 x 178 cm.). Samuel H. Kress Collection

486 **Francesco Guardi**: *Campo San Zanipolo*. 1782. Canvas, 14¾ x 12⅜" (37.5 x 31.5 cm.). Samuel H. Kress Collection

487 **Pietro Longhi** (Venetian, 1702–1785): *The Simulated Faint*. c. 1745. Canvas, 19¼ x 24" (49 x 61 cm.). Samuel H. Kress Collection

483

484

486

485

487

488 **Pietro Longhi** (Venetian, 1702–1785): *Blind-man's Buff.* c. 1745. Canvas, 19¼ x 24" (49 x 61 cm.). Samuel H. Kress Collection

489 **Bernardo Bellotto** (Venetian, 1720–1780): *The Castle of Nymphenburg.* c. 1761. Canvas, 26⅞ x 47⅛" (68.4 x 119.8 cm.). Samuel H. Kress Collection

490 **Bernardo Bellotto**: *View of Munich.* c. 1761. Canvas, 27¼ x 47⅛" (69.3 x 119.8 cm.). Samuel H. Kress Collection

488

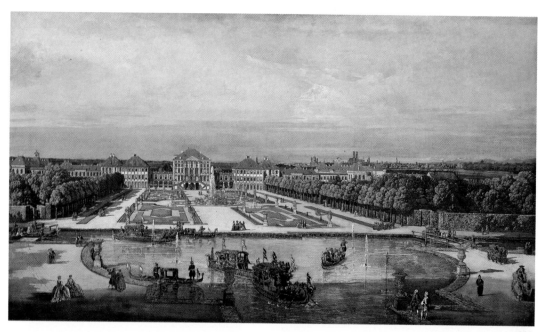

489

490

British &
American Schools

XVIII CENTURY

William Hogarth

(BRITISH, 1697–1764)

491 A SCENE FROM THE BEGGAR'S OPERA

With Hogarth the great period of English painting begins, and it begins with an unusual genre, pictorial satire. One of Hogarth's first significant works illustrates a scene from *The Beggar's Opera*, a play of 1728 that is itself satirical, a parody of Italian opera, then much in vogue. The painter, who was an avid theatergoer, has used the most dramatic moment to make a sardonic comment on society, law, and audiences. The caricatured notables converse, flirt, and occasionally glance at the spectacle. Many can be identified. In the box on the right, for example, is the actor and manager John Rich, talking to Christopher Cook, the auctioneer, and behind him is John Gay, the author of the opera.

In the center stands the highwayman Captain Macheath, who has been arrested, betrayed for a reward by Peachum, a despicable character and a notorious fence. On the left stands Peachum's fat colleague Lockit, a jailer, equally corrupt. Peachum's daughter, Mrs. Macheath, on the right, pleads with her father for clemency for her husband, and on the other side Lockit's daughter with equal passion begs her parent for the release of the captain, her lover. Meanwhile, Macheath, in fetters but imperturbable, sings those immortal lines

> How happy could I be with either
> Were t'other dear charmer away.

The sentiment has been echoed over the years by many an unfortunate man in the presence of two loves with whom he has entangled himself simultaneously.

The captain, though a thief, is obviously heroic, while the respectable-looking gangster and the jailer, also a crook, are the ones who should be hanged. The theme of *The Beggar's Opera* must have delighted Hogarth, as it has myriads of theatergoers ever since. Enormously successful, it occasioned a splendid double pun. It was said that it had made the author, Gay, rich and the producer, Rich, gay. So popular was Hogarth's painting that he repeated it six times between 1728 and the end of 1729. Of these the National Gallery's painting is the fourth, and Ronald Paulson says in his book on Hogarth, "It is the most expressive of all. . . . There is no wrong note, no distortion for effect."

One reason for the popularity of opera and painting was a scandal. The beautiful Lavinia Fenton, who played Polly Peachum, became the obsession of the Duke of Bolton, who, in later versions of the picture, sits in one of the boxes and ogles her. He was so smitten that he attended the play night after night and eventually took Miss Fenton as his second wife. A social uproar resulted, and Robert Walpole, the Prime Minister, removed the Duke from many of his important positions.

Collections: E. Cheney; F. Capel-Cure (1905); and by descent to Nigel Capel-Cure. *Paul Mellon Collection.* Painted c. 1728. Canvas, 20⅛ x 24⅛'' (51.1 x 61.2 cm.).

Thomas Gainsborough

(BRITISH, 1727-1788)

492   MRS. RICHARD BRINSLEY SHERIDAN

To understand this portrait, one must take into account its background in Whig society of the late eighteenth century—a society materialistic, rich, self-confident, yet with a love of learning and freedom and a special sensibility that sometimes verged on sentimentality. Mrs. Sheridan, the beautiful singer who married the wit, playwright, brilliant member of Parliament, and drunken favorite of Devonshire House, is a characteristic figure in that society. And this picture, at once charmingly pastoral (although nature is somewhat arranged, as the great Whig nobles liked it to be) and dashingly, artificially worldly, is a consummate expression of high Whig taste.

Gainsborough is known to have painted on occasion with brushes mounted on handles almost six feet long, in order to be the same distance from his model and his canvas. The consequent sketchiness of effect makes the certainty of each brush-stroke still more remarkable. This feature of his style impressed Sir Joshua Reynolds, who wrote, "This chaos, this uncouth and shapeless appearance, by a kind of magic, at a certain distance assumes form, and all the parts seem to drop into their proper places; so that we can hardly refuse acknowledging the full effect of diligence, under the appearance of chance and hasty negligence."

Collections: Richard Brinsley Sheridan, Bath, England; Baron Nathaniel de Rothschild, Tring, Hertfordshire, and heirs, until sold by Lord Rothschild, London. *Andrew W. Mellon Collection*, 1937. Painted probably 1785/86. Canvas, 86½ x 60½" (220 x 154 cm.).

493

494

495

496

497

498

Thomas Gainsborough, more than any other British painter, delights the spectator with his technique in oil. Usually the surfaces of his pictures have the transparency of watercolor and the delicacy of pastel. His thinly brushed canvases have lasted better than those of his contemporaries who used a thicker pigmentation. Portraiture was Gainsborough's vocation, but his avocation was landscape. His visions of an imaginary countryside, however, were largely unsalable, and masterpieces like *Landscape with a Bridge* (plate 496) filled his studio at his death.

Thomas Gainsborough   (British, 1727–1788)

493   *Master John Heathcote.* c. 1770/74. Canvas, 50 x 37⅞" (127 x 101.2 cm.). Given in memory of Governor Alvan T. Fuller by the Fuller Foundation

494   *Georgiana, Duchess of Devonshire.* Probably 1783. Canvas, 92¾ x 57⅝" (235.6 x 146.5 cm.). Andrew W. Mellon Collection

495   *Miss Catherine Tatton.* Probably 1785. Canvas, 30 x 25" (76 x 64 cm.). Andrew W. Mellon Collection

496   *Landscape with a Bridge.* c. 1785. Canvas, 44½ x 52½" (113 x 133 cm.). Andrew W. Mellon Collection

497   *The Honorable Mrs. Graham.* Probably 1775. Canvas, 36 x 28" (89.5 x 69 cm.). Widener Collection

498   *The Earl of Darnley.* Probably 1785. Canvas, 30 x 25" (76 x 63.5 cm.). Widener Collection

499   *Seascape.* Probably 1781. Canvas, 40¼ x 50⅜" (102.2 x 127.9 cm.). Ailsa Mellon Bruce Collection

499

357

Sir Joshua Reynolds

(BRITISH, 1723-1792)

500 LADY CAROLINE HOWARD

In the portrait of Lady Caroline Howard, Reynolds has stressed a certain aspect of childhood, its innocence, its unstudied gracefulness. It does not matter that the portrait may not be a precise likeness of Lady Caroline, nor even that he used a similar pose and setting in other paintings of children, notably in *The Age of Innocence* in the National Gallery, London. For "the great aim of the art," as he said addressing the Royal Academy, "is to strike the imagination." In the portrait of Lady Caroline the mind is captured and converted to the romantic concept of childhood, "trailing clouds of glory," thirty years before Wordsworth's poem. Needless to say Reynolds himself was a bachelor!

Reynolds, in spite of the classical creed expounded in his *Discourses*, proves himself in many ways a precursor of the Romantics. This is manifest not only in his tendency to sentimentality but also in his faltering technique, in that uncertainty of craftsmanship which was the plague of Romantic painting. Thus many of his canvases, because of his constant technical experiments and his constant use of bitumen, have cracked and faded. *Lady Caroline Howard*, however, has lasted with its original brilliance and freshness; and for that reason it gives an idea of the luminosity of tone which must have characterized Reynolds' portraits when they left his studio, an impression hard to gain from many of his pictures in their present condition.

Collection: Earl of Carlisle, Castle Howard, England. *Andrew W. Mellon Collection*, 1937. Painted c. 1778. Canvas, 56¼ x 44½" (143 x 113 cm.).

Lady Caroline Howard
Lady Cawdor

359

501

503

502

Sir Joshua Reynolds was the first president of the Royal
Academy, and his *Discourses*, comprising his annual
lectures before that institution, were taken as the gospel
of British painting for generations. They remain one of
the most comprehensive, sensible, and persuasive
aesthetic statements ever made. His portraits, though
never reaching the level of his theories, are the supreme
expression in the eighteenth century of the Grand
Manner, which was introduced by van Dyck a century
and a half earlier.

Sir Joshua Reynolds (British, 1723–1792)

501 *Lady Betty Hamilton.* 1758. Canvas, 46 × 33″ (117 × 84 cm.). Widener Collection

502 *Lady Elizabeth Delmé and Her Children.* 1777–80. Canvas, 94 × 58⅛″ (239.2 × 147.8 cm.). Andrew W. Mellon Collection

503 *Squire Musters.* 1777/80. Canvas, 93⅞ × 58″ (238.5 × 147.3 cm.). Given in memory of Governor Alvan T. Fuller by the Fuller Foundation

504 *Lady Elizabeth Compton.* 1781. Canvas, 94½ × 58½″ (240 × 149 cm.). Andrew W. Mellon Collection

505 *Lady Cornewall.* c. 1785. Canvas, 50 × 40″ (127 × 101.5 cm.). Widener Collection

506 **Thomas Gainsborough** (British, 1727–1788): *Mrs. John Taylor.* Probably c. 1778. Canvas, oval, 30 × 25″ (76 × 64 cm.). Andrew W. Mellon Collection

504

505

506

361

George Romney

(BRITISH, 1734–1802)

507   MISS WILLOUGHBY

If there were only a divining rod to point out those artists destined to be the Old Masters of the future, we might enjoy portraits of ourselves or our children and at the same time count on our descendants being copiously enriched. Miss Willoughby's parents in 1784 paid Romney less than one-thousandth part of the price his picture brought when it was acquired for the National Gallery of Art a few decades ago, and many families in Europe today owe their fortunes to the perspicacity with which their ancestors selected their portraitists.

But how can we tell what picture will gain in appreciation? Why has *Miss Willoughby*, for instance, come to be so highly treasured? It is merely the conventional and scarcely individualized portrait of a pretty child. Perhaps Romney was even bored with the commission, for he disliked portraiture, and the only sitter he seems to have taken pleasure in painting was Emma, Lady Hamilton, whose strange, restless magnetism enthralled and maddened him. When he painted other people his real interests lay in solving certain problems of color and design rather than in getting a likeness.

But then, who cares any longer what Miss Willoughby looked like? Her portrait is enjoyed today because of Romney's genius as a colorist and as a decorator. The harmonious tone of the picture is a lesson in the adroit use of a limited palette, in this case a palette of only three colors, red, yellow, and blue. The design is as simple as the color, but just as subtly ingenious. The gesture of the child seems spontaneous and unposed, but note the tilt of the head at just the right angle to suggest a diagonal movement crosscutting the diagonal of the sloping landscape in the background. Imagine it upright and the rhythm of the composition vanishes. And how satisfactory in scale is Miss Willoughby in relation to the canvas. These qualities of color and design, so frequently to be found in eighteenth-century English portraiture, are the antecedent facts which make it probable that a painting will continue to interest posterity.

Collection: Major Sir John Christopher Willoughby, fifth bart., Fulmer Hall, Slough, Buckinghamshire (sold 1906). *Andrew W. Mellon Collection*, 1937. Painted 1781–83. Canvas, 36⅛ x 28″ (91 x 71 cm.).

508

509

George Romney was one of the most popular of British portraitists, but he loathed portrait painting. He was interested in historical subjects, especially if there was some classical association. Nevertheless, he had to make his living, and sitters were queuing up to be painted. He gave the ladies who came to his studio charm and grace, and they were delighted. But in the artist's heart and mind only one face was stamped—that of Emma, the beautiful wife of Sir William Hamilton and the mistress

510

511

512

508   **George Romney** (British, 1734–1802): *Lady Broughton.* 1770/73. Canvas, 94 x 58″ (239 x 147 cm.). Andrew W. Mellon Collection

509   **George Romney:** *Lady Arabella Ward.* 1783–88. Canvas, 30 x 25″ (76 x 64 cm.). Widener Collection

510   **George Romney:** *Sir William Hamilton.* Probably 1783. Canvas, 30¼ x 25⅝″ (76.8 x 65.1 cm.). Ailsa Mellon Bruce Collection

511   **George Romney:** *Mrs. Davenport.* 1782–84. Canvas, 30⅛ x 25⅛″ (76.5 x 64 cm.). Andrew W. Mellon Collection

512   **Arthur Devis** (British, 1711–1787): *Conversation Piece, Ashdon House.* c. 1760. Canvas, 54½ x 77″ (138.5 x 195.6 cm.). Paul Mellon Collection

513   **John Hoppner** (British, 1758–1810): *The Hoppner Children.* c. 1790. Canvas, 60 x 50″ (152.5 x 127 cm.). Widener Collection

514   **John Hoppner:** *The Frankland Sisters.* Signed. 1795. Canvas, 61 x 49¼″ (155 x 125 cm.). Andrew W. Mellon Collection

of Britain's naval hero Lord Nelson. (Romney's painting of Sir William is reproduced in plate 510.) Romney painted some fifty portraits of Lady Hamilton; she provoked him with her coquetry and tantalizing loveliness until his health, never strong, broke under the emotional strain and he withdrew to Kendal in the north of England. His wife faithfully nursed him until he died.

513

514

Sir Henry Raeburn

(BRITISH, 1756–1823)

515   MISS ELEANOR URQUHART

Flaubert's admonition to artists, "Be regular and ordinary in your life, like a bourgeois, so that you can be violent and original in your work," might serve as a description of Sir Henry Raeburn. Art was a business to this most distinguished of Scottish painters, and from nine to five-thirty it kept him regularly in his studio, where he painted a succession of three to four sitters a day. When he left his easel, it was to speculate in real estate or to play golf. But conventional as was his life, there was nothing conventional about his portraiture.

As a young man Raeburn decided to record only what he saw in front of him and never to trust his memory even when painting a subordinate part of the picture. This practice, common today, was contrary to the regular procedure of eighteenth-century portraitists. They used instead a preestablished tone for flesh, a traditional arrangement of highlights and shadows, and other fixed conventions. Raeburn, relying on actual observation and not on a memorized formula, developed a style which foreshadows contemporary painting.

For while he anticipates the goal of modern portraitists, seizing in his best works on the salient features of the sitter and rendering them in the moment of conception, his technical performance at times goes beyond the attainments of any contemporary artist. It is amazing that in portraying Miss Urquhart, for example, he did not have to change a single brushstroke. Success in direct painting of this type depends on the swiftness and certainty of the artist's hand. The moment he falters, renders a false shadow, fails to find the correct contour, misses the right color, the passage must be repainted and the freshness is gone.

Raeburn himself failed more often than he succeeded, and his work frequently suffers from the same faults that plague modern portraitists: either the pigment is thick from reworking, or the shadows too black, or the colors dull. *Miss Urquhart* is an exception; and it is easy to imagine that on this occasion, fascinated by the beauty of his sitter, the artist forgot all hesitations and afterthoughts and put down *à premier coup* the image of an aristocratic and charming woman, creating spontaneously one of his supreme masterpieces.

Collection: Captain Michael Pollard-Urquhart, Craigston, Scotland. *Andrew W. Mellon Collection*, 1937. Painted c. 1793. Canvas, 29⅜ x 24¼″ (75 x 62 cm.).

367

516

517

516 **George Stubbs** (British, 1724–1806): *Colonel Pocklington with His Sisters.* Signed, and dated 1769. Canvas, 39⅛ x 49¾" (100.2 x 126.6 cm.). Gift of Mrs. Charles S. Carstairs in memory of her husband, Charles Stewart Carstairs

517 **Sir Thomas Lawrence** (British, 1769–1830): *Lady Templetown and Her Son.* c. 1801. Canvas, 84¾ x 58⅝" (215 x 149 cm.). Andrew W. Mellon Collection

518 **Sir Henry Raeburn** (British, 1756–1823): *The Binning Children.* c. 1811. Canvas, 50⅝ x 40⅜" (128.8 x 102.7 cm.). Given in memory of John Woodruff Simpson

519 **Sir Henry Raeburn:** *John Johnstone of Alva, His Sister, and His Niece.* c. 1805. Canvas, 40 x 47¼" (101.6 x 120 cm.). Gift of Mrs. Robert W. Schuette

520 **Sir Henry Raeburn:** *John Tait and His Grandson.* c. 1793. Canvas, 49½ x 39¾" (126 x 100 cm.). Andrew W. Mellon Collection

521 **Sir Henry Raeburn:** *David Anderson.* Probably c. 1790. Canvas, 60 x 46¼" (152.5 x 107.5 cm.). Widener Collection

522 **Sir Henry Raeburn:** *Colonel Francis James Scott.* c. 1800. Canvas, 50¼ x 40" (128 x 102 cm.). Andrew W. Mellon Collection

Every Scot above the level of a crofter seems to have had the means to have himself and his family portrayed by Raeburn. To maintain high standards and be so prolific was difficult, and the quality of Raeburn's work varies more than the exceptionally fine portraits reproduced here indicate. Although the Scots were willing to spend

518

519

money on their likenesses, their canniness remained, as is illustrated by plate 520. John Tait was painted in the 1790s, but later a grandson was born, and rather than pay for a new portrait, the family asked to have the child added. This presented Raeburn with a pictorial problem for which, as one can see, there was no satisfactory solution; but the painter was not deterred. He was delighted to have an additional payment.

520

The craving of the British for the immortality conferred by a portrait is a national characteristic. Two able portraitists not previously mentioned, Hoppner and Lawrence, helped to assuage this insatiable desire. With a few marvelous exceptions, however, their full-lengths are dull and repetitious. More interesting on the whole are the conversation pieces by artists like Devis and Stubbs. Even though the sitters themselves may be forgotten, we see these members of the squirearchy and the aristocracy in an Arcadian world we cannot but envy.

521

522

Benjamin West

(AMERICAN, 1738–1820)

523   COLONEL GUY JOHNSON

Although American painting in the eighteenth century was a colonial dependency of British painting, American artists, until they went abroad, saw very few European pictures. As Copley wrote, "I think myself peculiarly unlucky in Living in a place into which there has not been one portrait brought that is worthy to be call'd a Picture within my memory." Under the circumstances it is not surprising that our leading painters should have found it more congenial to live in England.

Of these expatriates Benjamin West was the first to settle abroad, where his success was extraordinary. He may well have appeared to Europeans as a perfect instance of the "noble savage," whose interest in art justified the theories of Jean-Jacques Rousseau. West's biographer John Galt relates that during the artist's visit to Rome in 1760, the Italians, thinking that he had received the education of a savage, became curious to see the effect the works of art in the Belvedere and Vatican would have on him. When, however, he compared the *Apollo Belvedere* to a young Mohawk warrior, and proceeded to explain the merits of the statue in terms of the analogy between it and the Mohawk Indians, the Italians were delighted with the excellence of the criticism and West's popularity was assured. Eventually he settled in London, where he came to be recognized as the foremost English historical painter. Elected to succeed Sir Joshua Reynolds, he became the second President of the Royal Academy.

West did many large historical canvases for George III and painted many notable portraits. Of these one of the finest is the portrait of Colonel Guy Johnson, who was the English Superintendent of Indian Affairs in the American Colonies. With him West has included an idealized figure of an Indian holding a peace pipe in contrast with the Englishman's gun. In the background is an idyllic scene of Indian family life before a huge waterfall, perhaps Niagara. The Indian has not been identified, and is probably intended merely as a "noble savage" advocating peace, a constant British hope throughout the Revolution.

The picture can be dated with some precision because we know from Ethan Allen's journal that Johnson and his famous Indian secretary, Joseph Brant, crossed with him to England late in 1775 on the *Adamant*, and that Johnson returned to the Colonies in the spring of 1776. Incidentally, on the voyage Allen, a prisoner of the British, was put into the charge of Brook Watson (see plate 552), whom he described as "a man of malicious and cruel disposition, and who was probably excited, in the exercise of his malevolence, by a junto of Tories who sailed with him to England; among whom were Col. Guy Johnson. . . ."

Collection: Dina E. Brown, Henfield, England. *Andrew W. Mellon Collection*, 1940. Painted 1776. Canvas, 79¾ x 54½" (203 x 138 cm.).

Benjamin West

(AMERICAN, 1738–1820)

524   THE BATTLE OF LA HOGUE

The Battle of La Hogue, one incident of which West has depicted, took place late in May 1692. In a series of encounters, the allied British and Dutch fleets defeated a French force on the northern and eastern sides of the Cotentin Peninsula. West has shown the final phase of the battle when the British Rear Admiral George Rooke (standing with sword upraised in the stern of the boat on the left) destroys with his flotilla the remaining French ships, which had sought refuge in the harbor of La Hogue. It was a decisive battle, the last effort of Louis XIV to invade England and restore James II. Thereafter William III was secure. The French troops ready for the invasion can be dimly seen on the cliffs between the burning hulks of the French fleet.

The terrified officer in blue leaping from a boat adorned with fleur-de-lis has lost his wig and seems to symbolize French impotence. By contrast there is the calm, imperious gesture of the British admiral. *La Hogue* was one of at least ten battle scenes commissioned by Lord Grosvenor, the ancestor of the Duke of Westminster, from whose collection the painting was acquired. Of this series the two most famous are the *Death of Wolfe* in the National Gallery of Canada in Ottawa and the *Battle of La Hogue*. Both illustrate victories over the French, and were probably intended to bolster British morale. For in the year 1778, when *La Hogue* was painted, General Burgoyne surrendered a third of the British army at Saratoga, and the same year France entered the war on the side of the colonists. It was a bitter moment for George III and his Minister, Lord North, and it was not an easy time for Benjamin West, an American expatriate dependent on royal favor.

The future President of the Royal Academy, however, continued to please the King, and according to an early historian of American art, William Dunlap, when West was painting *La Hogue* "an admiral took him to Spithead, and to give him a lesson in the effect of smoke in a naval engagement, ordered several ships of the fleet to manoeuvre as in action, and fire broadsides, while the painter made notes." In the eighteenth century a royal favorite like West was fortunate. Imagine an admiral today manoeuvering his ships and firing their guns so that a painter could envisage a naval battle!

Collections: Richard, first Earl Grosvenor, and his descendants the Dukes of Westminster. *Andrew W. Mellon Fund*, 1959. Painted 1778. Canvas, 60⅛ x 84⅜" (152.7 x 214.3 cm.).

525

Benjamin West was the tireless host of a swarm of American painters who came to London to study and also in search of fame and fortune. One of the first of these was Matthew Pratt, who escorted West's fiancée to London in 1764. West also taught Charles Willson Peale and kindly received the latter's son Rembrandt, whom he introduced to artists in London. Theus, a Swiss who crossed the ocean in the opposite direction, became the leading artist of Charleston, South Carolina, during the colonial period.

526

527

528

529

530

525 **Charles Willson Peale** (American, 1741–1827): *Benjamin and Eleanor Ridgely Laming.* 1788. Canvas, 42 x 60¼″ (106.6 x 152.9 cm.). Gift of Morris Schapiro

526 **Rembrandt Peale** (American, 1778–1860): *George Washington.* c. 1850. Canvas, 35⅞ x 28⅞″ (91.1 x 73.3 cm.). Gift of Mr. and Mrs. George W. Davison

527 **Mather Brown** (American, 1761–1831): *William Vans Murray.* Signed, and dated 1787. Canvas, 30⅛ x 25″ (77 x 64 cm.). Andrew W. Mellon Collection

528 **Benjamin West** (American, 1738–1820): *Self-Portrait.* Probably c. 1770. Canvas, 30¼ x 25⅜″ (77.3 x 64.4 cm.). Andrew W. Mellon Collection

529 **Jeremiah Theus** (American, 1719–1774): *Mrs. Cuthbert.* c. 1765. Canvas, 29¾ x 24⅞″ (75.4 x 63.1 cm.). Gift of Edgar William and Bernice Chrysler Garbisch

530 **Matthew Pratt** (American, 1734–1805): *The Duke of Portland.* Probably 1774 or later. Canvas, 30 x 25″ (76.7 x 64 cm.). Gift of Clarence Van Dyke Tiers

Gilbert Stuart

(AMERICAN, 1755–1828)

531   THE SKATER

In two hundred years America has produced several great painters, and among these at least one innovator of genius, Gilbert Stuart. Stuart, who arrived in London in 1775, a penniless young student, was trained by his compatriot Benjamin West. In West's studio he was taught accepted methods of eighteenth-century portraiture: a general tint for flesh, certain fixed places for highlights and deep shadows, and, often to improve the appearance of the sitter, touches of carmine in the nostrils and the corners of the eyes.

The Skater, a portrait of William Grant of Congalton, was Gilbert Stuart's first of major importance. It was painted in London while he was still working in West's studio. At the time it was said that he had learned to make "a tolerable likeness of the face, but as to the figure he could not get below the fifth button." Possibly it was to overcome such criticism that he determined his portrait of William Grant should be full-length. The sittings were arranged, and one wintry day Grant remarked that the weather seemed more suitable for skating than for painting. Stuart agreed, and both went to skate in Hyde Park. The ice cracked, however, and they were forced to return. It was then that Stuart had an inspiration. He decided to portray his sitter on skates.

When *The Skater* was sent to the Royal Academy in 1782, according to Stuart's account it caused a sensation. Grant went there dressed in his skating costume, and Stuart described how the crowd followed him so closely he was compelled to make his retreat, for everyone was exclaiming, "That is he! That is the gentleman!" Although Stuart was apt to exaggerate, it is true the portrait was much admired.

Nearly a century later the unsigned *Skater* was again exhibited at the Royal Academy. Controversy over its authorship raged. The *Daily Telegraph* attributed it to Romney, but the *Times* said it was too good for that artist and suggested Hoppner or Raeburn. The *Art Journal* reported, "A more graceful and manly figure was surely never painted by an English artist, and if Gainsborough were that artist, this is unquestionably his masterpiece." This was the most logical assumption, as the sketchy landscape in the background, showing Westminster Abbey in the distance, is rendered very much in the manner of Gainsborough.

Again, for half a century, *The Skater* vanished from public attention. Fortunately, however, it was located and purchased by the National Gallery of Art. It remains uniquely important in Stuart's career, for as he observed to Josiah Quincy it is rare for an artist to be "suddenly lifted into fame by a single picture."

Collections: Inherited by William Grant's granddaughter, through whose marriage it came into the Pelham-Clinton family, Moor Park, Stroud, Gloucestershire, and London. *Andrew W. Mellon Collection,* 1950. Painted 1782. Canvas, 96⅝ x 58⅛" (245.3 x 147.6 cm.).

532

533

Gilbert Stuart (American, 1755–1828)

532 *Lady Liston*. 1800. Canvas, 29⅛ x 24⅛″ (74 x 61.3 cm.). Gift of Chester Dale

533 *Sir Robert Liston*. 1800. Canvas, 29¼ x 24⅛″ (74.3 x 61.3 cm.). Gift of Chester Dale

534 *Sir Joshua Reynolds*. 1784. Canvas, 36 x 30″ (95 x 76 cm.). Andrew W. Mellon Collection

535 *Commodore Thomas Macdonough*. Probably 1818. Wood, 28½ x 23″ (72.3 x 58 cm.). Andrew W. Mellon Collection

536 *Mrs. Lawrence Lewis*. 1804/5. Canvas, 29 x 24¼″ (73.7 x 61.6 cm.). Loan and partial gift of H. H. Walker Lewis in memory of his parents, Mr. and Mrs. Edwin A. S. Lewis

537 *John Bill Ricketts*. 1793/99. Canvas, 29⅝ x 24¼″ (75.1 x 61.6 cm.). Gift of Mrs. Robert B. Noyes in memory of Elisha Riggs

534

535

536

Gilbert Stuart was one of the most original of eighteenth-century painters. His late portraits, such as *Commodore Thomas Macdonough* (plate 535), have the indistinctness of unfocused vision, with the planes of the face adumbrated rather than defined, that we find in Velázquez. Stuart said, "In the commencement of all portraits the first idea is an indistinct mass of light and shadows, or the character of the person as seen in the heel of the evening, in the grey of the morning, or at a distance too great to distinguish features with exactness." An earlier, very beautiful portrait is that of Mrs. Lewis (plate 536), who was Nellie Custis, granddaughter of Martha Washington.

537

Gilbert Stuart

(AMERICAN, 1755–1828)

538   MRS. RICHARD YATES

To quote a contemporary, Dunlap, soon after painting *The Skater* Stuart had "his full share of the best business in London, and prices equal to any, except Sir Joshua Reynolds and Gainsborough." But his earnings could not keep pace with his expenditures. Deeply in debt, he returned to America and spent the rest of his life painting the heroes of the new Republic and the increasingly wealthy merchants and their families.

He once said, "I want to find out what nature is for myself, and see her with my own eyes." Such freshness of vision was easier to achieve in the Colonies than in the mother country, for in America no formula for painting had yet been established. Patrons like Mrs. Yates, the wife of a New York merchant, wanted to see themselves as they really were, and they were perfectly willing that an artist should make technical experiments if these led to a more accurate portrayal. Thus, after his return to America in 1793, Stuart's power of observation increased, and he noted, among other facts of vision, that "good flesh coloring partook of all colors, not mixed, so as to be combined in one tint, but shining through each other, like the blood through the natural skin." Had there been the artists and the tradition of painting in America that there were in France, these innovations of Stuart's might have caused Impressionism to appear in the New World generations before it revolutionized art in Europe.

Collections: Carlisle Pollock II, grandson of the sitter, New Orleans; and by descent to Mrs. Louise Chiapella Formento; Dr. Isaac M. Cline, New Orleans; Thomas B. Clarke, New York. *Andrew W. Mellon Collection*, 1940. Painted 1793/94. Canvas, 30¼ x 25" (77 x 63 cm.).

539

540

541

539 Edward Savage (American, 1761–1817): *The Washington Family.* 1796. Canvas, 84⅜ x 111⅞" (213.6 x 284.2 cm.). Andrew W. Mellon Collection

Gilbert Stuart   (American, 1755–1828)

540 *Benjamin Tappan.* 1814. Wood, 28⅝ x 23¼" (72.8 x 59 cm.). Gift of Lady Vereker

541 *John Randolph.* 1805. Canvas, 29⅛ x 24⅛" (74 x 61 cm.). Andrew W. Mellon Collection

542 *George Washington (Vaughan Portrait).* 1795. Canvas, 29 x 23¾" (73.5 x 60.5 cm.). Andrew W. Mellon Collection

543 *Mrs. John Adams.* 1815. Canvas, 29 x 23¾" (73.7 x 60.5 cm.). Gift of Mrs. Robert Homans

544 *John Adams.* 1815. Canvas, 29 x 24" (73.7 x 61.3 cm.). Gift of Mrs. Robert Homans

When in 1793 Stuart was swept back to America by an avalanche of debts, he told his creditors, "I hope to make a fortune by Washington alone." He did. His Washington portraits were numerous, and came to be known as Stuart's hundred-dollar bills, his charge for a replica. To have a portrait of the first president hanging on one's wall was a certificate of patriotism eagerly sought after by many former Tories. Edward Savage likewise became prosperous—by the sale of innumerable engravings after his *Washington Family* (plate 539), which was to become one of the most popular and famous of all American icons.

542

543

544

John Singleton Copley

(AMERICAN, 1738–1815)

545   THE COPLEY FAMILY

The career of John Singleton Copley, the greatest American artist of the eighteenth century, was the reverse of that of Stuart. Copley got his start in Boston and did not settle in London, where he spent the rest of his life, until 1775.

His wife's father, Richard Clarke, was a consignee of the famous shipment of tea which was sent to America contrary to the wishes of the Colonists, only to be thrown into the harbor in the Boston Tea Party. Consequently Clarke, a loyal Tory merchant, left the Colonies in high dudgeon and low repute, taking with him Copley's family. Copley, who had been studying in Italy for a year, soon joined his family in London. Shortly after his arrival he painted the group portrait reproduced here.

Mrs. Copley and her father sit in the foreground, surrounded by the little Copleys, while the artist looks out pensively from behind and clutches all that remains of his New England prosperity—a few sheets of drawings. Copley had reached a crossroads in his life. He was settled in England, faced with the necessity of making his way in an alien country where standards were very different from those he had left behind in Boston. He decided to change his whole approach to portraiture. *The Copley Family* shows, side by side, his old and his new styles. The painting of his father-in-law, especially his face and hands, and the charmingly rendered doll in the corner of the picture are the last echoes of that visual truth which characterized his early work. The painting of his wife, of the children, the composition of the picture, all are reminiscent of Reynolds, of West, of the "grand manner" of portraiture, which Copley forced himself to adopt. For a period he was successful and was elected a member of the Royal Academy, but he fell out of fashion. And though he painted more industriously than ever, he was unable to gain back his reputation. The end of his life was sad, for he was constantly menaced by debts and seems to have felt that he had betrayed his original gifts.

Collections: Copley family, London and Boston. *Andrew W. Mellon Fund*, 1961. Painted 1776/77. Canvas, 72½ x 90⅜" (184.4 x 229.7 cm.).

546

Copley's style, before the Revolution drove him to England, is illustrated by plates 546–49. Note in the men's portraits how every wrinkle is accurately delineated. It must have taken Copley days on end to paint these sitters, and there are records of some protests, but on the whole, it was easy in the Colonies to persuade them to pose repeatedly. There was nothing more amusing to do! This willingness to give the painter time benefited Copley. As he wrote, "My pictures are almost always good in proportion to the time I give them provided I have a subject that is picturesk." Two more "picturesk" faces than those of Sargent and Tyng would be hard to find.

547

548

549

550

546 John Singleton Copley (American, 1738–1815): *Jane Browne.* Signed, and dated 1756. Canvas, 30⅛ x 25⅛″ (77 x 64.3 cm.). Andrew W. Mellon Collection

547 John Singleton Copley: *Epes Sargent.* c. 1760. Canvas, 49⅞ x 40″ (126.8 x 101.6 cm.). Gift of the Avalon Foundation

548 John Singleton Copley: *Eleazer Tyng.* Signed, and dated 1772. Canvas, 49¾ x 40⅛″ (126.5 x 101.2 cm.). Gift of the Avalon Foundation

549 John Singleton Copley: *Mrs. Metcalf Bowler.* c. 1763. Canvas, 50 x 40¼″ (127 x 102 cm.). Gift of Louise Alida Livingston

550 Winthrop Chandler (American, 1747–1790): *Mrs. Samuel Chandler.* c. 1780. Canvas, 54¾ x 47⅞″ (139.1 x 121.7 cm.). Gift of Edgar William and Bernice Chrysler Garbisch

551 Winthrop Chandler: *Captain Samuel Chandler.* c. 1780. Canvas, 54⅞ x 47⅞″ (139.5 x 121.7 cm.). Gift of Edgar William and Bernice Chrysler Garbisch

551

John Singleton Copley

(AMERICAN, 1738–1815)

552 WATSON AND THE SHARK

Watson and the Shark represents a horrible incident which occurred in 1749 when a young British sailor swimming in Havana Harbor was attacked by a shark. On the first strike all the flesh from his leg below the calf was torn away, on the second his foot was bitten off at the ankle, and a third assault is about to begin. It is a moment of terror. Will the youth be dead before the boathook stops the shark?

Actually, the mutilated swimmer, Brook Watson, was rescued. He stumped on his wooden leg through a successful life to become a prominent merchant, Commissary General to the British armies in America, a member of Parliament, and Lord Mayor of London. The picture was commissioned to commemorate his survival, and ultimately willed to Christ's Hospital, a boys' school, in order, as a long inscription on the frame states, "that it might serve a most usefull Lesson to Youth." One must suppose the lesson Watson had in mind is the folly of bathing in the Caribbean. It is difficult to find any other message.

At the Royal Academy in 1778 the success of the painting was immediate. The *St. James Chronicle* said, "We heartily congratulate our Countrymen [*sic*. The War of Independence was still being fought] on a Genius, who bids fair to rival the great Masters of the Ancient Italian Schools." The comparison to Italian art is an astute one, for the pyramidal composition with its apex the top of the uplifted boathook is typical of the High Renaissance. Also, Copley probably learned how to achieve the recession into the picture, by a series of zigzagging diagonals, from his study of Italian painting.

Watson and the Shark was studiously prepared. Though Copley had never seen Havana, he must have studied engravings and maps. He has depicted Moro Castle on the right with some accuracy. Of the city itself he has shown the dome of the Cathedral and the Convent towers, all recorded in a drawing of 1762 by R. Bishop. Five detailed drawings and one oil sketch of the figures have also been preserved, and probably more have vanished. Copley made a careful replica, now in the Museum of Fine Arts in Boston. This he kept in his studio the rest of his life, and in 1782 he painted a small vertical version, now in the Detroit Institute of Arts. It is not surprising that he valued the painting greatly, for just as Stuart, four years later, was to be "suddenly lifted into fame by a single picture," *The Skater* (plate 531), so *Watson and the Shark* drew Copley "from silent insignificance to the beam of general notice." Thereafter for many years his success in England was assured.

Collections: Sir Brook Watson, London; Christ's Hospital, London. *Ferdinand Lammot Belin Fund*, 1963. Signed, and dated 1778. Canvas, 71¾ x 90½" (182.1 x 229.7 cm.).

553   John Singleton Copley (American, 1738–1815): *The Death of the Earl of Chatham.* Signed, and dated 1779. Canvas, 20¾ x 25⅜" (52.4 x 65 cm.). Gift of Mrs. Gordon Dexter

554   John Singleton Copley: *The Red Cross Knight.* 1793. Canvas, 84 x 107½" (213.5 x 273 cm.). Gift of Mrs. Gordon Dexter

555   John Singleton Copley: *Baron Graham.* Signed. 1804. Canvas, 57¼ x 46⅞" (145.3 x 118.9 cm.). Gift of Mrs. Gordon Dexter

556   John Singleton Copley: *Colonel Fitch and His Sisters.* 1800–1801. Canvas, 101½ x 134" (259.1 x 340.2 cm.). Gift of Eleanor Lothrop, Gordon Abbott, and Katharine A. Batchelder

557   Thomas Sully (American, 1783–1872): *Lady with a Harp: Eliza Ridgely.* Signed (monogram), and dated 1818. Canvas, 84⅜ x 56⅛" (214.6 x 142.6 cm.). Gift of Maude Monell Vetlesen

558   Thomas Sully: *Captain Charles Stewart.* 1811–12. Canvas, 93¼ x 58¾" (237 x 149 cm.). Gift of Maude Monell Vetlesen

553

Copley's English period is exemplified by plates 553–56. In London the expatriated artist continued for a while to paint with the same observation of character which lends such distinction to his American portraits. But gradually he was forced to compromise, to adapt his style to the prevailing fashion of Reynolds, Gainsborough, and Lawrence. Often, he looked wistfully homeward, frequently inquiring whether it would be wise for him to return. Sully, by contrast, felt comfortable in the slick, English style, which became the vogue in America as sophistication increased.

554

555

556

557

558

John Trumbull

(AMERICAN, 1756–1843)

559   PATRICK TRACY

Detective work is one of the most amusing of curatorial activities, as I pointed out in the commentary to plate 239. The investigation of Trumbull's portrait of Captain Patrick Tracy is an example. It was once exhibited at the Museum of Fine Arts in Boston as by Copley. Then, in 1948, Theodore Sizer, the Trumbull authority, stumbled on the painter's own checklist. Under the year 1784 he found: "No. 15. Whole length of Mr. P. Tracy (father of Nat) leaning on an anchor—head copied—recd. 20 guineas." With this information the author of the portrait and the date it was begun were further established. But two curators of the Gallery were baffled by the words "head copied." Sizer had presumed that Trumbull had made a copy of the head, which, unless destroyed, should exist somewhere. A search for the picture, however, proved unavailing.

Then the detective work began in earnest. A family notebook was found with the entry: "Patrick Tracy, painted by John Trumbull. 20 gns. 1786." It was noted that the head was painted in the manner of Copley, whose work Trumbull at first imitated. Reynolds characterized this style as looking like "bent tin." Stung by this criticism, Trumbull changed almost overnight and began to paint more fluently. This occurred about 1785, a year after his arrival in London; and as Patrick Tracy's portrait reveals both methods, one in the head and the other in the body, it is logical to deduce that the painting was done over a period of time.

To understand the next deduction it is necessary to know something about the Tracy family in the eighteenth century. Patrick Tracy was a Massachusetts warehouse owner. His son, Nathaniel, Nat Tracy, as he was called, sailed on July 5, 1784, for England. But was his father also a passenger? Thomas Jefferson was on the boat on his way to his embassy in Paris, and in a letter to a friend shortly after his arrival he asks to be remembered to Nat, but no word of Patrick. Abigail Adams wrote at least seven letters in 1784 in which she speaks of seeing Nathaniel Tracy in London, but Patrick is never mentioned.

But if Patrick did not come to London, how then did he pose for Trumbull, who was in England during those years? The answer is that he did not. The mysterious words "head copied" probably mean that for Patrick Tracy's head Trumbull copied someone else's painting, perhaps a miniature brought to England by Nathaniel. "20 gns. 1786" indicates the painting was delivered that year. Thus Trumbull seems to have had the portrait in his studio for two years, which would explain the discrepancy in style between the head and the rest of the body. Like all denouements in good detective stories, the final explanation is simple.

Collections: Family of the sitter, Cambridge, Massachusetts. *Gift of Patrick T. Jackson,* 1964. Painted 1784–86. Canvas, 91½ x 52⅝" (232.5 x 133.7 cm.).

560

561

562

560 **Ralph Earl** (American, 1751–1801): *Daniel Boardman*. Signed, and dated 1789. Canvas, 81⅝ x 55¼" (207.5 x 140.5 cm.). Gift of Mrs. W. Murray Crane

561 **John Trumbull** (American, 1756--1843): *Alexander Hamilton*. Probably 1792. Canvas, 30¼ x 24⅛" (76.9 x 61.3 cm.). Gift of the Avalon Foundation

562 **Samuel L. Waldo** (American, 1783–1861): *Robert G. L. De Peyster*. Signed, and dated 1828. Wood, 33 x 25¼" (84 x 63.6 cm.). Andrew W. Mellon Collection

563 **John James Audubon** (American, 1785–1851): *Arctic Hare*. c. 1841. Pencil, watercolor, ink, and oil on paper, 24½ x 34¼" (62.2 x 87.1 cm.). Gift of E. J. L. Hallstrom

564 **John Neagle** (American, 1796–1865): *Thomas W. Dyott*. Probably 1836. Canvas, 30 x 25" (76 x 64 cm.). Andrew W. Mellon Collection

565 **Chester Harding** (American, 1792–1866): *Amos Lawrence*. c. 1845. Canvas, 84⅝ x 54" (215 x 137 cm.). Given in memory of the Rt. Rev. William Lawrence by his children

563

564

With the exception of the one by Earl, who belongs to an earlier generation, the portraits reproduced here represent a cross-section of the work of the most competent American painters in the decades preceding the Civil War. Much more interesting, however, than the paintings of these portraitists are the prints of John James Audubon, the great naturalist. His *Birds of America* and *Viviparous Quadrupeds of North America*, which were engraved by Havell, are, to quote Cuvier's famous remark, "Le plus magnifique monument que l'art ait encore elévé à la science." The *Arctic Hare* (plate 563) is one of Audubon's rare known studies in oil for these epoch-making publications.

565

Spanish &
British Schools

XIX CENTURY

Francisco de Goya

(SPANISH, 1746–1828)

566 THE MARQUESA DE PONTEJOS

Until Picasso, Goya was the last of Spain's great painters. He was influenced, as were the American Colonial artists, by British painting. True, he knew the works of Gainsborough and Reynolds only in mezzotint engravings, but from prints after their portraits he learned to convey an impression of elegance and luxury. However, as a society portraitist in the English sense, his character was flawed. He could not take his sitters seriously. The Marquesa is just a little ridiculous. She is a fashion plate, as much the product of artificial selection as her pug dog. Her tulle skirt was more amusing to Goya than her insipid face. It offered him an opportunity to paint her portrait in a mockingly light palette with piquant alternations of sweet and acid colors.

In this work of Goya's early years there appears for the first time a note that is sardonic, even cynical. This was to swell to the terrifying chord, the clash of horror, the rumble of social systems in collapse that is heard with such fearful force in the great masterpieces of Goya's later years. This combination of a much deeper seriousness and a bitter disbelief in all established things provided a basis for those revolutions in painting which, under his influence, took place in France in the next century.

Collections: Marquesa de Martorell y de Pontejos, Madrid; Marqués de Miraflores y de Pontejos, Madrid. *Andrew W. Mellon Collection*, 1937. Painted possibly 1786. Canvas, 83 x 49¾" (211 x 126 cm.).

567

568

Goya's cynicism was nurtured at the Spanish court. Ruled over by an otiose king and a scheming queen, its corruption was appalling. Goya has depicted these two rulers as ugly manikins: he irresolute, she dissolute. In their miserable way they destroyed their niece, Doña María Teresa, later known as the Chinchón, whom Goya had painted as a beautiful child of almost three (plate 568). They forced her to marry Manuel Godoy. Godoy, the king's closest friend and trusted adviser, also happened to be the queen's lover and was by reputation the most depraved libertine at court. After experiencing her husband's infidelities and cruelty, the Chinchón sat for Goya again. This second likeness, which is owned by the Prado in Madrid, is the most melancholy portrait in existence.

569

571

570

Francisco de Goya (Spanish, 1746–1828)

567 *Carlos IV of Spain as Huntsman.* Probably 1799 or shortly after. Canvas, 18¼ x 11¾″ (46 x 30 cm.). Andrew W. Mellon Collection

568 *Condesa de Chinchón.* 1783. Canvas, 53 x 46¼″ (134.7 x 117.5 cm.). Ailsa Mellon Bruce Collection

569 *María Luisa, Queen of Spain.* Probably 1799 or shortly after. Canvas, 18¼ x 11¾″ (46 x 30 cm.). Andrew W. Mellon Collection

570 *Victor Guye.* 1810. Canvas, 42 x 33½″ (106.7 x 85.1 cm.). Gift of William Nelson Cromwell

571 *Don Antonio Noriega.* Signed, and dated 1801. Canvas, 40⅜ x 31⅞″ (102.6 x 80.9 cm.). Samuel H. Kress Collection

Francisco de Goya

(SPANISH, 1746–1828)

572 DOÑA TERESA SUREDA

Sometimes a painting is more interesting when considered in conjunction with its pendant. To appreciate fully the portrait of Doña Teresa, look at plate 576, where a portrait by Goya of her husband is reproduced. He was a painter, one of the first Spanish lithographers, an authority on the manufacture of glass, porcelain, and textiles, and, from 1804 to 1808, the director of the royal porcelain factory of the Buen Retiro in Madrid, where he introduced the production of Sèvres porcelain. He was also Goya's friend, and they must in all probability have spent many late and companionable evenings together. On their return one can easily imagine that they were confronted by this icy, outraged woman. Goya has painted not only a portrait but a point of view—the intolerance of uncompromising rectitude. Note the stiff line of Doña Teresa's back and how her resentment is conveyed by her hard, staring eyes and her sullen mouth. Here is a whole novel in two pictures.

Goya's portraits are different from those of earlier artists. Velázquez, for example, portrays his sitters with complete detachment, imposing no mood whatever, permitting us to make our own judgment; Rembrandt sees his subjects as an opportunity to convey his own tragic feelings; Frans Hals presents his men and women with a photographic superficiality which makes them seem acquaintances who will never become friends. Goya, on the other hand, studies character in relation to social position and environment. Occasionally one seems even to sense the sitter's reaction to a particular situation. This type of analysis, a combination of sociology and psychology, was a distinct innovation in portraiture and a remarkable contribution to art.

Collections: The family of the sitter; Havemeyer family, New York. *Gift of Mr. and Mrs. P. H. B. Frelinghuysen in memory of her father and mother, Mr. and Mrs. H. O. Havemeyer, 1941.* Painted c. 1805. Canvas, 47⅛ x 31¼'' (119.8 x 79.4 cm.).

573

573 Attributed to Francisco de Goya (Spanish, c. 1827): *The Bullfight.* Canvas, 29 x 43¼" (73.9 x 109.9 cm.). Gift of Arthur Sachs

Francisco de Goya (Spanish, 1746–1828)

574 *The Bookseller's Wife.* Signed. c. 1805. Canvas, 43¼ x 30¾" (109.9 x 78.2 cm.). Gift of Mrs. P.H.B. Frelinghuysen

575 *The Duke of Wellington.* Probably 1812. Canvas, 41½ x 33" (105.5 x 83.7 cm.). Gift of Mrs. P.H.B. Frelinghuysen

576 *Don Bartolomé Sureda.* c. 1805. Canvas, 47⅛ x 31¼" (119.7 x 79.4 cm.). Gift of Mr. and Mrs. P.H.B. Frelinghuysen

577 *Señora Sabasa García.* c. 1806 or 1807. Canvas, 28 x 23" (71 x 58 cm.). Andrew W. Mellon Collection

574

575

577

576

The works reproduced here give some indication of the range of Goya's portraits. The Duke of Wellington has been transformed from an Englishman into a Spaniard, something he did not fancy. At the other end of the social scale is *The Bookseller's Wife* (plate 574), a handsome girl of the middle class, and a sitter more to Goya's taste. In between is Sabasa García, the niece of Spain's foreign minister. According to tradition, she entered Goya's studio while he was painting her uncle, and he was so struck by her dazzling beauty that he sent the foreign minister home and devoted himself to this portrait of a much more inspiring model.

John Constable

(BRITISH, 1776–1837)

578   WIVENHOE PARK, ESSEX

One function of art is to suggest a world perfectly attuned to human desires. During the Renaissance this earthly paradise was usually located in Greece, in a pastoral country known as Arcadia. Today the English countryside of a century or more ago has something of the same nostalgic appeal for us that the Hellenic world had for the humanists of the Renaissance. However, Arcadian shepherds are imaginary figures, whereas we know from a host of novelists how real was the English squirearchy, how actual its serene and stable environment.

"Arcadian realism" may seem a contradictory term, but it describes the charm of many of Constable's canvases. His scenes are filled with poetry, visions of the tranquil delight of an ideal rural existence. Yet, at the same time, they have an extraordinary reality, conveying as they do flashes of insight into the momentary moods of nature with that sensibility which is at the heart of modern landscape painting.

In a letter written in 1816 by Constable to his future wife, we sense how much owners of estates like Wivenhoe Park must have esteemed their possessions. "My dearest Love," Constable wrote, "I have been here since Monday and am as happy as I can be away from you. . . . I am going on very well with my pictures. The park is the most forward. The great difficulty has been to get so much in as they [the Rebows] wanted . . . so that my view comprehended too many degrees. But today I got over the difficulty and I begin to like it myself."

The wish of the owner to see as much as possible of his estate explains the unusually wide angle of the artist's view. But Constable, by the actuality he gives *Wivenhoe Park*, triumphs over this difficult composition and makes us agree with General Rebow that it would not be possible to see too much of so entrancing a scene. So there is no necessity for the twilight with which earlier landscapists gave a romantic aspect to their Arcadian scenery. Instead, Constable has found in a typical English day of scattered clouds and brilliant sunshine a new inspiration. He reveals "the infinite variety of natural appearances," and delights in the loveliness of flickering, sparkling light as it falls on leaves and grass and water. Painting was changed by such a fresh observation of landscape, just as poetry was changed at about the same time by Wordsworth's descriptions of nature.

Collection: Wivenhoe Park, Essex. *Widener Collection*, 1942. Painted 1816. Canvas, 22⅛ x 39⅞" (56.1 x 101.2 cm.).

579

579 John Constable (British, 1776–1837): *The White Horse*. Probably 1819. Canvas, 50 x 72" (127 x 183 cm.). Widener Collection

580 John Constable: *A View of Salisbury Cathedral*. Probably c. 1825. Canvas, 28¾ x 36" (73 x 91 cm.). Andrew W. Mellon Collection

581 George Morland (British, 1763–1804): *The End of the Hunt*. Signed. c. 1794. Canvas, 56 x 74" (142 x 188 cm.). Widener Collection

582 John Ferneley (British, 1782–1860): *In the Paddock*. c. 1830. Canvas, 36¼ x 60⅛" (92 x 152.6 cm.). Ailsa Mellon Bruce Collection

580

The White Horse, owned by the Frick Collection in New York City, is the first of the pictures Constable called his "six-footers." These canvases intended for the Royal Academy were preceded by paintings and drawings done directly from nature, followed by a full-scale sketch painted in the studio, and finally the picture to be exhibited—a procedure unusual if not unique among landscapists. Plate 579 reproduces the preliminary study for the Frick Collection painting. The final version was shown at the Academy in 1819 and bought by Archdeacon Fisher, the nephew of the Bishop of Salisbury and Constable's closest friend. Constable spent many weeks in the Bishop's palace painting his cathedral; one of the finest of these landscapes is plate 580.

581

582

Joseph Mallord William Turner

(BRITISH, 1775–1851)

583   MORTLAKE TERRACE

In 1827 Turner exhibited at the Royal Academy the picture reproduced here, which was titled *Mortlake Terrace, the Seat of William Moffatt, Esq.; Summer's Evening*. The preceding year he had exhibited the same site seen from the opposite direction and bathed in the light of an early summer morning, a picture now in the Frick Collection in New York. These two canvases were executed at a moment of significant change in Turner's style: a period when light and the rendering of a visible atmosphere were becoming his preoccupation, to the exclusion of his earlier interest in topography. Though he was doubtless fulfilling a commission in depicting Moffatt's garden terrace from opposite points and under contrasting illumination, Turner's whole effort was concentrated on the atmospheric envelope of the scene, on rendering the sun-filled mist of a hot afternoon. As one of the most astute of French critics, Théophile Thoré (W. Bürger), wrote in 1865, "Everything seems to be luminous with its own light and to throw its own rays and sparks. Claude, the master of luminosity, has never done anything so prodigious!"

How little Turner worried at this time about the design of his paintings is illustrated by the story of the dog on the parapet. The anecdote is recorded by Frederick Goodall, whose father engraved some of Turner's pictures. On Varnishing Day at the Royal Academy when Turner was out for lunch, Edwin Landseer, the animal painter, came in and noticed *Mortlake Terrace*. He saw at once that it needed an accent in the center, and so he cut out of paper a little dog and stuck it on the parapet. "When Turner returned," Goodall says, "he went up to the picture quite unconcernedly, never said a word, adjusted the little dog perfectly, and then varnished the paper and began painting it. And there it is to the present day." There is no doubt that the composition of the painting was saved by this accidental but highly successful collaboration, one of the most unusual in the history of art.

Collections: Perhaps William Moffatt, owner of Mortlake Terrace; Joseph Hamatt; Rev. Edward J. Daniel; Thomas Creswick, R.A.; E. B. Fripp; Samuel Ashton; Thomas Ashton; Mrs. Elizabeth Gair Ashton. *Andrew W. Mellon Collection*, 1937. Painted c. 1826. Canvas, 36¼ x 48⅛" (92 x 122.2 cm.).

584

Of these six pictures only *The Junction of the Thames and the Medway* belongs to Turner's first period. The change in his style over the years is extraordinary, and is well illustrated by the other reproductions. The somber colors of the early work are transformed into irridescent hues, the massive volumes of the waves to shimmering, glassy water, the dark, windswept clouds to dazzling light and translucent atmosphere. Turner in his paintings gradually transmutes the density of matter into the fluidity of air. His late pictures have been aptly described as "painted with tinted steam."

585

586

587

588

Joseph Mallord William Turner (British, 1775–1851)

584 *The Junction of the Thames and the Medway.* c. 1805/8. Canvas, 42¾ × 56½″ (108.8 × 143.7 cm.). Widener Collection

585 *Keelmen Heaving in Coals by Moonlight.* Signed with initials. Probably 1835. Canvas, 36¼ × 48¼″ (92.3 × 122.8 cm.). Widener Collection

586 *The Dogana and Santa Maria della Salute, Venice.* Signed with initials. Probably 1843. Canvas, 24⅜ × 36⅝″ (62 × 93 cm.). Given in memory of Governor Alvan T. Fuller by the Fuller Foundation

587 *Van Tromp's Shallop.* c. 1832. Canvas, 36⅜ × 48¼″ (92.3 × 122.5 cm.). Ailsa Mellon Bruce Collection

588 *Venice: Dogana and San Giorgio Maggiore.* Probably 1834. Canvas, 36 × 48″ (91.5 × 122 cm.). Widener Collection

589 *Approach to Venice.* c. 1843. Canvas, 24½ × 37″ (62 × 94 cm.). Andrew W. Mellon Collection

589

590

The Corinthian Maid (plate 590), by Joseph Wright of Derby, was commissioned by the famous porcelain manufacturer Josiah Wedgwood. It is the essence of Neoclassicism and could easily be translated into a bas-relief. The subject is an allegory of the invention of pictorial art. According to Pliny, the daughter of a Corinthian potter incised her lover's shadow on the wall. Her father made a clay mold of the image and baked it with his pottery. Hence the appeal of the story to Wedgwood. The subject of Henry Fuseli's painting (plate 591) is taken from Sophocles' *Oedipus at Colonus.* The exiled and self-blinded king of Thebes curses his son for abandoning him; by contrast, his two daughters (seen on either side), he declared, "preserve me, these my nurses, these who are men, not women, in true service." Here the emotional exaggerations indicate the growing strength of the Romantic movement, which displaced Neoclassicism.

590 Joseph Wright of Derby (British, 1734–1797): *The Corinthian Maid.* c. 1783–84. Canvas, 41⅞ x 51½" (106.3 x 130.8 cm.). Paul Mellon Collection

591 Henry Fuseli (Swiss, active in England, 1741–1825): *Oedipus Cursing His Son Polynices.* c. 1776–78. Canvas, 57 x 64" (137.1 x 162.6 cm.). Paul Mellon Collection

592 Arnold Boecklin (Swiss, 1827–1901): *The Sanctuary of Hercules.* Signed. 1884. Wood, 44⅞ x 71⅛" (113.8 x 180.5 cm.). Andrew W. Mellon Fund

591

A third echo of classical literature appears in *The Sanctuary of Hercules* (plate 592). Painted almost a century later by Arnold Boecklin, who like Fuseli was born in Switzerland, it melds the two movements, showing figures from the ancient world in a setting of romantic gloom. Three soldiers kneel at a shrine dedicated to Hercules, whose statue in profile can be seen at the back; one soldier stands and gazes defiantly at the ominous clouds on the horizon. Humility and defiance, twin aspects of the Romantic movement, are acted out before the mysterious sanctuary. An immense spiritual chasm separates Boecklin's introspective painting from the objectivity of Wright and the hyperbole of Fuseli.

592

French School

XIX CENTURY

Jacques-Louis David

(FRENCH, 1748–1825)

593 NAPOLEON IN HIS STUDY

How much our concept of historic personages depends upon the artists who portrayed them! Compared to Napoleon, men like Doge Gritti (see plate 246) or Giuliano de' Medici (see plate 59) were insignificant. Yet no one who painted the Emperor was able to give him an appearance of authority, of human grandeur. Perhaps Napoleon lived too late. The available artists were incapable of creating an image commensurate with his achievement. David tried, but has managed merely to supply a mass of external trappings.

The Emperor's uniform combines details of the Grenadiers of his famous Imperial Guard with an infantry general's epaulettes, a uniform worn by him on Sundays and special occasions. His medals are the insignia of the Legion of Honor and the Iron Cross of Italy, two orders which he himself had created. Beneath the table is a copy of Plutarch's *Lives*. The manuscript of the *Code Napoléon* is on the desk. The pen and scattered papers, the candles burning to their sockets, and the clock pointing to a quarter-past four, all indicate that the Emperor has just finished a hard night's work. This unmitigated flattery caused the Emperor to say to the artist, "You have understood me, David. By night I work for the welfare of my subjects, and by day for their glory."

Just as the portrait of Gritti probably held a special significance for Charles I, so this portrait of Napoleon, a masterpiece of political propaganda, must have had its own meaning for another Briton, the Duke of Hamilton, who looked upon himself as descended from James I and thus the rightful heir to the throne of Scotland. A Catholic, a Scottish nationalist, and a close friend of Napoleon's sister, Pauline Bonaparte, he considered the Emperor a potential ally in the restoration of the Stuarts. In his gallery the portrait of the archenemy of his country, which he had commissioned David to paint, was predominant.

Although the painting is signed and dated 1812, David's grandson said it was painted in Paris in 1810. But the correct date is established by the chair designed by David himself and delivered in 1812, as well as by correspondence which shows that the portrait was being worked on in the winter of that year, shortly before Napoleon embarked on his fatal Russian invasion. There were supposed to be four replicas of the Hamilton portrait, but only one, belonging to Prince Napoleon, can be definitely identified.

Collections: Marquess of Douglas (Alexander, tenth Duke of Hamilton), Hamilton Palace, near Glasgow; Archibald Philip, fifth Earl of Rosebery; Albert Edward, sixth Earl of Rosebery, London. *Samuel H. Kress Collection*, 1961. Signed, and dated 1812. Canvas, 80¼ x 49¼" (203.9 x 125.1 cm.).

417

594

595

596

594 Jacques-Louis David (French, 1748–1825): *Madame David*. Signed, and dated 1813. Canvas, 28¾ x 23⅜" (72.9 x 59.4 cm.). Samuel H. Kress Collection

595 Circle of Jacques-Louis David (French, early XIX century): *Portrait of a Young Woman in White*. Canvas, 49⅜ x 37½" (125.4 x 95.2 cm.). Chester Dale Collection

596 Pierre-Paul Prud'hon (French, 1758–1823): *David Johnston*. Signed, and dated 1808. Canvas, 21⅝ x 18⅜" (55 x 46.6 cm.). Samuel H. Kress Collection

597 Baron François Gérard (French, 1770–1837): *The Model*. c. 1790. Canvas, 24⅛ x 19¾" (61.2 x 50.2 cm.). Chester Dale Collection

598 Théodore Géricault (French, 1791–1824): *Trumpeters of Napoleon's Imperial Guard*. 1812/14. Canvas, 23¾ x 19½" (60.4 x 49.6 cm.). Chester Dale Collection

599 Georges Rouget (French, 1784–1869): *Jacques-Louis David*. Probably c. 1815. Canvas, 35⅛ x 26¼" (89.2 x 67.8 cm.). Chester Dale Collection

597

599

598

French painting in the first half of the nineteenth century was marked by three successive movements: Classicism, Romanticism, and Realism. David was founder of Classicism, and Gerard and Rouget were his followers. Ingres, as we shall see, was the greatest of all Classicists (see plates 600–603). Romanticism was introduced by Géricault, and its most brilliant exponent was Delacroix, whose works are to be seen in plates 605 and 606. Courbet (see plates 638–44) set himself up as the leader of the Realists, saying that his goal was to interpret the manners, ideas, and aspects of his own time.

Jean-Auguste-Dominique Ingres

(FRENCH, 1780–1867)

600   MADAME MOITESSIER

Fashion in feminine beauty is as variable as fashion in clothes. Occasionally this mutability of taste affects the appreciation of a work of art. Many people today, for example, would consider Mme Moitessier, as she appears in her portrait by Ingres, an ugly woman, corpulent and bovine. Their dislike of her appearance might even blind them to the merits of the painting. Yet to Ingres, the outstanding master of the French academic school, she was the reincarnation of a goddess of the ancient world, an archetype of the beautiful woman.

Although the portraitist often extolled his sitter's appearance, he seems to have had only a secondary interest in her personality. He worked for months on her portrait, finishing the dress and accessories; then he added the arms and hands; and finally he attached the head to the bare shoulders. Painting backward, so to speak, he treated his picture less as portraiture than as still life, and concentrated his immense virtuosity on painting Mme Moitessier's clothes, jewels, fan, and beside her the chair with gloves and fur jacket. It is Ingres' marvelous conjunction of eye and hand in such passages, the way he renders the subtle ellipses of flesh in the fat arms, the depth of translucence in the rubies and sapphires, the sheen of the pearl necklace, the subtle distinction between the gilt of the chair and the gold of the bracelets, that shows his mastery of realistic detail. This verisimilitude has remained, on his example, the principal goal of academic painting.

Character is certainly lacking in Mme Moitessier's somnolent face, but her cold and symmetrical beauty offered Ingres a solution to a conflict at the heart of his style. He was both a classicist and a realist; consequently his selective instinct impelled him toward models who recalled the canons of classical proportion, as we know them from the sculpture of Greece or Rome, and he was really happy only when depicting people who approached this ideal. Once at the opera a pupil, seeing the master restless and obviously disturbed, asked whether he did not admire the tenor's voice. "Yes, yes," Ingres answered, "it's a beautiful voice and beautifully produced but . . . his eyes are rather wide apart!" In looking at Mme Moitessier, however, he found no such fault. Her regular features and ample figure were an inspiration and a challenge. Théophile Gautier, the French critic, wrote after watching her pose for this portrait: "Never did beauty more regal, more magnificent, more stately, and of a more Junoesque type, offer its proud lines to the tremulous pencil of an artist."

Collections: M. and Mme Sigisbert Moitessier; Comtesse de Flavigny (née Moitessier); Vicomtesse O. de Bondy (née Moitessier); Comte Olivier de Bondy, Château de la Barre (Indre). *Samuel H. Kress Collection,* 1946. Signed, and dated 1851. Canvas, 57¾ x 39½" (146.7 x 100.3 cm.).

421

601

602

Raphael was the god of Classicism, whose most devout believer was Ingres. Ingres and his followers stressed probity of drawing, beauty of line, infrangibility of surface, and restraint of color. His artistic opponent, Delacroix, the leader of the Romantics, derived his art principally from Rubens, emphasizing richness of color, violence of movement, expressive brushwork, and exotic subject matter.

603

604

601 **Jean-Auguste-Dominique Ingres** (French, 1780–1867): *Pope Pius VII in the Sistine Chapel.* Signed, and dated 1810. Canvas, 29¼ x 36½″ (74.5 x 92.7 cm.). Samuel H. Kress Collection

602 **Jean-Auguste-Dominique Ingres**: *Ulysses.* Signed. c. 1827. Canvas on wood, 9¼ x 7¼″ (24.9 x 18.5 cm.). Chester Dale Collection

603 **Jean-Auguste-Dominique Ingres***: Monsieur Marcotte.* Signed, and dated 1810. Canvas, 36¾ x 27¼″ (93.5 x 69.3 cm.). Samuel H. Kress Collection

604 **Baron Antoine-Jean Gros** (French, 1771–1835): *Dr. Vignardonne.* Signed. 1827. Canvas, 31⅞ x 25¼″ (81 x 64.3 cm.). Chester Dale Collection

605 **Eugène Delacroix** (French, 1798–1863): *Columbus and His Son at La Rábida.* Signed, and dated 1838. Canvas, 35⅝ x 46⅝″ (90.4 x 118.3 cm.). Chester Dale Collection

605

Eugène Delacroix

606   ARABS SKIRMISHING IN THE MOUNTAINS

In 1832 Delacroix was attached to a French military mission sent to the Sultan of Morocco. His journey lasted five months. He arrived in Tangier exhausted from the competitive struggle which had marked his life since the Revolution of 1830. He had lost his appetite for work and was much in need of the refreshment and inspiration of new scenes. These he found in North Africa. He wrote a friend, "The thought of my reputation, of that Salon which I was supposed to be missing, never occurs to me. I'm even sure that the considerable sum of curious information that I shall bring back from here will be of little use to me. Away from the land where I discovered them, such particulars will be like trees torn from their native soil; my mind will have forgotten its impressions, and I shall disdain to give a cold and imperfect rendering of the living and striking sublimity that lies all about one here."

He was wrong. His mind always retained its impressions of North Africa. His sketches in the Louvre, small and fragile as they are, remain among the great treasures of French art. Throughout his life he turned to them repeatedly. *Arabs Skirmishing in the Mountains*, for example, was painted thirty-one years after his visit to Morocco, a few months before his death. It was his last important easel picture and was shown in the Centennial Exhibition of 1863.

Delacroix's feelings about the Arabs were ambivalent. In one letter just after his arrival he wrote, "This place is made for painters. . . ." By contrast, a month later he wrote, "I have spent most of my time here in utter boredom, because it was impossible to draw anything from nature openly, even the meanest hovel; if you so much as go on to the terrace you run the risk of being stoned or shot at. The Moors are fantastically jealous, and it is on these terraces that their women usually take the air or visit one another." But time alchemized these days of boredom into golden memories. He recalled the strong colors, the blinding light, the violence, all of which appealed deeply to his nature. In recollection he saw these Arabs as romantic heroes, fierce and courageous warriors, as wild and unbroken as their beautiful horses.

In 1865 Delacroix's first biographer wrote that the battle scene in the picture reproduced here represented a fight between tax collectors and their reluctant victims. As far as one can judge, the Sultan's emissaries are losing. But how much more picturesque they are than their tamer yet never defeated colleagues today! It has often amused me to think that this violent resistance to tax collecting now hangs a few blocks from the United States Bureau of Internal Revenue.

Collections: Edouard André, Paris; A. Smit, Paris; C. D. Borden, New York; James J. Hill, St. Paul; Louis W. Hill, St. Paul; Jerome Hill, New York. *Chester Dale Collection*, 1966. Signed, and dated 1863. Canvas, 36⅜ x 29⅜" (92.5 x 74.6 cm.).

Jean-Baptiste-Camille Corot

(FRENCH, 1796–1875)

607 AGOSTINA

Time may prove Corot to have been the most important painter of the nineteenth century. Certainly the admiration he has aroused in other artists has been unceasing, and his influence even on contemporary artists like Picasso, immense. He was one of the few artists of recent times to excel not only in landscape but also in figure painting, of which *Agostina* is an outstanding example. Here he combines an alertness of vision with a profound knowledge of Renaissance style. This Italian peasant girl, who stands with unself-conscious detachment, evokes the heroic women of Piero della Francesca. But she is also of her own century, for she has been observed by the artist with an enamored and penetrating scrutiny which brings her much closer to actuality, to the living model, than her fifteenth-century forebears.

The plastic values which distinguish Corot's best landscapes are due in part to his constant study of human form. This is of importance in understanding his work. There is a profound difference in style between those landscape painters who are either incapable of drawing the human form, or draw it in a perfunctory way, and those whose art is based on a knowledge of the body. In one category we have artists like Perugino, Claude Lorrain, most of the Dutch landscape painters with the significant exception of Rembrandt, and, in the nineteenth century, Turner and Monet, among others. All these artists could draw the human figure after a fashion, but none of them was a figure painter of any consequence. In their landscapes we find that such effects as the sweep of distance and the play of light are stressed, but in the beautiful iridescent spaces they create, everything is insubstantial, intangible. The other category, those artists like Corot who have mastered the hollows and bosses of the human form, its plastic shape, seem able to translate this knowledge of mass and volume into hills and rocks and trees. Painters like Rubens, Poussin, Rembrandt, Cézanne, and, at his best, Corot are intent on rendering the plastic character of nature. They model trees and rocks with the same studious gravity they show toward the human body. They seem to be in search of the tendons and sinews of nature.

Collections: Breysse, Paris; Faure, Paris; Paton, Paris; Bernheim-Jeune, Paris. *Chester Dale Collection*, 1962. Signed. Painted probably 1866. Canvas, 52¼ x 38⅜″ (132.8 x 97.6 cm.).

608

609

610

Jean-Baptiste-Camille Corot   (French, 1796–1875)

608   *Italian Peasant Boy.* Signed. 1825/26. Canvas, 10 x 12⅞″ (25.4 x 32.6 cm.). Chester Dale Collection

609   *Gypsy Girl with Mandolin.* Signed. Probably c. 1870/75. Canvas, 25 x 20″ (63.9 x 51 cm.). Gift of Count Cecil Pecci-Blunt

610   *The Artist's Studio.* Signed. c. 1855/60. Wood, 24⅜ x 15¾″ (62 x 40 cm.). Widener Collection

611   *Portrait of a Young Girl.* Signed, and dated 1859. Canvas, 10¾ x 9⅛″ (27.4 x 23.2 cm.). Chester Dale Collection

612   *Italian Girl.* Signed. c. 1871/72. Canvas, 25⅝ x 21⅝″ (65.1 x 52.4 cm.). Gift of the Avalon Foundation

613   *Madame Stumpf and Her Daughter.* Signed. 1872. Canvas, 41¾ x 29¼″ (106 x 74.2 cm.). Ailsa Mellon Bruce Collection

614   *River Scene with Bridge.* Signed, and dated 1834. Canvas, 9⅞ x 13⅜″ (25 x 33.8 cm.). Ailsa Mellon Bruce Collection

611

612

Corot was extensively collected in the United States, and it is not surprising that the National Gallery's collection of his works is among the richest outside the Louvre. Looking at the pictures reproduced here offers an opportunity to measure Corot's monumentality and plasticity against the great Renaissance masters, and also to judge the precision of his observation of the subject, which, in the *Portrait of a Young Girl* (plate 611) and *The Artist's Studio* (plate 610), challenges Vermeer in faultless modeling and accurate rendering of light.

613

614

Jean-Baptiste-Camille Corot

(FRENCH, 1796–1875)

615   A VIEW NEAR VOLTERRA

A View near Volterra belongs to Corot's earlier style. It is dated 1838, four years after he had visited the Etruscan site of Volterra. It is therefore a *souvenir d'Italie*, an evocation of a mood the artist had felt when he entered that strange, wild country, that *pays magnifique*, as he described it in his sketchbook. But the painting itself was based on careful studies and sketches made at the time, and it seems to fulfill the profession of a faith which Corot expressed in his youth when he wrote, *"Il ne faut laisser d'indécision dans aucune chose."* Consequently, we feel in the scene itself the same sense of a vivid reality which the artist experienced as he sketched one day in the early summer sunlight, yet we also feel that the emotion conveyed is an "emotion recollected in tranquillity," a mood revived long after the event by some nostalgia, some longing for the olive greens and soft, luminous skies of Italy. This has given to the painting qualities both of timelessness and of actuality, qualities which Corot himself seems to have appreciated; for we find that he often returned in this way to scenes he had enjoyed on his early Italian journeys. Led by these recollections, he painted from memory again and again the sights of classical civilization, the world of Horace and Vergil, whose feelings for nature were so akin to his own.

It is curious, however, how little these superb paintings of Italy were appreciated during Corot's lifetime. He sent a *View of Volterra* to the Salon of 1838, doubtless the picture now in the Timken Art Gallery, San Diego, and the critics found it cold, timid in execution, without distinction or brilliance. Probably they would have been equally critical of the Chester Dale picture, which was painted the same year. They failed to see the real importance of these paintings: that they were remarkable revivals of the classical tradition, and that they illustrated what Cézanne had in mind when he is quoted as saying, *"Imaginez Poussin refait entièrement sur nature."* For Corot's landscapes of this period possess the formal beauty of Poussin's style without his artificiality, his declamatory effects, his suggestion of stage scenery. It was the blindness of the critics, year after year, which caused Corot to compromise and to give the classical style a sentimental interpretation. But as the familiar gray mist spread through his landscapes, his extraordinary gift for the rendering of plastic volume disappeared.

Collection: Baronne Thénard, Paris. *Chester Dale Collection,* 1962. Signed, and dated 1838. Canvas, 27⅜ x 37½" (69.5 x 95.2 cm.).

616

Jean-Baptiste-Camille Corot (French, 1796–1875)

616 *Forest of Fontainebleau*. Signed. c. 1830. Canvas, 69⅛ x 95½" (175.6 x 242.6 cm.). Chester Dale Collection

617 *The Eel Gatherers*. Signed. c. 1860/65. Canvas, 23¾ x 32" (60 x 81 cm.). Gift of Mr. and Mrs. P.H.B. Frelinghuysen in memory of her father and mother, Mr. and Mrs. H. O. Havemeyer

618 *The Forest of Coubron*. Signed, and dated 1872. Canvas, 37¾ x 30" (96 x 76 cm.). Widener Collection

619 *Rocks in the Forest of Fontainebleau*. Signed. 1860/65. Canvas, 18 x 23" (45.9 x 58.5 cm.). Chester Dale Collection

620 *View near Epernon*. Signed. 1850/60. Canvas, 12¾ x 21" (32.5 x 53.5 cm.). Widener Collection

621 *Ville d' Avray*. Signed. c. 1867/70. Canvas, 19⅜ x 25⅝" (49.2 x 65.3 cm.). Gift of Count Cecil Pecci-Blunt

622 *River View*. Signed. Probably c. 1870. Wood, 12⅝ x 16⅜" (32.3 x 41.8 cm.). Gift of R. Horace Gallatin

617

618

619

620

621

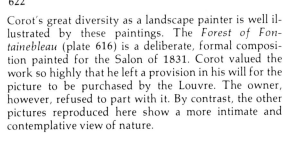

622

Corot's great diversity as a landscape painter is well il-lustrated by these paintings. The *Forest of Fon-tainebleau* (plate 616) is a deliberate, formal composi-tion painted for the Salon of 1831. Corot valued the work so highly that he left a provision in his will for the picture to be purchased by the Louvre. The owner, however, refused to part with it. By contrast, the other pictures reproduced here show a more intimate and contemplative view of nature.

Honoré Daumier

(FRENCH, 1808–1879)

623   ADVICE TO A YOUNG ARTIST

Corot's figure style influenced the work of his close companion, Daumier. The two artists had much in common—both sought and found the true tradition of painting in the Italian masters. Balzac said of Daumier, "He is a man who has something of Michelangelo in his blood." But this great talent had to be lavished on caricatures for various periodicals. Poverty left Daumier little time for painting, and with failing eyesight he could not draw and sell his famous cartoons fast enough to pay his rent, even for the dilapidated cottage he occupied at Valmondois. But he was fortunate in one thing—in friendship. Corot secretly bought Daumier's house, and wrote him as follows: "My old comrade—I had a little house for which I had no use at Valmondois near the Isle-Adam. The idea came into my head of offering it to you, and as I think it is a good idea, I have placed it in your name at the notary's. It is not for you that I do this, it is merely to annoy your landlord." It was a simple gesture, and it gave Daumier a few serene and tranquil years. But it meant that Corot painted fewer Agostinas and more misty lakes, fewer masterpieces and more potboilers. In return for this sacrifice, a few paintings like this, which once belonged to Corot, were all that Daumier could give his old friend, but into their execution he poured all the brilliant genius that a lifetime of poverty could not destroy.

Collections: J.-B.-C. Corot, Paris; Adolphe A. Tavernier, Paris; Cronier, Paris; Goerg, Rheims. *Gift of Duncan Phillips*, 1941. Signed. Painted probably after 1860. Canvas, 16⅛ x 12⅞" (41 x 33 cm.).

434

435

624

625

626

Honoré Daumier (French, 1808–1879)

624 *The Beggars.* Signed. c. 1845. Canvas, 23½ x 29⅛″ (59.7 x 74 cm.). Chester Dale Collection

625 *French Theater.* Signed. c. 1857/60. Wood, 10¼ x 13¼″ (25.9 x 35 cm.). Chester Dale Collection

626 *Wandering Saltimbanques.* c. 1847/50. Wood, 12⅞ x 9¾″ (32.6 x 24.8 cm.). Chester Dale Collection

627 *In Church.* Probably c. 1860. Wood, 6 x 8⅝″ (15 x 22 cm.). Rosenwald Collection

Daumier was the greatest lithographer and social critic of the nineteenth century. He had a genius for gesture and facial expression. In *French Theater* he contrasts the restrained interest of the prosperous family in the foreground with the excited eagerness of those in the cheaper seats. In *The Beggars* and *Wandering Saltimbanques* he shows by the postures and movements of the figures the resigned weariness of these impoverished and exhausted members of society.

627

Jean-François Millet

(FRENCH, 1814–1875)

628 LECONTE DE LISLE

Artists' reputations are in a state of constant revision, but none has been more mutable than that of Jean-François Millet. Although he lived to see himself the most famous of the painters who worked at Barbizon, during much of his life he was on the verge of penury. As a result of privation, he was subject all his life to fearful headaches and pains in his eyes. But he never complained. "Art is no diversion," he told a friend; "it is a conflict in which one is crushed." Yet Millet was responsible for one of the most popular pictures of the nineteenth century, *The Angelus*, a painting underappreciated today.

Before he went to Barbizon and attained his vast popularity, Millet executed a few portraits. These were painted as potboilers, and there is no evidence that he especially valued them; but in recent years they have been more sought after than the paintings which gained him fame. In many ways they are better than his peasant subjects, and some even rank among the finest achievements of nineteenth-century painting. Since color is less important in portraiture than in figure painting or landscape, Millet's outstanding weakness is here less apparent. Also, while his portraits show his magnificent power of construction, they are free from his subjective sadness, from that "dark pleasure of a melancholy heart" upon which he was wont to be overinsistent.

Because of its subject, the painting reproduced here is the most interesting of the few portraits by Millet. It was a happy coincidence that brought together these two young men of genius, Millet and Leconte de Lisle, one an unknown artist, the other a still inexperienced poet. Leconte de Lisle was born in 1818 in the West Indies, the son of a plantation owner. His father sent him to Brittany to be educated. Between 1837 and 1843 he lived with his uncle at Dinan and attended the University of Rennes. During those years and before he returned to the West Indies he apparently met Millet, who was also in his twenties and who spent the summers in Brittany with his family. There is a letter in which Leconte de Lisle mentions sightseeing with "three landscapists from Paris." Whether Millet was one of these artists, or however they met, the young poet proved an attractive subject. He appears a romantic figure as he stands with one arm resting on a wall, which bears the proud inscription *F. Millet*. This is one of the earliest commissions Millet executed, and it is the first important portrait we have of Leconte de Lisle. Thus the painting is doubly precious, as a portrait of exceptional beauty and as the likeness of one of the geniuses of French literature, whose poem *Le Manchy* Baudelaire considered a masterpiece without an equal.

Collections: Henri Rouart; Ernest Rouart, Paris. *Chester Dale Collection*, 1962. Signed. Painted probably 1842. Canvas, 46⅛ x 32″ (117.1 x 81.2 cm.).

Eugène Boudin

(FRENCH, 1824–1898)

629   THE BEACH AT VILLERVILLE

In a short autobiographical piece Boudin stated, to the consternation of his admirers, that his principal object had been for many years "to please the sovereign public." During the 1860s he discovered a genre which did just that: seascapes of fashionable bathing places adorned with a frieze of small, modishly dressed figures. These canvases evoke an enchanting past, the world Proust was to describe a few decades later. In the painting reproduced here, it is a late summer day in 1864, and a group of men and women, who seem to have stepped without change of apparel from boulevard to beach, stroll about or sit on stiff chairs. They have wrapped themselves in coats and capes, for the days are drawing in and there is a cool breeze from the sea. Charming as we find this diminutive society, to Boudin it was merely a means to an end, a way to make his marvelous renderings of sea and sky more palatable to collectors, and in this he succeeded. As he wrote a friend in 1863, "My little ladies on the seashore are very popular. Some people even think there is a vein of gold in these subjects ready to be exploited."

But Boudin came to despise himself for its exploitation. The turning point was a trip to Brittany in 1867 to visit his wife's relations. On his return he wrote the same friend, "Having just passed a month among people who on black bread and water devote their lives to rude labor in the fields, one feels . . . ashamed to paint these idlers, this band of gilded parasites, who seem to have such a triumphant air." Although he continued to depict an occasional beach scene, his heart was not in it, and after 1870 he abandoned his "gilded parasites" altogether and devoted the rest of his life to views of harbors and shipping.

Unfortunately, when Boudin exchanged the idlers of the seashore for the toilers of the sea, he lost his vein of gold. The treasure he had found, though he did not realize it, had been aesthetic as well as commercial. For the poetry, the evocation in a canvas like *The Beach at Villerville* lies in the very incongruity of these fashionable people seen against the majestic setting of sea and sky. They suggest an audience come to the edge of the world to watch a drama of cosmic splendor, which in the end bores them with its magnificence. But our sympathies are touched, our hearts moved by these spectators. The infinite radiance of sky, streaked by the setting sun and hung with ominous clouds, lends a melancholy poetry to their transience. The tragedy is that the painter himself saw only "a hideous masquerade" where in reality he had expressed the poignancy of the transitory, the pathos of the evanescent. Boudin was a victim of social consciousness, perhaps the first but certainly not the last in the history of art.

Collections: Henry C. and Martha B. Angell, Boston; Museum of Fine Arts, Boston. *Chester Dale Collection*, 1962. Signed, and dated 1864. Canvas, 18 x 30" (45.7 x 76.3 cm.).

630

631

Return of the Terre-Neuvier depicts the unloading of a fishing schooner which has arrived in France from the Grand Banks. To facilitate the task of transporting the salted fish from the ship's hold to the carts, it was the practice to run the ship aground and unload when the tide receded. Here Boudin is painting the workers he admired. The other reproductions, except for plates **633** and **636**, show the "gilded parasites" he despised.

632   633

634

Eugène Boudin   (French, 1824–1898)

630   *Return of the Terre-Neuvier.* Signed, and dated 1875. Canvas, 29 x 39⅝" (73.5 x 100.7 cm.). Chester Dale Collection

631   *The Beach.* Signed, and dated 1887. Wood, 4¼ x 10" (10.9 x 25.4 cm.). Ailsa Mellon Bruce Collection

632   *On the Jetty.* 1869/70. Wood, 7¼ x 10¾" (18.4 x 27.3 cm.). Ailsa Mellon Bruce Collection

633   *Washerwomen on the Beach of Étretat.* Signed, and dated 1894. Wood, 14⅝ x 21⅝" (37.2 x 54.9 cm.). Ailsa Mellon Bruce Collection

634   *Beach at Trouville.* Signed. 1864/65. Wood, 10¼ x 18⅞" (25.9 x 47.9 cm.). Ailsa Mellon Bruce Collection

635   *On the Beach, Trouville.* Signed, and dated 1887. Wood, 7½ x 12⅞" (18.4 x 32.7 cm.). Chester Dale Collection

636   *Women on the Beach at Berck.* Signed, and dated 1881. Wood, 9¾ x 14¼" (24.8 x 36.2 cm.). Ailsa Mellon Bruce Collection

637   *Yacht Basin at Trouville-Deauville.* Probably 1895/96. Wood, 18 x 14⅝" (45.8 x 37.1 cm.). Ailsa Mellon Bruce Collection

635

636

637

443

638

Impressionism in its love of fugitive atmospheric effects looks back to the out-of-door paintings of Boudin, and in its absorption in the actuality of the scene invokes the realism of Courbet. The landscapes reproduced here show how carefully Courbet observed a beach, a grotto, a forest. When working from a human model, he painted with equal realism. There is no idealization in the commonplace features of the woman reading (plate 640) or in the oxlike stolidity of *Portrait of a Young Girl* (plate 639).

639

640

641

642

643

644

Gustave Courbet (French, 1819–1877)

638 *The Stream.* Signed, and dated 1855. Canvas, 41 x 54″ (104.1 x 137.1 cm.). Gift of Mr. and Mrs. P.H.B. Frelinghuysen in memory of her father and mother, Mr. and Mrs. H.O. Havemeyer

639 *Portrait of a Young Girl.* Signed, and dated 1857. Canvas, 23¾ x 20⅝″ (60.4 x 52.4 cm.). Chester Dale Collection

640 *A Young Woman Reading.* Signed. 1868–72. Canvas, 23⅝ x 29¾″ (60 x 72.9 cm.). Chester Dale Collection

641 *La Grotte de la Loue.* Signed. c. 1865. Canvas, 38¾ x 51⅜″ (98.4 x 130.4 cm.). Gift of Charles L. Lindemann

642 *Beach in Normandy.* c. 1869. Canvas, 24⅛ x 35½″ (61.3 x 90.2 cm.). Chester Dale Collection

643 *Boats on a Beach, Étretat.* Signed. 1869. Canvas, 25½ x 36¼″ (64.9 x 92 cm.). Gift of the W. Averell Harriman Foundation in memory of Marie N. Harriman

644 *Landscape near the Banks of the Indre.* Signed, and dated 1856. Canvas, 24 x 28⅞″ (60.8 x 73.3 cm.). Gift of the W. Averell Harriman Foundation in memory of Marie N. Harriman

645 **Charles-François Daubigny** (French, 1817–1878): *The Farm.* Signed, and dated 1855. Canvas, 20¼ x 32″ (51.4 x 81.2 cm.). Chester Dale Collection

645

Edouard Manet

(FRENCH, 1832–1883)

646   THE OLD MUSICIAN

The principal pleasure to be gained from Manet comes from the beauty of his brushwork. He mixed on his palette the exact tone he needed and with swift and certain dexterity delineated on the canvas each area of light and shadow. In *The Old Musician* this virtuosity of handling can be seen most clearly in the trenchant strokes that define the folds in the shirt and trousers of the boy with the straw hat, or in the more caressing feather touch on the shawl of the girl holding the baby.

Manet's method of direct painting caused him to suppress the transitional tones of modeling which particularly suggest volume. Like Velázquez, who was also a master of brushwork, he chose an illumination which would flatten form as much as possible. Thus the light falls directly on the figures from behind the artist's head, and the shadows are reduced to a minimum. Through this arbitrary elimination of shadow Manet was able to state local color more freely. He attained, especially in such early works as *The Old Musician*, the most subtle harmonies of yellowish white and faded blue, here contrasted with warm browns and blacks and soft grays. This color scheme was as far as possible from the high intensities and broken colors of the Impressionists, which he adopted at the end of his life.

For Manet, in spite of a strong instinct for the traditional, became a leader of the Impressionists' revolt. The public attacked his pictures, as they attacked the other Impressionists, but less because of his method of painting than because of a certain outré quality in his subject matter. In *The Old Musician*, for instance, what is the meaning of the brooding octogenarian on the extreme right, who is bisected so unconventionally by the frame? Perhaps he was put there simply to balance the composition, for Théodore Duret, who knew Manet well, said he painted this troupe of beggars merely because it pleased him to preserve a record of them and for no other reason. And yet one senses a significance which just escapes, a hidden meaning which is baffling. In Manet's pictures these recurrent and tantalizing affectations infuriated his contemporaries and were in part the reason he never attained the popular admiration which he so desperately desired.

Collections: Manet family, Paris; Prince de Wagram, Paris; P. R. Pearson, Paris; Kunsthistorisches Museum, Vienna. *Chester Dale Collection*, 1962. Signed, and dated 1862. Canvas, 73¾ x 98" (187.5 x 249.1 cm.).

647

The paintings reproduced here show Manet's dexterity of brushwork, a quality most apparent perhaps in the *King Charles Spaniel*, where the texture of the dog's coat is brilliantly rendered. *The Dead Toreador* is a fragment the painter cut out of a large picture which was ridiculed at the Salon of 1864. *The Tragic Actor* and *The Plum* illustrate Manet's skill in finding the exact pose to express the character of the sitter.

648

650

Edouard Manet (French, 1832–1883)

647 *The Dead Toreador.* Signed. Probably 1864. Canvas, 29⅞ x 60⅜″ (75.9 x 153.3 cm.). Widener Collection

648 *The Plum.* Signed. c. 1877. Canvas, 29 x 19¾″ (73.6 x 50.2 cm.). Collection of Mr. and Mrs. Paul Mellon

649 *The Tragic Actor (Rouvière as Hamlet).* Signed. 1865–66. Canvas, 73¾ x 42½″ (187.2 x 108.1 cm.). Gift of Edith Stuyvesant Gerry

650 *A King Charles Spaniel.* Signed. c. 1866. Canvas, 18¼ x 15″ (46.4 x 38.2 cm.). Ailsa Mellon Bruce Collection

649

449

Edouard Manet

(FRENCH, 1832–1883)

651 **STILL LIFE WITH MELON AND PEACHES**

652 **BALL AT THE OPERA**

It is in still-life painting that Manet's three most admirable qualities are especially apparent: his dexterous brushwork, his superb control of value relations, and his mastery of texture. In front of a still life he painted with the utmost speed. As he once explained: "Don't bother about the background. Look for the values. When you look at [a still life], when you want to render it as you see it, that's to say give the public the same impression of it as it makes on you, you don't look at it, you don't stare at it, you don't see the stripes on the wallpaper behind it. . . . Do you count the grapes? Of course not! What's so striking about them is the clear amber of their tone, and the bloom that modulates and softens the outline. . . . What you have to decide about that cloth is the light, and then the places that are not directly touched by it. . . . The creases will indicate themselves. . . . Above all don't mix your tones!"

There is no mixture of tones in *Ball at the Opera*. It is a virtuoso performance on the theme of a single color, or the absence of color—black. Here the men's silk hats and their evening clothes offered Manet a unique opportunity, a chance to depict every variation of ebony. And these blacks are harmoniously interspersed with bouquets of flowers, girls in costume, and the varied hues of a punchinello on the extreme left. Manet's goal was to illustrate the daily life of Parisians. This he did superbly in many canvases but nowhere more successfully than in the *Ball at the Opera*.

Masked balls were given on Saturday nights in the "old" opera house, which burned down in 1873, the year Manet painted this picture. A few months earlier he had seen a newspaper illustration drawn by Alfred Grévin, which must have inspired him. It showed spectators and actresses talking together during an entr'acte or after the performance. From sketches done on the spot he painted a similar scene and included portraits of himself and many of his friends, among them the banker Albert Hecht, the critic Théodore Duret, and the composer Alexis Chabrier. Manet at this time felt himself on the verge of success. His confidence increased when Jean-Baptiste Faure, the famous singer, came to his studio and bought this picture with four others for 6,000 francs. But his optimism was short-lived: In 1874 when he sent the *Ball at the Opera* to the Salon it was turned down, the first rejection he had had in seven years.

651 collections: Léopold Beaugnée, Brussels. *Gift of Eugene and Agnes Meyer*, 1960. Signed. Painted c. 1866, Canvas, 27⅛ x 36¼" (69 x 92.2 cm.).

652 collections: Jean-Baptiste Faure, Paris; Havemeyer family, New York. *Gift of Mrs. Horace Havemeyer in memory of her mother-in-law, Louisine W. Havemeyer*, 1982. Painted 1873. Canvas, 23¼ x 28½" (59 x 72.5 cm.).

451

653

The still life by Manet reproduced in plate 654 cannot but stir the gastric juices of any oyster lover. If, on the other hand, one is a racing enthusiast, plate 653 will inevitably arouse the excitement of a close finish. Similarly, the viewer can almost smell the flowers in the vase in plate 656. Thus, in the originals of these reproductions, one experiences Manet's wonderful ability to create empathy between spectator and painting. But empathy is impossible for the spectator, as it was for the portraitist, confronted with the blank, bovine expression of Madame Michel-Lévy (plate 657). Here virtuosity in the use of pastel and paint together is the chief fascination.

655

654

656

Edouard Manet   (French, 1832–1883)

653   *At the Races.* Signed. c. 1875. Wood, 5 x 8½″ (12.5 x 21.5 cm.). Widener Collection

654   *Oysters.* Signed. 1862. Canvas, 15⅜ x 18⅜″ (39.1 x 46.7 cm.). Gift of the Adele R. Levy Fund, Inc.

655   *Portrait of a Lady.* c. 1879. Wood, 5¾ x 4½″ (15 x 11.5 cm.). Gift of Mrs. Charles S. Carstairs

656   *Flowers in a Crystal Vase.* Signed. c. 1882. Canvas, 12⅞ x 9⅝″ (32.6 x 24.3 cm.). Ailsa Mellon Bruce Collection

657   *Madame Michel-Lévy.* Signed, and dated 1882. Pastel and oil on canvas, 29¼ x 20⅛″ (74.4 x 51 cm.). Chester Dale Collection

657

Edouard Manet

(FRENCH, 1832–1883)

658   GARE SAINT-LAZARE

Why does this painting convey such a sense of gaiety? There is, of course, the marvelous observation of the little sleeping dog, one of the most enchanting puppies in art. There is also the pretty Victorine Meurend, whose beauty is more familiar to us from pictures of ten years earlier, *Olympia* and *Le Déjeuner sur l'herbe*. Dressed or undressed she is a joy, delighting us with the wonderfully candid gaze of a woman to whom shyness is unknown. But the real source of our pleasure, the heroine of the picture, is the little girl, the daughter of Manet's friend Alphonse Hirsch. From the way she holds the railing, from the angle of her head, from the beautiful line made by the curve of her neck, we know the intensity of her scrutiny. We share the excitement we felt in childhood at seeing trains and steam and smoke. Manet knew better than anyone else how to catch the fugitive charm of everyday life. He was a master of the informal composition. He had a keen sense of the immediacy this type of design can convey. The *Gare Saint-Lazare* is a family snapshot. But this moment of time, made timeless, is held with a beauty and intensity far beyond the possibilities of photography.

The painting was admitted, somewhat unexpectedly, to the Salon of 1874, where it aroused more protests than praise. It was the first large canvas Manet had executed mostly out-of-doors, perhaps acknowledging thereby his association with the younger Impressionists, Monet and Renoir especially, who had for some time been working in the open air. Thus it carried into the citadel of the official Salon the banner of their revolt.

Collections: Jean-Baptiste Faure, Paris; Havemeyer family, New York. *Gift of Horace Havemeyer in memory of his mother, Louisine W. Havemeyer*, 1956. Signed, and dated 1873. Canvas, 36¾ x 45⅛" (93.3 x 114.5 cm.).

Berthe Morisot

(FRENCH, 1841–1895)

659   THE MOTHER AND SISTER OF THE ARTIST

The question is constantly asked, "How should my son [or daughter] learn to be a painter?" When Mme Morisot put this question to Guichard about her daughter, Berthe, then age fifteen, the painter answered, "The first thing to do, Madame, is to get your daughter permission to work in the Louvre, where I shall give my instruction in front of the masters." The answer was not surprising, for the Louvre was the traditional art school of all French painters of ability. There, as Ingres said, they sought to draw out from the Old Masters, "le suc de la plante," that quintessential quality which is in all *great* art. This intelligent use of the Louvre explains to a large extent the superiority of French painting in the last century.

Berthe Morisot was an assiduous copyist. She began with the Old Masters and ended with Corot, whose work she had the advantage of discussing with the artist himself. In the Louvre she often saw Manet, the brother of her future husband. During the winter before the outbreak of the Franco-Prussian War, when she was just twenty-nine, she completed the portrait of her mother and sister and asked Manet to come to her studio to give her a criticism. He was delighted with the picture, but suggested a few changes and then seized the brush and spent the afternoon retouching it. His brushstrokes are still visible in the somewhat heavier touch around the eye and mouth of Mme Morisot and the thicker impasto of her dress. While Manet was working, the van to take the picture to the Salon arrived, and Berthe Morisot, though she was angry, could do nothing but send the painting as it was. Fortunately, the canvas was received with enthusiasm by many artists, especially by Fantin-Latour, and the painter herself became reconciled to the changes.

Among women Berthe Morisot's only peer was Mary Cassatt, and they had much in common. Both tried to fashion a modern style from a lifelong study of the masters of the past, one with the guidance of Manet, the other with the help of Degas. Berthe Morisot showed a piquant delicacy joined to a Parisian chic, Mary Cassatt a mastery of formal design combined with good taste. It is remarkable that the nineteenth century should have given us two women of such genius in art. How many, one wonders, will the twentieth century produce?

Collections: Mme Pontillon and Mme Forget (sister and niece of the artist), Paris. *Chester Dale Collection*, 1962. Painted during the winter of 1869–70. Canvas, 39¾ x 32¼" (101 x 82 cm.).

456

457

660

661

662

663

Until the twentieth century, the handicaps faced by a woman who wished to be a professional artist were nearly insurmountable. The whole social structure was against her. But as Berthe Morisot proves, there is a vision of the external world which is entirely feminine. These pictures could never have been painted by a man!

664

665

Berthe Morisot (French, 1841–1895)

660 *The Sisters.* Signed. 1869. Canvas, 20½ x 32″ (52.1 x 81.3 cm.). Gift of Mrs. Charles S. Carstairs

661 *The Artist's Daughter with a Parakeet.* Signed. 1890. Canvas, 25¾ x 20⅝″ (65.6 x 52.4 cm.). Chester Dale Collection

662 *In the Dining Room.* Signed. 1886. Canvas, 24⅛ x 19¾″ (61.3 x 50 cm.). Chester Dale Collection

663 *The Artist's Sister at a Window.* 1869. Canvas, 21⅝ x 18¼″ (54.8 x 46.3 cm.). Ailsa Mellon Bruce Collection

664 *The Harbor at Lorient.* Signed. 1869. Canvas, 17½ x 28¾″ (43.5 x 73 cm.). Ailsa Mellon Bruce Collection

665 *Young Woman with a Straw Hat.* 1884. Canvas, 21⅞ x 18⅜″ (55.5 x 46.7 cm.). Ailsa Mellon Bruce Collection

666 *Girl in a Boat with Geese.* Signed. c. 1889. Canvas, 25¾ x 21½″ (65.4 x 54.6 cm.). Ailsa Mellon Bruce Collection

666

459

Auguste Renoir

(FRENCH, 1841–1919)

667   A GIRL WITH A WATERING CAN

A Girl with a Watering Can, painted in 1876, is one of the most popular pictures in the National Gallery. It is evocative of sunlight and childhood, springtime and the breath of flowers, images and sensations which are in themselves attractive. But these are not enough. To be great a painting must have more than charm of subject matter; it must have certain aesthetic values as well. In the case of *A Girl with a Watering Can*, these values consist largely in the relationship of figure and landscape, in the way the two are fused by ingenious repetition of colors and a consistent treatment of detail. The whole picture is made up of a web of brilliantly colored brushstrokes, which from a distance are seen to be a child, roses, grass, a garden path. The little girl seems to merge with her surroundings, to become one with the variegated tones of nature. This creates a mysterious sense of interrelations, as though one substance permeated humanity, vegetation, and earth.

The unity of figure and background Renoir extends to a psychological unity between himself and the child. The scene is depicted from the level of the little girl's own vision, so that her outlook on nature is suggested. Thus the garden becomes the world seen through her eyes, narrow and circumscribed. By accepting her scale of observation, Renoir evokes, in an almost unique way, memories of childhood. This mood, this "remembrance of things past," is intensified by the pleasure of the painter in his subject, by the spontaneity and gaiety of his treatment of the scene. Renoir, in canvases like this, seems almost a pagan Fra Angelico. "I arrange my subject as I want it," he once said, "and then I go ahead and paint it like a child." He loved bright colors, joyous and pretty human beings, and nature drenched in sunshine. He was a painter moved to lyrical ecstasy by the beauty of the everyday world. His great gift was to catch on canvas

A strain of the earth's sweet being in the beginning . . .
Innocent mind and Mayday in girl and boy.

Collections: Paul Bérard, Paris; A. Rosenberg, Paris; Prince de Wagram, Paris. *Chester Dale Collection*, 1962. Signed, and dated 1876. Canvas, 39½ x 28¾" (100 x 73 cm.).

668

669

670

Auguste Renoir   (French, 1841–1919)

668   *Mademoiselle Sicot.* Signed, and dated 1865. Canvas, 45¾ x 35¼" (116 x 89.5 cm.). Chester Dale Collection

669   *Woman with a Cat.* Signed. c. 1875. Canvas, 22 x 18¼" (56 x 46.4 cm.). Gift of Mr. and Mrs. Benjamin E. Levy

670   *The Dancer.* Signed, and dated 1874. Canvas, 56⅛ x 37⅛" (142.5 x 94.5 cm.). Widener Collection

671   *Madame Henriot.* Signed. c. 1876. Canvas, 26 x 19⅝" (65.9 x 49.8 cm.). Gift of the Adele R. Levy Fund, Inc.

672   *Marie Murer.* Signed. 1877. Canvas, oval, 26⅝ x 22½" (67.6 x 57.1 cm.). Chester Dale Collection

673   *Oarsmen at Chatou.* Signed, and dated 1879. Canvas, 32 x 39½" (81.3 x 100.3 cm.). Gift of Sam A. Lewisohn

674   *Caroline Rémy ("Séverine").* Signed. c. 1885. Pastel, 24½ x 20" (62.3 x 50.8 cm.). Chester Dale Collection

671

672

The important canvases by Renoir reproduced in this
volume illustrate fully the artist's career, although they
do not represent entirely the Renoir collection of the
National Gallery of Art. Renoir was the most attractive
of the Impressionist painters, and more of his work is to
be seen in the United States than anywhere else in the
world. The earliest of his pictures in Washington is the
portrait of Mlle Sicot (plate 668). His training as a
decorator of porcelain is evident in the delicate nuances

674

of color in the flesh tones of the face. The sitter, an actress of the Comédie Francaise, was astute enough to
recognize Renoir's genius when he was only twenty-
four. The other portraits of women were also of
friends: Marie Murer (plate 672), the half-sister of a
pastry cook who owned a small, flourishing restaurant
and was one of Renoir's chief backers while he was still
unknown; Caroline Rémy ("Séverine") (plate 674), a
writer and feminist who also supported his early
endeavors; Madame Henriot (plate 671), another
enchanting actress of the Comédie Francaise; and
Madame Hagan (plate 678), the mistress of one of his
first patrons, Caillebotte. All these women are beautiful
and charming in different ways.

673

675

676

677

Auguste Renoir (French, 1841–1919)

675 *Girl with a Hoop.* Signed, and dated 1885. Canvas, 49½ x 30⅛" (125.7 x 76.6 cm.). Chester Dale Collection

676 *Young Woman Braiding Her Hair.* Signed, and dated 1876. Canvas, 21⅞ x 18¼" (55.6 x 46.4 cm.). Ailsa Mellon Bruce Collection

677 *Madame Monet and Her Son.* 1874. Canvas, 19⅞ x 26¾" (50.4 x 68 cm.). Ailsa Mellon Bruce Collection

678 *Madame Hagen.* Signed, and dated 1883. Canvas, 36¼ x 28¾" (92 x 73 cm.). Gift of Angelika Wertheim Frink

679 *Woman Standing by a Tree.* Signed with initials. 1866. Canvas, 9⅞ x 6¼" (25.2 x 15.9 cm.). Ailsa Mellon Bruce Collection

680 *Child with Brown Hair.* Signed. 1887/88. Canvas, 4⅝ x 4" (11.8 x 10.2 cm.). Ailsa Mellon Bruce Collection

681 *Woman in a Park.* Signed R. 1870. Canvas, 10¼ x 6⅜" (26.1 x 16.1 cm.). Ailsa Mellon Bruce Collection

678

679

680

681

465

Auguste Renoir

(FRENCH, 1841–1919)

682   PONT NEUF, PARIS

Renoir loved Paris, not only its streets, bridges, and buildings, but the Parisians themselves. When in 1872 he decided to paint the Pont Neuf, he took a room on the second floor of a nearby café and sat in the window on a gloriously sunny day. He happily watched the crowds crossing the Seine on foot, in horse-drawn trams, in carriages and wagons. He was fascinated by the stir and movement of a great city, but for a time he was baffled by the speed of all this ceaseless motion. No one stopped long enough for him to catch a likeness. The solution, however, was simple. He sent his brother out to question the passersby, to enquire the location of some street or to ask the time of day. This momentarily arrested the flux of people, and he was able to sketch individuals, to record their gestures and postures. He wanted more than the generalized impression of the scene which would have satisfied Monet or Pissarro. And it is this note of the specific which has given the *Pont Neuf* its immediacy, its sense of actuality, a quality which is lacking in many Impressionist canvases.

But in the 1870s his public considered such paintings "the negation of the most elementary rules of drawing and painting," to quote Emile Cardon, a contemporary critic. In 1875 when Renoir, along with Alfred Sisley and Berthe Morisot, decided to take a chance and hold an auction at the Hôtel Drouot of twenty paintings which they considered their best work, the sale brought in barely 2,000 francs. As Renoir later told Ambroise Vollard, "After it was over, the expenses had not even been covered; we actually owed money to the auctioneers! A certain Monsieur Hazard had had the courage to bid one of my pictures, a *Pont Neuf*, up to 300 francs. But nobody followed his example."

At about the same date an American paid 300,000 francs for Meissonnier's *1807*, a thousand times the amount that Renoir received. Today at auction the *Pont Neuf* would bring at least 6,000,000 new francs, or 20,000 francs for each franc M. Hazard invested. In terms of dollars this would mean that an outlay of $75 one hundred years ago would have a value of $1,500,000 today; whereas Meissonnier's charging cavalry, even if the seller were fortunate, would not reach its original price. The moral seems to be that the best hedge against inflation is an investment in the right painters. But the discovery of the "right" artists of one's time, while they are still unknown, requires taste, insight, and a strong element of luck. Nevertheless, as a rule of thumb it is wise to avoid the fashionable.

Collections: The artist; M. Hazard; G. Bernheim, Paris; R. M. Coe, Cleveland; C. Carstairs, New York; Marshall Field, New York; Dr. and Mrs. Robert Boggs (later Mrs. Peter Benziger), New York. *Ailsa Mellon Bruce Collection*, 1970. Signed, and dated 1872. Canvas, 29⅝ x 36⅞" (75.3 x 93.7 cm.).

467

683

685

684

For a true sensualist like Renoir, nudes were an inspiration. Once he had several pretty models pose for him naked, but the pictures went badly. Finally he exclaimed, "I must find Louison again." Louison was always vividly in his mind from the time nearly thirty years earlier when, as he said, "I saw her on the Boulevard Clichy with a blue ribbon at her neck." He did find her, and though her body had aged, it still recalled just the lines he needed. A painter benefits from a model, in Renoir's words, "well worked into his brushes."

His nudes, however, at first were not well received. *Diana* (plate 684), painted for the Salon of 1867, was refused, even though the attributes of a classical goddess were added to make the picture more acceptable to a classically minded jury. In 1870 he was more fortunate. His *Odalisque* (plate 688) was hung in the Salon. By then the jurors had come to admire Delacroix, whose influence is apparent; also, they were attracted by a certain element of eroticism, which Renoir cleverly evokes.

Auguste Renoir (French, 1841–1919)

683 *The Vintagers.* Signed, and dated 1879. Canvas, 21¼ x 25¾" (54.2 x 65.4 cm.). Gift of Margaret Seligman Lewisohn in memory of her husband, Sam A. Lewisohn

684 *Diana.* Signed, and dated 1867. Canvas, 77 x 51¼" (199.5 x 129.5 cm.). Chester Dale Collection

685 *Bather Arranging Her Hair.* Signed. 1893. Canvas, 36⅜ x 29⅛" (92.2 x 73.9 cm.). Chester Dale Collection

686 *Girl with a Basket of Fish.* Signed. c. 1889. Canvas, 51½ x 16½" (130.7 x 41.8 cm.). Gift of William Robertson Coe

687 *Girl with a Basket of Oranges.* Signed. c. 1889. Canvas, 51½ x 16½" (130.7 x 42 cm.). Gift of William Robertson Coe

688 *Odalisque.* Signed, and dated 1870. Canvas, 27¼ x 48¼" (69.2 x 122.6 cm.). Chester Dale Collection

686

687

688

469

689

691

690

692

470

693

694

Auguste Renoir   (French, 1841–1919)

689   *Regatta at Argenteuil.* 1874. Canvas, 12¾ x 18″ (32.4 x 45.6 cm.). Ailsa Mellon Bruce Collection

690   *Landscape at Vétheuil.* Signed. c. 1890. Canvas, 4½ x 6½″ (11.5 x 16.5 cm.). Ailsa Mellon Bruce Collection

691   *Head of a Dog.* Signed. 1870. Canvas, 8⅝ x 7⅞″ (21.9 x 20 cm.). Ailsa Mellon Bruce Collection

692   *Georges Rivière.* Signed, and dated 1877. Tile, 14½ x 11½″ (36.8 x 29.3 cm.). Ailsa Mellon Bruce Collection

693   *Picking Flowers.* Signed. 1875. Canvas, 21⅜ x 25⅝″ (54.3 x 65.2 cm.). Ailsa Mellon Bruce Collection

694   *Young Spanish Woman with a Guitar.* Signed, and dated 1898. Canvas, 21⅞ x 25⅝″ (55.6 x 65.2 cm.). Ailsa Mellon Bruce Collection

Edgar Degas

(FRENCH, 1834–1917)

695   MADAME RENÉ DE GAS

Some of the greatest paintings done by Degas, curiously enough, were painted in America, for he spent the winter of 1872–73 in New Orleans. His mother had been born there, and his uncle and brothers had established themselves in that city as cotton merchants. In a letter he describes his gratitude to one of his brothers, René, whose wife appears in the painting reproduced here. "I knew neither English nor the art of traveling in America; therefore I obeyed [René] blindly. What stupidities I should have committed without him! He is married and his wife, our cousin, is blind, poor thing, almost without hope. She has borne him two children, she is going to give him a third whose godfather I shall be, and as the widow of a young American killed in the War of Secession she already had a little girl of her own who is 9 years old."

With tactful subtlety Degas has suggested the blind, unfocused stare of his sister-in-law. The portrait seems unposed, the sitter unself-conscious. Thus Degas conveys that feeling of fortuitous objectivity which was his goal in portraiture. As he once said, he was interested in doing "portraits of people in familiar and typical attitudes, above all giving to their faces the same choice of expression as one gives to their bodies." Consequently, he sought to transcribe appearance accurately, to achieve photographic veracity, as though the camera had just clicked and the artist had transposed to the canvas his exact mental picture. But though the casual yet perfectly balanced design of this picture has the immediacy of a snapshot, the artist, because draftsmanship is more flexible than photography, has been able to eliminate all extraneous detail and to concentrate attention on the important features of his sitter. Unfortunately, contemporary portraiture has lost the secret of combining aesthetic perception with photographic likeness.

Collections: Degas' atelier until 1918; Henry D. Hughes, Philadelphia. *Chester Dale Collection*, 1962. Atelier stamp: Degas. Painted in the winter of 1872–73. Canvas, 28⅝ x 36¼" (72.7 x 92 cm.).

696

697

Edgar Degas (French, 1834–1917)

696 *Achille de Gas in the Uniform of a Cadet.* 1856/57. Canvas, 25⅜ x 20⅛″ (64.5 x 46.2 cm.). Chester Dale Collection

697 *Madame Dietz-Monnin.* 1879. Pastel, 23⅝ x 17¾″ (60 x 45.1 cm.). Gift of Mrs. Albert J. Beveridge in memory of her aunt Delia Spencer Field

698 *Edmondo and Thérèse Morbilli.* c. 1865. Canvas, 46⅛ x 35⅜″ (117.1 x 89.9 cm.). Chester Dale Collection

699 *The Races.* Signed. Before 1873. Canvas, 10½ x 13¾″ (26.5 x 35 cm.). Widener Collection

700 *Girl in Red.* c. 1866. Canvas, 38⅜ x 31⅞″ (98.9 x 80.8 cm.). Chester Dale Collection

701 *Madame Camus.* 1869/70. Canvas, 28⅝ x 36¼″ (72.7 x 92.1 cm.). Chester Dale Collection

698

699

Degas was the son of prosperous parents with some claim to aristocracy. Hence the occasional spelling of their name as de Gas, as it appears in the titles of plate 695 and an early work, *Achille de Gas in the Uniform of a Cadet* (plate 696). These family portraits reveal in their drawing and modeling the influence of Degas' hero, Ingres. But in the composition of his pictures Degas never emulated the great master of Classicism. The portrait of Degas' sister and her banker husband, Edmondo Morbilli (plate 698), shows, in the informal poses and the abrupt angle of the chair, a snapshot effect, a type of design which would have shocked Ingres. The picture was intentionally left unfinished; it is evident that any further detail would have spoilt it.

700

701

Edgar Degas

(FRENCH, 1834–1917)

702 FOUR DANCERS

Degas was the major exponent of a new type of design introduced by the Impressionists. Whereas earlier artists like Poussin had usually devised their compositions out of their imagination, Degas would watch the kaleidoscope of appearance, like a cat watching its prey, until this moving pattern would seem to resolve itself into a momentary significance. Such accidental, ready-made designs he would store up in his memory and use later for the compositions of his pictures. This pouncing upon the scene, holding an instantaneous pattern and giving it permanency, was the essence of Impressionism; but in return there was the necessary sacrifice of an enduring equilibrium, the structural design to be found in the compositions of the Old Masters.

Degas found a rich mine of casual yet perfectly balanced arrangements in the ballet, as one can see in the picture reproduced here. There is no question that he was helped to discover these ready-made compositions by Japanese prints. The Japanese printmakers sought to make their woodcuts a mirror of the passing world, and Impressionism had essentially the same goal. But the Impressionists, especially Degas, went far deeper into the study of appearance than the superficial actuality of Japanese prints. In a way that would have been inconceivable for Eastern artists, these French painters were scientists, intent upon analysis of vision. In his painting *Four Dancers* Degas is experimenting with effects of artificial illumination, with the appearance of these ballet dancers under beams of green and red spotlights, noting how flesh tones and drapery catch the mixture of these two lights, changing color either toward green tones or toward red tones.

Degas ranked this canvas among his finest achievements and would never part with it. It is one of his last large paintings in oil and shows the influence of his use of pastel, a medium which, because of failing eyesight, he employed for most of his later works.

Collections: Degas' atelier until 1918; Wilhelm Hansen, Copenhagen. *Chester Dale Collection*, 1962. Atelier stamp: Degas. Painted about 1899. Canvas, 59½ x 71" (151.1 x 180.2 cm.).

703

Edgar Degas (French, 1834–1917)

703 *Girl Drying Herself.* Signed, and dated 1885. Pastel, 31½ x 20⅛″ (80.1 x 51.2 cm.). Gift of the W. Averell Harriman Foundation in memory of Marie N. Harriman

704 *Before the Ballet.* Signed. 1888. Canvas, 15¾ x 35″ (40 x 89 cm.). Widener Collection

705 *Dancers at the Old Opera House.* Signed. c. 1877. Pastel, 8⅝ x 6¾″ (21.8 x 17.1 cm.). Ailsa Mellon Bruce Collection

706 *Ballet Dancers.* Signed. c. 1877. Pastel and gouache, 11¾ x 10⅝″ (29.7 x 26.9 cm.). Ailsa Mellon Bruce Collection

707 *Ballet Scene.* c. 1907. Pastel on cardboard, 30¼ x 43¾″ (76.8 x 111.2 cm.). Chester Dale Collection

708 *Dancers Backstage.* Signed. c. 1890. Canvas, 9½ x 7⅜″ (24.2 x 18.8 cm.). Ailsa Mellon Bruce Collection

Degas was a master at discovering beauty in the world around him. He particularly loved the opera and the ballet, but he loved them for professional reasons—for the fleeting gesture, the significance given to a passing moment. In the performance or the rehearsals of the ballerinas he found a kaleidoscope of shifting forms, which stimulated his sense of design. In the reproductions in this volume, especially in *Ballet Scene* (plate 707), a pastel painted in his last years, he reveals the plasticity of these young bodies and the motion of their complicated postures as no other artist has ever done.

704

705

706

707

708

Edgar Degas

(FRENCH, 1834–1917)

709   MADEMOISELLE MALO

Mlle Malo was a dancer, and with her Degas formed a close friendship. When he journeyed to New Orleans in 1872 to visit his uncle and brothers, who were in the cotton business, he corresponded with her. She puzzled him, and he communicated his bewilderment to a mutual friend. "I thanked her warmly for all her goodness to me. Why does she wish me more calmness in my ideas? Am I then an unusually excitable person?" When he returned to Paris he continued to see her, and during that period he painted the portrait reproduced here, which remained in his possession until he died.

Was there more than friendship in Degas' feeling for Mlle Malo? Probably not, for he seems never to have been in love. "This heart of mine has something artificial," he wrote. "The dancers have sewn it into a bag of pink satin, pink satin slightly faded, like their dancing shoes." His affections belonged not to a single ballerina but to the whole corps de ballet, not to an individual but to the *appearance* of all the performers at rest and at work.

Though Degas might deplore the artificiality of his heart, he could boast of the sincerity of his eye. And to the functioning of this organ, to its cold, analytical penetration, his personal life was sacrificed. From morning to night his single overwhelming passion was to record on paper or canvas what he had seen. But his vision had always been weak, and with incessant work he became almost blind. In the end he was a pathetic figure, wandering unkempt and careworn around Paris, unable to draw even with pastel, which he had come to use instead of oil as his eyesight faded.

He once advised Vollard to marry. "You do not realize how terrible it is to be alone as you grow old," he said. But, as for himself, he could not marry. "I could never bring myself to do it. I would have been in mortal misery all my life for fear my wife might say, 'That's a pretty little thing,' after I had finished a picture."

Degas never painted a "pretty" picture. Austere, detached, aristocratic, his art reembodies the high ideals of the Renaissance. He himself stood aloof from the fashion of his time. He believed "one should work for a few people, as for the others it is quite immaterial." If in his blindness he was lonely, he was also proud. Like Yeats he had "cast a cold eye on life, on death"; and the record of his observations gave him a deep sense of accomplishment. He knew that his detached, analytical vision, while it lasted, had enabled him to change the course of art, to introduce a new goal for painting: the realization of the essential gesture.

Collections: Degas' atelier until 1918; Henry D. Hughes, Philadelphia. *Chester Dale Collection*, 1962. Atelier Stamp: Degas. Painted about 1877. Canvas, 31⅞ x 25⅝" (81.1 x 65.1 cm.).

481

710

712

711

The contrast between the two directions taken by those painters generally called Impressionists is especially evident on these two pages. Degas, representing one tendency, did not share the preoccupation of Monet with light and atmosphere. Like his admirer and follower Jean-Louis Forain, Degas focused his interest on scenes of the everyday world: streets, shops, and theaters. Monet, though fundamentally a landscapist, occasionally revealed his private life, which for many years was poverty-stricken. When his son, shown lying in his cradle in plate 713, was born, Monet could not afford a ticket from Normandy to Paris to be with the child's mother, Camille Doncieux. His well-to-do father wished him to give up painting and to break immediately with his mistress. *Woman with a Parasol* (plate 714), painted eight years later, shows Camille again with her son Jean, now a young boy. In the meantime the artist had achieved a precarious success and was better able to support his family. *Woman with a Parasol* is a painting redolent of soft, grass-scented breezes. Few canvases match its enchanting joyousness, for it is rare that a painter is able to convey so intensely joi de vivre.

710 Jean-Louis Forain (French, 1852–1931): *Behind the Scenes.* Signed. c. 1880. Canvas, 18¼ x 15⅛" (46.4 x 38.4 cm.). Rosenwald Collection

711 Edgar Degas (French, 1834–1917): *Woman Ironing.* Signed. 1882. Canvas, 32 x 26" (81.3 x 66 cm.). Collection of Mr. and Mrs. Paul Mellon

712 Pierre Puvis de Chavannes (French, 1824–1898): *The Prodigal Son.* Probably c. 1879. Canvas, 41⅞ x 57¾" (106.5 x 146.7 cm.). Chester Dale Collection

713 Claude Monet (French, 1840–1926): *The Cradle— Camille with the Artist's Son Jean.* 1867. Canvas, 46 x 35" (116.8 x 88.9 cm.). Collection of Mr. and Mrs. Paul Mellon

714 Claude Monet: *Woman with a Parasol—Madame Monet and Her Son.* Signed, and dated 1875. Canvas, 39⅜ x 31⅞" (100 x 81 cm.). Collection of Mr. and Mrs. Paul Mellon

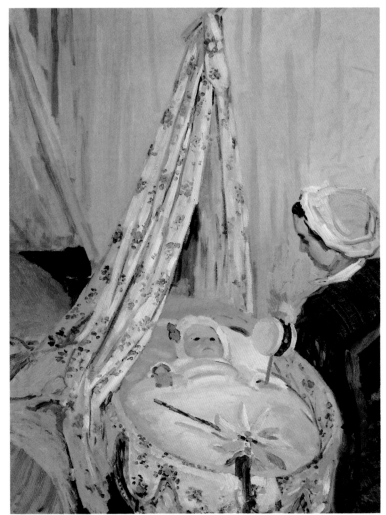

713

714

Claude Monet

(FRENCH, 1840–1926)

715   BAZILLE AND CAMILLE

In 1865 Monet decided to undertake an ambitious canvas measuring twenty feet. It was to be an outdoor scene, with the figures lifesize, a rival on a larger scale to Manet's *Déjeuner sur l'herbe* but with an important difference. Whereas Manet had borrowed his composition from a Renaissance engraving, Monet intended his picture to have the informality of an actual picnic. He left Paris and settled at Chailly near Fontainebleau, where he could paint unwearied by the constant aesthetic discussions of his Parisian friends.

But one of his admirers, Bazille, was persuaded to follow him to the country. He was a painter of considerable talent and of some means, to whom Monet often turned for financial help, as he did in 1868 when he wrote, "I have just been thrown out of an inn and stark naked at that. I have found shelter for Camille and my poor little Jean in the country for a few days. . . . I don't even know where I'll have a place to sleep tomorrow."

The hauntingly beautiful and consumptive Camille, to whom Monet refers, was a model who became his mistress and the mother of his two children. They were married in 1870, and her death in 1879 left Monet desolate.

The enormous canvas required for *Déjeuner sur l'herbe* was too large to carry into the forests of Chailly. Therefore Monet did a series of sketches out-of-doors using Bazille and Camille as models and recombined them in his studio. The picture reproduced here is one of these sketches.

The twenty-foot canvas, however, was a disaster. When it was nearly finished, Courbet appeared at Chailly. With the authority of his great reputation, backed by his irresistible self-confidence, he explained to Monet how certain passages should be repainted. The young and insecure artist took the master's advice; but when he had reworked the picture, he realized that he had ruined a painting that had occupied him for over a year. In disgust he took the canvas off its stretcher, rolled it up, and left it at the inn where he had been staying, as collateral for his debts. When he was able to redeem what must have been his most important work up to that time, only small sections could be salvaged. The rest had been ruined by damp.

He still had, however, the inspiration of Camille's beauty. They returned together to Paris, and Monet with uncharacteristic speed painted the portrait of her which is now in the Kunsthalle, Bremen. This he submitted to the Salon of 1866 in place of his ruined *Déjeuner sur l'herbe*. Camille's pose, seen from the back with her face turned in profile to the right, is very close to her attitude in the sketch and may have been inspired by it. The portrait was accepted for the Salon and had a success which Monet was not to repeat for many years.

Collection: E. Molyneux, Paris. *Ailsa Mellon Bruce Collection,* 1970. Signed. Painted about 1865. Canvas, 36⅝ x 27⅛" (93 x 69 cm.).

716

717

718

Working out-of-doors, Monet found that colors were constantly changing. To analyze these changes, he decided to paint a single subject at different times of day under different illumination. In over thirty canvases he showed how the color of Rouen Cathedral varies depending on the light that falls on it. Two of these Rouen paintings are reproduced here. A second observation, illustrated in all these reproductions, is that shadow is not colorless, is not brown or black, but is simply a less bright hue.

Claude Monet (French, 1840–1926)

716 *Rouen Cathedral, West Façade.* Signed, and dated 1894. Canvas, 39½ x 26″ (100.4 x 66 cm.). Chester Dale Collection

717 *Rouen Cathedral, West Façade, Sunlight.* Signed, and dated 1894. Canvas, 39½ x 26″ (100.2 x 66 cm.). Chester Dale Collection

718 *Bridge at Argenteuil on a Gray Day.* Signed. c. 1876. Canvas, 24 x 31⅝″ (61 x 80.3 cm.). Ailsa Mellon Bruce Collection

719 *The Bridge at Argenteuil.* Signed. 1874. Canvas, 23⅝ x 31⅜″ (60 x 79.7 cm.). Collection of Mr. and Mrs. Paul Mellon

720 *Argenteuil.* Signed. c. 1872. Canvas, 19⅞ x 25⅝″ (50.4 x 65.2 cm.). Ailsa Mellon Bruce Collection

721 *Ships at Anchor on the Seine.* Signed. 1872/73. Canvas, 14⅞ x 18⅛″ (37.8 x 46.6 cm.). Ailsa Mellon Bruce Collection

722 *The Artist's Garden at Vétheuil.* Signed, and dated 1880. Canvas, 59⅝ x 47⅝″ (151.4 x 121 cm.). Ailsa Mellon Bruce Collection

719

720

721

722

Claude Monet

(FRENCH, 1840–1926)

723   PALAZZO DA MULA, VENICE

In Venice substance often seems to dissolve into reflection, while light appears as material and palpable as the object it falls on. Then churches, palaces, and bridges are transmuted into curtains of colored light, wavering and trembling in their aqueous mirror; and nature, transformed by this amphibious atmosphere, becomes the imitator of art, creating scenery as insubstantially evanescent as the most impressionistic painting. No wonder that Claude Monet, when he finally reached Venice in 1908, wrote to Gustave Geffroy, "All this unusual light. . . . It is so beautiful! . . . I am having a delicious time here and can almost forget that once I was not the old man I am now!"

But looking at the *Palazzo da Mula* the question arises: has Monet gone too far in his interpretation of this light? At twilight did he actually see Venice as an architecture of amethysts, turquoises, emeralds, and rubies? Or is such a vision of intense color only a poetic invention and the reality much less colorful, much closer to the gray and black the average person sees? The answer is complicated and goes to the heart of the problem of Impressionism. What we see in the field of vision are relationships of areas of color and of light and shadow. These relationships the Impressionist painter wished to express, but he was hampered by the limitations of pigment. In the present scene, for instance, no oil paint could give the luminosity of the darkening water or the blackness of the velvety shadows as they actually appeared. Therefore many of the Impressionists, and Monet especially, decided to compensate for the deficiencies of paint, its narrower range of contrasting values, by using contrasting colors of an intensity greater than those they observed in the scenes they were painting. From this point of view the *Palazzo da Mula* is true to nature's organization of tones; yet it is a transposition into another key, one with a more limited scale of light and shadow but, as compensation, with a greater brilliance of color. Thus, though Monet never saw a building like this, a palace made of a rubble of precious stones, his canvas is still a close approximation to the relationship of light, shadow, and color in nature.

Collections: Arthur B. Emmons, Newport, Rhode Island; Henry D. Hughes, Philadelphia. *Chester Dale Collection*, 1962. Signed, and dated 1908. Canvas, 24½ x 32" (62.2 x 81.3 cm.).

724

725

726

Claude Monet (French, 1840–1926)

724 *Banks of the Seine, Vétheuil.* Signed, and dated 1880. Canvas, 28⅞ x 39⅝″ (73.4 x 100.5 cm.). Chester Dale Collection

725 *Vase of Chrysanthemums.* Signed, and dated 1880. Canvas, 39¼ x 28¾″ (99.6 x 73 cm.). Chester Dale Collection

726 *The Seine at Giverny.* Signed. c. 1885. Canvas, 32⅛ x 39⅝″ (81.6 x 100.3 cm.). Chester Dale Collection

727 *Waterloo Bridge, Gray Day.* Signed, and dated 1903. Canvas, 25⅜ x 39⅜″ (65.1 x 100 cm.). Chester Dale Collection

728 *The Houses of Parliament, Sunset.* Signed, and dated 1903. Canvas, 32 x 36⅜″ (81.3 x 92.5 cm.). Chester Dale Collection

729 *Woman Seated Under the Willows.* Signed, and dated 1880. Canvas, 31⅞ x 23⅝″ (81.1 x 60 cm.). Chester Dale Collection

727

Monet remained true to the Impressionist credo that an artist should transcribe visual sensations as experienced at a specific time and place. This reliance upon sense data as the sole basis of art represents the ultimate extension of nineteenth-century Realism. But there are implicit dangers in this theory: a tendency for scientific observation to replace human emotion, the recording power of the eye to replace the imaginative force of the mind, the analytical theorist to replace the sensuous human being.

729

728

Henri Fantin-Latour

(FRENCH, 1836-1904)

730   STILL LIFE

Many people do not understand why artists take such pleasure in still-life painting. For example, in the picture reproduced here, what was it that really interested Fantin-Latour? Obviously the rendering of actual appearance. But how is that done? The answer lies in the organization of detail, tone, and texture. Detail involves distance and time of vision. Should the artist paint what he would see when closely scrutinizing his subject through a magnifying glass, or when glancing at it quickly from a greater distance with half-closed eyes, or when looking at it repeatedly from a normal distance? The first method leads to those canvases in which a fly invariably crawls across a leaf or petal toward a drop of water, and the second to the broad abstract patterns which Cézanne has handed on to modern painting. Fantin-Latour, however, chooses the third and represents the amount of detail—the petals of the camellias, the skin of the fruit, the wicker of the basket—discernible by normal sight at the distance from which the picture is painted.

The same consistent naturalism appears in the organization of tones. There is a single source of light which defines the local color of each object. As these colors come into shadow each tone is altered consistently, so that the bright and the shadowy pink of the camellias maintains the same proportional relationship as the bright, shadowy green of their leaves, and this tonal accuracy is extended to the areas of light and shadow in the fruit, the basket, the cup, the book, and the table. Much of the reality of the painting depends on these delicate and immensely subtle adjustments.

The third element in conveying actual appearance, variety of texture, is difficult to achieve without destroying the organization of detail and tone. For where the painter wishes to suggest texture he is apt to paint too meticulously, and thus focus undue attention on that area of the picture (see, for example, ter Borch's *The Suitor's Visit*, plate 371). But Fantin-Latour avoids this error and yet manages to suggest the brittle substance of the porcelain cup, the waxy petals of the camellia, and the reticulated skin of the fruit. These three characteristics—consistent selection of detail, consonant organization of tone, and congruous rendering of texture—combine to make this still life one of the supreme expressions of what painters mean by the phrase "art for art's sake."

Collections: Reginald Davis, Paris; A. T. Hollingsworth, London. *Chester Dale Collection*, 1962. Signed, and dated 1866. Canvas, 24⅜ x 29½" (61.9 x 75 cm.).

731

732

731 Henri Fantin-Latour (French, 1836–1904): *Portrait of Sonia.* Signed, and dated 1890. Canvas, 43 x 31⅞" (109.2 x 81 cm.). Chester Dale Collection

732 Henri Fantin-Latour: *Self-Portrait.* Dated 1858. Canvas, 16 x 12⅞" (40.7 x 32.7 cm.). Chester Dale Collection

733 Henri Fantin-Latour: *Mademoiselle de Fitz-James.* Signed, and dated 1867. Canvas, 20⅛ x 16⅞" (51.1 x 42.8 cm.). Chester Dale Collection

734 Henri Fantin-Latour: *Duchesse de Fitz-James.* Signed. 1867. Canvas, 19¾ x 16⅝" (50.3 x 42.2 cm.). Chester Dale Collection

735 Paul Cézanne (French, 1839–1906): *Vase of Flowers.* Signed. c. 1876. Canvas, 28¾ x 23½" (73 x 59.8 cm.). Chester Dale Collection

733

734

Fantin-Latour was popular not only as a still-life painter but also as a portraitist. In his portraits he showed the same skill in observing precisely the amount of detail discernible at the distance from which the picture is painted that one finds in his still lifes. This method often gives his portraits a somewhat photographic look. The vast difference between Fantin-Latour's work and Cézanne's is well illustrated by plate 735. Fantin-Latour painted what he saw on the table in front of him, whereas Cézanne copied a vase of flowers from a magazine illustration and then transformed it into a seedpod which seems to explode with the fertility of nature.

735

Paul Cézanne

(FRENCH, 1839–1906)

736   STILL LIFE

The points made in the discussions on Fantin-Latour will be clearer if one compares the still life reproduced here with his still life in plate 730. In the painting by Fantin-Latour, the texture, tone, and color of the camellias, the fruit, the china, and the blue book are so skillfully organized that merely visual facts take on a quality of poetry. This is Impressionism insofar as the main interest on the part of the artist is in transcribing a visual impression as accurately as possible, using the highest key of color which can be consistently maintained. But it is also more traditional than the work of the Impressionists, closer to eighteenth-century painters like Chardin, who observe their subject with a steady gaze instead of the quick glance used by Impressionist artists (See Manet's advice to Eva Gonzalès, page 450). On the other hand, the still-life painting by Cézanne belongs to a different tradition. It is as far from Impressionism as it is from Chardin. It recalls instead the designs of the great Italian artists, for it has the same gravity and momentum of rhythm we find in the figure paintings of Giotto and Masaccio. The various objects which in Fantin-Latour's still life remain isolated are here united by continuous movement suggested by the pattern in the folds of the cloth and the napkin, a movement controlled and checked by the emphasized rectangular lines in the background. In Cézanne one finds again the permanent equilibrium characteristic of classical design. Cézanne is not dependent on visual memory for his composition as were Impressionists like Degas, for he had instead an extraordinary gift of visual imagination, of that genius for inventing compositions which we find in the major Renaissance artists. Thus the reaction of Cézanne against Impressionism resulted in a new emphasis on form, solidity, and structure—on qualities which were the bone and marrow of Renaissance art.

Collections: Ambroise Vollard, Paris; Maurice Gangnat, Paris; Emil Staub (Staub-Terlinden), Männedorf, Switzerland. *Chester Dale Collection*, 1962. Painted c. 1894. Canvas, 26 x 32¼″ (65.5 x 82 cm.).

737

738

739

740

741

The nineteen canvases by Cézanne in the collection of the National Gallery of Art form one of the most remarkable representations of his work in any museum. Particularly fine are the late paintings (see plates 737, 740, 742, 746, and 755). These show the deep resonances of color and the strong rhythmic design which Cézanne achieved in the last years of his life.

Paul Cézanne (French, 1839–1906)

737 *Still Life with Apples and Peaches.* c. 1905. Canvas, 32 x 39⅝" (81.2 x 100.6 cm.). Gift of Eugene and Agnes Meyer

738 *Man with Pipe.* 1892/96. Canvas, 10¼ x 8" (26.1 x 20.2 cm.). Gift of the W. Averell Harriman Foundation in memory of Marie N. Harriman

739 *At the Water's Edge.* c. 1890. Canvas, 28⅞ x 36½" (73.3 x 92.8 cm.). Gift of the W. Averell Harriman Foundation in memory of Marie N. Harriman

740 *Vase of Flowers.* 1900/1903. Canvas, 39⅞ x 32⅜" (101.2 x 82.2 cm.). Gift of Eugene and Agnes Meyer

741 *The Battle of Love.* c. 1880. Canvas, 14⅞ x 18¼" (37.8 x 46.2 cm.). Gift of the W. Averell Harriman Foundation in memory of Marie N. Harriman

742 *Still Life.* c. 1900. Canvas, 18 x 21⅝" (45.8 x 54.9 cm.). Gift of the W. Averell Harriman Foundation in memory of Marie N. Harriman

742

499

Paul Cézanne

(FRENCH, 1839–1906)

743 THE ARTIST'S FATHER

It is hard to imagine a more ambivalent relationship than that of Paul Cézanne and his father. Emile Zola, Paul's closest friend, describes the elder Cézanne as "mocking, republican, bourgeois, cold, meticulous, stingy. . . . He is, moreover, garrulous and, sustained by his wealth, doesn't care a rap for anyone or anything." This was probably also the younger Cézanne's judgment when in 1866 he was painting the portrait reproduced here; and yet twenty years later, according to friends, he venerated his parent, who had left him what he considered to be a large income.

Louis-Auguste Cézanne started his life as a manufacturer of hats, and by 1848 he had made enough money to buy the local bank, which was in financial difficulties because of the Revolution. He restored its prosperity and hoped his son, too, would become a banker. But when banking made Paul so obviously unhappy, and all he could think of was painting, his father gave him an allowance, small but sufficient to enable him to follow his unprofitable profession. He even agreed to act as a model for his son, whose work he never understood.

With time, relations between father and son, always variable, worsened, and the nadir was reached in 1872 when Paul had a son by Hortense Fiquet. His father was willing to support Paul as a bachelor but unwilling to have a family kept at his expense, especially one his son would not acknowledge. Yet eventually he accepted even this, and in 1886 when Paul at last married Hortense he signed the register.

Paul Cézanne painted his father at least three times and drew him often. Of these likenesses the National Gallery portrait is the most overwhelming. The massive body of the sitter suggests such weight and solidity, gives such an effect of three-dimensional existence, that it is difficult to find a comparable portrait by any other artist. These formal qualities are linked to an indefinable tenderness, "as though," to quote John Rewald, "while contemplating him, often without the model's knowledge, the painter had felt the deep-rooted links that nature or fate had established between him and this old man."

Father and son always shared a certain toughness—a revulsion from all sentimentality. When the banker was trying to persuade his son to give up painting, he used to say, "Think of the future; one dies with genius, but one eats with money." After his father's death, Paul, perhaps with subconscious irony, altered this aphorism into his only eulogy for his parent: "My father was a man of genius; he left me an income of twenty-five thousand francs."

Collections: Auguste Pellerin, Paris; Mme René Lecomte, Paris. *Collection of Mr. and Mrs. Paul Mellon,* 1970. Painted 1866. Canvas, 78⅛ x 47" (198.5 x 119.3 cm.).

744

These four portraits illustrate Cézanne's power of characterization, which is especially apparent in the portraits of two boys who were close friends, the painter's son (plate 748) and his playmate Louis Guillaume (plate 747). Did the son of the artist really look stolid and practical and his companion dreamy and artistic, or was this merely Cézanne's sense of irony? The subjects of the other portraits reproduced here, one by Bastien-Lepage (plate 744) and the other by Frédéric Bazille (plate 749) are also well characterized. Hayem, a banker, is typical of the French bourgeoisie and Blau, a poet, of the intellectuals of the time.

746

745

747

748

749

744 **Jules Bastien-Lepage** (French, 1848–1884): *Simon Hayem.* Signed. 1875. Canvas, 15⅞ x 12⅞" (40.4 x 32.6 cm.). Chester Dale Collection

745 **Paul Cézanne**: *Antony Valabrègue.* Signed. 1866. Canvas, 45¾ x 38¾" (116.3 x 98.4 cm.). Collection of Mr. and Mrs. Paul Mellon

746 **Paul Cézanne**: *The Sailor.* c. 1905. Canvas, 42¼ x 29⅜" (107.4 x 74.5 cm.). Gift of Eugene and Agnes Meyer

747 **Paul Cézanne**: *Louis Guillaume.* c. 1882. Canvas, 22 x 18⅜" (55.9 x 46.7 cm.). Chester Dale Collection

748 **Paul Cézanne**: *The Artist's Son, Paul.* 1885/90. Canvas, 25¾ x 21¼" (65.3 x 54 cm.). Chester Dale Collection

749 **Frédéric Bazille** (French, 1841–1870): *Édouard Blau.* Signed, and dated 1866. Canvas, 23½ x 17⅛" (59.7 x 43.5 cm.). Chester Dale Collection

Paul Cézanne

(FRENCH, 1839-1906)

750   HOUSE OF PÈRE LACROIX

Paul Cézanne's life was consecrated to painting. In his lonely retreat at Aix he once wrote to Emile Bernard, "I have sworn to die painting"; and he carried out his vow, for he was found after a torrential downpour of rain, unconscious beside his easel. A passerby carried him home in a laundry cart; yet the next morning he struggled back to his studio, was again stricken, and died a few days later.

What was the vision he followed with such passion and such relentlessness? As nearly as words can describe such matters, his quest was twofold: to discover a means of transcribing the weft of color that in nature covers and yet indicates mass, and to find a way of conveying an impression of space without destroying these color relations. In the present landscape, for example, which he painted at Auvers, near Paris, in 1873, he wished to show the trees and the walls of the cottages not only as the colored patterns of light and shade which would have satisfied an Impressionist painter but also to communicate his perception of their volumes, the dense mass of the foliage and the solidity of the buildings. Similarly, he wished to transcend Impressionism in the rendering of space. Instead of allowing the colors to fade into a misty background, the conventional method of suggesting recession, he wanted to maintain chromatic intensity even in the distance. Thus local color in the *House of Père Lacroix* retains its strength in every plane; and space is created not by diminution of tonal contrast but by the position and scale of the trees, the cottages, and the hill which make up the scene. The magic of Cézanne's style consists in his power to suggest, through selection of color and organization of form, solid volumes in a sequence of planes, aspects of vision which we experience more intensely in his paintings than we do when we look directly at nature.

Collections: Alphonse Kann, St.-Germain-en-Laye, France; Auguste Pellerin, Paris. *Chester Dale Collection*, 1962. Signed, and dated 1873, and exhibited in the Salon of 1873. Canvas, 24¼ x 20″ (61.5 x 51 cm.).

505

751

752

Paul Cézanne   (French, 1839–1906)

751   *Houses in Provence.* c. 1880. Canvas, 25⅝ x 32″ (65 x 81.3 cm.). Collection of Mr. and Mrs. Paul Mellon

752   *Riverbank.* c. 1895. Canvas, 28¾ x 36⅜″ (73 x 92.3 cm.). Ailsa Mellon Bruce Collection

753   *Landscape near Paris.* c. 1876. Canvas, 19¾ x 23⅞″ (50.2 x 60 cm.). Chester Dale Collection

754   *Mont Sainte-Victoire.* c. 1887. Canvas, 26½ x 36″ (67.2 x 91.3 cm.). Gift of the W. Averell Harriman Foundation in memory of Marie N. Harriman

755   *Le Château Noir.* 1900/1904. Canvas, 29 x 38″ (73.7 x 96.6 cm.). Gift of Eugene and Agnes Meyer

Cézanne once wrote, "One can't be too scrupulous, too sincere, or too submissive to nature, but one ought to be nonetheless master of his model and above all of his means of expression. Penetrate to what is before you and express yourself as logically as possible." This might apply to all the landscapes by Cézanne which are reproduced in this volume.

753

754

755

756

Camille Pissarro   (French, 1830–1903)

756 *Boulevard des Italiens, Morning, Sunlight.* Signed, and dated 1897. Canvas, 28⅞ x 36¼" (73.2 x 92.1 cm.). Chester Dale Collection

757   *Peasant Girl with a Straw Hat.* Signed, and dated 1881. Canvas, 28⅞ x 23½" (73.4 x 59.6 cm.). Ailsa Mellon Bruce Collection

758 *Orchard in Bloom, Louveciennes.* Signed, and dated 1872. Canvas, 17¾ x 21⅝" (45 x 55 cm.). Ailsa Mellon Bruce Collection

759 *Peasant Woman.* Signed, and dated 1880. Canvas, 28¼ x 23⅝" (73.1 x 60 cm.). Chester Dale Collection

760 *The Bather.* Signed, and dated 1895. Canvas, 13⅞ x 10¾" (35.3 x 27.3 cm.). Chester Dale Collection

761 *Hampton Court Green.* Signed, and dated 1891. Canvas, 21⅜ x 28¾" (54.3 x 73 cm.). Ailsa Mellon Bruce Collection

757

758

759

Pissarro was much less a "master of his model" than Cézanne, but he was nonetheless admired and respected by the significant artists of his generation. Cézanne wished his landscapes to have the permanence of his favorite motif, Mont Sainte-Victoire (plate 754), whereas Pissarro wished his pictures to suggest the scene exactly as photographed by the retina of the eye. Sisley shared Pissarro's goal but achieved it less often. In *Meadow* (plate 765), however, he has created one of his rare masterpieces.

760

761

762

763

764

510

762   Camille Pissarro (French, 1830–1903): *The Artist's Garden at Eragny.* Signed, and dated 1898. Canvas, 29 x 36⅜″ (73.6 x 92.3 cm.). Ailsa Mellon Bruce Collection

763   Camille Pissarro: *Place du Carrousel, Paris.* Signed, and dated 1900. Canvas, 21⅝ x 25¾″ (54.9 x 65.4 cm.). Ailsa Mellon Bruce Collection

Alfred Sisley   (French, 1839–1899)

764   *Street at Sèvres.* Signed, and dated 1872. Canvas, 15½ x 23½″ (39.5 x 59.6 cm.). Ailsa Mellon Bruce Collection

765   *Meadow.* Signed, and dated 1875. Canvas, 21⅝ x 28¼″ (54.9 x 73 cm.). Ailsa Mellon Bruce Collection

766   *The Banks of the Oise.* Signed. 1877/78. Canvas, 21⅜ x 25½″ (54.3 x 64.7 cm.). Chester Dale Collection

767   *The Road in the Woods.* Signed. 1879. Canvas, 18¼ x 22″ (46.3 x 55.8 cm.). Chester Dale Collection

765

766

767

Georges Seurat

(FRENCH, 1859–1891)

768   THE LIGHTHOUSE AT HONFLEUR

769   SEASCAPE AT PORT-EN-BESSIN, NORMANDY

These two paintings belong to a group of landscapes that Seurat painted between 1886 and 1888. Many are devoted to interpreting the aqueous light of the seashore; all have carefully thought out compositions. The key to the design of *The Lighthouse at Honfleur* (plate 768) is the sawhorse in the foreground. It introduces the theme of cross-cut angles, repeated by the boats, roofs, shoreline, retaining wall, and even shadows on the sand. If you hide the sawhorse with your hand the picture becomes empty and meaningless. Similarly, cover the two cranes in the upper left-hand corner of *Seascape at Port-en-Bessin* (plate 769) and the structure of the picture will vanish.

In large part Seurat accurately recorded what he was painting, as is proved by photographs taken of the same scenes; but he carefully chose the exact location from which to paint. Photographic veracity, however, does not apply to the subordinate details of the scenes. On the beach at Honfleur the sawhorse, the broken wheel, the rowboat in the middle distance, and the sailboat further away—all intrinsic elements of the design—were arbitrarily arranged by the artist, as were the two cranes and the clouds blown into undulating lines by an improbable wind in the Port-en-Bessin landscape.

Both pictures were executed in the Divisionist technique Seurat developed. He would place at the top of his palette a line of pure primary colors and at the bottom the same number of dabs of white pigment. Between the two lines was a third row of tints, a blend he made by mixing the prismatic hues at the top and the colorless white blobs at the bottom. Dots and strokes from these three sequences of pigment were then placed on the canvas side by side to meld together in the spectator's vision. Seurat was interested in the science of color, a subject much discussed during his lifetime. He read and absorbed the theories of the French scientist Eugène Chevreul and of the American Ogden Rood. These were the most advanced texts on optical color then available.

Such Divisionist paintings, although basically photographic, shocked contemporary taste, and during his short life of thirty-one years Seurat sold almost nothing. The two National Gallery paintings are exceptions.

768 collections: Emile Verhaeren; Curt von Mützenbecher; R. Goetz; Wilhelm Lowenstein; Etienne Bignou, Paris; Sir Alfred Chester Beatty, Dublin. *Collection of Mr. and Mrs. Paul Mellon.* Signed. Painted 1886. Canvas, 26¼ x 32¼" (66.7 x 81.9 cm.).

769 collections: Mme Seurat; Léon Appert; Léopold Appert; Félix Fénéon, Paris. *Gift of the W. Averell Harriman Foundation in memory of Marie N. Harriman,* 1972. Signed. Painted 1888. Canvas, 25⅝ x 31⅞" (65.1 x 80.9 cm.).

770

771

772

773

John Rewald has aptly remarked, "Redon lived in a world of beautiful and disquieting dreams that were indistinguishable from reality." But the painter himself wrote, "I have always felt the need to copy nature in small objects, particularly the casual and accidental." The first quotation explains paintings like *Pandora*, *St. Sebastian*, and the puzzling portrait entitled *Evocation of Roussel*; the second explains the three beautiful still lifes of flowers, which delight the eye and present no problem to the brain.

Odilon Redon (French, 1840–1916)

770 *Pandora.* Signed. 1910/12. Canvas, 56½ x 24¾"
(143.6 x 62.9 cm.). Chester Dale Collection

771 *St. Sebastian.* Signed. 1910/12. Canvas, 56¾ x
24¾" (144 x 62.8 cm.). Chester Dale Collection

772 *Flowers in a Vase.* Signed. c. 1910. Canvas, 22 x
15½" (55.9 x 39.4 cm.). Ailsa Mellon Bruce Collection

773 *Pansies.* Signed. c. 1905. Pastel, 21½ x 18" (54.6
x 45.7 cm.). Gift of the Adele R. Levy Fund, Inc., as a
tribute to Lessing J. Rosenwald

774 *Evocation of Roussel.* Signed. c. 1912. Canvas,
28⅞ x 21⅜" (73.4 x 54.3 cm.). Chester Dale Collection

775 *Wildflowers.* Signed. c. 1905. Pastel, 24⅜ x 18⅞"
(61.9 x 47.9 cm.). Gift of Loula D. Lasker

776 **Georges Seurat** (French, 1859–1891): *Study for
"La Grande Jatte."* 1884/85. Wood, 6¼ x 9⅞" (15.9 x
25 cm.). Ailsa Mellon Bruce Collection

774

775

776

515

Vincent van Gogh

(DUTCH, 1853–1890)

777   LA MOUSMÉ

Cézanne was not the only artist to react against Impressionism, against its absorption in the facts of vision. Van Gogh also wished to escape the Impressionist tyranny of the eye, to go beyond the mere transcriptions of appearance. A study of Japanese prints liberated him. From them he learned to paint in masses of flat tone or masses of but slightly broken color, and to treat the picture surface as decoration.

Van Gogh wrote his brother, Theo, "I envy the Japanese the extreme clearness which everything has in their work. It is never tedious, and never seems to be done too hurriedly. Their work is as simple as breathing, and they do a figure in a few sure strokes with the same ease as if it were as simple as buttoning your coat." But van Gogh never attained this facility. He wrote again in July 1888 of *La Mousmé*, "It took me a whole week, I have not been able to do anything else, not having been very well either . . . but I had to reserve my mental energy to do the *mousmé* well. A *mousmé* is a Japanese girl—Provençal in this case—12 to 14 years old." Creation was easier for the Japanese artist. He was a member of a group, where everyone worked in the same tradition, but van Gogh was a lonely individual, never sure of his way, only certain that he must follow his self-destroying search for beauty. It was a quest that cost him first his sanity and then his life, but he knew in the end that he had found the Grail he sought.

Collections: Mme J. van Gogh-Bonger, Amsterdam; Carl Sternheim, La Hulpe, Belgium; Alphonse Kann, St.-Germain-en-Laye, France; J. B. Stang, Oslo. *Chester Dale Collection*, 1962. Painted 1888. Canvas, 28⅞ x 23¾" (73.4 x 60 cm.).

Vincent van Gogh

(DUTCH, 1853–1890)

778   GIRL IN WHITE

Every picture by an artist of deep feeling is itself a piece of autobiography. The painting reproduced here was finished less than a month before van Gogh committed suicide. He had been released from the asylum at St-Remy and had placed himself in the care of Dr. Gachet at Auvers-sur-Oise. It was the last stage in a losing battle, the last effort to paint and remain sane.

For a time he seemed better. He liked his new doctor. He painted his portrait. He felt a deep sympathy for a man who also had "the heartbroken expression of our time," as he wrote Gauguin. Although always fearful of another attack, van Gogh seemed happy in his work, hopeful that at last he could resist. Gradually, however, his mind grew clouded again. His letters to Theo became less coherent, tinged with a deepening melancholy. He found that he could paint only "sadness and the extreme of loneliness."

His demon of despair had found him out once more. Perhaps in this picture he decided to paint the portrait of his familiar spirit, to embody all his sorrow in the features of a young peasant girl. It is one of the most beautiful and touching of his pictures. The girl's frail body, her long thin arms with their large, awkward hands, the droop of her shoulders, the huge eyes, vacant and staring, convey an effect of tranquil sadness. All around her is the tender green of early summer. She stands in the midst of nodding heads of wheat like some unhappy spirit of the fields.

In the last few weeks of his life, wheat fields held a deep fascination for van Gogh. He found them hard to paint. As he wrote Gauguin, "It is a question of different greens, of the same value, so as to form a green ensemble which, by its vibration, will make you think of the gentle rustle of ears of wheat swaying in the breeze."

As background in this portrait, they are rendered by the most abstract notation, but with that mystical intensity described by Traherne, "The corn was orient and immortal wheat, which never should be reaped, nor was ever sown." To hold this vision van Gogh worked more feverishly than ever. He knew the danger in this. Shortly before he shot himself he wrote his brother, "Well, my own work, I am risking my life for it and my reason has half foundered in it—that's all right." He was resigned. "Painters have more and more their backs to the wall," he admitted. At last he was ready to accept the terrible truth Emerson has expressed: "The artists must be sacrificed to their art. Like the bees, they must put their lives into the sting they give."

Collections: Mme J. van Gogh-Bonger, Amsterdam; Richard Kisling; Mme H. Glatt-Kisling, Zurich. *Chester Dale Collection*, 1962. Painted 1890. Canvas, 26⅛ x 17⅛" (66.3 x 45.3 cm.).

519

779

779 Vincent van Gogh (Dutch, 1853–1890): *Roulin's Baby.* 1888. Canvas, 13¾ x 9⅜" (35 x 23.9 cm.). Chester Dale Collection

780 Vincent van Gogh: *The Olive Orchard.* 1889. Canvas, 28¾ x 36¼" (73 x 92 cm.). Chester Dale Collection

781 Vincent van Gogh: *Farmhouse in Provence, Arles.* 1888. Canvas, 18⅛ x 24" (46.1 x 60.9 cm.). Ailsa Mellon Bruce Collection

782 Paul Gauguin (French, 1848–1903): *Madame Alexandre Kohler.* Signed. 1887/88. Canvas, 18¼ x 15" (46.3 x 38 cm.). Chester Dale Collection

780

781

Van Gogh's "sadness and the extreme of loneliness" are evident even in paintings where one would normally expect cheerfulness. *Roulin's Baby* has all the chubbiness of infancy, but the gaiety one associates, perhaps wrongly, with roly-poly babies is absent. Instead, those huge, staring eyes hold a premonition of sorrow to come. Sad too is the subdued color of *The Olive Orchard*. The low tonality of this landscape, however, is explained by the painter in a beautiful analogy, "It is a canvas worked at from memory because I wanted something very far away like a vague memory softened by time."

782

Paul Gauguin

(FRENCH, 1848–1903)

783 **BRETON GIRLS DANCING**

784 **FATATA TE MITI**

Paul Gauguin, when already a man of middle age, abandoned his prosperous brokerage business, his wife and children, and ultimately all civilized life to devote himself to painting. Some demon of creativity drove him toward an exotic world, first to Panama, where he worked as a digger on the canal, hating every moment, and then to Martinique, where the climate nearly killed him. Still ill, he signed on as a seaman in a sailing ship and returned to Paris. The sea air on the trip reinvigorated him, and he recovered his usual optimism. Having finally sold some pictures, he came to a vital decision. "I'm going to Pont-Aven for six months. I must get under the skin of the people and the country—that is essential in painting." It was in Pont-Aven that he first showed his genius. In *Breton Girls Dancing* (plate 783), of 1888, he has "gotten under the skin" of these children. They are peasants: uncouth, awkward as dancers, their faces dour and at once young and old. But above all they are real children, innocent and appealing. It is as though one could hear the clatter of their wooden shoes. As Gauguin said, "When my sabots echo on the granite I hear the sound, dull and strong, that I'm looking for in painting."

Sounds always had a deep meaning for him. When he left France again and traveled to Tahiti, he developed his theories of the analogy of color to music. "Are not these repetitions of tone," he was later to ask, "these monotonous color harmonies (in the musical sense) analogous to Oriental chants sung in a shrill voice, to the accompaniment of pulsating notes which intensify them by contrast?"

Fatata te Miti (plate 784) was painted a few months after Gauguin's first arrival at Tahiti. He had withdrawn to the interior of the island to live among the natives. Tehura, a beautiful Polynesian, became his *vahine* and probably posed for the figure of the girl on the right removing her sarong.

In all his canvases painted in the South Seas, complementary colors—orange and blue, yellow and violet, green and red—at their highest intensities and without modulation of values, are balanced harmoniously against each other, forming beautiful, almost abstract patterns. *Fatata te Miti* may have been the picture which Mallarmé, the symbolist poet, had in mind when he said of a canvas by his friend Gauguin, "It is a musical poem, it needs no libretto."

783 collections: Boussod et Valadon, Paris; Ambroise Vollard, Paris; William A. Cargill, London. *Collection of Mr. and Mrs. Paul Mellon.* Signed, and dated 1888. Canvas, 28¾ x 36½" (73 x 92.7 cm.).

784 collections: Ambroise Vollard, Paris; Louis Horch, New York. *Chester Dale Collection.* Signed, and dated 1892. Canvas, 26¾ x 36" (68 x 91.5 cm.).

785

786

Paul Gauguin   (French, 1848–1903)

785   *Parau na te Varua'ino (Words of the Devil)*. Signed, and dated 1892. Canvas, 36⅛ x 27″ (91.7 x 68.5 cm.). Gift of the W. Averell Harriman Foundation in memory of Marie N. Harriman

786   *Te Pape Nave Nave (Delectable Waters)*. Signed, and dated 1898. Canvas, 29⅛ x 37½″ (74 x 95.3 cm.). Collection of Mr. and Mrs. Paul Mellon

787   *Brittany Landscape*. Signed, and dated 1888. Canvas, 28 x 35¼″ (71.1 x 89.5 cm.). Chester Dale Collection

788   *The Bathers*. Signed, and dated 1898. Canvas, 23¾ x 36¾″ (60.4 x 93.4 cm.). Gift of Sam A. Lewisohn

789   *Self-Portrait*. Signed, and dated 1889. Wood, 31¼ x 20¼″ (79.2 x 51.3 cm.). Chester Dale Collection

790   *Haystacks in Brittany*. Signed, and dated 1890. Canvas, 29¼ x 36⅞″ (74.3 x 93.6 cm.). Gift of the W. Averell Harriman Foundation in memory of Marie N. Harriman

787

788

789

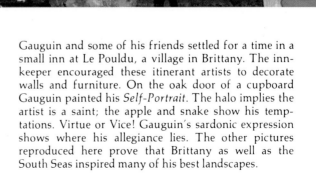

790

Gauguin and some of his friends settled for a time in a small inn at Le Pouldu, a village in Brittany. The innkeeper encouraged these itinerant artists to decorate walls and furniture. On the oak door of a cupboard Gauguin painted his *Self-Portrait*. The halo implies the artist is a saint; the apple and snake show his temptations. Virtue or Vice! Gauguin's sardonic expression shows where his allegiance lies. The other pictures reproduced here prove that Brittany as well as the South Seas inspired many of his best landscapes.

Henri de Toulouse-Lautrec

(FRENCH, 1864–1901)

791   QUADRILLE AT THE MOULIN ROUGE

After the opening of an art exhibition, Toulouse-Lautrec sent a friend his impressions with this note: "What a crush! . . . A hurly-burly of gloved hands carrying pince-nez framed in tortoise-shell or gold. . . . Here are some observations I made among all those elbows." He saw the world at elbow height. He was a dwarf.

But there is no self-pity in his observations. He enjoyed the hurly-burly of men and women. Day and night he drew and painted his *comédie humaine*. For an artist who lived only thirty-seven years, the corpus of his work is enormous. More than any other painter he has given us our imagery of Paris and Parisians at the turn of the century. They are all there: writers, painters, singers, dancers, sportsmen, prostitutes, poor and rich, the whole crush of human beings looming above a tiny draftsman.

He was perhaps the last great artist to be preoccupied with humanity. Though he represented members of his own class—for he was a descendant of the Counts of Toulouse—the specifically human quality he sought was more apparent elsewhere. He found it strongest at the theater, at the races, in cabarets, in brothels, among artists and their impresarios, or among the vicious and their victims, wherever genius had left the strong lines of character or degradation, the numb look of indifference.

He was fascinated by spontaneous wickedness. He destroyed himself with dissipation and drink. "He was," the singer Yvette Guilbert once said, "the genius of deformity." But he drew the strange contours, both physical and spiritual, of the men and women he portrayed with the same witty detachment he showed toward his own illness. He made no moral comment. He retained at all times his detached vision.

Painted in 1892, the figures of *Quadrille at the Moulin Rouge* have been identified, from left to right, as Valentin le Désossé, Mlle Lucie Bellanger, and Gabrielle, a dancer in Montmartre. The painting once belonged to Louis Bouglé, who posed for several portraits. He was a bicycle enthusiast and a member of the sporting set of Tristan Bernard.

Collection: Louis Bouglé, Paris. *Chester Dale Collection*, 1962. Signed with monogram. Painted 1892. Gouache on cardboard, 31½ x 23¾" (80 x 60.5 cm.).

792

793

As a draftsman Toulouse-Lautrec ranks with the greatest nineteenth-century artists. With marvelous economy of brushwork he has immortalized his friends. A few supple strokes, for instance, and he has caught the provocative charm of Jane Avril. A dancer at the Moulin Rouge, she was a constant companion of the painter in the sordid life of Montmartre. *Rue des Moulins, 1894* is symbolic of this world of petty vice. It depicts two prostitutes awaiting their medical inspection, a squalid but deeply moving picture.

794

795

796

Henri de Toulouse-Lautrec (French, 1864–1901)

792 *Rue des Moulins, 1894.* Signed with initials. Cardboard mounted on wood, 32⅞ x 24⅛" (83.5 x 61.4 cm.). Chester Dale Collection

793 *Alfred la Guigne.* Signed. 1894. Gouache on cardboard, 25¾ x 19¾" (65.6 x 50.4 cm.). Chester Dale Collection

794 *Maxime Dethomas.* Signed, and dated 1896. Gouache on cardboard, 26½ x 20¾" (67.3 x 52.7 cm.). Chester Dale Collection

795 *Jane Avril.* Signed. 1892. Cardboard mounted on wood, 26¾ x 20⅞" (67.8 x 52.9 cm.). Chester Dale Collection

796 *Carmen Gaudin.* 1885. Wood, 9⅛ x 5⅞" (23.8 x 14.9 cm.). Ailsa Mellon Bruce Collection

797 *Lady with a Dog.* Signed, and dated 1891. Cardboard, 29½ x 22½" (75 x 57.2 cm.). Gift of the W. Averell Harriman Foundation in memory of Marie N. Harriman

797

Henri de Toulouse-Lautrec

(FRENCH, 1864–1901)

798   A CORNER OF THE MOULIN DE LA GALETTE

The Moulin de la Galette was for Toulouse-Lautrec a favorite haunt, a catchall of the types he liked to paint. It was an unpretentious wineshop, which still survives near the summit of Montmartre. On certain days it was frequented by petty gangsters and streetwalkers, on other days by a more conservative set. Lautrec in the picture reproduced here seems to have painted the less rowdy clientele. Catching them in a moment of repose, he has drawn the bourgeois men and women with the utmost simplicity and without his usual distortions.

It is a brilliant composition. The casual juxtaposition of seven figures is seized on to form an intricately balanced design. Although only four faces are clearly seen, the mood of each of the seven is conveyed, even of the tall man whose head is so daringly cut by the frame. The edge of the face of the woman seen from behind suggests her smile; the toss of the next woman's head carries its invitation; the sideburn of the man with the beret gives his character; the fixed and purposeless gaze of the three central figures in the foreground suggests their dreary tragedy of boredom. It is also a profound painting, a masterly study in loneliness. The figures are crowded together in space but isolated in their own thoughts. No one looks at anyone else. Our attention is focused on the young girl standing in the center behind a table. In spite of her ugly, mannish clothes, she has a latent beauty rarely found in Lautrec's women.

In stature she seems hardly more than a child but with a face prematurely lined and saddened. Did Lautrec glimpse for a moment a woman perfectly formed but almost of his own size, someone else who knew what it was to make observations among elbows? Lautrec had a passionate nature and was in constant search of affection—not friendship only, for which he had a genius, but something deeper and more intimate. In his treatment of this tired, dispirited, but still beautiful woman one feels a mood of sympathy, even of tenderness. There is an overtone which almost approaches compassion and which, combined with Lautrec's other qualities of incisive vision, makes the *Moulin de la Galette* one of his greatest achievements, a masterpiece of nineteenth-century painting.

Collections: Depeaux; Gerstenberg, Berlin. *Chester Dale Collection*, 1962. Signed, and dated 1892. Cardboard mounted on wood, 39½ x 35⅛" (100.3 x 89.1 cm.).

799

800

801

799   Jean-Francois Raffaëlli (French, 1850–1924): *The Flower Vendor.* Signed. Canvas, 31⅞ x 25½" (80.8 x 65 cm.). Chester Dale Collection

800   Jean-Jacques Henner (French, 1829–1905): *Alsatian Girl.* Signed, and dated 1873. Wood, 10¼ x 7⅛" (27.2 x 18.7 cm.). Chester Dale Collection

801   Jean-Jacques Henner: *Madame Uhring.* 1890. Wood, 10¾ x 7⅜" (27.3 x 18.7 cm.). Chester Dale Collection

802   Henri de Toulouse-Lautrec (French, 1864–1901): *The Artist's Dog Flèche.* Signed, with initials. c. 1881. Wood, 9¼ x 5½" (23.4 x 14.1 cm.). Ailsa Mellon Bruce Collection

803   Alfred Stevens (Belgian, 1823–1906): *Young Woman in White Holding a Bouquet.* Signed, with initials. c. 1865/75. Wood, 11¼ x 8⅛" (28.7 x 20.5 cm.). Chester Dale Collection

804   Adolphe Monticelli (French, 1824–1886): *Madame Cahen.* Signed, and dated 1869. Canvas, 51⅞ x 38½" (131.8 x 97.9 cm.). Chester Dale Collection

802

Toulouse-Lautrec once said of Jean-Jacques Henner that "it would be impossible to be more nebulous without becoming mushy." This statement applies to Henner's redheaded nudes, popular two generations ago. By contrast, the *Alsatian Girl* (plate 800) is a jewel, a study of Victorian childhood, sensitive in interpretation, delicate yet solid in modeling. Real connoisseurship consists in finding not only the achievements of genius but the occasional flashes of inspiration that light up the work of less gifted artists, as one can see in these reproductions.

803

804

Henri Rousseau

(FRENCH, 1844–1910)

805   THE EQUATORIAL JUNGLE

It is significant that an obscure inspector of customs should have changed the course of painting in our time almost as much as Michelangelo or Rubens did in theirs. None of the Post-Impressionists, with the possible exception of Cézanne, anticipated or influenced the direction of the modern French School to the same degree as did the self-taught Rousseau. His admirers and disciples included most of the leading artists of the first quarter of the twentieth century: Picasso, Braque, Derain, de Chirico, Vlaminck, to mention a few. For Rousseau brought to painting the qualities that these artists admired: directness of vision, innocence of technique, and naïveté of spirit. He was one of the very few unself-conscious painters of modern times. When a critic was preparing a *Who's Who* of French artists, Rousseau appeared with his self-portrait and his biography. Speaking of himself, he said: "He has perfected himself more and more in the original manner which he adopted and he is in the process of becoming one of our best realist painters. As a characteristic mark he wears a bushy beard."

It is surprising to find that Rousseau considered his paintings realistic, but we know from many sources that he wished to render nature accurately and that he envied the academic painters their greater skill. But still more important than realism to his mind was the artist's emotional response to his vision. Apollinaire, the French poet, describes how the *douanier*, when painting a terrifying subject, would quite genuinely become frightened by his own creation and rush trembling to open a window. His pictures had for him a life of their own. He once said that he did not mind sleeping in his uncomfortable studio, for, as he put it, "You know, when I wake up, I can smile at my canvases."

And it is this curious inner life which makes *The Equatorial Jungle*, which he painted in 1909, the year before his death, so fascinating a picture. The wilderness Rousseau depicts is overfecund and sinister. Leaves and flowers are magnified even beyond the fantastic fertility of the tropics. Interwoven and interlocking, they form a barrier and convey a sense of the impenetrability of the jungle. Within this jungle and furtively peering out is a hidden life, menacing and full of small sounds. The rhythmic beauty of the repeated leaf shapes in Rousseau's landscape is extraordinary, and as a decorator he is difficult to surpass; but the real wonder of the painting lies in its imaginative realism, in its powerful conception, in the degree to which the artist is possessed by his subject until the scene he depicts comes alive in a strange, almost magical way.

Collection: Robert Delaunay, Paris. *Chester Dale Collection*, 1962. Signed, and dated 1909. Canvas, 55¼ x 51" (140.3 x 129.5 cm.).

806

Henri Rousseau (French, 1844–1910)

806 *Rendezvous in the Forest.* Signed. 1889. Canvas, 36¼ x 28¾″ (92 x 73 cm.). Gift of the W. Averell Harriman Foundation in memory of Marie N. Harriman

807 *Boy on the Rocks.* Signed. 1895/97. Canvas, 21¾ x 18″ (55.4 x 45.7 cm.). Chester Dale Collection

Le Douanier Rousseau, as he was called, though technically naive was psychologically sophisticated. His spectral *Boy on the Rocks* and his bizarre *Rendezvous in the Forest* afford glimpses into the nightmare world of the unconscious. One senses that Freud and Jung are in the offing.

807

American School

XIX AND EARLY XX CENTURY

808

809

808 **Unknown Painter** (American, 19th century): *Miss Arnold Holding an Apple*. c. 1830. Wood, 32¼ x 23⅜" (81.7 x 59.5 cm.). Gift of Edgar William and Bernice Chrysler Garbisch

809 **Unknown Painter** (American, 19th century): *Miss Arnold Knitting*. c. 1830. Wood, 35¼ x 22¾" (89.4. x 58 cm.). Gift of Edgar William and Bernice Chrysler Garbisch

810 **Unknown Painter** (American, 19th century): *Portrait of a Man*. Probably 1829. Wood, 19½ x 13½" (49.5 x 33 cm.). Gift of Edgar William and Bernice Chrysler Garbisch

811 **Unknown Painter** (American, 19th century): *Blue Eyes*. c. 1840. Wood, oval, 18 x 12¾" (45.8 x 32.5 cm.). Gift of Edgar William and Bernice Chrysler Garbisch

812 **Unknown Painter** (American, 19th century): *The Dog*. Canvas, 35¼ x 41½" (89.4 x 105.3 cm.). Gift of Edgar William and Bernice Chrysler Garbisch

813 **Unknown Painter** (American, 19th century): *The Sargent Family*. 1800. Canvas, 38⅜ x 50⅜" (96.5 x 127.9 cm.). Gift of Edgar William and Bernice Chrysler Garbisch

810

811

The hallucinatory effects that appear in the paintings of Rousseau (see plates 805–7) are also to be found in the work of many American anonymous artists. *The Dog*, a typical American primitive painting, might equally be ascribed to Rousseau. Occasionally, however, these native folk painters anticipate European artists of great sophistication. *Blue Eyes*, for example, is a premature Modigliani.

812

813

Linton Park

(AMERICAN, 1826–1906)

814   FLAX SCUTCHING BEE

Rousseau would have felt sympathy and understanding for the American folk-painters. These self-taught and often anonymous artists who flourished chiefly in the nineteenth century, though talented practitioners are to be found from earliest Colonial times, established a native style.

There are many designations of this style, the most satisfactory of which seems to be primitive painting. It is a method of delineation that is realistic but not naturalistic. It is an objective statement of fact to which lack of technical accomplishment adds a touch of fantasy. It is an idea of a person, a place, or an object, around which the artist, so to speak, puts a line. But such representation is rarely achieved without a certain stress and strain. Part of the charm of these pictures lies in the tension between a recalcitrant image and the artist's determination to get it down on his canvas or panel.

Flax Scutching Bee represents a gathering of neighbors to prepare flax for weaving into linen. On the left can be seen a machine used to smash the stalks that enclose the flax fibers. As shown on the right, the fibers were then removed from the stalks by being beaten with a wooden knife against a board set vertically into the ground, a process known as scutching. The buildings are interesting. The one on the left is a log-house with shingled roof, glass windows, and chimney made of sticks of wood and clay. The one on the right is a double-pen barn. The spaces between the logs have not been filled in, to permit ventilation. The resulting circulation of air helped to dry the hay or grain.

Collections: John Houk, Indiana, Pa; Mrs. Bessie B. Mollard, Harmony, Pa.; Michael de Sherbinin, New York City. *Gift of Edgar William and Bernice Chrysler Garbisch*, 1953. Painted 1885. Bed ticking, 31¼ x 50¼″ (79.5 x 127.7 cm.).

815

816

Naive painting flourished in the American climate. In Europe academies were so firmly entrenched that they affected artists to a degree unknown in this country. America in the eighteenth and nineteenth centuries was predominantly rural; consequently many native artists were itinerant, moving from village to village, self-taught and ignorant of professional standards. To them metropolitan fashions meant nothing.

817

818

819

820

815 **L. M. Cooke** (American, last quarter 19th century): *Salute to General Washington in New York Harbor.* Signed. Date illegible. Canvas, 27 x 40¼" (68.7 xk 102.1 cm.). Gift of Edgar William and Bernice Chrysler Garbisch

816 **Francis Alexander** (American, 1800–1880): *Ralph Wheelock's Farm.* c. 1822. Canvas, 25⅛ x 48⅛" (64 x 122.3 cm.). Gift of Edgar William and Bernice Chrysler Garbisch

817 **W. H. Brown** (American, active last quarter 19th century): *Bareback Riders.* Signed, and dated 1886. Cardboard, 18½ x 24½" (46.4 x 62.2 cm.). Gift of Edgar William and Bernice Chrysler Garbisch

818 **Asahel L. Powers** (American, active 1813–1840): *Mrs. J. B. Sheldon.* c. 1835. Wood, 41 x 30¾" (104.1 x 78.2 cm.). Gift of Edgar William and Bernice Chrysler Garbisch

819 **Joshua Johnston** (American, active 1796–1824): *The Westwood Children.* c. 1807. Canvas, 41⅛ x 46" (105 x 117 cm.). Gift of Edgar William and Bernice Chrysler Garbisch

820 **Edward Hicks** (American, 1780–1849): *The Cornell Farm.* Signed, and dated 1848. Canvas, 36¾ x 49" (93.3 x 124.4 cm.). Gift of Edgar William and Bernice Chrysler Garbisch

George Inness

(AMERICAN, 1825-1894)

821 THE LACKAWANNA VALLEY

Recently on an ever-increasing scale the patronage of art has come from commercial firms; and the ancient problem of the relation between patron and artist, how much the one should dictate and the other acquiesce, has arisen again. In painting the roundhouse at Scranton for the Delaware and Lackawanna Railroad in 1855, George Inness was confronted with this immemorial conflict. He painted one picture and it was unsatisfactory. He had shown only one line of rails, all that existed at the time, but the president of the railroad wanted him to show the additional three or four planned for the future. Also he was told to depict four trains, the entire rolling stock of the company, and to paint the letters D. L. & W. on a locomotive. He protested as an artist but gave in as the head of a family. He needed the seventy-five dollars he was to be paid. Later the railroad sold the painting, and Inness as an old man recovered it in a junk shop in Mexico.

Who is right, railroad or artist? Most people today would stand behind the painter and say he should not be interfered with by his patrons. Yet many of the greatest works of art were executed in accordance with the strictest contracts, how many figures to be shown, where they were to stand, how much gold, how much blue, how much red to be used. Within this rigid framework the painter exerted his genius to create a work of beauty, and he succeeded more often in reaching his goal than many modern artists with a blank canvas and nothing to do but express their own ideas.

Commercial patronage may also have helped Inness. Out of the actual scene he was compelled to paint he has created a vision of ordered beauty. Today *The Lackawanna Valley* is more highly prized than the misty landscapes he painted at the end of his life, when he had no patron to dictate.

Collections: Delaware, Lackawanna & Western Railroad; George Inness, the artist; Mrs. Jonathan Scott Hartley, the artist's daughter, New York. *Gift of Mrs. Huttleston Rogers*, 1945. Signed. Painted 1855. Canvas, 33⅞ x 50⅛" (86 x 127.3 cm.).

822

American artists were in love with the novelty of their surroundings, in love with a flamboyantly picturesque subject matter. Cropsey, for example, shows all too vividly the colors of an American autumn, and Cole similarly exaggerates the glamour of Crawford's Notch in the White Mountains of New Hampshire, while Doughty and Church give hyperbolic, if misty, expression to their basically conventional scenes. Inness once remarked, "A work of art is beautiful if the sentiment is beautiful," to which these artists would have said *amen*. Yet it is a hazardous doctrine, as Ryder, the greatest genius among American Romantic painters, was to prove. Interested only in "sentiment," he violated all the laws of his craft, which in the end proved disastrous. His poetic canvases, overloaded with pigment, have cracked and darkened until they threaten to vanish entirely.

823

824

825

826

827

822 Frederic Edwin Church (American, 1826–1900): *Morning in the Tropics.* Signed, and dated 1877. Canvas, 54⅜ x 84⅛" (138.1 x 201.9 cm.). Gift of the Avalon Foundation

823 Jasper Francis Cropsey (American, 1823–1900): *Autumn—On the Hudson River.* Signed, and dated 1860. Canvas, 60 x 108" (152.1 x 259.2 cm.). Gift of the Avalon Foundation

824 Albert Pinkham Ryder (American, 1847–1917): *Siegfried and the Rhine Maidens.* Signed. 1888/91. Canvas, 19⅞ x 20½" (50.3 x 52.1 cm.). Andrew W. Mellon Collection

825 Thomas Cole (American, 1801–1848): *The Notch of the White Mountains (Crawford Notch).* Signed, and dated 1839. Canvas, 40 x 61½" (101.5 x 147.6 cm.). Andrew W. Mellon Fund

826 Thomas Doughty (American, 1793–1856): *Fanciful Landscape.* Signed, and dated 1834. Canvas, 30⅛ x 39⅞" (76.5 x 101.2 cm.). Gift of the Avalon Foundation

827 George Inness (American, 1825–1894): *View of the Tiber near Perugia.* Dated 1874. Canvas, 38⅝ x 63¾" (98 x 161.5 cm.). Ailsa Mellon Bruce Fund

828 John Quidor (American, 1801–1881): *The Return of Rip Van Winkle.* Signed, and dated 1829. Canvas, 39¾ x 49¾" (100.6 x 125.3 cm.). Andrew W. Mellon Collection

828

547

829

830

831

George Catlin   (American, 1796–1872)

829   *The White Cloud, Head Chief of the Iowas.* c. 1845. Canvas, 27¾ x 22¾" (70.2 x 58 cm.). Paul Mellon Collection

830   *A Pawnee Warrior Sacrificing His Favorite Horse.* 1857/69. Cardboard, 18½ x 24½" (47.1 x 62.3 cm.). Paul Mellon Collection

831   *Buffalo-Lancing in the Snow Drifts—Sioux.* Before 1830. Canvas, 17½ x 23½" (44.5 x 59.8 cm.). Paul Mellon Collection

George Catlin as a young man visited some forty-eight tribes; he lived with Indians in North and South America, persuaded them to sit for their portraits, and accompanied them on hunting trips (plate 831). After exhibiting his paintings and artifacts in the eastern United States, he took his collection to Europe, where there was an even greater fascination with Indian lore. Several of his Indian portraits were shown at the Paris Salon of 1846, and were much admired there by the critic Charles Baudelaire, who commented that "with their fine attitudes and easy movements, these savages make antique sculpture comprehensible."

A similar romanticism led other American artists to paint South America. Frederic Church worked there (see plate 822). Martin Johnson Heade saw the surf of one of the world's most beautiful bays breaking in an undulating and decorative line and in the jungle interiors he found exotic flowers of piercing loveliness (plates 832, 833). The luminist painters Fitz Hugh Lane and John Frederick Kensett depicted the landscapes of their native land with the sharp focus of a laser beam. Although they represented nature objectively, they, too, convey romantic and nostalgic emotions (plates 834, 835).

832

833

834

832 Martin Johnson Heade (American, 1819–1904): *Rio de Janeiro Bay.* Signed, and dated 1864. Canvas, 17⅞ x 35⅞″ (45.1 x 91 cm.). Gift of the Avalon Foundation

833 Martin Johnson Heade: *Cattleya Orchid and Three Brazilian Hummingbirds.* Signed, and dated 1871. Wood, 13¾ x 18″ (34.8 x 45.6 cm.). Gift of the Morris and Gwendolyn Cafritz Foundation

834 John Frederick Kensett (American, 1816–1872): *Beacon Rock, Newport Harbor.* Signed with initials, and dated 1857. Canvas, 22½ x 36″ (57.1 x 91.5 cm.). Gift of Frederick Sturges, Jr.

835 Fitz Hugh Lane (American, 1804–1865): *Lumber Schooners at Evening on Penobscot Bay.* Signed, and dated 1860. Canvas, 24⅝ x 38⅛″ (62.5 x 96.8 cm.). Andrew W. Mellon Fund and Gift of Mr. and Mrs. Francis W. Hatch, Sr.

835

Thomas Eakins

(AMERICAN, 1844–1916)

836   THE BIGLIN BROTHERS RACING

Thomas Eakins was the most intellectual artist America has produced, and yet *The Biglin Brothers Racing*, which he painted probably in 1873, looks at first glance as fortuitous and casual as a colored snapshot. Where did the intellectual element in Eakins' painting show itself? What is the difference between a realistic painting of this kind and a good color photograph? Although Eakins himself was a pioneer photographer, he used the camera only as a mechanical means of gathering data about appearance, not as a basis for his pictures. This scene of a rowing race about to begin, for example, was put together in the studio from sketches and from memory. The picture seems photographic because painter and camera have the same goal, to show, as Eakins said, "What o'clock it is, afternoon or morning, winter or summer, and what kind of people are there, and what they are doing and why they are doing it."

But these facts the painter can convey more convincingly than the camera. A photograph taken on a sunny day indicates sunshine; but Eakins' careful study of reflected light taught him how to exaggerate the sparkle of sunlight on water until the waves seemed to catch the rays of the sun itself. A photograph indicates depth but Eakins' precise perspective, worked out mathematically, draws the spectator's vision into this depth, makes him part of the scene. And a photograph sometimes fixes in the kaleidoscope of appearance a satisfactory design; but it almost never achieves, as in *The Biglin Brothers Racing*, an integrated composition in which no object can be altered or removed without destroying the whole effect.

Collections: Mrs. Thomas Eakins; Whitney Museum of American Art, New York. *Gift of Mr. and Mrs. Cornelius Vanderbilt Whitney*, 1953. Painted probably 1873. Canvas, 24 x 36 " (61 x 91.5 cm.).

Thomas Eakins continued in his portraits the tradition of the early works of Copley. Probing, analytical, uncompromising, these likenesses are often as detached and unseductive as a psychiatric report. Even when painting a child, as in *Baby at Play* (plate 841) of 1876, he made no attempt to render the subject pretty or the model cunning. Instead, because the head is in shadow the effect is almost somber, which is unusual in the portrait of a child. The same passion for visual realism marked American still-life painters, the greatest of whom was William Harnett. As he said, "The whole effect of still-life painting comes from its tone, and the nearer one attains perfection, the more realistic the effect will be." It is because Harnett was able to render this proportional relationship of tones, exactly as they are perceived in nature, that his pictures come so close to ocular truth.

838

837

839

837 **Thomas Eakins** (American, 1844–1916): *Archbishop Diomede Falconio.* 1905. Canvas, 72⅛ x 54¼″ (183.2 x 138 cm.). Gift of Stephen C. Clark

838 **Thomas Eakins:** *Louis Husson.* Signed, and dated 1899. Canvas, 24 x 20″ (61.3 x 50.6 cm.). Gift of Katharine Husson Horstick

839 **Thomas Eakins:** *Mrs. Louis Husson.* Signed with initials. c. 1905. Canvas, 24 x 20″ (61.3 x 50.6 cm.). Gift of Katharine Husson Horstick

840 **William M. Harnett** (American, 1848–1892): *My Gems.* Signed, and dated 1888. Wood, 18 x 14″ (45.7 x 35.5 cm.). Gift of the Avalon Foundation

841 **Thomas Eakins:** *Baby at Play.* Signed, and dated 1876. Canvas, 32¼ x 48⅜″ (81.9 x 122.9 cm.). John Hay Whitney Collection

840

841

Winslow Homer

(AMERICAN, 1836–1910)

842   BREEZING UP

The distinguished achievement of American painting in the second half of the nineteenth century was due in no small part to Winslow Homer, who shares with Thomas Eakins a preeminent position in the tradition of American realism. Homer was trained as an illustrator, and an element of illustration appears in his pictures from beginning to end. His earliest significant work was drawn for *Harper's Weekly* during the Civil War, when he was detailed to the Army of the Potomac as a correspondent. Working for a magazine, he learned to make his illustrations clear and specific. Throughout his life he presented his subjects graphically and made them appear to exist convincingly. Such objective recording has now almost vanished from art; and Homer's pictorial style with its simple, lucid statements has had little if any influence in recent years.

Yet Homer was able to suggest mood, feeling, atmosphere, as vividly as any Abstract Expressionist. Three small boys and a fisherman in a sailboat evoke the pleasure of sailing before a fair breeze; a dory with men peering over the side into a foggy sky conveys the loneliness and vastness of the sea; a huntsman with his dog silhouetted against the mountain suggests the exhilaration of sport. One could elaborate endlessly.

But the important point is that a certain mood is induced in the spectator's mind by recognizable images. Representation in the visual arts is, of course, traditional. The basic language of painting with rare exceptions has always been representational, an imagery of identifiable objects. At times, however, painting has tried to usurp the function of other arts: poetry, for example, with the Pre-Raphaelites, and music with the Abstract Expressionists. With Winslow Homer, there is no confusion of the arts. He simply represents actual scenes with such vividness, with such grasp of significance, that their pervading mood is inescapable.

Collections: Charles Stewart Smith, New York; Howard Caswell Smith, Oyster Bay, New York. *Gift of the W. L. and May T. Mellon Foundation*, 1943. Signed, and dated 1876. Canvas, 24⅛ x 38⅛" (61.5 x 97 cm.).

843

Two streams of American painting, the romantic and the realistic, are illustrated by these reproductions. Blakelock is a romantic. In the gathering dusk his garden glows with a murky light. A commonplace scene is imbued with a mystery and melancholy foreshadowing the artist's madness and suicide. By contrast, nothing could be more realistic than the paintings by Winslow Homer and Thomas Moran nor more matter-of-fact than the interior by Eastman Johnson. James McNeill Whistler at the beginning of his career also recorded with precision what he saw. *Wapping on Thames* (plate 848) is an early picture of a group of friends seated in an inn overlooking a busy harbor. The girl on the left is Joanna Hiffernan (often spelled Heffernan), his mistress, whose full-length portrait is the next illustration. The man with the beard is Alphonse Legros, painter, sculptor, and engraver. The sailor on the right is unidentified. How far Whistler, under the influence of Japanese and Spanish art, departed from this early realism can be seen in plates 850–52.

844

845

843 **Winslow Homer** (American, 1836–1910): *Hound and Hunter*. Signed, and dated 1892. Canvas, 28¼ x 48⅛″ (71.8 x 122.2 cm.). Gift of Stephen C. Clark

844 **Winslow Homer:** *Right and Left*. Signed, and dated 1909. Canvas, 28¼ x 48⅜″ (71.8 x 123 cm.). Gift of the Avalon Foundation

845 **Thomas Moran** (American, 1837–1926): *The Much Resounding Sea*. Signed, and dated 1884. Canvas, 25 x 62″ (64 x 148.8 cm.). Gift of the Avalon Foundation

846 **Ralph Albert Blakelock** (American, 1847–1919): *The Artist's Garden*. Signed. c. 1880. Canvas, 16 x 24″ (40.5 x 61.3 cm.). Chester Dale Collection

847 **Eastman Johnson** (American, 1824–1906): *The Brown Family*. Signed, and dated 1869. Believed to have been painted 1860–64. Paper, mounted on canvas, 23⅝ x 28½″ (59.3 x 72.4 cm.). Gift of David Edward Finley and Margaret Eustis Finley

848 **James McNeill Whistler** (American, 1834–1903): *Wapping on Thames*. Signed, and dated 1861. Canvas, 28½ x 40¼″ (72.4 x 102.2 cm.). John Hay Whitney Collection

846

847

848

James McNeill Whistler

(AMERICAN, 1834–1903)

849   THE WHITE GIRL (SYMPHONY IN WHITE, NO. 1)

There have always been two opposed traditions in American painting. Eakins and Homer represent one: a rugged, native vitality; Whistler and Mary Cassatt illustrate the second: a genteel, Europeanized urbanity. Although Whistler's fame is brighter in Europe than in America, his sophisticated selection of what seems best, wherever found, is of exceptional significance to this country, for it marks the coming of age of American painting.

Only at the beginning of his career as a painter would Whistler have understood or approved of Homer's or Eakins' works. Later on, he tried to avoid what they sought, qualities he described as "damned realism, and beautiful nature and the whole mess." He preached a return to "that wondrous thing called the masterpiece, which surpasses in perfection all that they [the gods] have contrived in what is called Nature." In other words, Whistler wished to demonstrate that the inventive force of the artist is more important than the recording power of his eye. To do this he combined the patterns of Japanese prints with that mastery of value relations which distinguishes the painting of Velázquez. This eclecticism is predictable from even so early a work as *The White Girl,* a portrait of his mistress Joanna Hiffernan. It was shown in 1863 at the Salon des Refusés with what we now consider to be many of the finest French paintings of the second half of the nineteenth century. It proved to be the sensation of that exhibition, the most revolutionary held in France in a hundred years.

True, the public was hostile, and Zola has reported how people nudged one another and became almost hysterical with laughter in front of the painting. But the wisest connoisseurs and critics were enthusiastic, and with *The White Girl* Whistler became the first American painter since the eighteenth century to attain renown and leadership among European artists.

Collection: Thomas Whistler, Baltimore. *Harris Whittemore Collection,* 1943. Signed, and dated 1862. Canvas, 84½ x 42½" (214.7 x 108 cm.).

850

851

852

Whistler's style was a curious hybrid, partly Japanese and partly derived from Velázquez, a style of fastidious elegance and of soft, vaporescent beauty, a twilight world of disembodied figures. For him nature sings in tune when forms are dimly discerned, when twilight or night has lent a vagueness to the scene. He was admired by other American artists like Chase and Henri; but they were more vigorous, more explicit, more American in a certain dash and boldness of handling, which, in the case of Henri, would have seemed to Whistler vulgar.

853

850 **James McNeill Whistler** (American, 1834–1903): *Chelsea Wharf: Grey and Silver.* c. 1875. Canvas, 24¼ x 18⅛″ (61.5 x 46 cm.). Widener Collection

851 **James McNeill Whistler:** *Brown and Gold: Self-Portrait.* Signed with butterfly. c. 1900. Canvas, 24½ x 18¼″ (62.2 x 46.2 cm.). Gift of Edith Stuyvesant Gerry

852 **James McNeill Whistler:** *L'Andalouse, Mother-of-Pearl and Silver.* Signed with butterfly. c. 1894. Canvas, 75⅜ x 35⅜″ (191.5 x 90 cm.). Harris Whittemore Collection

853 **William Merritt Chase** (American, 1849–1916): *A Friendly Call.* Signed, and dated 1895. Canvas, 30⅛ x 48¼″ (76.5 x 122.5 cm.). Chester Dale Collection

854 **Robert Henri** (American, 1865–1929): *Young Woman in White.* Signed. 1904. Canvas, 78¼ x 38⅛″ (198.8 x 96.9 cm.). Gift of Violet Organ

855 **Robert Henri:** *Catharine.* Signed. 1913. Canvas, 24 x 20⅛″ (61.3 x 51 cm.). Given in memory of Mr. and Mrs. William J. Johnson

854

855

Mary Cassatt

(AMERICAN, 1844–1926)

856   THE BOATING PARTY

How great a sacrifice should a woman make to become an artist? The life of Mary Cassatt poses this question. The daughter of wealthy parents, she renounced a conventional existence in America for a lifetime of study in Europe and a career of painting. In Paris she was early fascinated by the work of Degas, which she first saw in the window of a picture dealer. "I used to go," she wrote a friend, "and flatten my nose against that window and absorb all I could of his art. It changed my life." It spurred her to tireless self-discipline, especially in drawing. On seeing some of her work, Degas once said that he would not have admitted that a woman could draw so well. As for the use she made of her perfected technique, no one since the Renaissance has painted the relation of mother and child with such tender inventiveness. In pictures like the one reproduced here, Miss Cassatt has brought a new interpretation to a traditional theme. She avoids the sentimental; she sees the mother as busy, proud of her child, but very matter-of-fact. This, and many similar canvases, will assure Miss Cassatt a high place in the history of painting. And yet after those long hours of physical labor at the easel, after the strain and the fight for recognition for her own work and the work of her friends, the Impressionists, was the sacrifice she made worthwhile? She ended her life a lonely woman, living in self-imposed exile, surrounded in her château by beautiful works of art which blindness, the lot of so many painters, prevented her from seeing. Miss Cassatt has left us the suggestion of an answer to the question of why maternity is the subject which occurs most frequently in her work. "After all," she said to a friend, "woman's vocation in life is to bear children."

Collections: In the possession of the artist until at least 1914; Durand-Ruel, New York. *Chester Dale Collection*, 1962. Painted 1893/94 at Antibes. Canvas, 35½ x 46¼" (90.2 x 117.5 cm.).

857

858

Mary Cassatt (American, 1844–1926)

857 *Girl Arranging Her Hair.* 1886. Canvas, 29½ x 24½" (75 x 62.3 cm.). Chester Dale Collection

858 *Portrait of an Elderly Lady.* c. 1887. Canvas, 28⅝ x 23¾" (72.7 x 60.4 cm.). Chester Dale Collection

859 *The Loge.* Signed. 1882. Canvas, 31⅜ x 25⅛" (79.7 x 63.8 cm.). Chester Dale Collection

860 *Miss Mary Ellison.* Signed. c. 1880. Canvas, 33½ x 25¾" (84.8 x 65.3 cm.). Chester Dale Collection

861 *Woman with a Red Zinnia.* Signed. 1891. Canvas, 29 x 23¾" (74 x 60.4 cm.). Chester Dale Collection

862 *Two Children at the Seashore.* Canvas, 38½ x 29¼" (98 x 74.5 cm.). Ailsa Mellon Bruce Collection

859

860

861

Mary Cassatt, like her friend Degas, studied the old masters assiduously. This is evident in *Girl Arranging Her Hair*, which was shown in 1886 in the last Impressionist exhibition. Miss Cassatt has taken an awkward adolescent and placed her in the pose of Michelangelo's *Bound Slave*, a statue she had often seen in the Louvre. Degas, entranced with her blending of the contemporary and the classical, bought the painting and kept it until he died. But the picture is not characteristic of Miss Cassatt's work. More in her usual style is *The Loge*. It shows her particular qualities: an elaborate and fragile refinement, a mood of social fastidiousness, which suggests the novels of her fellow expatriates Henry James and Edith Wharton.

862

John Singer Sargent

(AMERICAN, 1856-1925)

863   MRS. ADRIAN ISELIN

Sargent's painting of Mrs. Iselin epitomizes the American mothers described in the novels of Henry James: ruthless guardians of their young, determined managers of financial and social advancement. Thirty years after Sargent had painted this portrait he was asked if he remembered it. He thought for a moment before he replied, "Of course! I cannot forget that dominating little finger." And with what skill he has shown it tapping the edge of the table!

Mrs. Iselin's grandson has recounted how reluctant she was to have her portrait painted. When Sargent came for the first sitting, she entered the room in an extremely irritated manner, followed by her maid carrying her best French frocks, and haughtily told the artist to choose a dress. Sargent replied that he wanted to paint her just as she was. He did not mention that he intended to portray her resentful expression at having to pose, her air of contempt for the painter, and her large and ugly ear.

In those early days the young portraitist was more courageous and less bored than he would become in later years. He painted his sitters as he saw them, disregarding their feelings and their wishes. He was at his best when the character and the mood he wanted to portray were obvious. Mrs. Iselin was a perfect model. She was firm, self-confident, perhaps a little aggressive. One admires her without feeling the least sympathy for her forceful personality, which Sargent has caught unforgettably.

Technically the painting is brilliant, but it reveals the flaw which Henry James astutely perceived and described in an essay published the year before the portrait was painted. After praising Sargent's astounding dexterity, the novelist asked, "Yes, but what is left?" He observed that "it may be better for an artist to have a certain part of his property invested in unsolved difficulties." And he concluded his essay saying, "The highest result [in portraiture] is achieved when to this element of quick perception a certain faculty of brooding reflection is added." This "faculty of brooding reflection" was exactly what Sargent lacked, and as a consequence his work for all its brio remains superficial.

Collections: Family of the sitter, New York City and New Rochelle. *Gift of Ernest Iselin,* 1964. Signed, and dated 1888. Canvas, 60½ x 36⅝" (153.7 x 93 cm.).

567

864

865

866

864 **John Singer Sargent** (American, 1856–1925): *Mrs. Joseph Chamberlain*. Signed, and dated 1902. Canvas, 59¼ x 33" (150.6 x 83.9 cm.). Gift of the sitter, Mary Endicott Chamberlain Carnegie

865 **John Singer Sargent**: *Street in Venice*. Signed. 1882. Wood, 17¾ x 21¼" (45.1 x 53.9 cm.). Gift of the Avalon Foundation

866 **John Singer Sargent**: *Mrs. William Crowninshield Endicott*. Signed, and dated 1901. Canvas, 64¼ x 45⅛" (163.6 x 114.3 cm.). Gift of Louise Thoron Endicott in memory of Mr. and Mrs. William Crowninshield Endicott

867 **Childe Hassam** (American, 1859–1935): *Allies Day, May 1917*. Signed, and dated May 17, 1917. Canvas, 36¾ x 30¼" (93.2 x 77.3 cm.). Gift of Ethelyn McKinney in memory of her brother, Glenn Ford McKinney

868 **John Singer Sargent**: *Repose*. Signed, and dated 1911. Canvas, 25⅛ x 30" (63.8 x 76.2 cm.). Gift of Curt H. Reisinger

867

868

John Singer Sargent was at his best in sketches like. *Repose* and *Street in Venice*, painted for his own pleasure. He enjoyed displaying his virtuousity of brushwork, especially when he felt no responsibility for a portrait. Compromising more and more in his portraits of the rich and famous, he painted not what he saw in front of him, but what his sitter thought his or her appearance to be. Artists in the past have done this, but they did not have Sargent's wish to match what he observed of variations of shadow, and alterations of color. The task of copying appearance yet trying to flatter the sitter became too tedious, and Sargent at the end of his life abandoned portraiture and took up architectural decoration, for which he had no talent whatever.

869

Few artists have been proficient athletes, but George Bellows was an exception. He starred at school and college in basketball and baseball, and in the opinion of friends might have gone on to play in the major leagues. From an early age, however, he was determined to be a painter. He enrolled in the New York School of Art and studied under Robert Henri, who taught him that "anything . . . which has the power to hold or receive human attention may be the subject of a work of art." He enjoyed painting prizefights, depicting, as he said, "two men trying to kill each other"; and in his painting of a fight at Tom Sharkey's Athletic Club, near the artist's studio in New York City (plate 869), he has shown not only a vicious combat but also the frenzied delight of the spectators. These half-demented faces are brilliantly exe-

cuted, with Hogarth's sense of exaggeration and the slashing brushwork of Goya's nightmare scenes. The title was undoubtedly intended as an ironic commentary on a device to circumvent a New York State law that made public boxing illegal from 1900 to 1910. Fights were therefore staged at "private" clubs, where both spectators and boxers were members, the latter usually only for the night of the fight.

Hopper was born the same year as Bellows and was for a time his fellow student. He once said his aim in painting "has always been the most exact transcription possible of my most intimate impressions of nature." But he qualified this by saying that *Cape Cod Evening* (plate 870) "is no exact transcription of a place, but pieced together from sketches and mental impressions of things in

870

the vicinity.... In the woman I attempted to get the broad, strong-jawed face and blond hair of a Finnish type of which there are many on the Cape. The man is a dark-haired Yankee. The dog is listening to something, probably a whippoorwill or some evening sound."

There is a strange stillness in the picture. The man and the woman seem isolated; and their isolation creates a mood that occurs often in Hopper's paintings, a feeling of loneliness. Human beings may exist side by side, the painter seems to say, without ever making contact. In this canvas only the dog is alert. His attention is fixed, perhaps, by the song of a whippoorwill, but one feels he is aware of an existence outside himself. The vitality of his arrested motion gives the human figures by contrast something of the rigidity of death.

869 George Bellows (American, 1882–1925): *Both Members of This Club*. Signed. 1909. Canvas, 45¼ x 63⅛″ (115 x 160.5 cm.). Chester Dale Collection

870 Edward Hopper (American, 1882–1967): *Cape Cod Evening*. Signed. 1939. Canvas, 30¼ x 40¼″ (77 x 102.5 cm.). John Hay Whitney Collection

871 **George Bellows** (American, 1882–1925): *The Lone Tenement.* Signed. 1909. Canvas, 36⅛ x 48⅛" (91.8 x 122.3 cm.). Chester Dale Collection

872 **William Glackens** (American, 1870–1938): *Family Group.* 1910–11. Canvas, 72 x 84" (182.8 x 213.3 cm.). Gift of Mr. and Mrs. Ira Glackens

873 **George Bellows:** *Club Night.* 1907. Canvas, 43 x 53" (109.5 x 134.5 cm.). John Hay Whitney Collection

874 **George Luks** (American, 1866–1933): *The Miner.* Signed. 1925. Canvas, 60¼ x 50⅜" (153.1 x 128 cm.). Chester Dale Collection

875 **Robert Henri** (American, 1865–1929): *Snow in New York.* Signed, and dated Mar 5 1902. Canvas, 32 x 25¾" (81.2 x 65.3 cm.). Chester Dale Collection

876 **John Sloan** (American, 1871–1951): *The City from Greenwich Village.* 1922. Canvas, 26 x 33¾" (66 x 85.7 cm.). Gift of Helen Farr Sloan

871

872

873

572

874

875

George Bellows, although not one of the original members, later became closely associated with a group known as The Eight, which included the best American painters working just before and after World War I. Robert Henri was their teacher and spokesman, and the most gifted members were William Glackens, George Luks, and John Sloan. All at one time or another held jobs as cartoonists or magazine illustrators, and the atmosphere of the "city desk" colors their interpretation of the American scene. Their brushwork is vehement and their point of view often tough, with something of the truculence of the newspaper reporter. They were dubbed with considerable aptness, "The Ashcan School."

The Eight were instrumental in bringing together in New York an exhibition of contemporary American painting (including Glackens's *Family Group*) and Post-Impressionist, Fauve, and Cubist works from Europe. The show opened at the Armory in February 1913, and it had a tremendous impact on artists and public alike. Walt Kuhn, Marsden Hartley, and Max Weber were among those who felt the influence of the Armory Show, and they represent the new trend toward Modernism in American painting.

876

877

878

877 **Walt Kuhn** (American, 1877–1949): *The White Clown*. 1929. Canvas, 40¼ x 30¼″ (102.3 x 76.9 cm.). Gift of the W. Averell Harriman Foundation in memory of Marie N. Harriman

878 **Max Weber** (American, 1880–1961): *Rush Hour, New York*. 1915. Canvas, 36¼ x 30¼″ (92 x 76.9 cm.). Gift of the Avalon Foundation

879 **Marsden Hartley** (American, 1877–1943): *The Aero*. c. 1914. Canvas, 39½ x 32″ (100.3 x 81.2 cm.). Andrew W. Mellon Fund

880 **Marsden Hartley**: *Mount Kitadhin*. 1942. Oil on Masonite, 30 x 40⅛″ (76 x 101.9 cm.). Gift of Mrs. Mellon Byers

879

880

XX Century

Pierre Bonnard

(FRENCH, 1867–1947)

881   THE LETTER

The styles of Bellows and Bonnard provide a study in contrasts. Bellows was sometimes too brutal, Bonnard occasionally too bland. *Both Members of This Club*, (plate 869) is strident, virile, explicit; *The Letter* is subtle, feminine, intimate.

Intimacy in art is a quality difficult to convey. The subject matter of the intimate picture is, of necessity, slight, made up of recurring incidents in everyday life, scenes so fleeting that they pass almost without notice. But these must be seen with tenderness and sympathy. They must stimulate us to enter imaginatively the small, serene world in which they take place. Only a painter like Bonnard, gifted with exceptional sensitivity, can catch in his memory the instantaneous gesture, the unconscious pose, the singularity of appearance essential to such subjects.

In the picture reproduced here, Bonnard was fascinated by the appearance of a girl sitting at her desk. She seems absorbed and puzzled. One senses she is not writing a love letter. Perhaps it is only a thank-you note. Her shadow of a smile suggests that she wants it to be a little unconventional, a little whimsical but there is a momentary hesitation, her thought remains elusive. Her mood is conveyed by the hovering pen, the slight smile, the way the eyes seem to reread what has been written.

Bonnard never painted from a model. For this reason he was constantly making quick notations of things seen, notes in pen, pencil, and ink of each salient feature of the motif. These sketches, often indecipherable to anyone but himself, would fix in his mind the significant image caught by his alert vision. From these he would construct a formal harmony of line and color. His problem, however, was to preserve the spontaneity of his first inspiration, to hold, in spite of careful calculations, his gay, almost impish reaction to his subject.

This may explain his unconventional way of painting, as though the very informality of his methods would assist him in retaining the freshness of his original conceptions. He almost never worked at an easel. He tacked his canvases on the wall, indifferent to even the brightest wallpapers. At times he worked in his dining room, at times in a hotel bedroom, but hardly ever in a studio. He would often paint several pictures on one canvas and then cut them apart. Cursory as these methods may seem, Bonnard was at the same time exacting in self-criticism. He would, for example, go to a museum where his pictures were hanging and, while a friend distracted the guard, repaint certain passages which displeased him!

Collection: Alexandre Natanson, Paris. *Chester Dale Collection*, 1962. Signed. Painted about 1906. Canvas, 21⅝ x 18¾" (55 x 47.5 cm.).

882

883

Bonnard, particularly in his early work, wanted to catch the character of the scenes he painted, and to express their inner meaning even if this entailed a certain awkwardness in the composition. But he was basically a decorator. As Albert Aurier astutely observed, Bonnard is "a delightful ornamentalist, as skillful and resourceful as a Japanese and capable of embellishing all the ugly things of our life with the ingenuous and iridescent flowerings of his imagination."

Pierre Bonnard (French, 1867–1947)

882 *Bouquet of Flowers.* Signed. c. 1926. Canvas, 27⅝ x 18⅝" (70.3 x 47.4 cm.). Ailsa Mellon Bruce Collection

883 *The Artist's Sister and Her Children.* Signed, and dated 1898. Cardboard on wood, 12 x 10" (30.5 x 25.4 cm.). Ailsa Mellon Bruce Collection

884 *The Cab Horse.* Signed. c. 1895. Wood, 11¾ x 15¾" (29.7 x 40 cm.). Ailsa Mellon Bruce Collection

885 *Two Dogs in a Deserted Street.* Signed. c. 1894. Wood, 13⅞ x 10⅝" (35.1 x 27 cm.). Ailsa Mellon Bruce Collection

886 *Stairs in the Artist's Garden.* 1942/44. Canvas, 24⅞ x 28¾" (63.3 x 73.1 cm.). Ailsa Mellon Bruce Collection

887 *Children Leaving School.* Signed. c. 1895. Cardboard on wood, 11⅜ x 17⅜" (28.9 x 44 cm.). Ailsa Mellon Bruce Collection

888 *A Spring Landscape.* c. 1935. Canvas, 26⅝ x 40½" (67.6 x 103 cm.). Ailsa Mellon Bruce Collection

884

885

886

887

888

Edouard Vuillard

(FRENCH, 1868–1940)

889   THÉODORE DURET

Bonnard we associate with youth, with pictures like *The Letter*; but Vuillard, his close friend, was at his best when he was exploring the increasing frailty and infirmity of age. He seems to have felt a tender sympathy for those who were on the downward slope of life, and repeatedly painted them as they hastened onward at an ineluctably faster speed. He observed his mother in scores of paintings, noting her face with its ever deepening lines; her back bending more and more, from rheumatism; the gradual graying of her hair; and her growing resemblance to his grandmother, whom he drew when he was a young man.

Old men equally fascinated him. His likeness of Théodore Duret, the art critic and champion of the Impressionists, is among the most sensitive representations of age since the late portraits of Rembrandt. Duret sits in his study, surrounded by his works of art. Directly behind him are three paintings, the smaller ones unidentified, the larger one, *Telemachus and Mentor* by Tiepolo, now belonging to the Rijksmuseum, Amsterdam. Reflected in the mirror is Duret's portrait by Whistler, later acquired by the Metropolitan Museum, New York. In Whistler's painting, Duret is shown carrying over his arm a pink cloak, which is the key to Vuillard's own color scheme, and in his hand an opera hat. He looks a typical boulevardier. Thirty years pass, and Duret has totally changed. He appears meager; his hands seem to tremble; his eyes are red rimmed. His weightless, insubstantial body is rendered no more definitely than his surroundings. Thus this apparition of old age dissolves into its chromatic constituents, takes on the protective coloration characteristic of Vuillard's figures, and becomes one substance with all the other details of the scene. There is an effect of imprecision, enhanced by the use of cardboard as a ground. Because of its absorbency, outlines are blurred, and the result is a uniformity of texture, which Vuillard loved.

That nothing is precisely seen does not affect the precision of the design. The carefully constructed composition defines the mood of the portrait. Vuillard wished to indicate the claustral life of a scholar. Consequently Duret is shown as tightly constricted by the angles of the desk piled high with books, papers, reviews, the paraphernalia of his trade. The two wings of the writing table are like the blades of a scissors, seemingly ready to sheer the sitter in two, to destroy him. His favorite cat, Lulu, sits on his knee, an intimation of his solitude, his loneliness. It is a masterpiece of psychological portraiture; as Claude Roger-Marx has said, it "is worthy of inclusion with the great portraits of writers at work—with the Zola of Manet, the Duranty of Degas, and the Gustave Geffroy of Cézanne."

Collection: Théodore Duret, Paris. *Chester Dale Collection*, 1962. Signed, and dated 1912. Cardboard mounted on wood, 37½ x 29½" (95.2 x 74.8 cm.).

890

891

Vuillard was a more delicate and subtle colorist than Bonnard, whose late paintings (see plates 886 and 888) are an explosion of the most vivid hues. Both artists, however, shared an ability to charm with unexpected improvisations, as in *Child Wearing a Red Scarf* (plate 894). Vuillard was more of a poet, depicting ironically yet tenderly typical scenes of middle-class life. *The Visit* (plate 892) might be an illustration for Colette's *Gigi*. Is the young girl standing between the two older women, one wonders, being told her value as marriageable merchandise in a market of men?

892

Edouard Vuillard (French, 1868–1940)

890 *Vase of Flowers on a Mantelpiece.* Signed. c. 1900. Cardboard on wood, 14¼ x 11⅝" (36.2 x 29.5 cm.). Ailsa Mellon Bruce Collection

891 *The Artist's Paint Box and Moss Roses.* Signed. 1898. Cardboard, 14¼ x 16⅞" (36.1 x 42.9 cm.). Ailsa Mellon Bruce Collection

892 *The Visit.* Signed. 1931. Canvas, 39⅜ x 53¾" (100.1 x 136.4 cm.). Chester Dale Collection

893 *Repast in a Garden.* Signed. 1898. Gouache on cardboard, 21⅜ x 20⅞" (54.3 x 53.1 cm.). Chester Dale Collection

894 *Child Wearing a Red Scarf.* Signed. c. 1891. Cardboard on wood, 11½ x 6⅞" (29.2 x 17.5 cm.). Ailsa Mellon Bruce Collection

895 *The Yellow Curtain.* Signed. c. 1893. Canvas, 13¾ x 15⅜" (34.9 x 39 cm.). Ailsa Mellon Bruce Collection

893

894

895

Amedeo Modigliani

(ITALIAN, 1884–1920)

896   CHAIM SOUTINE

If I were asked to choose the greatest portrait painter of the twentieth century, I would unhesitatingly pick Modigliani. For he has solved beyond any of his contemporaries the basic problem of portraiture: how to represent the human face both as a likeness of an individual and as an element of formal design. His entire life was devoted to this study. Other artists painted still lifes, figure compositions, landscapes, but Modigliani restricted himself virtually to portraiture. Even his rare and beautiful nudes are essentially portraits of the model.

To combine a formal stylization with a telling likeness, this was the goal of the great Renaissance masters, who were his heroes. Modigliani would have been accepted into their Pantheon, whereas Sargent would have been rejected. Take, for example, the portrait of Chaim Soutine. The sitter is rendered in Modigliani's highly idiomatic style as a formal pattern within the rectangle of the canvas, but if one compares the portrait with a photograph of the artist, one realizes how successful Modigliani has been in catching the curious dichotomy of his appearance: that of an uncouth peasant with a thick nose and coarse, asymmetrical features, joined to a sensitive artist with slender wrists and tapering fingers.

Modigliani also did a drawing of Soutine now in a Los Angeles collection. It has the beautiful rhythm of lines he always attained, but it is less convincing as a likeness. When he came to paint a portrait he scrutinized his sitter more carefully. He stressed the distinctive features of his model: in this case his friend's long neck, his broad nostrils, his black, unruly hair, and his clasped hands, suggestive of insecurity and of an underlying diffidence.

Between the two artists there must have been a deep affinity. Both were drawn to Paris, one from Lithuania, the other from Italy. Both were Jewish, Soutine the son of an indigent mender of clothes, Modigliani of a middle-class stockbroker and dealer in hides and coal. Both knew extreme poverty, and both were kept from starvation by the same Polish picture peddler, Zborowski, who tried tirelessly to sell their paintings to the more important dealers. But Modigliani did not have Soutine's peasant physique. Destitution, combined with alcohol and drugs, killed him at thirty-six. Jean Cocteau has described seeing him on the terrace outside the Rotonde always drawing people's faces. He reminded the poet "of the proud contemptuous gypsies, who sit down at your table and read your hand . . . Modigliani did not paint to order, and he exaggerated his drunkenness, his outbursts of fury, and his incongruous laughter as a defense against [those] who were offended by his haughtiness."

Collections: Léopold Zborowski, Paris; Jacques Netter, Paris. *Chester Dale Collection*, 1962. Signed. Painted 1917. Canvas, 36⅛ x 23½" (91.7 x 59.7 cm.).

585

897

Amedeo Modigliani (Italian, 1884–1920)

897 *Nude on a Blue Cushion.* Signed. 1917. Canvas, 25¾ x 39¾" (65.4 x 100.9 cm.). Chester Dale Collection

898 *Gypsy Woman with Baby.* Signed. 1919. Canvas, 45⅝ x 28¾" (115.9 x 73 cm.). Chester Dale Collection

899 *Girl in a Green Blouse.* Signed. 1917. Canvas, 32 x 18⅛" (81.3 x 46 cm.). Chester Dale Collection

900 *Café Singer.* Signed. 1917. Canvas, 36⅜ x 23¾" (92.4 x 60.3 cm.). Chester Dale Collection

901 *Madame Amédeé (Woman with Cigarette).* Signed. 1918. Canvas, 39½ x 25½" (100.3 x 64.8 cm.). Chester Dale Collection

902 *Nude on a Divan.* Signed. 1918. Canvas, 23⅝ x 36⅛" (60.2 x 91.7 cm.). Chester Dale Collection

For proof of Modigliani's genius look at the nine portraits of women reproduced on pages 586–89. One can guess at the character of each. Adrienne will take advantage of men. The café singer and the girl in the green blouse will be taken advantage of by men. Madame Kisling probably preferred women. Madame Amédée doubtless exploited women, possibly the girls who posed for the two nudes. Whereas the gypsy woman and the woman with the red hair, one imagines, would have made excellent wives. In real life none of these generalizations might hold up, but what the sitter was in actuality is unimportant. The portraitist's ultimate fame depends on his ability to convey character; whether his evaluation be true or false doesn't matter.

898

899

900

901

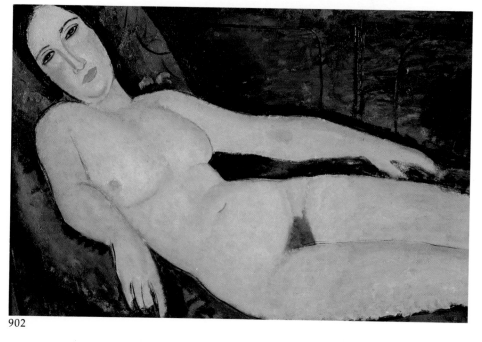

902

904

903

Amedeo Modigliani (Italian, 1884–1920)

903 *Woman with Red Hair.* Signed. 1917. Canvas, 36¼ x 23⅞″ (92.1 x 60.7 cm.). Chester Dale Collection

904 *Adrienne (Woman with Bangs).* Signed. 1917. Canvas, 21¾ x 15″ (55.3 x 38.1 cm.). Chester Dale Collection

905 *Monsieur Deleu.* 1916. Canvas, 31⅞ x 18⅜″ (81.1 x 46.7 cm.). Chester Dale Collection

906 *Léon Bakst.* Signed. 1917. Canvas, 21¾ x 13″ (55.3 x 33 cm.). Chester Dale Collection

907 *Madame Kisling.* Signed. c. 1917. Canvas, 18¼ x 13⅛″ (46.2 x 33.2 cm.). Chester Dale Collection

905

906

907

908

ROBERT DELAUNAY

909

Although Paris in the last three hundred and fifty years has produced no Rubens, Rembrandt, or Velázquez, it has been, all in all, the most creative city for painting over the longest period in history. These reproductions show the work of a few of the artists who, in this century, formed the School of Paris. With Modigliani, Matisse, Braque, and Picasso, they provided for many years

908 **Robert Delaunay** (French, 1885–1941): *Political Drama.* Signed. 1914. Collage, 35 x 26″ (88.7 x 67.3 cm.). Gift of the Joseph H. Hazen Foundation, Inc.

909 **André Derain** (French, 1880–1954): *Charing Cross Bridge, London.* Signed. 1905–6. Canvas, 31⅝ x 39½″ (80.5 x 100.5 cm.). John Hay Whitney Collection

910 **André Derain:** *The Old Bridge.* Signed. 1910. Canvas, 31⅞ x 39½″ (81 x 100.3 cm.). Chester Dale Collection

911 **André Derain:** *Flowers in a Vase.* Signed. 1932. Canvas, 29½ x 37″ (75 x 94 cm.). Chester Dale Collection

912 **Maurice Utrillo** (French, 1883–1955): *Marizy-Sainte-Geneviève.* Signed. c. 1910. Canvas, 23½ x 31⅞″ (59.7 x 81 cm.). Chester Dale Collection

913 **Maurice Utrillo:** *Street at Corte, Corsica.* Signed. 1913. Canvas, 24 x 31¾″ (60.8 x 80.7 cm.). Ailsa Mellon Bruce Collection

914 **Raoul Dufy** (French, 1877–1953): *Regatta at Cowes.* Signed, and dated 1934. Canvas, 32⅛ x 39½″ (81.6 x 100.3 cm.). Ailsa Mellon Bruce Collection

915 **Chaim Soutine** (Russian, 1893–1943): *Portrait of a Boy.* Signed. 1928. Canvas, 36¼ x 25⅝″ (92.1 x 65.1 cm.). Chester Dale Collection

910

911

912

the dominant movements in the art of our time, whether Expressionism, Cubism, abstraction, or the more conventional vision of Utrillo and Derain after his Fauve period. Until World War II, when New York became a new center of creativity, these painters, Parisian by birth or adoption, dominated the world of art.

913

914

915

Henri Matisse

(FRENCH, 1869–1954)

916   BEASTS OF THE SEA

More than seventy years ago Henri Matisse, king of the Fauves or "Wild Beasts," as he and his friends were called, challenged the doctrine generally accepted since the Renaissance that the suggestion of a third dimension through modeling is basic in painting. He pointed out that shading and perspective, at least as taught in art schools, tend to weaken the effect of line, color, and pattern. Instead he wished "to study each element of construction separately: drawing, color, values, composition; to explore how these elements could be combined into a synthesis without diminishing the eloquence of any one of them by the presence of the others."

Matisse's mastery of two-dimensional representation led logically to his exploration of the possibilities of collage. His first use of scissors and paper was in 1931, but only as a means to an end. He wanted to work out the placement of the figures in his decorations for the Barnes Gallery in Merion, Pennsylvania. Toward the end of his life, however, in ill health and unable to work at his easel, he turned to collage as an art in itself. He found, as he explained, that by using colored paper and scissors, "instead of establishing a contour, and then filling it with color . . . I draw directly in the color."

In 1950, when he was over eighty, he cut out one of his most beautiful collages, which he called *les bêtes de la mer*. It is a memory of the South Seas, which he had visited twenty years earlier. There are symbols of the aquatic life at the bottom of the ocean, of the surface of the water, of the island itself (perhaps Tahiti) and of the sky above. Matisse has described looking into a lagoon. He recounts how the water was "greyish jade-green, colored by the bottom, which lies very close, the branched coral and their variety of soft pastel tints, around which pass shoals of small fish, blue, yellow, and striped with brown, looking as though they were enamelled. And dotted about everywhere the dark brown of the sea-cucumbers, torpid and almost inert . . ." In the artist's description note that the colors of nature are muted, like the pastel tints he mentions, but in the collage colors blaze forth vividly. The artist observing his visual data, in Matisse's words, "must render the emotion they awaken . . . the emotion of the ensemble, the specific character of every object—modified by its relation to the others—all interlaced like a cord or a serpent." In other words the artist's transcription from nature must never be literal.

In *Beasts of the Sea* Matisse combines the most dissonant colors. Playing them against each other, he attains tonal resonances unique in art. Such chromatic harmonies in pigment and collage are Matisse's great contribution to painting; and they explain why he, of all contemporary artists, had the greatest influence on the color painters of the nineteen-sixties.

Collection: Family of the artist. *Ailsa Mellon Bruce Fund*, 1973. Constructed 1950. Paper on canvas (collage) 116⅜ x 60⅝" (295.5 x 154 cm.).

592

les bêtes de la mer...
H. matisse 50

917

918

919

920

Henri Matisse   (French, 1869–1954)

917   *Pot of Geraniums.* Signed. 1912. Canvas, 16¼ x 13⅛″ (41.3 x 33.3 cm.). Chester Dale Collection

918   *Still Life with Pineapple.* Signed. 1924. Canvas, 19⅞ x 24¼″ (50.5 x 61.5 cm.). Gift of the W. Averell Harriman Foundation in memory of Marie N. Harriman

919   *Woman with Amphora and Pomegranates.* 1952. Paper on canvas (collage), 96 x 37⅞″ (243.6 x 96.3 cm.). Ailsa Mellon Bruce Fund

920   *Les Gorges du Loup.* Signed. 1920/25. Canvas, 19¾ x 24″ (50.2 x 60.9 cm.). Chester Dale Collection

921   *La Coiffure.* Signed. 1901. Canvas, 37½ x 31½″ (95.2 x 80.1 cm.). Chester Dale Collection

922   *Odalisque with Raised Arms.* Signed. 1923. Canvas, 25⅝ x 19¾″ (65.1 x 50.2 cm.). Chester Dale Collection

923   *Palm Leaf, Tangier.* Signed. 1912. Canvas, 46¼ x 32¼″ (117.5 x 81.9 cm.). Chester Dale Collection

924   *Still Life: Apples on Pink Tablecloth.* Signed. c. 1922. Canvas, 23¾ x 28¾″ (60.4 x 73 cm.). Chester Dale Collection

921

922

Matisse's painting bears a superficial and deceptive resemblance to the work of a child. But the revolution he introduced into art is rooted in studies which began when he was a copyist in the Louvre, and which he continued to do through his last years, when he executed his greatest designs—for a Dominican chapel at Vence, in southern France. Like Michelangelo, however, Matisse was always at pains to hide the effort that had gone into his work. He wished his paintings "to have the lightness and joyousness of springtime, which never lets anyone suspect the labor it has cost." In this statement he described his greatest gift: almost alone among twentieth-century artists he was able to convey his own delight in a person, or a place, or a flower, to communicate a joyousness of vision which eighty-five years and two wars did not diminish.

923

924

Georges Braque

(FRENCH, 1882–1963)

925   NUDE WOMAN WITH BASKET OF FRUIT

Braque's father and grandfather were housepainters, and he learned from them the meaning of craftsmanship. They gave him his command of texture, and above all they taught him patience and perseverance. He was always slow but determined. He used to box with Derain, and he would wear him down with a ponderous and impenetrable defense until his more powerful but wilder opponent could be felled with a single well-aimed blow. This tenacious slowness was characteristic of Braque's approach to painting. As he said, "Progress in art consists not in extending one's limits, but in knowing them better."

His fortieth birthday occurred in 1922, when the Salon d'Automne held a special exhibition in recognition of his achievement. The same year, at the height of his powers, he began his series of Canephori (Ceremonial Basket Bearers). Sensuality as we find it in the Old Masters, the late works of Titian and Rubens, for example, is difficult, though not impossible, to combine with the increasing abstraction characteristic of contemporary painting. And yet Braque's monumental, partially draped figures, abstract as they are, have a compelling eroticism that is impossible to forget. The giantess reproduced here might well represent "wide-bosomed Earth, the everlasting foundation of us all," as John Russell has pointed out, or conjure up "member-loving Aphrodite." In either role she suggests some modern symbol of fertility.

But the remarkable fact is the way these two-dimensional goddesses with their deliquescent outlines seem to have a visionary existence. Although nothing is modeled and there is no deviation from the flatness of the *espace pictural*, yet skillfully selected color patches and brilliantly related contours suggest volume, so that one can easily imagine the figures translated into sculpture, statues such as one sees in the gardens of Versailles. Apollinaire once said, "No one is less concerned than he [Braque] with psychology, and I fancy a stone moves him as much as a face does." Such indifference to personality led him to create universal types of femininity.

The series of the Canephori ended around 1927. According to Jean Leymarie, "Among many variants of unequal value, some less firmly designed than others, though all are imbued with a decorative stateliness, the finest is the Canephorus of 1926 in the Chester Dale Collection in Washington, outstanding for its power and robust vigour." And also, I might add, for its amplitude and fluidity of form.

Collection: Paul Rosenberg, Paris. *Chester Dale Collection*, 1962. Signed, and dated 1926. Canvas, 63¾ x 29¼" (162 x 74.3 cm.).

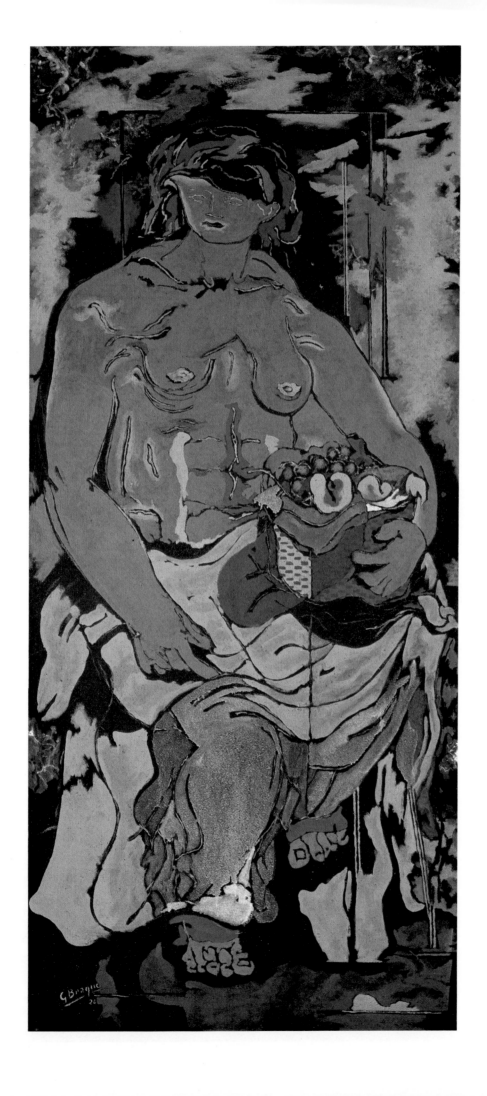

926

927

Braque was a master of powerful, chromatic tonalities, subdued in intensity, yet so strong in effect that one has difficulty in hanging his paintings beside those of other artists. Just as he used to knock out Derain when they were sparring, so his pictures knock out Derain's when their work is juxtaposed. But Derain had a facility denied to Braque. His still life shows how cleverly he manages to combine Cubism with representation.

928

929

930

Georges Braque (French, 1882–1963)

926 *Nude Woman with Fruit.* Signed, and dated 1925. Canvas, 39½ x 32″ (100.3 x 81.3 cm.). Chester Dale Collection

927 *Peonies.* Signed, and dated 1926. Wood, 22⅛ x 27¼″ (56.2 x 69.3 cm.). Chester Dale Collection

928 *Still Life: The Table.* Signed, and dated 1928. Canvas, 32 x 51½″ (81.3 x 130.8 cm.). Chester Dale Collection

929 *Still Life: Le Jour.* Signed, and dated 1929. Canvas, 45¼ x 57¾″ (115 x 146.7 cm.). Chester Dale Collection

930 **André Derain** (French, 1880–1954): *Harlequin.* Signed. 1919. Canvas, 29⅛ x 24″ (74 x 61 cm.). Chester Dale Collection

931 **André Derain**: *Still Life.* Signed. 1913. Canvas, 28⅞ x 36⅜″ (73.4 x 92.4 cm.). Chester Dale Collection

931

599

Pablo Picasso

(SPANISH, 1881–1973)

932 FAMILY OF SALTIMBANQUES

In 1905 Picasso intended to paint two large pictures but completed only one, the *Family of Saltimbanques*. Roughly seven feet square, it is the most impressive achievement of his early period. His many studies of the friends he had made at the Cirque Medrano—clowns, jugglers, and strolling players—are here gathered together in an empty, treeless landscape under a blue sky from which a fog seems to be clearing. On one side is a group comprising Harlequin holding the hand of a little girl, next to him the director of the troupe with a heavy paunch, dressed in red tights and wearing the mock crown of the bronze jester sculptured at about the same time, and at his side two adolescent acrobats. The composition is balanced precariously by a solitary girl (inspired perhaps by a Tanagra statuette), who is seated further in the foreground. These detached figures are unified by their mood of contemplation and by their inner loneliness.

Harlequin has the profile of Picasso himself. Jung has pointed out that the artist's desire to paint himself repeatedly in this disguise reveals a subconscious wish to play the role of Harlequin, "to juggle with everything," as Roland Penrose has perceptively said, "while remaining aloof and irresponsible."

The enigma of these circus people standing together as though awaiting some command or some mysterious event fascinated the German poet Rainer Maria Rilke. In 1918 he asked a friend who owned the painting whether he might live in the same room with it. Later he told her that the *Saltimbanques*, "the loveliest Picasso in which there is so much Paris that for moments I forget," had inspired him to write the fifth of his *Duino Elegies*, which begins:

> But tell me, who *are* they, these acrobats, even a little
> more fleeting than we ourselves—so urgently, ever since childhood,
> wrung by an (oh, for the sake of whom?)
> never-contented will? That keeps on wringing them,
> bending them, slinging them, swinging them,
> throwing them and catching them back; as though from an oily
> smoother air, they come down on the threadbare
> carpet, thinned by their everlasting
> upspringing, this carpet forlornly
> lost in the cosmos.

Collections: André Level, Paris; "Peau de l'Ours," Paris; Hertha von Koenig, Munich. *Chester Dale Collection*, 1962. Signed. Painted 1905. Canvas, 83¾ x 90⅜" (212.8 x 229.6 cm.).

934

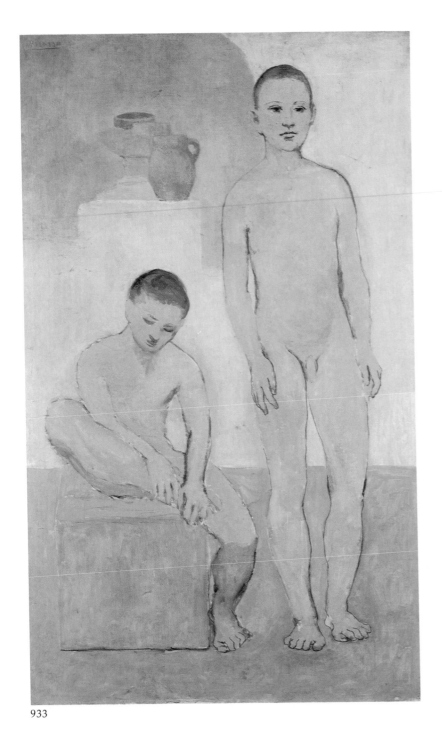

933

Pablo Picasso (Spanish, 1881–1973)

933 *Two Youths.* Signed. 1905. Canvas, 59⅝ x 36⅞″
(151.5 x 93.7 cm.). Chester Dale Collection

934 *Le Gourmet.* Signed. 1901. Canvas, 36½ x 26⅞″
(90.2 x 68.3 cm.). Chester Dale Collection

935 *Juggler with Still Life.* Signed. 1905. Gouache on
cardboard, 39⅜ x 27½″ (100 x 69.9 cm.). Chester Dale
Collection

936 *The Tragedy.* Signed, and dated 1903. Wood,
41½ x 27⅛″ (105.4 x 69 cm.). Chester Dale Collection

937 *Pedro Manach.* Signed. 1901. Canvas, 41⅜ x
27⅞″ (100.5 x 67.6 cm.). Chester Dale Collection

The Chester Dale Collection contains eleven master-pieces by Picasso. None dates after 1941. These reproductions illustrate his early style. *Pedro Manach*, depicting the face of an archetypal revolutionary, is the earliest painting, executed before Picasso left Spain. *Le Gourmet*, *The Tragedy*, and the *Juggler with Still Life* are all from the Blue Period, when Picasso often tends toward the sentimental, though his is a sentimentality of a noble kind. But in the sun-drenched painting *Two Youths* from his Rose Period his excessive sensibility seems to have been burned away by the hot Mediterranean light.

936

935

937

Pablo Picasso

(SPANISH, 1881-1973)

938   LADY WITH A FAN

Lady with a Fan was painted only a few months after the *Saltimbanques*, but during that period one of Picasso's protean changes had taken place. In the summer of 1905 he had gone to Holland to visit a Dutch writer named Schilperoort. He was amazed by the opulent beauty of the Dutch girls. Their robust figures swept from his mind the emaciated acrobats he had been painting. His thoughts also turned to sculpture, and for a time his enthusiasm for modeling seemed to take preference over painting. Introspection gave way to objectivity, the elongations of Romanesque art to the canons of Greek sculpture. The *Lady with a Fan*, one of his loveliest achievements, is typical. There is a serenity and a hieratic formality in her gesture which recall the stately dignity of archaic Greek reliefs.

This new period in Picasso's work, when he painted more broadly, modeled his figures more solidly and placed them in more studied poses, lasted only about a year. The next change begins to appear in the *Portrait of Gertrude Stein*, who once owned the *Lady with a Fan*. Picasso in 1906 discovered the beauty of pre-Roman Iberian sculpture in the bronzes excavated at Ossuna and especially in the portrait bust known as the *Lady of Ossuna*. Finding a new visual excitement and vitality in the works of art shown in the less explored sections of the Louvre, he went from these to an investigation of more primitive artifacts, particularly African art. In 1907 he startled and shocked his friends by painting *Les Demoiselles d'Avignon*, which Matisse at first considered an attempt to ridicule modern art. It was instead an effort to find a modern vocabulary for figure painting, and above all it was an introduction to the inspiration of ethnological exhibits.

After a few years, however, he tired of the barbaric and primitive and returned to a study of the Old Masters. Throughout his long life Picasso has been the perfect cicerone. Through his brilliant interpretations he has shown us qualities in Egyptian, Greek, Iberian, Romanesque, and African sculpture we might never have noticed, and he has translated into his own idiom with amazing virtuosity the attainments of the painters he has admired: Poussin, Le Nain, Cranach, El Greco, Courbet, Delacroix, and, most recently, Velázquez. Many artists have intensified our appreciation of nature; Picasso in a unique way has enhanced our enjoyment of museums.

Collections: Gertrude Stein; Paul Rosenberg, Paris. *Gift of the W. Averell Harriman Foundation in memory of Marie N. Harriman, 1972. Signed, and dated 1905. Canvas, 39½ x 32" (99 x 81.3 cm.).*

Pablo Picasso

(SPANISH, 1881–1973)

939 NUDE WOMAN

In the evolution of European art there have been certain epoch-making breaks with tradition. One occurred in Florence when Giotto shattered the Byzantine formula, as we have seen. The fracturing of the whole history of Western painting took place about 1908 in the little Catalan village of Cadaqués. It was caused by the introduction of a style known as Analytical Cubism. Picasso was its foremost exponent, and *Nude Woman* its masterpiece. Apollinaire spoke of Picasso "assassinating" anatomy "with the science and technique of a great surgeon."

Picasso once said, "There is no abstract art. You must always start with something. Afterward you can remove all traces of reality." In the picture reproduced here he has transformed the contours, volumes, and silhouettes as they exist in traditional figurative painting. The figure is rendered with planes and transparent openings. The linear structure is horizontal, with some diagonal and vertical elements, and others curved into hooks and spheres. All are intermingled with muted tones of gray and brown stippled and hatched with short brushstrokes. The result is a design of shapes with which Picasso conveys his analysis of his vision of the object. The model is thus partially obscured; yet its image, in the words of the artist, "will have left an indelible mark." The mirror that Western painting for thousands of years has held up to nature is shattered. In its place there is the basis of a new art of abstraction, which has made possible the work of artists like Mondrian and Feininger, and which later, in a different form, would dominate style.

Any effort, however, to explain Picasso's work earned the contempt of this artist. "Everyone wants to understand art," he once commented. "Why not try to understand the songs of a bird? Why does one love the night, flowers, everything around us, without trying to understand them? But in the case of painting people have to *understand*. If only they would realize above all that an artist works of necessity, that he himself is only a trifling bit of the world, and that no more importance should be attached to him than to plenty of other things which please us in the world, though we can't explain them. People who try to explain pictures are usually barking up the wrong tree. Gertrude Stein joyfully announced to me the other day that she had at last understood what my pictures of the three musicians was meant to be. It was a still life!"

There is a great deal of truth in what Picasso has said. His words seem a suitable and humbling conclusion to my endeavor to explain the masterpieces of painting reproduced in this volume.

Collections: Mrs. Meric Callery, New York; Frua dei Angeli, Milan. *Ailsa Mellon Bruce Fund*, 1972. Signed. Painted 1910. Canvas, 73¾ x 24" (187.3 x 61 cm.).

940 Pablo Picasso: *Guitar.* 1926. Panel, with paper, string, charcoal, tacks, etc., 51¼ x 38¼″ (130 x 97 cm.). Chester Dale Collection

941

Pablo Picasso (Spanish, 1881–1973)

941 *Still Life*. Signed. 1918. Canvas, 38¼ x 51¼"
(97.2 x 130.2 cm.). Chester Dale Collection

942 *Madame Picasso*. Signed, and dated 1923. Canvas, 39⅞ x 32¼" (100.3 x 82 cm.). Chester Dale Collection

943 *Classical Head*. Signed, and dated 1922. Canvas,
24 x 19¾" (61 x 50.2 cm.). Chester Dale Collection

944 *The Lovers*. Signed, and dated 1923. Canvas,
51¼ x 38¼" (130.2 x 97.2 cm.). Chester Dale Collection

945 *Dora Maar*. Signed, and dated 1941. Canvas,
28¾ x 23¾" (73 x 60.2 cm.). Chester Dale Collection

942

943

944

Between 1908 and 1914 Picasso and Braque worked closely together to develop Cubism. After World War I their works are still similar, and *Still Life* might be taken for a work by either were it not for its colors. Braque continued developing the same style all his life, but Picasso abandoned Cubism, and for a time painted such classical canvases as *Madame Picasso, Classical Head,* and *The Lovers.* Much later, in the 1930s, he began his personal deformations of the human form, but in the midst of these distorted images, often of a nightmare violence, he painted a serene portrait of his mistress Dora Maar, which has the timelessness of Egyptian art (plate 945).

945

946

Kandinsky and Feininger had a great deal in common. Although one was a Russian born in Moscow, and the other an American born in New York, they became friends and lived much of their lives in Germany. At the beginning of this century, they were looked on as avant-garde painters, leaders of radical groups of artists; but today, when everyone is avant-garde, their paintings seem almost conventional. Both taught at the Bauhaus, and both were driven from Germany by Hitler—Kandinsky to Paris in 1933 and Feininger to the United States in 1937.

Kandinsky is considered the father of abstract painting. He proposed as early as 1910 that the artist should not be tied to representation but should express spontaneously his inner feelings. This became a central principle of modern art and is illustrated by *Improvisation 31 (Sea Battle)* (plate 946). Two sailing vessels confront each other diagonally across the center of the composition, with the water and the smoke of their cannons represented symbolically. The painting, difficult as it is to decipher, is the artist's emotional response to thoughts of a naval conflict.

947

About Feininger's *Zirchow VII* (plate 947), a letter from the son of the artist is enlightening. "The date of the painting, 1918, marks a period in Lyonel Feininger's life almost completely overshadowed by his horror of the world war. . . . In this particular painting, a depth of structural unity, of interpenetration of light and substance, presented in deeply glowing color, is achieved which is indeed outstanding in even this, one of my father's very strongest, periods. He therefore rightly considered this to be one of his very major works. It was painted in Zehlendorf, that small suburb of Berlin, in those years an almost rural village, in which he was, as an 'enemy alien,' severely restricted in his movements and, nominally, under daily police surveillance. . . . The theme, the church of Zirchow, a Thuringian village, was sketched by my father in the happy times he had spent in Weimar in the years 1905, 1913, and 1914. . . . It is essential for the understanding of Feininger's art to realize that the underlying thought of it is religious in the deepest and truest sense of the word, and that this has nothing whatever to do with membership in church or synagogue, both of which my father repudiated as almost blasphemously contradicting the spirit of the bible. For the period of world war I one may say that his outlook was Tolstoyian."

946 Wassily Kandinsky (Russian, 1866–1944): *Improvisation 31 (Sea Battle)*. 1918. Canvas, 55⅜ x 47⅛" (145.1 x 119.7 cm.). Ailsa Mellon Bruce Fund

947 Lyonel Feininger (American, 1871–1956): *Zirchow VII*. 1918. Canvas, 31¾ x 39⅝" (80.7 x 100.6 cm.). Gift of Julia Feininger

Piet Mondrian

(DUTCH, 1872–1944)

948 LOZENGE IN RED, YELLOW, AND BLUE

It is noteworthy that the roots of modern Expressionism can be traced to a Dutch artist, Vincent van Gogh, and that the opposite stylistic trend, coldly intellectual and purely optical, can be traced to another Dutchman, Piet Mondrian.

The painting reproduced here, dated 1921–25, is one of sixteen paintings by Mondrian that are square and stand on one corner. The first was done in 1918, but most were painted in 1925 and 1926. He returned to this compositional pattern at the end of his life with *Victory Boogie-Woogie* (Collection of Mr. and Mrs. Burton G. Tremaine), which he was working on when he died.

Mondrian's abstractions are exercises in optical balance. Around an imaginary center the primary colors, blue, red, and yellow, to which he limited his palette, are carefully equalized in their placing, value, intensity, and amount. Thus the eye is drawn equally over the whole of the picture's surface. This gives the effect of dynamic movement held in tension.

Such paintings represent the complete dehumanization of art. Mondrian "systematically eliminated the world of nature and man." As he said once, "Yes, all in all, Nature is a damned wretched affair. I can hardly stand it."

Mondrian's ideas parallel those of Spinoza. It is interesting that the philosopher and the painter, separated by 250 years, should have arrived at much the same conclusion, to quote from Spinoza's *Ethics,* "that the mind can create of its own force, sensations of ideas which do not belong to anything." Here one finds the philosophical basis of Mondrian's work.

The psychological background, however, is more interesting and perhaps more significant. Mondrian grew up in the shadow of a domineering father who was a gifted draftsman and academic realist. Much of the son's progress toward complete abstraction may well have been a rebellion against paternal and family influences. It is interesting to note that he kept his diploma from the State Academy of Fine Arts in Amsterdam until his death—proof to himself that he was as competent an academic painter as either his father or his uncle, who had been his teachers. Nevertheless, he had to express his own personality, to destroy the academic tradition which had been thrust upon him. Many artists of Mondrian's generation were engaged, figuratively speaking, in blowing up the academies, but pictures like the one reproduced sparked the most effective explosions.

Collections: Bienert, Dresden; Jon Nicholas Streep, New York; John L. Senior, Jr., New York. *Gift of Herbert and Nannette Rothschild,* 1971. Painted 1921–25. Canvas on fiberboard, 56¼ x 56" (142.8 x 142.3 cm.).

Jackson Pollock

(AMERICAN, 1912–1956)

949 **NUMBER 1, 1950 (LAVENDER MIST)**

Pollock was the most original painter America has produced. He began his career under the tutelage of conventional and realistic painters; but inspiration finally appeared in the person of a Mexican muralist, David Alfaro Siqueiros. He was the catalytic agent who set off an explosion in Pollock and made him a great artist. From Siqueiros, Pollock learned the beauty of new pigments, among others, cellulose lacquers and silicons, and new ways of applying these materials: pouring them, splattering them, even hurling them at the picture surface. There resulted an endless variety of pictorial effects. All these procedures had been tried by other artists. Pollock's originality was to use them as final statements, to make his paintings in their ultimate form a combination of drip, splatter, and thrown pigment stirred with a stick or dry brush. Paradoxically, he imposed on the essential spontaneity of his technique a surprising discipline.

Lavender Mist, one of his masterpieces, he created in 1950, employing these technical innovations. This was a period when he substituted tranquilizers for alcohol to relieve the tension he had felt since childhood. These two years were his most creative period. When actually painting, Pollock knew that absolute sobriety was essential, a principle he followed in spite of the important element in his pictures of what might be termed "automatic response." This procedure is described by the artist himself: "When I am *in* my painting, I'm not aware of what I'm doing. It is only after a sort of 'get acquainted' period that I see what I have been about. I have no fears about making changes, destroying the image, etc., because the painting has a life of its own."

But the painting's "life of its own" requires a perfect conjunction of eye and hand. *Lavender Mist* is a splendid example of this. It is a complex skein of paint fused into a delicate and unified surface. Pollock worked on the picture from all four sides, moving like a ballet dancer around a huge canvas stretched on the floor. There is beauty in every square foot. Modern painters, unlike the Old Masters, rarely produce beautiful details; but photographs of individual parts of Pollock's best work are delectable in themselves. They have the same impress of personal style, the same calligraphic distinction one finds in a piece of drapery by Botticelli or tresses of hair by Leonardo.

Collections: Alfonso A. Ossorio and Edward F. Dragon, New York. *Ailsa Mellon Bruce Fund,* 1976. Signed, and dated 1950. Canvas, 87 x 118″ (221 x 299.7 cm.).

950

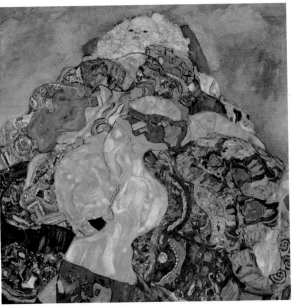

951

952

When the National Gallery of Art opened in 1941, nothing was on view except work by artists who had been dead for at least twenty years. This policy was altered when Chester Dale bequeathed to the Gallery one of the great collections of contemporary art, which was especially rich in paintings by Modigliani, Braque, and Picasso. Since then, a small but very distinguished collection of modern art has been assembled. It is the intention of the Gallery hereafter to keep abreast of the various movements in contemporary painting, sculpture, and the graphic arts but to focus on those artists who appear to have a permanent significance. Thus, there will be represented under one roof eight centuries of creativity, and this span of time will increase as the future discloses new talent.

953

950 Juan Gris (Spanish, 1887–1927): *Fantômas*. Signed, and dated 1915. Canvas, 23½ x 28⅞" (59.8 x 73.3 cm.). Chester Dale Collection

951 Gustave Klimt (Austrian, 1862–1918): *Baby*. 1917–18. Canvas, 43⅝ x 43½" (110.9 x 110.4 cm.). Gift of Otto and Franciska Kallir with the help of the Carol and Edwin Gaines Fullinwider Fund

952 Arshile Gorky (American, 1904–1948): *The Artist and His Mother*. c. 1929–c. 1936. Canvas, 60 x 50" (152.3 x 127 cm.). Ailsa Mellon Bruce Fund

953 Mark Rothko (American, 1903–1970): *Orange and Tan*. Signed, and dated 1954. Canvas, 81¼ x 63¼" (206.4 x 160.6 cm.). Gift of Enid A. Haupt

Sculpture

XIII TO XX CENTURY

Sculpture

The National Gallery of Art possesses a broad array of masterworks representing all sculptural media from the fourteenth century to the twentieth. The earliest of the works illustrated in this section are capital examples of northern and southern Italian relief-carvings of the Trecento, while international developments in late medieval sculpture are represented by two exceptional stone groups—the *Trinity* and *St. George,* both made to Spanish commissions. (The *St. George* is the largest freestanding Nottingham alabaster at present known.) The Gallery's greatest concentration of sculptural masterpieces represents the cultural flowering of Renaissance Italy. The stars in this constellation are a possible early work by Jacopo della Quercia; the finest example of a widespread type of half-length Madonna composition; the famous Martelli *David* and a fine group of relief plaquettes associated with Donatello; in addition to works by Desiderio, Antonio Rossellino, Verrocchio, Francesco di Giorgio (including a group of bronzes incorporating perhaps his finest relief), Riccio, and Mino (repre-

954 Attributed to Adriaen de Vries (Dutch-Florentine, c. 1560–1627): *Mercury.* c. 1603/13. Bronze, without base, 69⅝ x 19 x 37¼" (177 x 48.5 x 94.9 cm.). Andrew W. Mellon Collection

sented by four wonderful marbles culminating in one of the earliest dated busts of the Florentine Renaissance, his *Astorgio Manfredi* of 1455).

This singular density of first-rate Quattrocento figural sculpture provides a splendid foil to a composite collection of Renaissance small bronzes, medals, and especially plaquettes, in which the Gallery's holdings are unmatched in breadth and quality. With almost 1,500 of these rare treasures of miniature sculpture, among them such unique specimens as Costanzo's medal of Mohammed II, and with the superlative portrait of Leon Battista Alberti taking pride of place in a group of reliefs and plaquettes acknowledged to be the finest such series in existence, the National Gallery's collection puts Washington in a rank with Florence, Vienna, and London as an internationally important center for the enjoyment and study of Renaissance bronzes.

The sixteenth century is more selectively but still impressively represented, by fine works associated with the Venetian period of Jacopo Sansovino, by the noble terra-cotta *Knight* of his contemporary Vittoria, by masterpieces from Florence, such as Danti's *Descent from the Cross,* and by beautiful works from central and northern Europe such as Riemenschneider's *St. Burchard,* and Vischer's *Orpheus* relief.

A series of rare seventeenth-century masterworks is inaugurated with Adriaen de Vries's signed and dated *Empire Triumphant over Avarice* of 1610, a sequence continued with a celebrated youthful bust by Bernini, with the graceful fountains designed by Le Brun for the Théâtre de l'Eau at Versailles, and with Foggini's elaborate marble portraits of the Florentine Grand Ducal rulers. Much of the Gallery's recent activity has been focused on expanding these areas of High Renaissance and Baroque sculpture, so that we have now added to our holdings such treasures as Antonio Lombardo's important *Allegory* of 1512 and an early terra-cotta bust as well as a bronze relief by Algardi.

Eighteenth- and nineteenth-century sculpture is another area of long-standing strength for the Gallery. In addition to splendid Italian productions such as the Berninesque *Thetis,* it houses masterpieces by many preeminent French artists, including cabinet and garden figures, Academy reception-pieces such as Robert Le Lorrain's *Galatea,* and portraits of royal figures as well as of other individuals representing many levels of eighteenth-century society. The Gallery's collection of maquettes and early marbles and bronzes by Rodin is outstanding, and fine works by Carpeaux, Gauguin, and Saint-Gaudens provide a wider chronological and geographic frame of reference for the later nineteenth century.

From more recent times, the Gallery's collection includes an entirely autograph late masterpiece by Lehmbruck; an early and magnificent marble *Bird*—together with a large portrait—by Brancusi; an important Surrealist sculpture which Giacometti executed at the turning point of his career; and a strikingly beautiful *Cubi* by David Smith. These later works dramatically extend the significance of the sculpture holdings at the National Gallery of Art. Already the repository of one of the greatest Renaissance collections, its interest and appeal is thus carried forward, at the same astonishing level of quality, to the threshold of our own day.

Douglas Lewis
Curator of Sculpture

955

956

955 Giovanni di Balduccio (Pisan, active 1317–1349): *Charity.* 1328–34. Marble relief, 17¾ x 13⅞" (45.1 x 35.3 cm.). Samuel H. Kress Collection

956 **English School** (last quarter XIV century): *St. George and the Dragon.* Alabaster, painted and gilded, 32 x 23¾ x 8⅛" (81.5 x 60.5 x 20.5 cm.). Samuel H. Kress Collection

957

958

959

957 **English School** (early XIV century): *The Holy Trinity.* c. 1300. Alabaster, 33½ x 14 x 11½″ (85.3 x 35.7 x 29.2 cm.). Samuel H. Kress Collection

958 **Tino di Camaino** (Tuscan, c. 1285–1337): *Madonna and Child with Queen Sancia, Saints and Angels.* c. 1335–45. Alabaster relief, 20¼ x 14⅞″ (51.4 x 37.8 cm.). Samuel H. Kress Collection

959 **Jacopo della Quercia** (Sienese, 1367?–1438): *Madonna of Humility.* Early XV century. Marble, 22⅞ x 19¼ x 11⅛″ (58.4 x 48.8 x 28.3 cm.). Samuel H. Kress Collection

960 Florentine School (XV century): *Madonna and Child.* 1425. Terra-cotta, painted and gilded, 40⅜ x 24½″ (125 x 62.3 cm.). Samuel H. Kress Collection

961 Leon Battista Alberti (Florentine, 1404–1472): *Self-Portrait.* c. 1435. Bronze plaque with black patina, 7⅞ x 5⅜″ (20.1 x 13.6 cm.). Samuel H. Kress Collection

962 Florentine School (XV century): *Madonna and Child.* c. 1425. Terra-cotta, painted and gilded, 47½ x 18½ x 13⅛″ (120.8 x 47.2 x 33.5 cm.). Andrew W. Mellon Collection

963 **Mino da Fiesole** (Florentine, 1429–1484): *Chari-ty*. c. 1465–70. Marble relief, 49¾ x 17″ (126 x 43 cm.). Andrew W. Mellon Collection

964 **Mino da Fiesole**: *Faith*. c. 1465–70. Marble relief, 49¾ x 17″ (126 x 43 cm.). Andrew W. Mellon Collection

965

966

967

965 **Mino da Fiesole**: *Astorgio Manfredi*. Dated 1455. Marble, 20¼ x 21¼ x 10⅞" (51.5 x 54.2 x 27.7 cm.). Widener Collection

966 **Upper Rhenish School**: *The Dead Christ Supported by an Angel (The Trinity)*. c. 1440. Alabaster relief, painted and gilded, 12¼ x 8⅞ x 3⅞" (31.1 x 22.6 x 9.8 cm.). Gift of Mrs. Ralph Harman Booth

967 **Mino da Fiesole**: *The Virgin Annunciate*. c. 1458. Marble, 20 x 14½ x 5⅜" (51 x 37 x 13.6 cm.). Samuel H. Kress Collection

968 Antonio Rossellino (Florentine, 1427–1478/79): *The Young St. John the Baptist.* c. 1470. Marble, 13⅝ x 11¾ x 6¼" (34.7 x 29.8 x 16.1 cm.). Samuel H. Kress Collection

969 Antonio Rossellino: *Madonna and Child.* c. 1477–81. Marble relief, 33 x 22" (84 x 56 cm.). Samuel H. Kress Collection

970 Desiderio da Settignano (Florentine, 1428–1464): *St. Jerome in the Desert.* c. 1461. Marble relief, 16¾ x 21½ (42.7 x 54.8 cm.). Widener Collection

971 Desiderio da Settignano: *Bust of a Little Boy.* c. 1455–60. Marble, 10⅜ x 9¾ x 5⅞" (26.3 x 24.7 x 15 cm.). Andrew W. Mellon Collection

972 Desiderio da Settignano: *The Christ Child.* c. 1460–64. Marble, 12 x 10⅜ x 6⅜" (30.5 x 26.5 x 16.3 cm.). Samuel H. Kress Collection

969

968

970

971

972

974

973

975

976

977

978

973 Donatello (Florentine, c. 1386–1466): *The David of the Casa Martelli.* Third quarter XV century. Marble, 64 x 19¾ x 16⅝″ (162.8 x 50.4 x 42.4 cm.). Widener Collection

974 Francesco di Giorgio (Sienese, 1439–1501/2): *St. Jerome.* c. 1475–85. Bronze relief, 21⅝ x 14¾″ (55 x 37.3 cm.). Samuel H. Kress Collection

975 Costanzo da Ferrara (worked chiefly in Naples, XV century): *Mohammad II, Sultan of the Turks.* c. 1481. Bronze medal, obverse, diam. 4⅞″ (12.3 cm.). Samuel H. Kress Collection

976 Francesco di Giorgio: *St. John the Baptist.* Last quarter XV century. Bronze plaquette with black patina, diam. 8″ (20.3 cm.). Samuel H. Kress Collection

977 Francesco di Giorgio: *St. Sebastian.* Last quarter XV century. Bronze plaquette with black patina, diam. 8″ (20.3 cm.). Samuel H. Kress Collection

978 Lorenzo di Pietro, called Vecchietta (Sienese, c. 1412–1480): *Winged Figure Holding a Torch.* Probably 1460s or 1470s. Bronze, without base, 17⅞ x 6⅞ x 8¼″ (45.6 x 17.7 x 21 cm.). Samuel H. Kress Collection

980

979 **Andrea della Robbia** (Florentine, 1435–1525):
The Adoration of the Child. c. 1480. Glazed terra-cotta
relief, including base, 50⅜ x 30½" (127.8 x 77.4 cm.).
Samuel H. Kress Collection

980 **After Andrea del Verrocchio**: *Alexander the
Great.* XVI century. Marble relief, 21 x 14½" (55.9 x
36.7 cm.). Gift of Therese K. Straus

981

983

982

981 **Studio of Benedetto da Maiano:** *St. John the Baptist.* c. 1480. Terra-cotta, painted, 19¼ x 20½ x 10¼″ (48.9 x 52 x 26 cm.). Andrew W. Mellon Collection

982 **Domenico Gagini** (Lombard, mentioned 1448–1492): *The Nativity.* c. 1458. Marble relief, 35½ x 20½″ (90 x 52 cm.). Andrew W. Mellon Collection

983 **Andrea del Verrocchio** (Florentine, c. 1435–1488): *Giuliano de' Medici.* c. 1475. Terra-cotta, 24 x 26 x 11⅛″ (61 x 66 x 28.3 cm.). Andrew W. Mellon Collection

984 **Andrea del Verrocchio:** *Lorenzo de' Medici.* c. 1485. Terra-cotta, painted, 25⅞ x 23¼ x 12⅞″ (65.8 x 59.1 x 32.7 cm.). Samuel H. Kress Collection

984

985

985 **Il Riccio (Andrea Briosco)** (Paduan, c. 1470–1532): *The Entombment.* c. 1505–15. Bronze relief, 19⅞ x 29¾″ (50.4 x 75.5 cm.). Samuel H. Kress Collection

986 **Francesco da Sant'Agata (?)** (Paduan, active 1491–1528): *Hercules and Antaeus.* Bronze, 15 x 4¾ x 10½″ (38 x 12 x 26.5 cm.). Widener Collection

987 **Francesco da Laurana** (Venetian, c. 1425–1502): *A Princess of the House of Aragon.* 1472–75. Marble, 17½ x 17¾ x 8⅝″ (44.4 x 45.2 x 22.1 cm.). Andrew W. Mellon Collection

988 **Giovanni Antonio Amadeo** (Lombard, 1447–1522): *Lodovico Sforza, Called Il Moro.* 1491–94. Marble relief, diam. 24″ (61 cm.). Andrew W. Mellon Collection

989 **Pietro Lombardo** (Lombard-Venetian, c. 1435–1515): *A Singing Angel.* c. 1490. Marble, 33⅞ x 11 x 11¾″ (86 x 28 x 30 cm.). Samuel H. Kress Collection

986

987

988

989

990

990   Antonio Lombardo (Venetian, c. 1458–1516):
*Peace Establishing Her Reign: Allegory of the Victory
of Ravenna.* 1512. Bronze, 15⅞ x 13¼ x 30″ (40.6 x
33.9 x 76 cm.). Ailsa Mellon Bruce Fund

991   Jacopo Sansovino (Florentine-Venetian, 1486–
1570): *Venus Anadyomene.* c. 1527. Bronze, 65½ x
17¼ x 13¼″ (166 x 44 x 33.7 cm.). Andrew W. Mellon
Collection

992   Peter Vischer the Younger (German, 1487–
1528): *Orpheus and Eurydice.* c. 1515. Bronze, 7¾ x
5¾″ (19.5 x 15 cm.). Samuel H. Kress Collection

993   Tilman Riemenschneider (German, c. 1460–
1531): *St. Burchard of Würzburg.* c. 1510. Wood, 32⅜
x 18½ x 11⅞″ (82.3 x 47.2 x 30.2 cm.). Samuel H. Kress
Collection

994   Benedetto da Rovezzano (Florentine, 1474–c.
1554): *Relief from an Altar or Tabernacle.* c. 1505–13.
Marble, 22 x 51″ (56 x 129.5 cm.). Widener Collection

991

992

993

REX REGVM ET
DOMINVS
DOMINANTIVM

994

995

996

995   Giovanni Francesco Rustici (Florentine, 1474–1554): *Pietro Strozzi.* 1548. Bronze, 25½ x 24¾ x 15½″ (64.6 x 62.7 x 39.4 cm.). Gift of Stanley Mortimer

996   Paduan School (XVI century): *A Jurist.* c. 1550. Bronze, 32¼ x 28⅛ x 13½″ (82 x 71.5 x 34.3 cm.). Widener Collection

997   Vincenzo Danti (Florentine-Umbrian, 1530–1576): *The Descent from the Cross.* c. 1560. Bronze relief, 17½ x 18½″ (44.5 x 47.1 cm.). Widener Collection

998   Circle of Guglielmo della Porta (?) (Lombard-Roman, c. 1515(?)–1577): *Cup with Allegorical Scenes and Este Arms.* Mid-XVI century. Bronze, height 5⅛″ (13 cm.), diam. 7½″ (14 cm.). Widener Collection

999   Alessandro Vittoria (Venetian, 1525–1608): *Portrait of a Young Knight.* Third quarter XVI century. Terracotta, traces of gilding, 35½ x 24¼ x 12¾″ (90.2 x 61.6 x 32.3 cm.). Samuel H. Kress Collection

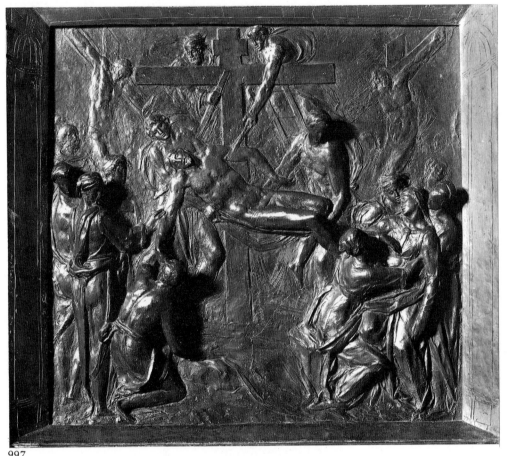

997

998

999

1000

1002

1001

1003

1000 Gian Lorenzo Bernini (Roman, 1598–1680): *Monsignor Francesco Barberini.* c. 1624–25. Marble, 31⅛ x 26 x 10½″ (79.2 x 66.1 x 26.7 cm.). Samuel H. Kress Collection

1001 Jean Baptiste Tubi (Italo-French, 1630/36–1700): *Cherubs Playing with a Swan.* c. 1674. Lead, traces of gilding, 47 x 59″ (119 x 150 cm.). Andrew W. Mellon Collection

1002 Giovanni Battista Foggini (Florentine, 1652–1725): *Vittoria della Rovere, Wife of Ferdinando II.* c. 1685. Marble, 32⅝ x 28 x 13⅜″ (83 x 71.2 x 34 cm.). Widener Collection

1003 Giovanni Battista Foggini: *Ferdinando II de' Medici, Grand Duke of Tuscany.* c. 1685. Marble, 31¼ x 28¾ x 15¾″ (79.5 x 73.2 x 40 cm.). Widener Collection

1004 Adriaen de Vries (Dutch-Florentine, c. 1560–1627): *Empire Triumphant over Avarice.* Signed, and dated 1610. Bronze, 30⅜ x 13⅝ x 12½″ (77.3 x 34.8 x 31.8 cm.). Widener Collection

1004

1005   1006

1005   School of Gian Lorenzo Bernini (Roman, XVII century): *Thetis.* c. 1700. Marble, 80¼ x 36 x 23¾" (204.2 x 91.6 x 60.3 cm.). Samuel H. Kress Collection

1006   Alessandro Algardi (Bolognese-Roman, 1595–1654): *St. Matthias.* c. 1640. Terra-cotta, 15 x 12¾ x 7¾" (38 x 32.4 x 19.8 cm.). Ailsa Mellon Bruce Fund

1007   French School (XVIII century): *Louis, Duc de Bourgogne.* c. 1702. Marble, without base, 29½ x 29¾ x 17⅛" (74.8 x 75.7 x 43.5 cm.). Samuel H. Kress Collection

1008   After Desjardins (French, XVII century): *Louis XIV, "The Sun King."* 1688–93 and 1698–99. Bronze, 22¼ x 8⅝ x 15¾" (56.6 x 21.9 x 40 cm.). Andrew W. Mellon Fund

1009   After Desjardins: *Louis of France, the Grand Dauphin.* 1698–99. Bronze, 22⅜ x 8⅜ x 16½" (57 x 21.3 x 41.8 cm.). Andrew W. Mellon Fund

1007

1008

1009

1010

1011

1010 Jean-Louis Lemoyne (French, 1665–1755): *A Companion of Diana*. Signed, and dated 1724. Marble, 71¾ x 30⅛ x 22¾" (182.5 x 76.5 x 57.8 cm.). Widener Collection

1011 François Coudray (French, 1678–1727): *St. Sebastian*. 1712. Bronze, 35½ x 14½ x 14¾" (90.5 x 36.8 x 37.6 cm.). Ailsa Mellon Bruce Fund

1012 Jean-Pierre-Antoine Tassaert (French, 1727–1788): *Painting and Sculpture*. 1775–78. Marble, 38⅝ x 34¼ x 25⅛" (98.3 x 87.2 x 63.8 cm.). Samuel H. Kress Collection

1013 Edmé Bouchardon (French, 1698–1762): *Cupid*. Signed, and dated 1744. Marble, height 29" (73.9 cm.), diam. of base, 13½" (34.5 cm.). Samuel H. Kress Collection

1014 Robert Le Lorrain (French, 1666–1743): *Galatea*. Signed, and dated 1701. Marble, 29½ x 14¾ x 17¾" (75.1 x 37.7 x 45.1 cm.). Samuel H. Kress Collection

1013

1012

1014

643

1015

1016

1017

1015 Jean-Antoine Houdon (French, 1741–1828): *Giuseppe Balsamo, Conte di Cagliostro.* Signed, and dated 1786. Marble, 24¾ x 23 x 13½" (62.9 x 58.9 x 34.3 cm.). Samuel H. Kress Collection

1016 Jean-Antoine Houdon: *Diana.* Signed, and dated 1778. Marble, with base 32⅛ x 17¾ x 12⅝" (81.6 x 45.1 x 32.2 cm.). Gift of Syma Busiel

1017 Clodion (French, 1738–1814): *A Vestal.* Signed, and dated 1770. Marble, 37½ x 16½ x 13¾" (95.5 x 42.1 x 35 cm.). Samuel H. Kress Collection

1018 Clodion: *The Surprise.* Signed, and dated 1799. Terra-cotta, including base, 14½ x 10⅛ x 8" (37 x 25.9 x 20.3 cm.). Gift of Mrs. Jesse Isidor Straus

1019 Jean-Antoine Houdon: *Alexandre Brongniard.* Signed, and dated 1777. Marble, 15⅜ x 11¼ x 7⅜" (39.2 x 28.7 x 19 cm.). Widener Collection

1020 Jean-Antoine Houdon: *Louise Brongniard.* 1777. Marble, 14⅛ x 9⅞ x 7⅝" (37.7 x 25.3 x 19.5 cm.). Widener Collection

1018

1019

1020

1021   Jean-Baptiste Carpeaux (French, 1827–1875): *Neapolitan Fisherboy.* Signed, and dated 1861. Marble, 36¼ x 16½ x 18⅜″ (92 x 42 x 47 cm.). Samuel H. Kress Collection

1022   Jean-Baptiste Carpeaux: *Girl with a Shell.* Signed, and dated 1867. Marble, 40¾ x 16⅞ x 20¼″ (103.5 x 43 x 51.5 cm.). Samuel H. Kress Collection

1022

1023   Paul Gauguin (French, 1848–1903): *Eve.* 1890. Ceramic, painted, 23⅞ x 11 x 10¾″ (60.6 x 27.9 x 27.3 cm.). Ailsa Mellon Bruce Fund

1024   Auguste Rodin (French, 1840–1917): *The Evil Spirits.* Signed. 1899. Marble, 28 x 29¾ x 23¼″ (71.2 x 75.7 x 59 cm.). Gift of Mrs. John W. Simpson

1025   Auguste Rodin: *Bust of a Woman.* Signed, and dated 1875. Terra cotta, 19¼ x 14⅛ x 10⅝″ (48.9 x 35.6 x 33.6 cm.). Gift of Mrs. John W. Simpson

1021

1023

1024

1025

1026

1027

1026 Amedeo Modigliani (Italian, 1884–1920): *Head of a Woman.* c. 1910. Limestone, 25¾ x 7½ x 9¾" (65.2 x 19 x 24.8 cm.). Chester Dale Collection

1027 Wilhelm Lehmbruck (German, 1881–1919): *Seated Youth (The Friend).* Signed, and dated 1917. Composite tinted plaster, 40⅝ x 30 x 45½" (103.2 x 76.2 x 115.5 cm.). Andrew W. Mellon Fund

1028 Augustus Saint-Gaudens (American, 1848–1907): *Diana of the Tower.* Signed, and dated 1899. Bronze, 38 x 19½ x 11⅜" (96.6 x 48.5 x 28.9 cm.). Pepita Milmore Memorial Fund

1029 Alberto Giacometti (Swiss, 1901–1966): *The Invisible Object: Hands Holding the Void.* Signed, and dated 1935. Bronze, blond patina, 60¼ x 13 x 12" (153 x 32.6 x 29.8 cm.). Ailsa Mellon Bruce Fund

1028

1029

1030

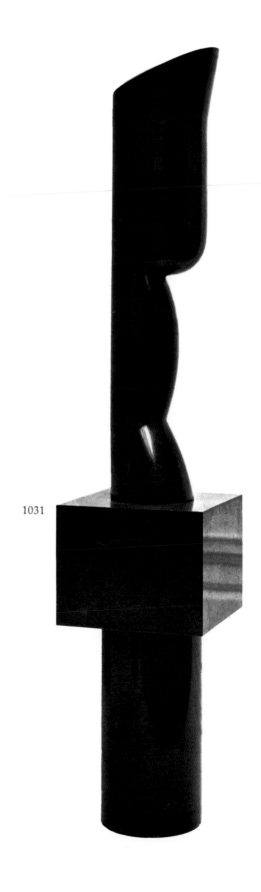

1031

1032

1030 Constantin Brancusi (Rumanian, 1876–1957): *Bird in Space.* 1925. Marble, stone and wood, height 136½″ (344.6 cm.). Gift of Eugene and Agnes Meyer

1031 Constantin Brancusi: *Agnes E. Meyer.* 1929. Black marble, height 90⅝″ (230.1 cm.). Gift of Eugene and Agnes Meyer

1032 David Smith (American, 1906–1965): *Cubi XXVI.* 1965. 9′ 11⅜″ x 12′ 7¼″ (303.2 x 384.2 cm.). Ailsa Mellon Bruce Fund

Drawings

XIII TO XX CENTURY

Drawings

A major collection of graphic arts, in contrast with paintings and sculpture, necessarily includes many more individual works, and usually depends upon the generosity of many more individual donors. In this introduction, it may be most useful to give a summary account of the coming to the National Gallery of the many thousands of works of graphic art that constitute its collection. With the generous support of numerous friends, the Gallery's holdings have grown with striking rapidity.

At the time of this interim report on our progress, the collections of the Department of Graphic Arts comprise prints, drawings, illustrated books, and photographs. Since this section can reproduce only a small selection, the choice has been restricted to drawings, even excluding many types of works that are normally grouped under this heading. A number of our later pastels, gouaches, and collages appear above in the paintings section, for example, the fine works by La Tour, Degas, Renoir, Toulouse-Lautrec, Vuillard, and Matisse. We have not included our monotypes, nor impressions of prints with drawings over them. From the fine group of medieval and Renaissance miniatures and drawings for illumination in the Rosenwald Collection, we have included only a token, the magnificent thirteenth-century leaf from the Arenberg Psalter.

The first gifts of graphic art to the new National Gallery of Art, in 1941, consisted mainly of old master prints donated by Ellen Bullard, Philip Hofer, Paul Sachs, and especially W. G. Russell Allen, whose contribution provided a large and excellent survey. Our first important gift of drawings came in 1942, from Mrs. John W. Simpson: eight fine Rodins which exemplify his marvelous economy of line, a touchstone for authentic Rodins in that most of them had been given directly to the Simpsons by the artist. The first truly major gift, Joseph E. Widener's superbly select collection of graphic art, followed in the fall of the same year. With the exception of a few early works, the beautiful Dürer *Young Woman in Netherlandish Dress* and eight fine Rembrandts, the main strength of the Widener collection is in the eighteenth-century. An extraordinary group of eighteenth-century French illustrated books—with so many special copies, early proofs, and luxurious bindings typical of the period—is complemented by an equally fine collection of French prints and spiced with large groups of drawings for the book illustrations, including designs by Boucher, Gravelot, Eisen, and Moreau le Jeune.

Within a year of the Widener donation came the first of the most important series of gifts the department has received to date, the extraordinary collection of Lessing J. Rosenwald. For the next three decades this amazingly generous man was the foremost figure in graphic arts at the National Gallery. Mr. Rosenwald's collection, with its remarkable range and depth and superlative high points of quality, immediately lifted the Gallery's graphic arts collection into the rank of the half-dozen greatest print rooms in the country. While Mr. Rosenwald is known primarily for his prints, the importance of his drawings may be judged by the fact that even in this limited selection they account for so many fine examples. Beginning with the earliest medieval illuminations, every century is represented in his drawings. For example, such early works as the beautiful Franco-Flemish silverpoint, Schongauer's striking monk, and the lyrical Bartolommeo landscape are followed by eight extremely fine sheets providing a survey of Rembrandt's styles and subjects, and completed by one of the Gallery's greatest twentieth-century drawings, Matisse's *Young Girl with Long Hair*.

As Lessing Rosenwald constantly stressed, no graphic arts collection can be truly balanced and built by depending on the taste and ability of only a few people. Fortunately for the collection, the gifts to the Nation named above were continually supplemented through the generosity of numerous other friends of the Gallery. In 1944 Myron Hofer gave, among other works, Daumier's wonderfully wry *Two Lawyers* and Lancret's lovely *Seated and Standing Figures*. The next year Mrs. Walter B. James donated her complete presentation set, with proofs corrected by the artist, of Audubon's *Birds of America*. Major groups of old-master and modern prints also came in the 1940s from R. Horace Gallatin and Addie Burr Clark, further supplemented by gifts from John Thacher, Elizabeth Achelis, and Mrs. J. Watson Webb. During this same period there were a number of gifts of works by single artists: George Matthew Adams donated thirty drawings and numerous prints by Legros; Frank Crowninshield provided four pen drawings and almost five hundred print and book illustrations by Segonzac; and, in addition to the magnificent "key" set of Stieglitz's photographs, Georgia O'Keeffe gave three large and beautiful Marin watercolors of the late 1920s. The Marin group was strengthened in 1967 with five major early watercolors of New York scenes from Eugene and Agnes Meyer, and a spirited pencil sketch from Mr. and Mrs. Frank Eyerly. The Eyerlys continued their support with drawings including a fine Feininger and the Gallery's best Miró.

In the 1950s, Howard Sturges donated several important eighteenth-century drawings, among which were two Mengs and the Watteau *Violinist*. At a similar time, Jane C. Carey made numerous significant additions to the Addie Burr Clark collection, including the technically fascinating Degas *Jockey*. In the early 1960s the department received three major donations in rapid succession: seventeen of Homer's most beautiful and fresh watercolors, from Mrs. Charles R. Henschel; Samuel H. Kress's extensive group of eighteenth-century French drawings and his Canaletto from the famous series of twelve ceremonies of the Venetian Doge; and Chester Dale's nineteenth- and twentieth-century French drawings, including the major pastels mentioned earlier. The Dale drawings have been further supplemented by numerous smaller works in the same field given by Ailsa Mellon Bruce. Then, in the later 1960s a new development in the Gallery's history began with its first purchases of drawings, initially very few, but select: Rembrandt's *Saskia in Bed*, Rubens's *Venus Lamenting Adonis* and his *Lion*, van Dyck's *Edge of the Wood*, and Gorky's *The Plow and the Song*.

Based upon the numerous previous donations, in the early 1970s a major program of serious building in our collection of graphic arts was begun in Washington. The primary goal is to make this collection as fine in its field as the Gallery's collection is in the field of painting. This effort is taking many forms: continuation of the great series of scholarly exhibitions and catalogues of prints, which have set new standards in their field; careful expansion of the professional staff; provision of regular funds for purchases to increase the department's holdings systematically in depth and to add outstanding single items; and especially the vast expansion in the range of collecting and in the development of new friends who will help the Gallery to build.

As it has always been truly national in its programs of loans and exhibitions, publications, and educational activities, so now the Gallery hopes to become truly national in the quality and range of its graphic arts collection and in the support given to that collection by friends and donors throughout the country. One may still single out major expansions accomplished through individual gifts: in old masters, the magnificent Callot collection donated by Rudolf Baumfeld; in American Primitives, the select survey from Edgar William and Bernice Chrysler Garbisch; in the earlier twentieth century, the wide-ranging group given by Mr. and Mrs. Burton Tremaine; and in artists of great contemporary interest, the extensive Escher collection of C. V. S. Roosevelt. One may also point to some major future gifts of drawings and other graphic art promised by individuals: from Armand Hammer, his magnificent series representing high points in drawing from the Renaissance to the twentieth century; from Mr. and Mrs. Robert Smith, a select group by the best draftsmen of the seventeenth through the early nineteenth centuries; from Mr. and Mrs. Paul Mellon, some of the finest works of the later nineteenth-century French draftsmen; from Mr. and Mrs. Lionel Epstein, the best and most extensive collection of Munch graphics in private hands; and from Ruth Cole Kainen, a collector's survey culminating in the intense works of German Expressionism, with special strength in Kirchner. However, the most important element in the story of the past few years, of the presently promised gifts, and of the future of this national collection, lies in the new dozens of great friends and donors throughout the country—happily, too many to mention in brief—who are helping to build a truly great collection of graphic arts at the National Gallery of Art.

Andrew Robison
Curator of Graphic Arts
1975

1033

1033 **Anonymous German, Lower Saxony**: *Paradise with Christ in the Lap of Abraham.* 1239(?). Tempera on vellum, 8⅞ x 6¼″ (22.4 x 15.7 cm.). Rosenwald Collection

1034 **Anonymous Franco-Flemish Artist**: *The Death of the Virgin.* c. 1390. Silverpoint on blue prepared paper, 11⅝ x 15⅞″ (28.8 x 40.2 cm.). Rosenwald Collection

1035 **Attributed to Hugo van der Goes** (Flemish, c. 1440–1482): *St. George and the Dragon.* Pen and sepia ink, 7⅞ x 6½″ (20 x 16.6 cm.). Rosenwald Collection

1036 **Martin Schongauer** (German, c. 1450–1491): *Bust of a Monk Assisting at Communion.* Pen and brown ink, 5 x 4⅛″ (12.5 x 10.3 cm.). Rosenwald Collection

1037 **Albrecht Dürer** (German, 1471–1528): *An Oriental Ruler Seated on His Throne.* 1494/95. Pen and black ink, 12 x 7¾″ (30.6 x 19.7 cm.). Ailsa Mellon Bruce Fund

1034

1035

1036

1037

1038

1039

1040

1041

1038 **Albrecht Dürer** (German, 1471–1528): *Young Woman in Netherlandish Dress.* 1521. Brush drawing in water and body color, 11⅛ x 7¾" (28.3 x 19.7 cm.). Widener Collection

1039 **Albrecht Dürer**: *The Entombment.* 1504. Pen and brownish-gray ink, 11½ x 8¼" (29.2 x 21 cm.). Syma Busiel Fund

1040 **Albrecht Dürer**: *Tuft of Cowslips.* 1526. Gouache on vellum, 7⅝ x 6⅝" (19.2 x 16.8 cm.). Promised Gift of the Armand Hammer Foundation

1041 **Anonymous Nuremberg Artist** (German, 1524–c. 1560): *River Landscape.* 1544. Pen and black and white ink on red-brown prepared paper, 8¼ x 12½" (21 x 31.8 cm.). Ailsa Mellon Bruce Fund

1042 **Wolf Huber** (German, c. 1485–1553): *Annunciation to Joachim.* 1514. Pen and dark brown ink, 8⅝ x 5¾" (22 x 14.7 cm.). Rosenwald Collection

1043 **Pieter Bruegel the Elder** (Flemish, c. 1528/30–1569): *Landscape with the Penitence of St. Jerome.* 1553. Pen and brown ink, 9⅛ x 13¼" (23.2 x 33.6 cm.). Ailsa Mellon Bruce Fund

1042

1043

1044

1045

1044 **Fra Bartolommeo** (Florentine, 1472–1517): *Two Friars on a Hillside*. Pen and brown ink, 11⅜ x 8⅝" (28.9 x 21.7 cm.). Rosenwald Collection

1045 **Leonardo da Vinci** (Florentine, 1452–1519): *Sheet of Studies*. c. 1478–80 (?). Pen and brown ink over traces of black chalk, 6½ x 5⅞" (16.4 x 13.8 cm.). Promised Gift of the Armand Hammer Foundation

1046 **Andrea Mantegna** (Paduan, 1431–1506): *Bird on a Branch*. Pen and brown ink, 4⅛ x 4½" (10.4 x 11.5 cm.). Andrew W. Mellon Fund

1047 **Raphael** (Umbrian, 1483–1520): *Study for the Prophets Jonah and Hosea*. Pen and brown wash heightened with white over preparation in black chalk and stylus, squared with stylus and red chalk, 10½ x 7¾" (26.2 x 19.8 cm.). Promised Gift of the Armand Hammer Foundation

1048 **Giulio Romano** (Roman, 1499–1546): *St. Michael and the Devil*. c. 1528. Pen and brown ink, 15¼ x 11⅜" (38.6 x 29 cm.). Ailsa Mellon Bruce Fund

1046

1047

1048

1049

1049 Correggio (School of Parma, 1489/94): *Sketch for the Madonna della Scodella.* c. 1523–24. Red chalk, pen and brush in brown ink, 8¼ x 5½" (21 x 14 cm.). Promised Gift of the Armand Hammer Foundation

1050 Michelangelo (Roman, 1475–1564): *Male Nude Striding Forward.* c. 1550. Black chalk, 9⅛ x 3⅞" (23.3 x 10 cm.). Promised Gift of the Armand Hammer Foundation

1051 Lorenzo Lotto (Venetian, c. 1480–1556): *Martyrdom of Saint Alexander of Bergamo.* Early 1520s. Pen and brown ink, squared in black chalk, 10⅝ x 7¾" (27.1 x 19.6 cm.). Ailsa Mellon Bruce Fund

1052 Titian (Venetian, c. 1477–1576): *Study of an Eagle.* Pen and brown ink on white paper, 3¾ x 3⅝" (9.3 x 9.2 cm.). Anonymous Promised Gift

1053 Domenico Campagnola (Venetian, 1500–1564): *Landscape with a Boy Fishing.* Pen and brown ink, 6½ x 9¾" (16.4 x 24.7 cm.). Rosenwald Collection

1050

1051

1052

1053

1054

1054 Luca Cambiaso (Genoese, 1527–1585). *The Martyrdom of St. Lawrence*. Before 1581. Pen and brown ink and wash, 15¼ x 9⅝″ (38.8 x 24.4 cm.). Ailsa Mellon Bruce Fund

1055 Agostino Carracci (Bolognese, 1557–1602): *Wooden Landscape with a Boat*. c. 1585–90. Pen and brown ink, 8½ x 12⅞″ (21.6 x 32.7 cm.). Anonymous Promised Gift

1056 Jacopo Tintoretto (Venetian, 1518–1594): *Standing Youth with His Arm Raised, Seen from Behind*. Black chalk on buff paper, 14¼ x 8⅝″ (36.3 x 21.9 cm.). Ailsa Mellon Bruce Fund

1056

1057

1057   Bartholomeus Breenbergh (Dutch, 1599–1658/9): *Landscape with Large Rock.* 1619–c. 1629. Pen and brown ink and wash, some black chalk, 9¾ x 10⅝″ (24.9 x 27 cm.). Ailsa Mellon Bruce Fund

1058   Rembrandt van Ryn (Dutch, 1606–1669): *Self-Portrait.* c. 1637. Red chalk, 5⅛ x 4¾″ (12.9 x 11.9 cm.). Rosenwald Collection

1059   Jacques de Gheyn II (Flemish, 1565–1629): *Landscape with Sleeping Peasants.* c. 1603. Pen and brown ink on buff paper, 10⅛ x 15¼″ (25.7 x 38.7 cm.). Anonymous Promised Gift

1058

1059

1060

1061

Rembrandt van Ryn (Dutch, 1606–1669)

1060 *Saskia Lying in Bed.* c. 1638. Pen and brush in bistre, wash, 4⅞ x 7⅛" (12.5 x 18 cm.). Ailsa Mellon Bruce Fund

1061 *The Preacher Jan Cornelius Sylvius.* c. 1644/45. Pen and bistre drawing, 5¼ x 4⅞" (13.4 x 12.2 cm.). Rosenwald Collection

1062 *View over the Amstel from the Rampart.* c. 1646. Pen and wash of brown india ink, 3½ x 7¼" (8.9 x 18.5 cm.). Rosenwald Collection

1063 *Landscape with Cottage and Hay Barn.* c. 1650. Pen and gray-brown bistre, wash, 4⅛ x 7" (10.5 x 17.9 cm.). Rosenwald Collection

1064 *Eliezer and Rebecca at the Well.* c. 1640–50. Pen and brown ink and brown wash with white body color, 8 x 12⅞" (20.4 x 32.6 cm.). Widener Collection

1065 *Lot and His Family Leaving Sodom.* c. 1655. Pen and bistre, 7¼ x 11" (19.7 x 27.9 cm.). Widener Collection

1062

1063

Elieser et Rebeca gen. 24. V.14.

1064

1065

1066

1067

1068

1066 **Peter Paul Rubens** (Flemish, 1577–1640): *Lion.* c. 1614–15. Black chalk with white heightening and yellow chalk, 10 x 11⅛″ (25.4 x 28.2 cm.). Ailsa Mellon Bruce Fund

1067 **Peter Paul Rubens**: *Venus Lamenting Adonis.* c. 1612. Pen and brown ink, 12 x 7¾″ (30.5 x 19.8 cm.). Ailsa Mellon Bruce Fund

1068 **Jacob Jordaens** (Flemish, 1593–1678): *Design for a Wall Decoration.* c. 1640–45. Brown brush and wash with watercolor over black chalk, 12½ x 7½″ (31.7 x 18.8 cm.). Ailsa Mellon Bruce Fund

1069 **Jacob Jordaens**: *The Martyrdom of St. Sebastian.* c. 1617. Pen and brown ink with brown wash, 7⅜ x 6″ (18.8 x 15.3 cm.). Ailsa Mellon Bruce Fund

1070 **Gian Lorenzo Bernini** (Roman, 1598–1680): *Self-Portrait.* c. 1614–15. Red and black chalk with white highlights, 12½ x 9⅛″ (31.7 x 23.1 cm.). Ailsa Mellon Bruce Fund

1071 **Guercino** (Bolognese, 1591–1666): *A Fisherman with His Net.* Black chalk with white highlights, 15⅞ x 10⅞″ (40.3 x 27.7 cm.). Pepita Milmore Fund

1070

1069

1071

1072 Sir Anthony van Dyck (Flemish, 1599–1641): *Edge of the Wood*. After 1631. Pen, brown ink, brown wash, 7⅞ x 10¼" (20 x 26.1 cm.). Syma Busiel Fund

1073 Claude Lorrain (French, 1600–1682): *Landscape with Ruins, Pastoral Figures and Trees*. c. 1650–55. Black chalk, pen and brown ink, brown wash, heightened with white, on pink prepared paper, 8 x 10½" (20.2 x 26.6 cm.). Syma Busiel and Pepita Milmore Funds

1074 Canaletto (Venetian, 1697–1768): *Ascension Day Festival at Venice*. 1766. Pen and sepia with bluish-gray wash, 13¼ x 21⅞" (33.8 x 55.7 cm.). Samuel H. Kress Collection

1075 Giovanni Battista Tiepolo (Venetian, 1696–1770): *St. Jerome in the Desert Listening to Angels*. Pen and brown ink, brown wash, heightened with white, over black chalk on buff paper, 16¾ x 10⅞" (42.5 x 27.6 cm.). Promised Gift of the Armand Hammer Foundation

1076 Giovanni Battista Tiepolo: *Virgin and Child Adored by Bishops, Monks, and Women*. c. 1740. Pen and brown wash over black chalk on white paper, 16¾ x 11⅞" (42.5 x 30 cm.). Promised Gift of the Armand Hammer Foundation

1072

1073

1074

1075

1076

1077

1078

1079

1077 **Antoine Watteau** (French, 1684–1721): *The Violin Player*. Sanguine and conté crayon, 11⅞ x 8⅜" (30 x 21.3 cm.). Gift of Howard Sturges

1078 **Antoine Watteau**: *Three Women's Heads*. c. 1715. Red and black chalk, pencil, brown wash, 7¼ x 6⅜" (18 x 16 cm.). Samuel H. Kress Collection

1079 **Antoine Watteau**: *Couple Seated on a Bank*. Red, black, and white chalk on buff paper, 9½ x 13¾" (24.1 x 34.9 cm.). Promised Gift of the Armand Hammer Foundation

1080 **François Boucher** (French, 1703–1770): *Tête-à-Tête*. 1764. Black chalk heightened with white, 13⅛ x 9⅛" (33.3 x 22.9 cm.). Widener Collection

1081 **François Boucher**: *Danaë Receiving the Golden Shower*. 1757. Red, white, and black chalk, 12¼ x 18¾" (31.1 x 47.6 cm.). Samuel H. Kress Collection

1080

1081

675

1082

1083

1084

1085

1082   **Jean-Honoré Fragonard** (French, 1732–1806): *Grandfather's Reprimand.* Gray-brown wash over black chalk, 13½ x 17¾″ (34.3 x 45.1 cm.). Promised Gift of the Armand Hammer Foundation

1083   **Jean-Honoré Fragonard** : *Le Coucher.* Brown washes over black chalk, 9½ x 14½″ (24 x 36.8 cm.). Samuel H. Kress Collection

1084   **William Blake** (British, 1757–1827): *Queen Katherine's Dream.* Watercolor, 16⅛ x 13½″ (41 x 34.2 cm.). Rosenwald Collection

1085   **Nicolas Lancret** (French, 1690–1743): *Seated Figure and Standing Figure.* Sanguine and white chalk, 7¼ x 11⅝″ (18.4 x 29.3 cm.). Gift of Myron A. Hofer in memory of his mother, Mrs. Charles Hofer

1086   **William Blake**: *The Great Red Dragon and the Woman Clothed with the Sun.* c. 1805–10. Watercolor, 15¾ x 12¾″ (40 x 32.4 cm.). Rosenwald Collection

1086

1087 **Eugène Delacroix** (French, 1798–1863): *Tiger.* Watercolor, 5½ x 9⅞″ (14 x 25.2 cm.). Rosenwald Collection

1088 **Pierre-Paul Prud'hon** (French, 1758–1823): *Venus.* 1810. Black chalk with white chalk heightening on blue paper, 22½ x 16¾″ (57 x 42.3 cm.). Ailsa Mellon Bruce Fund

1089 **Pierre-Paul Prud'hon**: *Adonis.* 1810. Black chalk with white chalk heightening on blue paper, 22½ x 16¾″ (57 x 42.3 cm.). Ailsa Mellon Bruce Fund

1090 **Jean-Auguste-Dominique Ingres** (French, 1780–1867): *Portrait of Auguste-Jean-Marie Guénepin.* 1809. Pencil, 7⅞ x 6⅜″ (20.1 x 16.3 cm.). Gift of Robert H. and Clarice Smith

1091 **Jean-Auguste-Dominique Ingres**: *Portrait of Mrs. Charles Badham, née Margaret Campbell.* 1816. Pencil, 10¼ x 8¼″ (26 x 21 cm.). Promised Gift of the Armand Hammer Foundation

1088

1087

678

1089

1090

1091

1092

1093

1092 Honoré Daumier (French, 1808–1879): *Two Lawyers.* Crayon and gray and brown and pink washes, 10½ x 9¼″ (26.5 x 23.5 cm.). Gift of Myron A. Hofer in memory of his mother, Mrs. Charles Hofer

1093 Edouard Manet (French, 1832–1883): *The Man in the Tall Hat.* Watercolor, 14⅛ x 10⅛″ (35.7 x 25.7 cm.). Rosenwald Collection

1094 Edgar Degas (French, 1834–1917): *The Artist's Brother, René.* 1855. Pencil, 11½ x 9″ (29.3 x 23 cm.). Promised Gift of Mr. and Mrs. Paul Mellon

1095 Edgar Degas: *Jockey.* c. 1898. Washed pastel and brown wash, 11 x 7⅞″ (28 x 20.1 cm.). Gift of Mrs. Jane C. Carey for the Addie Burr Clark Memorial Collection

1096 Mary Cassatt (American, 1844–1926): *Tramway.* c. 1891. Black crayon, 14⅜ x 10⅝″ (36.5 x 27 cm.). Rosenwald Collection

1094

1095

1096

1097

1098

1099

1100

1097   **Vincent van Gogh** (Dutch, 1853–1890): *Harvest–The Plain of La Crau*. c. 1888. Reed pen, 9⅝ x 12½″ (24.3 x 31.6 cm.). Promised Gift of Mr. and Mrs. Paul Mellon

1098   **Paul Gauguin** (French, 1848–1903): *Nave Nave Fenua*. c. 1894–1900. Ink drawing with watercolor, 16½ x 10¼″ (41.9 x 26 cm.). Rosenwald Collection

1099   **Winslow Homer** (American, 1836–1910): *Incoming Tide: Scarboro, Maine*. 1883. Watercolor, 15 x 21½″ (38.1 x 54.8 cm.). Gift of Mrs. Charles R. Henschel in memory of her husband

1100   **Winslow Homer**: *Sketch for Hound and Hunter*. 1892. Watercolor, 13⅞ x 20″ (35.4 x 50.8 cm.). Gift of Mrs. Charles R. Henschel in memory of her husband

1101   **Odilon Redon** (French, 1840–1916): *Head of a Veiled Woman*. Charcoal on tan paper, 20½ x 14¾″ (52.2 x 37.5 cm.). Rosenwald Collection

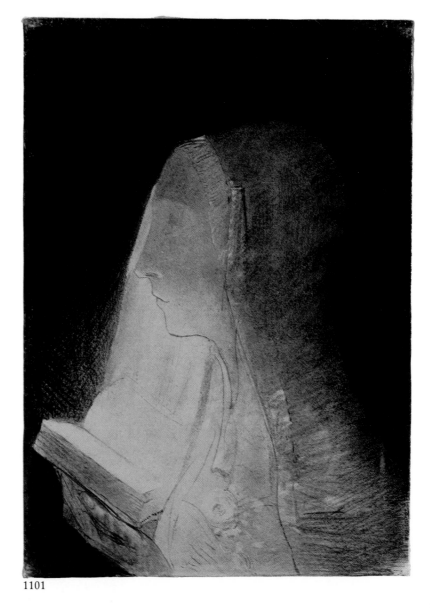

1101

1102

1103

1104

1105

1102   Edvard Munch (Norwegian, 1863–1944): *Two Women's Heads.* Colored crayon, 11¼ x 14⅞" (28.3 x 37.4 cm.). Anonymous Promised Gift

1103   Pablo Picasso (Spanish, 1881–1973): *Self-Portrait.* c. 1902. Crayon and watercolor, 12 x 9⅜" (30.4 x 23.8 cm.). Ailsa Mellon Bruce Collection

1104   Auguste Rodin (French, 1840–1917): *Dancing Figure.* 1905. Pencil with brown wash, 12¾ x 9⅞" (32.5 x 25 cm.). Gift of Mrs. John W. Simpson

1105   Henri Matisse (French, 1869–1954): *Young Girl with Long Hair.* 1926. Pencil, 21¼ x 14½" (54 x 37 cm.). Rosenwald Collection

1106   Egon Schiele (Austrian, 1890–1918): *Seated Nude.* 1918. Black crayon, 17 x 11" (43 x 27.5 cm.). Anonymous Promised Gift

1106

1107

1107 Ernst Ludwig Kirchner (German, 1880–1938): *Nude Woman in Tub.* c. 1923. Pen, wash, colored crayon, 21½ x 14⅛″ (52 x 36 cm.). Anonymous Promised Gift

1108 Joan Miró (Spanish, born 1893): *Three Women.* 1934. Ink and pastel, 24½ x 18″ (62.2 x 45.7 cm.). Gift of Frank and Jeannette Eyerly

1109 Arshile Gorky (American, 1904–1948): *The Plow and the Song.* 1947. Pencil, charcoal, pastel, and oil on paper, approximately 48 x 59″ (121.9 x 142.2 cm.). Gift of the Avalon Foundation

1110 John Marin (American, 1870–1953): *Woolworth Building No. 29.* Watercolor, 18¾ x 15⅝″ (47.6 x 39.8 cm.). Gift of Eugene and Agnes Meyer

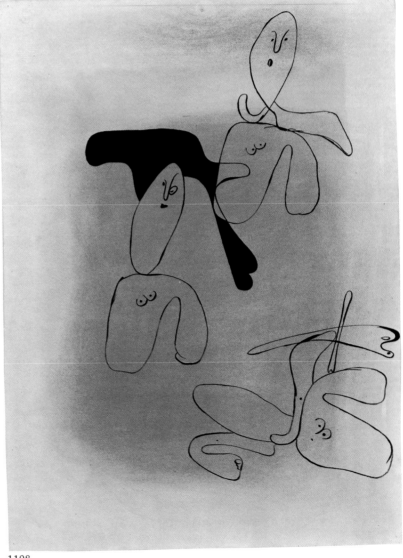

1108

1109

1110

Index to the Text

All numbers in this Index refer to *pages*.